PHILOSOPHY OF RELIGION

"As a contemporary introduction to philosophy of religion, it is a God-send or, if you prefer, a dharma-gift. Keith Yandell succeeds admirably in producing a textbook which has clarity, wit and rigour and that engages religion in its historical and cultural diversity . . . He grasps that religious traditions are irreducibly different: they make different types of claims, argue from different sorts of grounds, cultivate diverse values and aim at divergent goals."

John Clayton, *Boston University*

"The central strength of the book is its willingness to argue points out in detail rather than just reporting on arguments. It is a model of rigorous argument applied to questions of religion."

Mark Wynn, *Australian Catholic University, Brisbane*

Philosophy of Religion is one of the first comprehensive textbooks to consider the subject with reference to religions other than Christianity. As an experienced textbook author and an established generalist in philosophy of religion, Keith Yandell deals lucidly and constructively with representative views and competing issues from Judaism, Christianity, Islam, Buddhism and Jainism. He also shows how such issues and competing views can be rationally assessed. He includes discussion of major philosophical figures in religious traditions as well as important contemporary philosophers. This engaging text will appeal to students of both philosophy and religion as well as to the general reader interested in the subject.

Keith E. Yandell is Professor of Philosophy at the University of Wisconsin at Madison. He has written widely on philosophy and philosophy of religion and among his most recent books are *Hume's "Inexplicable Mystery"* (1990) and *The Epistemology of Religious Experience* (1995).

Routledge Contemporary Introductions to Philosophy

Series Editor:
Paul K. Moser
Loyola University of Chicago

This innovative, well-structured series is for students who have already done an introductory course in philosophy. Each book introduces a core general subject in contemporary philosophy and offers students an accessible but substantial transition from introductory to higher-level college work in that subject. The series is accessible to nonspecialists and each book clearly motivates and expounds the problems and positions introduced. An orientating chapter briefly introduces its topic and reminds readers of any crucial material they need to have retained from a typical introductory course. Considerable attention is given to explaining the central philosophical problems of a subject and the main competing solutions and arguments for those solutions. The primary aim is to educate students in the main problems, positions and arguments of contemporary philosophy rather than to convince students of a single position. The initial eight central books in the series are written by experienced authors and teachers, and treat topics essential to a well-rounded philosophy curriculum.

Epistemology
Robert Audi

Ethics
Harry Gensler

Metaphysics
Michael J. Loux

Philosophy of Art
Noel Carroll

Philosophy of Language
William G. Lycan

Philosophy of Mind
John Heil

Philosophy of Religion
Keith E. Yandell

Philosophy of Science
Alexander Rosenberg

PHILOSOPHY OF RELIGION

A contemporary introduction

Keith E. Yandell

London and New York

Thanks are due to Karen Buege Yandell for
illustrations of the various Digitators.

First published in 1999
by Routledge
11 New Fetter Lane, London EC4P 4EE

Simultaneously published in the USA and Canada
by Routledge
29 West 35th Street, New York, NY 10001

Typeset in Aldus Roman by RefineCatch Limited, Bungay, Suffolk
Printed and bound in Great Britain by
TJ International Ltd, Padstow, Cornwall

British Library Cataloguing in Publication Data
A catalogue record for this book is available from the British Library

Library of Congress Cataloging in Publication Data
A catalog record for this book has been requested

ISBN 0–415–13213–4 (hbk)
ISBN 0–415–13214–2 (pbk)

To Alvin Plantinga
– he led the way.

Contents

PART IV: ARGUMENTS CONCERNING NONMONOTHEISTIC CONCEPTIONS 237

Preface

Contemporary academia is secular. The idea that religious views of any traditional sort should guide the research or inform the worldview of any discipline is rejected out of court. Things were not always so. Professor John Bascom, former President of my own university, used to give a capstone undergraduate course in how to prove the existence and nature of God; his practice was more typical than surprising. Times have changed.

A student of mine once published a paper he wrote for a seminar he took with me. It argued that there is reason to reject a particular set of religious beliefs. In effect, the responses of his former professors ranged from *we all know that stuff is false* through *considering whether religious claims are true or false isn't part of the academic game* to *saying someone's religious beliefs are false is impolite and politically unwise*. None of these responses is atypical.

Nonetheless, both traditionally and currently, the philosophy of religion has made rational assessment of religious claims central to its purposes. Endeavoring to determine the meaning, and the truth value – the *sense* and the *truth-or-falsity* – of religious claims is part and parcel of this discipline. Some philosophers have denied that there are any religious claims, proposing that what seem to be such really are meaningless. Other philosophers have held that religious traditions can only be understood in their own terms, each describing a conceptual world inaccessible to any other so that there is no "neutral place" from which assessment can be offered. (As we will see, this misleading metaphor disguises a perspective whose incoherence has, alas, not mitigated its influence.) Taking either the *all supposed religious claims are nonsense* or the *every religion its own conceptual world unrelated to all others* line is itself opting for some philosophical views as opposed to others. Those outside of philosophy who assume one line or the other assume what desperately needs proof. In so doing, they draw intellectual drafts on empty accounts. These days, the *nonsense* line[1] is seldom heard but the *own conceptual world* line is everywhere. The best way to show that the *nonsense* and the *own conceptual world* lines are utterly mistaken is to offer the sorts of assessments that these lines suppose impossible. That is the basic task before us. This task has three components: presentation of data, assessment of arguments, and reflection on experiences.

Presentation of data

We begin by saying what religion is and what philosophy is. There are no noncontroversial answers to these questions. Nonetheless, clarity about how religion and philosophy are construed in this text should be helpful for understanding the rest of what is said. Then we consider what kinds of religions there are, what religious experience is, and what kinds of religious experience there are. Some religious experiences, for example, are seen as experiences of God; others are not. Some religions are monotheistic; they hold that God exists and has very strong powers. Others hold that ultimate reality is not God, but something else. Both sorts of religious traditions not surprisingly offer accounts of what persons are, and one tradition typically offers a different view of this matter than another. Such differences are philosophically as well as religiously significant, and they require our attention. There is more than one concept of God, and so more than one kind of monotheism. Similarly, nonmonotheistic religions differ in terms of how they conceive of what exists and has religious importance. So we need to look at different notions of ultimate reality, conceived as divine or not.

Since the variety of religions is great, no one book could responsibly deal with philosophy of religion in connection with all of them. Our scope will include representative views from Judaism, Christianity, Islam, Hinduism, Buddhism, and Jainism. Each of these traditions is itself complex, and while we can hope to be fair, we cannot pretend to be exhaustive. One great divide among religious traditions comes between those that are monotheistic and those that are not. Our discussion will be divided along these lines with no suggestion that "nonmonotheism" is more than a label of convenience; each variety of nonmonotheism we discuss, like each variety of monotheism, will be positively characterized in terms of its own indigenous perspective.

Without any suggestion that this is their only or primary importance, religions provide the raw material for philosophical reflection. At this point, we will have our raw data for philosophical reflection. Once we have reflected briefly on how arguments can be constructed and assessed, and on how appeal to experience as evidence may be crafted and evaluated, we can turn to asking what reason, if any, there is to think that the religious perspectives already described might be true.

Escaping incoherence

There are academic circles in which talk of truth, let alone religious perspectives being true, is about as popular as a teetotal sermon at a local pub. For this to be the line to take, it must be true (in the sense of "true" that was supposedly dismissed) that talk of truth is somehow so problematic as to require its abandonment. This line thus appears to be incoherent; it appears so because it is.[2]

The devotees of a religious tradition typically take what their sacred texts say to be true. Nor is it beyond their ability to think what this "being true" might amount to. Monotheists will take *God exists* to be true – they will suppose that an omnicompetent being exists on whom the world depends. Some religious nonmonotheists will think this claim false, and will think that such claims as *Persons are indestructible* or *Persons are nothing more than momentary states* are true. As Aristotle once said, a proposition is true if things are as it says they are, and not otherwise. Aristotle, and most devotees of most traditions, have no difficulty in understanding what this means. It is possible to educate oneself out of all possibility of learning anything. Aristotle and ordinary religious people have not suffered this injury.

Using the data (I)

Arguments have been offered for, and others against, religious beliefs. This is so regarding both monotheistic traditions and nonmonotheistic traditions. Far from such arguments going deeply against the grain of the religious traditions, sincere and admired devotees of such traditions have offered arguments for their own perspective and against other perspectives. If it is true that some religious believers have rejected any such idea as needless if not inappropriate, others have entered enthusiastically into the enterprise. The idea that offering such arguments is somehow inherently against all religious thought and practice is not substantiated by the history of these traditions. Many of these arguments are provocative and powerful; they deserve our attention. Some of these arguments concern the existence and nature of God; others concern the nature of persons. In each case, such disputes tie in tightly with different views of salvation and enlightenment, of what one may expect and hope. The arguments interact significantly with the traditions in ways often ignored.

Related to the possibility of such arguments are competing notions of faith, of reason, and of their connections. Also related are competing views of the capacities and limits of religious language. If all claims about God, for example, are nonliteral, how does this affect what sorts of arguments can be offered on behalf of these claims? Does this place them simply beyond argument altogether? *Are* all claims about God nonliteral? Hence, along with considering arguments, we must discuss issues concerning the nature and scope of religious language.

Using the data (II)

People claim to have religious experiences. We thus ask what evidence, if any, such experience provides for religious belief? Appeal to at least apparent experience of God, for example, can but need not be another version of an argument for God's existence. One could argue: *people seem to have experience of God; the best explanation of this fact is that God causes those experiences; hence there is reason to think that God exists.* Similarly, one could argue: *there seems to be a computer in front of me; the best explanation of things so appearing is that there is a computer in front of me; so there is reason to think a computer is there.* But I seem simply to see the computer; my belief that it is there is a matter of at least seeming to see it and having no reason to think that things are not as they seem. I neither see something else from which I infer to my computer nor offer claims about best explanations. Similarly, many have claimed to experience God, not to have some experience of something from which they can then properly infer that God exists. We will consider religious experience, viewed as evidence for God's existence by virtue of its being a matter of "seeing God" rather than simply as a matter of its being the source of a premise in a proof of God's existence.

Differing views of persons are also supported by appeals to experience, particularly to introspective and enlightenment experiences. How such experiences should be described, and what significance they bear, is a matter of central dispute, particularly between such nonmonotheistic traditions as Jainism and Buddhism. Further, competing accounts of what persons are connect closely with diverse accounts of morality and of value generally. These close connections are no insignificant part of what gives the disputes their importance to the traditions involved. Discerning these traditions widens one's understanding of the views involved, and enriches the sorts of possible assessments of competing appeals to experience. Closely connected with these topics are competing notions of human survival of death and whether any of them have any basis or support.

Summary

The core of philosophy of religion, as of philosophy generally, is metaphysics and epistemology, systematic attempts to give defensible answers to the questions *What is there?* and *How can we know what there is?* At the core of any religious tradition is its own answer to these questions, construed as and embedded in an answer to the basic problem to which the tradition addresses itself as the rationale for its existence. Thus our own concentration on accounts of religious reality and religious knowledge. How is ultimate reality conceived, and how are human persons viewed in relation to ultimate reality? With what consequences for salvation or enlightenment, morality, and any afterlife there may be? What arguments are offered for, and what against, these views? What appeals to experience are made for one view and against another? What assessment should be offered of these arguments and appeals?

In sum, our intent is to describe the basic perspectives concerning ultimate reality and our relations to it as seen by several of the major religious traditions, and to ask what, if anything, there is by way of reason or evidence to think any of the claims that define these perspectives are true, or are false. The underlying conviction is that an academia in which such questions are not somewhere raised, and competing answers debated, illegitimately ignores issues of great importance, and does so without decent excuse.

Besides being important, philosophy of religion is fun. One gets to learn what people in quite different cultural contexts believe about God, the nature of persons, good and evil, salvation, enlightenment, to see what they take to follow from these beliefs, and to think as clearly and well about them as one can. Perhaps this is not everyone's cup of tea, but for those at all inclined to it, it should be a thoroughly enjoyable project. I hope that this volume is as much serious fun to read as it was to write.

Annotated reading

Alston, William (1967) "Problems of Philosophy of Religion," *Encyclopedia of Philosophy*, Volume 6, New York: Macmillan. A brief issue-oriented summary of the field.

Bascom, John (1980) *Natural Theology*, New York: G. P. Putnam's Sons. A presentation of arguments for the existence of God by an early president of the University of Wisconsin.

Collins, James (1967) *The Emergence of the Philosophy of Religion*, New Haven: Yale University Press. A history of the field that finds its recent roots in nineteenth-century philosophy.

Lewis, H. D. (1967) "History of the Philosophy of Religion," *Encyclopedia of Philosophy*, Volume 6, New York: Macmillan. A brief historically oriented summary of the field.

CHAPTER 1
Introduction

If part of philosophy is visiting intellectual museums, an equally important part is engaging in criticism of what one finds there. Visits without criticism are not philosophical visits.

1
Introduction

Does God exist? Is there any reason to think that God exists? Is there no God? Is there any good reason to believe that? What makes us persons? What do the world religions teach about God, human persons, and life after death? How can what they say be evaluated? If God knows in advance what we will do, can we be free? Must we be free if we are responsible for what we do? Can a person survive the death of her body? Is the existence of evil evidence against God's existence? How are religion and morality related? Is faith inherently irrational? Such questions are the stuff of the philosophy of religion. Our task here is to look carefully at the issues they raise.

In Part I, four topics are considered:

1 what is the philosophy of religion (which involves our saying what philosophy and religion are, and how they intersect)?;
2 what sorts of religion, or religious traditions, are there?;
3 what sorts of religious experience are there?;
4 has religious doctrine real religious importance?

The notions of a *sort* of religion, and a *sort* of religious experience, come up for discussion and definition. Part I contends for a certain way of approaching religion, arguing from different angles (doctrine, experience, function) that it is false that all religions are the same. We argue that from a religious viewpoint as well as from a philosophical, doctrine matters.

Philosophy's task is the construction and assessment of worldviews. A worldview contains an account of the basic kinds of things there are and how they are related. These are the concern of *metaphysics*. It also contains an account of what knowledge is, what reasonable belief is, and how one identifies knowledge and reasonable belief. These are the concern of *epistemology*. It also gives an account of value, especially moral value. This is the concern of *ethics*.[1] There is no need for philosophy to construct such accounts from scratch. The common sense and cultural beliefs one encounters from one's youth contain theses and themes that, sometimes explicitly and sometimes implicitly, make commitments regarding what there is, what is known, and what is good.[2] Philosophers of course are free to offer their own accounts of these matters. It is an essential feature of philosophy that views offered on philosophical issues are also assessed. There is no such thing as philosophy without argument. Assertion without assessment is not philosophy.

A religion offers a diagnosis of what it tells us is our deep and paralyzing problem. It also offers a solution. This combination of diagnosis-and-cure itself makes assumptions about what there is, what can be known, and what has positive worth. It inherently contains the seeds of a full-grown worldview. At the very least, it contains commitments as to what there is, what must be known, and what has worth that can be consistently developed into some worldviews but not into others.

Judaism, Christianity, and Islam agree that our deep problem is that we are sinners in need of divine forgiveness and renewal. Advaita Vedanta, a variety of Hinduism, holds that our deep problem lies in our ignorance of our identity to Brahman, a qualityless ultimate reality. Theravada Buddhism claims that our deep problem is that we mistakenly think of ourselves as enduring self-conscious beings and the cure is seeing that we are composed of only momentary states. Jainism maintains that our deep problem is that we regard ourselves as inherently dependent on something else and having limited knowledge, whereas in fact we are enduring self-conscious beings that are inherently independent and capable of unlimited knowledge. These diagnoses and cures involve commitments as to what there is, what is known, and what has ultimate worth. These commitments differ from one diagnosis-and-cure to another in such a way that the correctness of one diagnosis-and-cure entails the incorrectness of the others. A central part of the philosophy of religion involves understanding these competing diagnoses-and-cures and examining what can be said for and against the views to which they are committed. This investigation involves getting the data about competing religious traditions straight. This, in turn, involves offering an accurate account of the kinds of religious experience these traditions include. It includes providing a fair, clear description of the doctrines that are an essential part of these traditions.

A view that is very popular in some Religious Studies circles is incompatible with the basic approach of this text. Religious Pluralism endeavors to escape any necessity for assessing competing religious traditions by claiming that, in any straightforward sense of the term, all religious doctrines are false or meaningless. Religious traditions are to be assessed simply in terms of whether or not people come closer to Religious Pluralism's moral ideal by virtue of accepting them. The overall argument of this book is a refutation of this view. Nonetheless, given its popularity, we have devoted a chapter to showing that Religious Pluralism is both self-refuting and self-contradictory.

In Part II, we consider the philosophical content of religious traditions.

Monotheism takes God alone to be an independently existing creator; nonetheless, there is more than one variety of monotheism. Advaita Vedanta holds qualityless Brahman to be the only ultimate reality, a status that Jainism gives to persons and physical elements while denying that there is a God. Theravada Buddhism takes the basic elements of the world to be co-dependent and transitory. These doctrines are presented and explained.

A monotheist can hold that God is in time or that God lacks all temporal properties. A purely philosophical monotheism may simply hold that the world depends for its existence on God though God does not choose to create. On this view, God and the world exist beginninglessly and God's existence is necessary and sufficient for the world's existence without God's doing anything. A religious monotheist accepts a doctrine of creation. She may hold that the world beginninglessly depends on God, that the world was created by God after some time had elapsed, or that creating the world automatically includes the creation of time. In any case, the world exists because God chose to create it. Religious monotheism holds God to be providential, concerned with and active in the course of history. A monotheist can hold that God has, or that God lacks, logically necessary existence. She will hold that it is logically impossible that God be caused to exist or depend for existence on anything else. Advaita Vedanta Hinduism asserts that these views about God should be replaced by the view that all that exists is a being without qualities.

Jainism accepts one view of persons. Theravada Buddhism holds another. The views in question are different and incompatible. The Buddhist view goes as follows. A core Buddhist doctrine is that everything[3] is impermanent. Hence persons are impermanent. At a time, a person is one or more purely momentary states. Over time, a person is a series of such bundles. The Jain view is that persons are permanent. Nothing that happens can destroy a mind, which is the essential person. A person is an enduring, indestructible self-conscious being. Strictly speaking, for the Buddhist the world's history is a matter of one set of states being replaced by another set which in turn is replaced by another. *Change* is a matter of something gaining or losing a quality; an item at one time has different qualities than those it has at another. This requires that the item in question endures through time. If everything is impermanent, nothing endures.[4] On the Jain view, change occurs. The Jain view entails that persons retain personal identity into enlightenment. The Theravada view entails that personal identity is not retained in the ultimate enlightenment state.

In Part III, we consider what can be said for and against monotheistic belief. The existence of evil is the most influential consideration against the existence of God. Wrong choices, debilitating disease, war, and suffering are evil. Is it even logically possible that a world created by God contains these evils? Does the fact that such evils exist provide evidence against the existence of God? While it has seemed to some that the answers to these questions cast severe doubt on monotheism, others have thought they do not. Evil is genuinely tragic only if persons have great worth. If human persons are created in the image of God then they have this worth. If it less clear that they have this worth on nonmonotheistic views,[5] then perhaps at least part of the apparent force of the problem of evil rests on monotheism being true after all.

Various features of the world have been explained by reference to God:

Fact 1: There are things that do exist that might not have existed. In fact, everything around us might not have existed. It is logically possible, for example, that nothing material exists. Plainly, material things do exist. It is logically possible that finite minds do not exist. But they do.

Fact 2: The world is orderly in a manner accessible to our intelligence. Lots of worlds that might have existed would not have had this feature. In them, neither science nor successful planning could occur.

Fact 3: There are moral standards, criteria for good and evil that were not invented by us. There are actions and persons which are appropriately assessed by reference to these standards. This might not have been so.

If God exists, this explains these facts. Arguments for God's existence typically appeal to these facts. Further, experiences occur in different ages and cultures which their subjects take to be experiences of God. These experiences are often said to provide evidence that God exists. We consider both the considerations against and those for monotheism.

In Part IV, we consider nonmonotheistic traditions. Appeals to argument and appeals to experience are made in defense of the Advaita Vedanta claims that only qualityless Brahman exists and that each person is identical to qualityless Brahman. The main consideration typically presented on its behalf is the occurrence of an esoteric religious experience.[6] The Jain thesis that self-conscious, enduring minds enjoy independent existence entails that persons are at least enduring and self-conscious. This claim is defended by both specific Jain arguments and by appeal to everyday experience and Jain enlightenment. Similarly, the Buddhist doctrine that everything is impermanent and co-dependent entails that a person at a time is one collection of momentary elements and over time a person is a series of such collections. This claim is defended by argument and appeal to Buddhist enlightenment experience. We discuss these appeals to argument and experience in some detail.

In Part V, we turn to religion and morality, and faith and reason. Religion and morality are related in different ways. Particularly significant is whether the ultimate religious values include moral values. This is closely related to the status of persons in a religion's conception of salvation or enlightenment. Faith typically involves belief or acceptance of some propositions. In monotheism this is accompanied by trust in God. We offer an account of a relationship between reason, or rational assessment, and faith, or acceptance of a religious worldview.

Along the way other issues arise. For example, the existence and nature of human freedom and the relationship between divine foreknowledge and human freedom come up for consideration. Of course, not everything in Philosophy of Religion is discussed here. A wide range of issues are covered. The methods used in covering them apply to the other issues as well.

As the reader will discover, there is an overall argument in what follows. Each chapter makes its own contribution to that argument. "Philosophy" refers to a long tradition of texts, ideas, arguments, and worldviews. It also refers to the effort we make to assess the contents of these texts, ideas, arguments, and worldviews. In philosophy, "old" is not to be equated with "outdated" let alone with "false." "New" is not to be equated with "better" let alone with "true." Neither can we assume that what is old is true. For one thing, there are lots of claims that have been made for some time, and some are incompatible with others. Further, lots of claims that have been made for a long time are false.

Introducing someone to Philosophy, or increasing their acquaintance with it, typically and properly involves exposing her to some of the ideas, arguments, and worldviews philosophers (and others) have accepted. It also involves engaging her in an effort to rationally assess these ideas, arguments, and worldviews. The author's view is that the best way to do this is not simply to say "Here is this argument, here is that one, and people disagree" but to offer a sustained assessment of competing claims and arguments for those claims. Philosophy is best learned by informed philosophizing. Informed philosophizing is best learned by observing someone philosophizing and joining in the endeavor. The purpose of this book is to provide material for the student who wants to learn what it is to do philosophy as well as learning what it is that philosophers do.

PART I

Philosophy and religion

CHAPTER 2
What is philosophy? What is religion? What is philosophy of religion?

2

What is philosophy? What is religion? What is philosophy of religion?

Philosophy

What is philosophy?

No noncontroversial answer is possible, and this is not a book about what philosophy is. So I will just say what I take philosophy to be, and go on to do philosophy.[1] Philosophy is the enterprise of constructing and assessing categorial systems. The tasks necessary to this enterprise are thus philosophical tasks, and the requisite skills are philosophical skills. The tasks in question, and the skills, need not be uniquely philosophical.[2]

A categorial system is, not surprisingly, a system of categories. A category is a basic concept, primitive in the sense that it is not analyzable in terms of other concepts. The categories of a full-blown philosophical system will be concepts of things or entities (in the broadest sense of *thing* or *entity*), thoughts, or values.[3] Philosophy is the enterprise of constructing and assessing categorial systems. Much of Ancient, Medieval, and Modern philosophy was deliberately pursued systematically. Plato, Aristotle, Aquinas, Descartes, Leibniz, Spinoza, Locke, Berkeley, Hume, and Kant all constructed complex systems of philosophy. Their intent was, as a later philosopher put it, "to see things, and see them whole" – to develop an integrated account of things, of knowledge, and of ethics. Much of contemporary philosophy has been suspicious of any such large-scale endeavors and has tended to stick to particular problems. Nonetheless, in dealing with particular problems, these philosophers too accepted general claims that placed constraints on what they could consistently accept elsewhere; even philosophy in the particularist mode is implicitly general.

I take religious claims to be neither more nor less open to rational assessment than any other sorts of claims. Any difference there is concerns difficulty, not possibility. Nor do I see any reason to think that offering rational assessment of religious claims is in principle harder than, say, assessing attempts to offer a unified theory for all of physics, or to solve the problems of the foundations of modal logic. Contrary to the preferences of some philosophers, some Religious Studies professors, and even some religious thinkers themselves, religious traditions do make claims. They are anything remotely like what they claim to be only if what they say is true. I shall offer respect to the diversity of religious traditions by taking those claims seriously enough to try to see what can be said for and against them.

One can easily ask *How can you tell whether a religious belief is true or not?*, try to think of some general way in which this could be done, and give up. That question is a paralysis question. There is no single answer to it; religious claims are made about quite a diversity of things, and some must be assessed in one way and others in other ways. The only sensible way to proceed is on a claim-by-claim, case-by-case, basis; given enough cases, one may then be able to generalize. In what follows, I will try to understand, and then assess, a variety of religious beliefs. The sorts of assessments offered will typically be relevant to other, similar claims not mentioned here. There are simply too many religions to deal with all of them in one book, even if one knew enough to do that. If you like to think in terms of books having agendas, my major agenda is to show, by detailed argument, that it is possible to assess religious beliefs rationally. In this respect, it runs against a belief that is very popular in our culture, namely that matters of religion are simply private affairs concerning how you feel about big things. This belief seems to me patently false.

It also runs against the tendency in some (certainly not all) Religious Studies circles, and (worse) even among some philosophers, to the effect that to think of religions as making claims at all is to misunderstand them. While it is possible to reply to such philosophers on their own terms, I find it more interesting and relevant to doing philosophy of religion to show the falsity of this view by looking at the actual authoritative texts of religious traditions. As to the suspicion that trying to assess religious beliefs is not really polite, something no nice person would do, I note that those who possess these standards for politeness or nicety do not find much support in the religious traditions themselves. I confess to taking such notions of politeness and nicety as cases of failure of nerve and unwillingness to think hard about some of the most important matters there are.

The book that follows offers a sustained argument. It does not offer a particular philosophical system, though no doubt its philosophical commitments (as would any others) considerably constrain the sort of system that one who accepts them could consistently accept. It seems to me that some sorts of religious tradition come off a lot better under rational assessment than do others, and as the argument develops it will become clear which ones I take those to be.

Objectivity

Objectivity is rightly prized in philosophy as elsewhere. To be objective in the relevant sense is, roughly, to accept or reject a belief on the basis of what can be said in favor of, and what can be said against, its truth, no matter whether one would prefer the belief to be true or not. It neither requires nor precludes one's caring deeply about what the truth is. One can, for example, be fully objective about whether one's dog has cancer, while caring very much whether or not she does. There are two false views about objectivity. On one account, a book on the philosophy of religion can be objective only if it conforms to the pattern "Tradition A says this, Tradition B says that, Philosopher C argues against this in this way, but Philosopher D argues against the same thing like this, and now everybody decide for themselves without the author interfering." The assumption is that description can be objective, but assessment cannot be. Of course the author or authors of such a text have had to decide what was important enough to be favored by their attention, which interpretations of the traditions so favored were probably accurate, what arguments were the more interesting and forceful, what could properly be said about these arguments, and the like. It remains baffling as to why one should suppose *these* assessments can be objective whereas assessments of the religious beliefs themselves are impossible, particularly since offering the relevant descriptions involves tasks very similar to those included in making assessments. If it is granted that one can be objective about description, it is arbitrary to think that one cannot be objective about assessment. The other view is that objectivity is impossible to obtain about anything. There is obviously no reason to take this view seriously. It proclaims *Objectivity about any belief is impossible to obtain* and so if its proponents are right, they are just being so kind as to share a small bit of their autobiographies, something on the level of *I don't like seafood*, which of course has no philosophical relevance whatever. If they are wrong, then again we need not worry about their claim. The truth about objectivity is that it is hard to achieve, especially about things that matter, and that one can do one's best to try. Sometimes one succeeds. For example, the objective truth is that if James says *Nothing said in English is ever true*, either what he says is true or false. But if it is true, then it is false. So, either way, it is false.

Religion

What is religion?

Our world contains a perplexing diversity of religious traditions. Increasingly, representative congregations or conclaves of these traditions can be found in any major city. Our question is simply *What is religion?* Responsible answers will reflect what one finds in traditions universally agreed to be religious.[4]

A definition of religion

Broadly speaking, definitions of "religion" tend to fall into one of two classes. One sort of definition is substantial or doctrinal; a given religion is defined in terms of the beliefs its adherents accept that make them adherents of that religion, and religion generally is characterized in terms of beliefs that all religions are alleged to share. Another sort of definition is functional or pragmatic; "religion" is defined in terms of what it is alleged that all religions do or what the social function of religion is alleged to be. Some definitions, of course, are somewhat less than objective. Marx's claim that religion is the opiate of the people is not proposed as a scholarly and neutral definition of religion – or, even if it is presented as neutral, it isn't. It is a functional definition rather than a substantial definition. "Religion is the superstitious acceptance of the belief that God exists" is a non-neutral substantial definition. "Religion is the act of getting right before God" is a non-neutral definition that is partly substantial and partly functional.

As a basis for answering our question, we need a neutral definition. A neutral definition will not presuppose some particular answer to any of our substantial philosophical questions. It will not presuppose that some particular religious tradition is true (or false) or that no religious traditions are true (or false). For reasons that will become clear shortly, it will be nice if the definition can be both functional and also recognize the important point made by attempts to give a substantial definition. I offer this definition: *a religion is a conceptual system that provides an interpretation of the world and the place of human beings in it, bases an account of how life should be lived given that interpretation, and expresses this interpretation and lifestyle in a set of rituals, institutions, and practices*. This is a functional definition; it views religions as providing persons with accounts of their world and their place in it – interpretations that are relevant to day-to-day living and that are given life in institutions, practices, and rituals. It recognizes the importance of religious activities. It also recognizes the importance of a doctrinal element in religious traditions. If doctrines without rituals are empty, then rituals without doctrines are blind. I should add that by "rituals" here one should not think only of a Catholic Mass or a highly liturgical Anglican or Lutheran service. A Plymouth Brethren celebration of the Lord's Supper or a Baptist celebration of adult baptism is a ritual in the sense of being a religious activity charged with theological meaning. My intent is that this definition be neutral in the sense recently characterized. Social science treatments of religion tend to focus on the institutions, rituals, and practices, viewed either collectively as cultural artifacts or individually as sources of personal meaning. Philosophical discussions of religion tend to focus on the doctrines that religions offer and live by. These approaches are supplementary, not competitive, though academics often play down, or even deny, the importance of what they do not happen to study.

Another definition

A different, but compatible, characterization of religion makes use of the notions of diagnosis and cure. A religion proposes a *diagnosis* (an account of what it takes the basic problem facing human beings to be) and a *cure* (a way of permanently and desirably solving that problem): one basic problem shared by every human person[5] and one fundamental solution that, however adapted to different cultures and cases, is essentially the same across the board. Religions differ insofar as their diagnoses and cures differ. For example, some religions are monotheistic and some are not. Hence some diagnoses are offered in terms of alienation from God and cures are presented that concern removing that alienation, while other diagnoses and cures make no reference to God.

Philosophy of religion

What is philosophy of religion?

Metaphysics, epistemology, and ethics are disciplines within philosophy. Metaphysics is the enterprise of constructing and assessing accounts of what there is. Epistemology is the enterprise of constructing and assessing accounts of what knowledge is and how it can be attained. Ethics is the enterprise of constructing and assessing accounts of what makes actions right or wrong, what makes persons good or evil, what possesses intrinsic worth, what sort of life is worth living, and how these matters are related.[6]

Philosophy of religion combines these enterprises in offering philosophically accessible accounts of religious traditions and assessing those traditions. Nothing very complex is involved in offering philosophically accessible accounts of religious traditions; the idea is simply to offer clear and literal[7] expressions of key doctrines.

A further feature of philosophy is worth highlighting. As Edmund Gettier once remarked in conversation, in philosophy you do not understand a position unless you understand the arguments for it.[8] Such claims as *All that exists is minds and ideas, If a proposition P is necessarily true then "P is necessarily true" is also necessarily true,* or *The existence of evil is logically compatible with the existence of God,* are such that one does not understand them unless one also grasps the reasons that can be offered on their behalf. This is why trying to teach philosophy without discussion of arguments is like trying to teach mathematics without reference to numbers. The reason, then, why we will pay attention to arguments is that this is a book on philosophy.

Questions for reflection

1 Explain what "Philosophy is the construction and assessment of categorial systems" means.
2 Explain and assess the claims that "The claim that objectivity is impossible is self-defeating" and "Objectivity is possible."
3 Distinguish between functional and substantial definitions of religion.
4 Offer and explain a definition of *religion*.
5 Offer and explain a definition of *philosophy of religion*.

Annotated reading

The works cited below are some of the best older studies in the philosophy of religion; some of the best newer studies are noted at the end of Part I.

Bertocci, Peter (1951) *An Introduction to the Philosophy of Religion,* Englewood Cliffs, NJ: Prentice-Hall. Covers a wide range of issues in the philosophy of religion with a detailed discussion of the teleological argument.

Bertocci, Peter (1970) *The Person God Is,* London: George Allen and Unwin, Ltd. Detailed presentation of theistic personalism (the view that persons are irreducible – not a complex made up of simpler things – and (in the case of God) ultimate).

Brightman, E. S. (1940) *A Philosophy of Religion,* New York: Prentice-Hall. Also covers a wide range of issues, arguing for the view that God is finite.

Burtt, E. A. (1951) *Types of Religious Philosophy*, New York: Harper and Brothers. After discussing Greek and biblical thought considers major traditions and some issues in philosophy of religion.

MacIntosh, H. R. (1940) *The Problem of Religious Knowledge*, New York: Harper and Brothers. Discussion of wide range of theories of religious knowledge.

Patterson, Robert Leet (1970) *The Philosophy of Religion*, Durham, NC: Duke University Press. An account of the natures of philosophy and religion followed by a discussion of issues in the philosophy of religion.

Thomas, George F. (1970) *Philosophy and Religious Belief*, New York: Charles Scribner's Sons. Discussion of grounds of belief, God and the world, and freedom and grace.

Thomas, George F. (1973) *Religious Philosophies of the West*, New York: Charles Scribner's Sons. Discusses the positions of "Western" philosophers of religion from Plato through Tillich, with glance beyond.

Thompson, Samuel (1955) *A Modern Philosophy of Religion*, Chicago: Henry Regnery. Another account of the natures of philosophy and religion followed by a discussion of issues in the philosophy of religion.

Wieman, H. N. and Meland, Bernard Eugene (eds) (1936) *American Philosophers of Religion*, Chicago: Willett, Clark, and Co. Varieties of philosophies of religion held in American culture.

1. Philosophy is coming up with a construct, sometimes about the whole of things and then assessing that construct. Philosophy is presented in systematic categories to be analyzed and argued.

CHAPTER 3
What sorts of religion are there?

What sorts of religion are there?

Different religions offer differing diagnoses and cures. Given that criterion, there are a good many religions. The diagnosis that a particular religion articulates asserts that every human person has a basic nonphysical illness so deep that, unless it is cured, one's potential is unfulfilled and one's nature cripplingly flawed. Then a cure is proffered. The diagnosis and cure assume[1] (or, if you prefer, entail) the essential structure of a religion's view of what there is, at least insofar as what there is has religious importance.

Not only are there different religions; there are different *sorts* of religion. The notion of a *sort* or kind of religion is not a paradigm of clarity. Perhaps this criterion will lend it some clarity:

Criterion 1: Religion A is of a *different sort* from Religion B if one can have the problem that A diagnoses without having the problem that B diagnoses, one can have the problem that B diagnoses without having the problem that A diagnoses, the cure that A proffers would not cure the disease that B diagnoses, and the cure that B proffers would not cure the disease that A diagnoses.

A different criterion that nonetheless will yield results that at least largely overlap those we get from applying Criterion 1 is:

Criterion 2: Religion A is of a *different sort* from Religion B if what must exist if A's diagnosis and cure are correct can exist without what must exist if B's diagnosis and cure are correct, and conversely.

A stronger version goes:

Criterion 3: Religion A is of a *different sort* from Religion B if what must exist if A's diagnosis and cure are correct cannot co-exist with what must exist if B's diagnosis and cure are correct, and conversely.

To offer an even partial answer as to what sorts of religion there are, examples are crucial. Consider, then, four traditions that are generally accepted as being religious: Christianity, Advaita Vedanta Hinduism, Jainism, and Theravada Buddhism. Christendom contains an incredible variety of perspectives. Hinduism, even if it is not the invention of nineteenth-century British scholars, is at least as diverse as Christendom. Buddhism is also a collection of quite diverse traditions and even Jainism has its complications. Nonetheless, there is such a thing as *orthodox* Christianity ("orthodox" with a small "o"), and an absolutist variety of Hinduism, Advaita Vedanta, whose greatest figure is Shankara. Indian Buddhism splits into Mahayana or "Great Vehicle" as well as Hinayana or "Small Vehicle;" our present concern is with Hinayana or Theravada Buddhism, the "Tradition of the Elders." Jainism, by contrast, is doctrinally uniform. A description of each of these four traditions in terms that would be accepted by its own adherents[2] will tell us a good deal about what sorts of religion there are. Each tradition represents a distinct sort of religion.[3]

Monotheism

Christianity

Christianity, of course, is a variety of monotheism. It shares with Judaism the exhortation to "Hear, O Israel, the Lord is one God." Like Judaism and Islam, it holds that an omnipotent, omniscient, and morally perfect God created the world and is providential over it.[4] God depends for existence on nothing else, and everything else that exists[5] depends on God for its existence. The created world is real, not illusory, and that it exists is a good, not an evil, state of affairs. Human beings are created in God's image, and thus have some degree of knowledge, power, and (potential) goodness. This has two consequences. One is that every person, as a person, has (in Immanuel Kant's terms) dignity and not price – if you like, has irreplaceable worth by virtue of being in God's image. Persons having inherent worth as creatures made in God's image is different from their being inherently morally good; whether a person becomes morally good or not depends on his or her choices. We might put the point this way: *being created in God's image* comprises a *metaphysical* goodness that is a gift provided in the very circumstance of being created; *being morally virtuous* constitutes *moral* goodness and it is not involved in the very act of being created. The other consequence is that the basis of morality lies in realizing one's nature by imitating the behavior biblically ascribed to God, insofar as this is humanly possible. God is holy, so we are to be holy. God unselfishly loves, so we ought to love unselfishly. Human individuality is real, not illusory, and it is good not evil, that individuals exist. God loves all persons in the sense of willing their ultimate good and acting for it. Central to being made in God's image is having the capacity for loving others and oneself in the sense of willing their and our ultimate good and acting for it. Love in this sense is primarily volitional, not primarily emotional. God is providential in the sense of governing the course of history and moving it toward the Kingdom of God, so that time is real and the historical process is real and one-directional (not cyclical).[6] It is a good, not an evil, that there are temporal and historical events. God is holy both in the sense of being unique, alone worthy of being worshipped, and of being morally pure or righteous. Thus worship is not a preliminary religious experience to be later transcended; its appropriateness is built into the nature of the distinction between Creator and creature, which is not a dissolvable distinction. As God is righteous, God judges sin. Sin is freely performed action that violates God's moral law; sin also is a defect of our nature due to our living in a world in which sinful actions proliferate. Sin prevents one's realizing his or her nature as made in God's image. Since God loves all persons, God hates what harms persons, and hence hates sin. Intolerance of sin is not opposed to, but follows from, the nature of divine love. Thus human sin and guilt are real, not illusory, and it is better that persons act freely and exercise moral agency than that they be made unable to sin. The basic religious problem is sin, and the deepest religious need is for forgiveness. Forgiveness is provided by God's grace or unmerited favor; it is not earned by human effort. God has acted in history at real times and in real places to reveal information that otherwise we would not have had and to act on our behalf. Central religious doctrines make *essential* reference to certain persons and events. Religious knowledge, at least in part, is gained through revelation rather than through reflection, meditation, self-abasement, or the like.

Much or all of this applies as well to Judaism and Islam, at least in their more orthodox varieties. What is distinct about Christianity, not surprisingly, is the life, death, and resurrection of Christ. In the Apostle Paul's summary of the basic Christian Gospel, he tells his audience: "I delivered unto you what I also received, that Christ died for our sins according to the Scriptures, and was buried, and rose again from the dead, according to the Scriptures."[7] That Christ lived sinlessly, that Christ died "the Just for the Unjust in order to bring us to God," that "Christ, who knew no sin, was made to be sin for us," that "Christ bore our sins in his own body on the tree," and that Christ bodily rose from the dead, are claims central to – indeed, they *are* – the Christian Gospel, the content of the Christian message.

Transition

Vedanta, Jainism, and Theravada Buddhism at root are Indian religions. Each has its own sacred texts.[8] Advaita Vedanta and Theravada Buddhism rather considerably qualify what is meant by reincarnation and karma, but they begin with these as assumptions. There is a story that, in its Jain version, goes as follows:

> A traveller was journeying through a dense forest when he encountered a mad elephant which charged him with upraised trunk. As he turned to flee, a terrible demoness with a naked sword in her hand appeared before him and barred his path. There was a great tree near the track, and he ran up to it, hoping to find safety in its branches, but he could find no foothold in its smooth trunk. His only refuge was an old well, covered with grass and weeds, at the foot of the tree, and into this he leapt. As he fell, he managed to catch hold of a clump of reeds which grew from the wall, and there he hung, midway between the mouth of the well and its bottom. Looking down, he saw that the bottom did not contain water, but was surrounded by snakes, which hissed at him as he hung above them. In their midst was a mighty python, its mouth agape, waiting to catch him when he fell. Raising his head again, he saw two mice, one white and the other black, busily eating away at the roots. Meanwhile, the wild elephant ran up to the well and, enraged at losing its victim, began charging at the trunk of the tree. Thus he dislodged a honeycomb which hung from a branch above the well, and it fell upon the man hanging there so precariously. Angry bees swarmed round his head and tormented him with their stings. But one drop of honey fell on his brow, rolled down to his face, and reached his lips. Immediately, he forgot his peril and thought of nothing more than of obtaining another drop of honey.[9]

Reincarnation and karma

Common to Hinduism, Jainism, and Theravada Buddhism are two familiar assumptions. Each accepts as a basic framework the doctrines of *reincarnation* (that each person is beginninglessly born and dies and is reborn and redies, and that this will occur endlessly short of one's achieving enlightenment) and *karma* (that one's right actions will be rewarded and one's wrong actions will be punished, without exception, save as this is qualified in some varieties of Vedanta by a doctrine of divine grace). Thus for each of these perspectives a religion should tell you how to 'escape the wheel' or stop the otherwise endless sequence of births and deaths.

From the perspective of a reincarnation/karma view, there might seem to be a highly attractive alternative open to us all. By living morally decent lives, according to this perspective, we can guarantee that we are reborn in pleasant circumstances; there is no necessary end to this process. Thus by living according to a decent moral code, we can look forward to an unending travel program under positive circumstances. Why isn't this a recommended alternative?

One reason is that on the relevant perspective one cannot, in this lifetime, make a decision that is irrevocably effective over one's future lifetimes; perhaps in the very next lifetime one will opt for drunken stupors and drug trips over endeavor for enlightenment. But there is also a deeper reason.

A Hindu text[10] reads as follows:

> In this ill-smelling body, which is a conglomerate of bone, skin, muscle, marrow, flesh, semen, blood, mucus, tears, rheum, feces, urine, wind, bile, and phlegm, what is the good of enjoyment of desires? . . . In this body, which is afflicted with desire, anger, covetousness, delusion, fear, despondency, envy, separation from the desirable, union with the undesirable, hunger, thirst, senility, disease, sorrow, and the like, what is the good of the enjoyment of desires? . . . we see that this whole world is decaying . . . In this sort of cycle of existence, what is the good of the enjoyment of desires, when after a man has fed on them there is seen repeatedly his return here to earth? . . . in this cycle of existence I am a frog in a waterless well.

A Theravada text[11] says:

> What then is the Holy Truth of Ill? Birth is ill, decay is ill, sickness is ill, death is ill. To be disjoined from what one likes means suffering. Not to get what one wants also that means suffering. In short, all grasping at any of the five Skandas [the elements of personality] involves suffering.

Being a frog in countless waterless wells, or suffering in endless cosmic variety, in these views, only prolongs a problem to which religion should provide a solution. An everlasting series of reincarnations would be the analogue to hell. Life is viewed as inherently unsatisfactory or unsatisfying – one scholar uses "unsatisfactoriness" rather than "suffering" in dealing with the sort of Buddhist text just quoted. Hinduism, Jainism, and Theravada Buddhism, then, each offers an escape from the Wheel of reincarnations.

The point of the story of the traveller in the forest now becomes clear. Most people are like the traveller. We focus our attention on "the things of this world" as the traveller focuses simply on the sweet taste of the honey. But the honey gives no solution to his deep, real problem. So most of us pay no attention to our deep religious problem. "The things of this world" provide no solution to that problem, whether we live grandly or barely survive. This is the point of the story. On that point, at least, religious traditions typically agree.

Advaita Vedanta

Advaita Vedanta is one of three main schools of Vedantic Hinduism; the other two are monotheistic. Popular Advaita Vedanta tends to polytheistic or monotheistic practices. Nonetheless, Advaita Vedanta takes monotheism to belong to *the realm of appearance* rather than to *the realm of reality*. There are two major ways of trying to explain what this distinction amounts to. One way treats the appearance/reality distinction epistemologically or relative to human knowledge, and speaks of *levels of truth*. Another way treats the appearance versus reality distinction metaphysically or in terms of what exists independent of human thought, and speaks of *levels of being*. The levels of being view goes something like this.

Suppose that something A depends for its existence on B, and B does not depend for its existence on anything else. Then one might (somewhat misleadingly) say that B has more reality than A, although strictly what is true is that B's existence is more secure than A's. Suppose, further, that B has more power, and knowledge, and goodness than A, or is more complex than A, or the like – suppose that B's properties are in some way more glorious than A's. Then one might say that B is "more real" than A in the sense of being more valuable than A, more worth imitating than A, or the like. It seems less open to misunderstanding to say all of this in terms of the greater existential security and the higher value that attaches to B, but insofar as what was intended was consistent, these sorts of things seem to be what philosophers who have talked about "degrees of existence" have had in mind. But this – the levels of being line – cannot be the way to understand Shankara. For if appearance depends on Reality, then appearance and Reality are such that appearance bears a genuine and non-illusory or non-apparent relationship to Reality; both appearance and Reality exist, and the former depends on the latter. On Shankara's view,

Reality can bear no such relationship to anything. Further, the properties of Reality can be more glorious than appearance's properties only if Reality has more glorious properties than those of appearance, and so on this view Reality has properties. But according to Shankara, Reality is *nirguna* or qualityless. So the levels of being line will not do as an exposition of Advaita Vedanta.

There remains the levels of truth line. Some elementary points regarding this are: (1) strictly, truth has no degrees; as a property of propositions, which seems what is here relevant, it is either present or not; (2) no doubt "more true" can be given some use, and if one is very careful no doubt this will cause no confusion; then we need to ask exactly what this sense is: compare "more perfect;" (3) if two propositions are contradictory then one must be true and the other false.

Now on a levels of truth view, the truth about Reality is one level of truth and the truth about appearance is another level of truth. Reality is qualityless Brahman. Thus when Brahman is described as being, consciousness, and bliss – *sat, cit, ananda* – this (if Brahman is really qualityless) is but to deny that Brahman has the properties of being non-existent, unconscious, and miserable. The truth about Reality, on Shankara's view, is that Brahman exists, and for any property, Brahman lacks it. This is a bit sparse, but it is the truth at the level of reality. The other level concerns appearance. There is something funny about the phrase "the truth about appearance" when used in this context. The reason for this is simple: strictly speaking, appearance does not exist. *That* is the truth about it. Perhaps, then, appearance is simply the way Reality looks to the unenlightened. But the unenlightened are *part* of appearance. Thus *they* do not exist, and so cannot be appeared to. The levels of truth view is that Reality appears to be one way and is another; there are perceptual experiences but they are all unreliable or misleading and there are perceivers but they are misled. But then these misleading experiences and misled perceivers must be real. But strictly they do not exist; they are not merely less glorious than the Real, but altogether non-existent. It is thus not easy to see how the lower level of truth is to be conceived. On it, appearance is as hard to make out as Reality.

Having spent some time in indicating some of the complexity involved in interpreting Advaita Vedanta, and given some indication of the sort of features that lead to objections by such non-Advaitic figures as Ramanuja and Madhva, let me turn to offering a brief and fairly straightforward description of this tradition. There is an ultimate and independent reality that is apersonal. To say that God is infinite is not, as in monotheistic contexts, to say that God is omnipotent, omniscient, and morally perfect. Rather, it is to say that everything is divine. For monotheism, "infinite" is an adjective, and to speak of "the Infinite" is to raise the question "The

Infinite *what*?" For Advaita Vedanta, "the Infinite" is a noun referring to Brahman. Persons seem to be enduring mental substances, and the objects of sensory perception seem to be enduring physical substances. This indeed is how they are to be viewed unless we turn to the level of Reality. Then the truth is that each Atman or enduring self is identical to Brahman; "Thou art that." The basic religious problem is ignorance – taking appearance to be Reality. Escape from this ignorance requires that one attain *moksha*, an esoteric experience in which it is alleged that no subject/conscious/object or subject/object distinction can be made. Personal identity obviously is not retained in one's solving one's religious problem; indeed, strictly, personal identity is viewed as always illusory and you cannot retain what you never had. Achieving *moksha* is due to one's efforts; salvation is essentially a do-it-yourself project for Advaita Vedanta, as it is for Jainism and Theravada Buddhism.[12] An Advaita Vedanta text tells us that "the man who has once comprehended Brahman to be the [real] self does not belong to this transmigratory world . . . There prevails the false notion that the Lord [i.e. Brahman] and the transmigrating soul are different."[13] The description of Advaita Vedanta offered here is, in effect, an explanation of what this passage means according to an Advaitic interpretation.

Jainism

Jainism is a particularly interesting religion in that it holds to the immortality of the soul without being monotheistic. It holds that the self or person or *jiva* is an enduring mental substance that is inherently immortal. Human persons *appear to be* enduring mental substances because they *are* enduring mental substances, just as physical objects appear to be enduring physical substances because they are. A Jaina text says straightforwardly that "modifications cannot exist without an abiding or eternal something – a permanent substance."[14] But persons seem to have limitations that they do not have, and by attaining an esoteric state of enlightenment – *kevala* – one can see that these limitations are illusory. Thus in the *Jaina Sutras*[15] one reads that when the Venerable Ascetic Mahavira had become enlightened, he was

> omniscient and comprehending all objects; he knew and saw all conditions of the world, of gods, men, and demons: whence they come, whither they go, whether they are born as men or animals . . . or become gods or hell-beings . . . the ideas, the thoughts of their minds, the food, doings, desires, the open and

> secret deeds of all living beings in the whole world; he the Arhat, for whom there is no secret, knew and saw all conditions of all living beings in the world, what they thought, spoke, or did at any moment.

Occasionally it is claimed that one who reaches *kevala* even learns that he or she is omnipotent; at any rate, one learns that one is omniscient and dependent for one's existence on nothing external to oneself. The same *Sutras* say of the soul that "since it possesses no corporeal form, it is eternal."[16] This is not a variety of monotheism; there is no reference to God or (as in monotheistic Hinduism) to Brahman with qualities. Nor does it posit an identity between the soul and qualityless Brahman. Another Jaina text says that

> Liberation is the freedom from all karmic matter, owing to the non-existence of the cause of bondage and to the shedding of the *karmas*. After the soul is released, there remain perfect right-belief, perfect right-knowledge, and the state of having accomplished all.[17]

Thus personal identity is retained in enlightenment; a mental substance that once existed under severe epistemic and other constraints is freed from those constraints.

Buddhism

Theravada Buddhism

A Buddhist text says that

> Nagasena [or any other personal proper name] is but a way of counting, term, appellation, convenient designation, mere name for the hair of my head, hair of my body . . . brain of the head, form, sensation, perception, the predispositions and consciousness. But in the absolute sense there is no ego.[18]

An individual person is a set of elements, each momentary and transitory, and everything else is made up of momentary, transitive states as well. There is no *atman* or *jiva* or enduring self – no enduring mental substance – nor is there an unchanging ultimate Brahman. Thus one reads that

> Misery only doth exist, none miserable. No doer is there; naught save the deed is found. Nirvana is, but not the man who seeks this. That path exists, but not the man who seeks this. That path exists, but not the traveller on it.[19]

We are told that as

> the word "chariot" is but a name for pole, axle, wheels, chariot-body, and banner staff . . . [the proper name] "Nagasena" is but a . . . mere name for the hair of my head, brain of the head, form, sensation, perception, the predispositions, and consciousness. But in the absolute sense there is no ego to be found.[20]

In a this-life experience that prefigures final nirvana the enlightened one learns this truth concerning impermanence. Final nirvana is the cessation of even this transitory self with consequent release from all desire. Nirvana alone is changeless.

Comparison

It may aid comprehension if we compare and contrast our Indian traditions. For Advaita Vedanta, there is a distinction between the apparent self and the real; one cannot escape transmigration without knowing the nature of this distinction – namely, that the real self is identical with qualityless Brahman. For Jainism, there is a distinction between the way the self appears regarding knowledge and dependence and the way the self is regarding knowledge and dependence; we are omniscient and independent, and one cannot escape transmigration without knowing this. For Theravada, we tend to believe that there is an enduring ego or self, and there is none; one cannot escape transmigration without knowing this. In each case, the religious problem we all face is said to be ignorance of our own nature. Each religious tradition has its own account of the truth about what our nature is. Correspondingly, each has its own cure, namely the recognition of and appropriate reaction to the truth about ourselves.

The criteria applied

According to Christianity, our sickness is that we have sinned against God and the cure is that God provide forgiveness and restoration. According to Advaita Vedanta, the sickness is our ignorance of our being identical with

Brahman and the cure is gaining this knowledge. According to Jainism, the sickness is that we think we are ignorant and dependent and the cure is learning that we are omniscient and existentially independent. According to Theravada Buddhism, our sickness is that we take ourselves to be enduring substances and the cure is learning that we are only transitory states. While brief, lacking subtlety and detail, these remarks are also accurate.

We can summarize the diagnoses and cures as follows:

- Christianity: sinners, divine forgiveness and restoration;
- Advaita Vedanta: ignorance of Brahman, knowledge of Brahman;
- Jainism: assumed ignorance and dependence, knowledge of independence and omniscience;
- Theravada Buddhism: assumed status as enduring substances, knowledge of transitory states.

Earlier, three criteria were offered of what it might mean to speak about different *sorts* of religions. The first of these was:

Criterion 1: Religion A is of a *different sort* from Religion B if one can have the problem that A diagnoses without having the problem that B diagnoses, one can have the problem that B diagnoses without having the problem that A diagnoses, the cure that A proffers would not cure the disease that B diagnoses, and the cure that B proffers would not cure the disease that A diagnoses.

Assuming that it is logically possible that any one of these diagnoses be correct, and logically possible that any one of these cures works regarding its target disease, it is obviously possible to have any of the alleged diseases – sin, ignorance of Brahman, assumed dependence and ignorance, assumed enduring substance and actual transitory states – without having any of the others. Further, no one cure would work for any of the sicknesses save the one with which it is correlated by the religious tradition that suggests it. So, by Criterion 1, we have four distinct sorts of religions.

The second criterion was:

Criterion 2: Religion A is of a *different sort* from Religion B if what must exist if A's diagnosis and cure is correct can exist without what must exist if B's diagnosis and cure are correct, and conversely.

What must exist if the diagnoses and cures are correct can be represented as follows:

- Christianity: God, persons created by God;
- Advaita Vedanta: only qualityless Brahman;
- Jainism: independently existing persons;
- Theravada Buddhism:[21] only transitory states.

Assuming that each account of what there must be if the diagnoses and cures are correct is possibly true, it is obvious that each could exist without the others existing.

The third criterion was:

Criterion 3: Religion A is of a *different sort* from Religion B if what must exist if A's diagnosis and cure are correct cannot co-exist with what must exist if B's diagnosis and cure are correct, and conversely.

Plainly, in the context of its overall religious tradition, each account of what there is has this feature: if it is true, the others are not.[22]

Given the discussion just concluded, it is clear that Christianity, Advaita Vedanta, Theravada Buddhism, and Jainism are, given any of these criteria, different sorts of religions. One may like, dislike, or be indifferent to this fact; but it is a fact. These are neither all the religions nor all the sorts of religion that there are. But we have made progress in laying out data relevant to philosophical reflections about religion.

Questions for reflection

1 What are the core doctrines of monotheistic religions? What philosophical issues do they raise?
2 What are the core doctrines of Christian monotheism? Do these doctrines raise any philosophical issues not also raised by monotheism alone?
3 What are the core doctrines of Theravada Buddhism? What philosophical issues do they raise?
4 What are the core doctrines of Jainism? What philosophical issues do they raise?
5 What are the core doctrines of Advaita Vedanta? What philosophical issues do they raise?
6 Are the criteria offered for religions being of different sorts philosophically neutral and accurately applied?

Annotated reading

Christian, William (1972) *Opposition of Religious Doctrines*, New York: Herder and Herder. An account of how we can discover and may understand doctrinal differences between religions.

Larsen, Gerald James and Deutsch, Elliot (eds) (1988) *Interpreting across Boundaries*, Princeton, NJ: Princeton University Press. Investigates some of the challenges and rewards of considering religion in a cross-cultural context.

Schmidt, Wilhelm (1931) *The Origin and Growth of Religion*, London: Methuen and Company. A controversial but very interesting defense of the view that monotheism is the earliest religion.

Smart, Ninian (1960) *A Dialogue of Religions*, London: SCM Press. Presents the views of various religions on central topics in the form of a dialogue.

Smart, Ninian (1964) *Doctrine and Argument in Indian Philosophy*, London: Allen and Unwin. Clear and comprehensive presentation of the basic claims of different Indian philosophical systems.

CHAPTER 4
What sorts of religious experience are there?

Structure and content

Descriptions

Criteria and their application

Questions for reflection

Annotated reading

4

What sorts of religious experience are there?

Structure and content

The interest of religious experiences for the philosophy of religion lies in whatever potential they may have for providing information about what there is. Those who think that there are experience-independent material objects typically suppose that perceptual experience – seeing, hearing, tasting, smelling, and touching[1] – are on the whole a reliable source of information about these objects.[2] Moral experience typically is taken by moral realists – roughly, those who think that there actually are obligations, duties, right and wrong ways of behaving, ways of being a good or an evil person, and the like – to have similar information potential. The discussion that follows is governed by an underlying query: what sort of information about what there is might religious experience provide, and how could one tell? While this underlying question does not receive direct attention until later chapters, the presentation here looks forward to the discussion there.

Not only are there various sorts of religion; there are also various sorts of religious experience. The notion of a *sort* of experience is not immediately obvious. Let us begin with two criteria for experiences being of a different sort. One has to do with structure, the other with content. Consider such experiences as feeling nauseous, dizzy, or disoriented; consider also generalized anxiety and generalized euphoria, where the force of "generalized" is to cancel out the idea that there is something in particular that one is anxious or euphoric about. These experiences do not seem to their subjects to be matters of sensing something external, something that exists independent of the subject and, so to say, causes her to take notice of itself. In that respect, these experiences differ from seeing a tree, hearing a bell, or smelling the perking coffee. The former experiences are *subject/content*; the experience's "owner" feels a certain way. The latter experiences are *subject/consciousness/object*; the experience's "owner" senses (or seems to sense) a particular object – a tree, a bell, or coffee. To have generalized anxiety or euphoria, panic attacks, or a headache is to have subject/content experience. To be anxious about the large dog pulling at his chain, euphoric at the thought of buttermilk doughnuts, or pained by a friend's harsh words is to have a subject/consciousness/object experience. This leads us to our first criterion.

Criterion 1: Experience A is of a different sort from experience B if A is of subject/consciousness/object structure and B is of subject/content structure, or conversely.

Whether there are other experiential structures besides the two we have mentioned or not, an experience possessing one of the two identified structures is of a different sort from one that has the other sort of identified structure.

The second criterion has to do with experiential content. One way of understanding "different sort of content" is to consider different sensory modalities. Since there seems not to be much by way of different modalities relevant to religious experience, such considerations are of no help in understanding the notion of a sort of religious experience. An easily formulated criterion concerns what philosophers sometimes call *hedonic content* – the pleasantness or unpleasantness of an experience. Is having the experience a matter of pleasure or of pain? So, where the different hedonic content types are *being pleasurable, being painful,* and *being neutral regarding pleasure and pain,* one can offer:

Criterion 1a: Experience A is of a different sort from experience B if they have different hedonic content.

But this criterion has little relevance to our concerns.

Phenomenologically, *as-experienced* so to say, color content is one thing and auditory content another. True, different sensory content arises from different sensory sources, the deaf can see colors and the blind can hear sounds, and it is logically possible that there be a world without colors but with sounds, or a world without sounds but with colors. But after one has recited such things, the difference between color experience and sound experience that makes us think of them, if we do, as of different sorts lies in their intrinsic phenomenological difference, their experienced quality. More generally, color and sound experiences differ from each other and from taste experiences because colors, sounds, and tastes are themselves of different sorts. Recognized phenomenological distinctness is here the basis of discerned difference in experiential kind.[3] Recognition of phenomenological differences, of course, is not limited to noting differences in sensory content.

Descriptions

It may be helpful here to have some descriptions of religious experiences to hand before offering what is a more helpful criterion than Criterion 1a. The descriptions indicated by an asterisk seem more clearly first-person reports, and those not so designated seem more a matter of comments about what is true of a sort of experience particularly prized by the tradition in question, though it is very likely that these comments themselves are affected by reports by people who claim to have had such experiences.

*Experience 1**: Moses, tending the flock of his father-in-law Jethro, sees a bush that apparently is burning and not consumed by the fire. Then, the text of Exodus tells us: And Moses said, "I will turn aside and see this great sight, why the bush is not burnt." When the Lord saw that he turned aside to see, God called to him out of the bush, "Moses, Moses!" And he said, "Here am I." Then he [God] said, "Do not come near; put off your shoes from your feet, for the place on which you are standing is holy ground." And he said, "I am the God of your Father, the God of Abraham, the God of Isaac, the God of Jacob." And Moses hid his face, for he was afraid to look at God. (Exodus 3: 3–6)

*Experience 2**: In the year that King Uzziah died I saw the Lord, high and holy and lifted up; and his train filled the temple. Above him stood the seraphim; each had six wings: with two he covered his face, and with two he covered his feet, and with two he flew. And one called to another and said: "Holy, holy, holy is the Lord of Hosts; the whole earth is full of His glory." And the foundations of the thresholds shook at the voice of him who called, and the house was filled with smoke. And I said: "Woe is me! For I am lost; for I am a man of unclean lips and I dwell in the midst of a people of unclean lips; for my eyes have seen the king, the Lord of hosts!" Then flew one of the seraphims to me, having in his hand a burning coal which he had taken with tongs from the altar. And he touched my mouth, and said: "Behold, this has touched your lips; your guilt is taken away, and your sin forgiven." And I heard the Lord saying, "Whom shall I send, and who will go for us?" Then I said, "Here I am! Send me." And he said, "Go . . ."

(Isaiah 6:1–9)

*Experience 3**: I [John] was in the Spirit on the Lord's day, and I heard behind me a loud voice like a trumpet saying, "Write what you see in a book and send it to the seven churches . . . Then I turned to see the voice that was speaking to me, and on turning I saw seven golden lampstands, and in the midst of the lampstands one like a son of man, clothed with a long robe and with a golden girdle round his breast; his head and his hair were white as wool, white as snow; his eyes were like a flame of fire, his feet were like burnished bronze, refined as in a furnace, and his voice was like the sound of many waters; in his right hand he held seven stars, from his mouth issued a sharp two-edged sword, and his face was like the sun shining in full strength. When I saw him, I fell at his feet as though dead. But he laid his right hand upon me, saying "Fear not, I am the first and the last, and the living one; I died, and behold I am alive forevermore, and I have the keys of Death and Hades."

(Revelation 1:10–18)

*Experience 4**: Father of all, Master supreme, Power supreme in all the worlds, Who is like thee? Who is beyond thee? I bow before thee. I prostrate before thee, and I beg thy grace, O glorious Lord. As a father to his son, as a friend to his friend, as a lover to his lover, be gracious unto me, O God. In a vision I have seen what no man has seen before; I rejoice in exultation, and yet my heart trembles with fear. Have mercy upon me, Lord of Gods, refuge of the whole universe: show me again thine own human form. I yearn to see thee again with thy crown and scepter and circle. Show thyself to me in thine own four-armed form, thou of arms infinite, Infinite Form.

(*Bhagavagita [Song of the Blessed Lord]*
Chapter 11, paragraphs 43–6)

Experience 5: This monk life leads to complete detachment, to freedom from desire, to peace, to superknowledge, to the highest insight, to nibbana.

(*Digha Nikaya* II, 251)

Experience 6: This is peace, this is the highest, namely the calming of the activities, the rejection of all attachment, the destruction of craving, the freedom from desire, nibbana.

(*Anguttara Nikaya* V, 110)

Experience 7: Freedom from pride, restraint of thirst, uprooting of attachment, cutting off of the cycle of existences, destruction of craving, freedom from desire, ceasing, nibbana.

(Ibid. I, 88)

*Experience 8**: But when I comprehended, as it really is, the satisfaction of the world as satisfaction, the misery as misery, and the escape as escape, then I understood fully and accepted full Buddha status, and the knowledge and the vision arose in me: sure is the release of my mind: this is my last birth.

(Ibid. I, 259)

Experience 9: With the knees high and the head low, in deep meditation, he [Mahavira, a founder of Jainism] reached Nirvana, the complete and full, the unobstructed, unimpeded, infinite and supreme, best knowledge and intuition, called Kevala . . . he was a Kevalin, omniscient and comprehending all objects, he knew all conditions of the world, of gods, men, and demons; whence they come, where they go, whether they are born as men or animals, or become gods or hell-beings; their food, drink, doings, desires, open and secret deeds, their conversation and gossip, and the thoughts of their minds; he saw and knew all conditions in the whole world of all living beings.

(*Jaina Sutras* I, 201, 202)

Experience 10: With supreme knowledge, with supreme intuition, with supreme conduct, . . . with supreme uprightness, with supreme mildness, with supreme dexterity, with supreme patience, with supreme freedom from passions, with supreme control, with supreme contentment, with supreme understanding, on the supreme path to final liberation, which is the fruit of veracity, control, penance, and good conduct, the Venerable One meditated on himself for twelve years. During the thirteenth year, in the second month of summer, in the fourth fortnight . . .

on its tenth day, when the shadow had turned towards the east and the first wake was over . . . [the Venerable One] in a squatting position, with joined heels, exposing himself to the heat of the sun after fasting two and a half days without drinking water, being engaged in deep meditation, reached the highest knowledge and intuition called Kevala, which is infinite, supreme, unobstructed, unimpeded, complete, and full . . . he was a Kevalin, omniscient and comprehending all objects; he knew and saw all conditions of the world, of gods, men, and demons; whence they come, whither they go, whether they are born as men or as animals or become gods or hell-beings, the ideas, the thoughts of their minds, the food, doings, desires, the open and secret deeds of all the living beings in the whole world; he the Arhat, for whom there is no secret, knew and saw all conditions of all living beings in the world, what they thought, spoke, or did at any moment . . . [This is] final liberation.

(Ibid. I, 263, 271)

Experience 11: Mahavira quitted the world, cut asunder the ties of birth, old age, and death; become a Siddha, a Buddha, a Mukta, a maker of the end [to all misery], finally liberated, freed from all pains.

(Ibid. I, 264, 265)

Experience 12: Mahavira obtained the highest knowledge and intuition, called Kevala, which is infinite, supreme, . . . complete, and full.

(Ibid. I, 265, 266)

Experience 13: The highest knowledge and intuition, called Kevala, which is infinite, supreme, unobstructed, unimpeded, complete, and full . . . final liberation.

(Ibid. I, 265, 266)

Experience 14: He reached Nirvana, the complete and full, the unobstructed, unimpeded, infinite and supreme, best knowledge and intuition, called Kevala.

(Ibid. I, 201)

Experience 15: (The liberated) with their departing breath reach absolute perfection, wisdom, liberation, final Nirvana, the end of all misery.

(Ibid. I, 94)

Experience 16: Having annihilated his Karman [= karma] both meritorious and sinful, being steadfast (self-controlled) . . . [the enlightened one] crossed the ocean-like flood of worldly existence and obtained exemption from transmigration.

(Ibid. I, 111, 112)

Experience 17: What is called Nirvana, or freedom from pain, or perfection, which is in view of all; it is the safe, happy, and quiet place which all the great sages reach. This is the eternal place, in view of all, but difficult of approach. Those sages who reach it are free from sorrow, they have put an end to the stream of existence.

(Ibid. I, 128)

Experience 18: [Kevalins] have obtained perfection, enlightenment, deliverance, final beatitude, and . . . an end to all misery.

(Ibid. II, 158)

Experience 19: [A Kevalin] obtains perfection, enlightenment, deliverance, and final beatitude and puts an end to all misery.

(Ibid. II, 173)

Experience 20: When a seer sees the brilliant Maker, Lord, Person, the Brahman-source, then, being a knower, shaking off good and evil, stainless, he attains supreme identity with Him.

(*Mundaka Upanishad* III, i, 3)

Experience 21: Not by sight is it grasped, not even by speech, not by any other sense-organs, austerity, or work, by the peace of knowledge, one's nature purified – in that way, however, by meditating, one does behold him who is without parts.

(Ibid. III, i, 8)

Experience 22: That which is the finest essence – the whole world has that as its self. That is Reality. That is Atman. That art thou.

(*Chandogya Upanishad* VI, ix, 4)

Experience 23: Now, when one is sound asleep, composed, serene, and knows no dreams – that is the self [Atman] . . . that is the immortal, the fearless. That is Brahman.

(Ibid. VIII, xi, 1)

Experience 24: Then Usasta Cakkayan questioned him. "Yajnavalkya," said he, "explain to me who is Brahman present and not beyond our ken, him who is the self in all things." [Yajnavalkya replies:] Verily, he is the great, unborn self, who is this (person) consisting of knowledge among the senses. In the space within the heart lies the ruler, the lord of all, the king of all.

(*Brhadaranyaka Upanishad* III, iv, 1)

Criteria and their application

Tim's experience of *at least seeming to see a whale* is veridical if there is the whale Tim seems to see, and he sees it. Mia's experience of *at least seeming to hear the bell ringing* is veridical if the bell is ringing, and Mia hears it. Now consider:

Criterion 2: Experience A is of a different sort from experience B if: (i) experience A is veridical, then X exists; (ii) experience B is veridical, then Y exists; and (iii) X exists, and Y exists, then X and Y belong to different fundamental kinds.

Understanding Criterion 2 obviously requires our being able to make sense of the notion of *fundamentally different kinds*. We may as well define this notion in a way relevant to our overall concerns.

Part of this task is easy. Consider this criterion of *beings of fundamentally different kinds* (FDK):

> Being X is of a fundamentally different kind from being Y if (i) X has the property[4] *existing independent of anything else* or *not depending on anything else for existence* and Y has the property *existing dependent on something else* or *depending on something else for existence*; (ii) X has the property *being immaterial* and Y has the property *being material*; (iii) X has the property

being alive and Y has the property *not being alive*;[5] (iv) X has the property *being capable of consciousness* and Y has the property *not being capable of consciousness*; (v) X has the property *being capable of self-consciousness* and Y has the property *not being capable of self-consciousness*; (vi) X has the property *being capable of being a moral agent* and Y has the property *not being capable of being a moral agent*.

Obviously FDK is open-ended; one can think of additions – for example *being abstract* and *being concrete*. But the important general idea is clear enough; there are stateable differences in property that constitute differences in kind or sort, and some at least of these are fairly readily recognizable. Further, experiences differing in any of the ways that FDK describes are sufficient for them to be of different kinds.

The next question concerns whether understanding Criterion 2 along the lines of FDK will allow us to distinguish between different sorts of experiences. Let us look at our descriptions of religious experiences. Experiences 1 through 4 naturally fall together; in each case the subject at least seems to experience a being distinct from experience and experiencer – each is subject/consciousness/object in structure.

An interesting if incidental feature of the fourth description is that the being who at least seems to be experienced is said to have a thousand arms. This sort of description will go down better in Delhi than in Detroit, where the notion of something having a thousand arms will be associated with things that exterminators exterminate. Considerable difference in metaphor need not be accompanied by considerable difference in doctrine; Old Testament writers refer to God as having "a strong right arm" and the *Bhagavadgita* refers to Brahman as having a thousand arms, but both have in mind divine power; indeed, divine omnipotence.

In any case, the response to the being in question is worship. In contrast to some popular songs, there is nothing here of the flavor of "the Man Upstairs" and there is no suggestion of a cosmic Santa. Instead, "it is a fearful thing to fall into the hands of the living God." Leaving aside for now the question of exactly how to frame a detailed description or relate the descriptions offered here to standard theological claims (matters discussed in a later chapter), at least this much seems clear: if any of Experiences 1 through 4 are veridical, then there is a self-conscious being of impressive holiness whose presence elicits a tendency to worship. Consider, then, this instantiation of Criterion 2:

Criterion 2a: Experience A is of a different sort from experience B if:

(i) A is veridical, there is a self-conscious being of

> impressive holiness whose presence elicits a tendency to worship, whereas it is false that if experience B is veridical then there is a self-conscious being of impressive holiness whose presence elicits a tendency to worship.[6]

Consider next the descriptions of Experiences 5 through 8. Here one finds a focus on such psychological features as peace, calm, and freedom from desire, and the association with these features of a claim to have reached the last of one's rebirths and an achievement of nirvana – technically, of an experience now that is alleged to guarantee that one "goes to nirvana" when one dies. These experiences, by Criterion 2a, are of a different sort from Experiences 1–4. Further, they do not claim exactly an awareness of nirvana; the link between experiences with the psychological features mentioned comes through the acceptance of certain doctrines that provide the backing for a claim to the effect that (N) *If one has experiences of a certain psychological sort under certain conditions, then one has achieved enlightenment*. The evidential force, if any, of Experiences 5 through 8 rests on the status of the doctrines that provide the backing for (N).

This, in turn, illustrates a point of some importance. An experience can provide evidence for a claim *directly*, as my seeing my computer screen does for the claim that my computer screen still exists. An experience can provide evidence for a claim *indirectly*, as in the case in which observing squiggles in a cloud chamber provides evidence that electrons are passing through the chamber. Here, there is a theory that says that under certain conditions, there will be observable squiggles in the chamber that are best explained as caused by electrons – or, if you like, observing the squiggles *is* observing the electrons. Either way of putting things depends on there being a theory connecting observation (perceptual experience) to claim (that there are electrons present). In cases of indirect evidence, the evidence is only as good as the theory that links experience to claim.

Experiences 9 through 19 include descriptions of psychological states similar to those given of Experiences 5 through 8, but there is an interesting additional feature. There is a report to the effect that the subject can "see" his own past lives and a remarkable range of things besides – in effect, that the subject has become at least something like omniscient, knowing the entire history of the world. This is a different sort of claim – a claim that the subject has, not merely a sense of calm and bliss, but knowledge of a truly formidable range. It ascribes a *cognitive* state of knowledge that is quite distinct from any merely *affective* state of feeling. It is apparently reported on behalf of someone else (a follower of the Jain saint and founder Mahavira reports it regarding an experience that Mahavira is said to have had; a similar experience is ascribed to Gotama Buddha).

Experiences 20 through 24 are like the preceding two groups in that they ascribe psychological states of calm and bliss to their subjects, but unlike either in that a further report is offered. It at least appears to the subject of the experience that he experiences a being that is ineffable or beyond all description [see 21], or a being who is "Maker, Lord" [see 20], with whom the subject is identical. These cases raise especially difficult questions regarding interpretation. Let us note but one element of them, an element specified in all these descriptions but one [namely, 21] – that the subject is identical to the being apparently experienced.

There are various issues to be considered regarding Experiences 1–24. It is reasonable to suppose that there have been experiences. It isn't likely that such descriptions are simply made up. Further, experiences like these have been reported by monks and mystics, cross-culturally and cross-temporally. Strictly, after all, what has been quoted is a set of descriptions of experiences or of comments about experiences. Now consider this expansion of Criterion 2a.

*Criterion 3**: Experience A is of a different sort from experience B if: (i) A is veridical, there is a self-conscious being of impressive holiness whose presence elicits a tendency to worship, whereas it is false that if experience B is veridical then there is a self-conscious being of impressive holiness whose presence elicits a tendency to worship; or (ii) A is veridical, then one is something like omniscient, whereas it is false that if B is veridical then one is something like omniscient; (iii) A is veridical then one is identical to the apparent object of one's experience whereas if B is veridical then it is false that one is identical to the apparent object of one's experience.[7]

It seems clear that Criteria 1 through 3 do distinguish what, if they actually occur, will be different sorts of experiences, where their being of different sorts is relevant to what their information potential, if any, turns out to be. Further, if there actually do occur experiences of the sort that authoritative-within-their-traditions religious texts claim have occurred, those experiences will be of different sorts. Finally, since those experiences, if they have occurred, are taken to be soteriologically central by the traditions in which they are alleged to have occurred; it is assumed that those sorts of experiences not only have occurred, but have made a significant difference to the diagnosis and solution of the fundamental problem the traditions in question assert us to have. So it seems plainly appropriate to call these *religious* experiences. If there are, then, the experiences that religious traditions claim there are, they are experiences of different kinds or sorts.

Questions for reflection

1 Are the criteria offered for religious experiences being of different kinds philosophically neutral and applied fairly?
2 What is a phenomenological description of a religious experience, and why is it important that there be such descriptions?
3 Experiences that no one would think of as religious are also distinct in kind according to the criteria presented. What are some examples of different kinds of experience? For what sorts of claims do these experiences provide evidence?
4 What can be learned about what different kinds of religious experiences can provide evidence for by reflecting on what different kinds of non-religious experiences can provide evidence for?

Annotated reading

Bowker, John (1973) *The Sense of God,* Oxford: Oxford University Press. This book and the next discuss "experience of God" and social science theories, denying that we have good reason to think that such experiences are merely subjective.
Bowker, John (1978) *The Religious Imagination and the Sense of God,* Oxford: Clarendon Press. See previous reference.
Griffiths, Paul J. (1991) *An Apology for Apologetics,* Maryknoll, NY: Orbis Books. Defends the propriety of talking about religion in rational terms.
Smart, Ninian (1964) *Philosophers and Religious Truth,* London: SCM Press. A discussion of the central views of Aquinas, Freud, Hume, and Wittgenstein.
Smart, Ninian (1973) *The Science of Religion and the Sociology of Knowledge,* Princeton, NJ: Princeton University Press. Argues the attempts to reduce claims about knowledge to claims about what is believed in a culture are self-defeating.

CHAPTER 5
The importance of doctrine and the distinctness of religious traditions

5

The importance of doctrine and the distinctness of religious traditions

Doctrine

Agreement on the importance of doctrine

It is fairly well known that the New Testament contains such passages as that in which Jesus says "I am the Way, the Truth, and the Life; no one comes to the Father but by me."[1] One reads that "he who believes in the Son has eternal life; he who does not obey the Son shall not see life, but the wrath of God abides on him."[2] St Peter asserted "There is salvation in no one else [but Jesus Christ], for there is no other name under heaven given among men by which we must be saved."[3] It is less well known that the other religious traditions we have discussed have similar emphases. The Advaita Vedantin Shankara, for example, forthrightly says that "if the soul . . . is not considered to possess fundamental unity with Brahman – an identity to be realized by knowledge – there is not any chance of its obtaining final release."[4] A text from the *Jaina Sutras* bluntly tells us that

> Those who do not know all things by *kevala* [knowledge], but who being ignorant teach a law [of their own], are lost themselves, and work the ruin of others in this dreadful, boundless Circle of Births. Those who know all things by the full Kevala knowledge, and who are practicing meditation and teach the whole law, are themselves saved and save others.

A Buddhist text speaks plainly to this effect:

> If one does not proceed in this manner [to "proceed in this manner" is to "develop the understanding which results from the study of the (Buddhist) teachings"], inasmuch as meditation on some erroneous idea cannot even clear away doubt, recognition of reality will not arise and consequently meditation will

> be profitless like that of the Tirthikas [i.e., non-Buddhists, especially Jains].[5]

The theme of these passages is clear enough. To put them in one jargon: there is a heaven to gain and a hell to shun; there is one way to gain heaven and shun hell, and there are plenty of ways to shun heaven and gain hell.

This insistence on the importance of doctrine comes out in another way. It is not an accident that, as we have noted, the experiences that are religiously central to our traditions are typically called *enlightenment* experiences or they are said to yield knowledge of God;[6] they are described as *cognitive*. An Advaitin description of *moksha* goes like this: "When a seer sees . . . the Brahman-source, then, being a knower, shaking off good and evil, stainless, he attains supreme identity with Him."[7] The *Jaina Sutras* speak of "the highest knowledge and intuition, called 'Kevala' which is . . . final liberation."[8] A Theravada text says that "The monk life leads to complete detachment, to freedom from desire, to cessation, to peace, to superknowledge, to the highest insight, to nibbana."[9] Correspondingly, the New Testament says that "We know that the Son of God has come and has given us understanding so that we may know Him who is true."[10]

This feature of religion is often regarded with sadness or disapproval, an unfortunate but accidental feature that can be removed from religious traditions with gain and without loss. Such suggestions fail to understand what a religion is. A doctor who diagnoses Mary as having migraine headaches and proposes Darvon and stress reduction as a cure differs from a doctor who diagnoses Mary as feigning pain and recommends psychoanalysis. The one thinks that Mary's pain is real and requires medical attention; the other thinks that Mary has no pain and is faking it and thus offers no remedy for pain at all. The first doctor, if she is competent and confident of her diagnosis, will predict continuing anguish for Mary as long as her migraine headaches are ignored. The second doctor, if he is competent and confident of his diagnosis, will predict continuing fakery on Mary's part until she faces her childhood. This is what one would expect; it does not arise from either or both of the doctors being immoral, loving controversy, or taking pleasure in the thought of the suffering of others.

One who sincerely embraces a religious tradition accepts that tradition's diagnosis and cure of what it takes to be a deep problem in dire need of treatment. The founders, authorities, texts, doctrines, and experiences of the tradition are focused on properly diagnosing and successfully curing the believer's illness, which it takes to be an illness we all share. A sincere Christian, Advaita Vedantin, Theravada Buddhist, and Jain will differ as to the diagnoses they accept and the cures they embrace. Each will take the others' diagnoses to be in error and the others' cures to be ineffective regarding what the real problem is.

To believe that John is a sinner in need of God's forgiveness, or that John is unknowingly identical to qualityless Brahman, or that John at a time is but a cluster of momentary states and over time a series of such clusters and will unfortunately remain so unless he recognizes his nature and enters nirvana, or that John is actually an enduring and indestructible self-conscious being whose embodiment hides his omniscience and existential security, is also to think that anything incompatible with the diagnosis and cure that one accepts is false. If it is true (as it is) that the National Basketball franchise that has won the most championships is the Boston Celtics, it is not *another* thing for it to be false that the Celtics are not this franchise. If my view is that we are in need of God's gracious forgiveness, and that this is the basic religious problem that I share with all others, then if my belief is true it is not *another* thing for it to be false that this is not the basic religious problem that I share with all others. The same holds for the truth about any other proposed diagnosis. Any diagnosis is either true or not true. The same applies to any cure.

It could be contended that, just as different people have different diseases, so they may have different religious problems. In some sense, no doubt, they may. But religious traditions focus on what they take to be the deepest religious illness and suppose it to be shared by all human beings. This is not arbitrary on their part – the problem, however construed, is one viewed by these traditions as closely connected to human nature. On their view, the problem *is* human nature, or it is due to a universal misuse of capacities, possession of which is constitutive of being human, or the like. They take it that everyone lives in the same cosmos, has the same nature, and so is disjointed or warped in essentially the same way. From their perspective, to propose seriously that different persons have different religious problems at the deepest level is tantamount to suggesting that not all human beings are members of the same species. This suggestion is incompatible with at least most religious traditions, and there is little if any reason to think it true.

The viewpoints expressed in the passages recently quoted, then, is exactly what one would expect from anyone who was sincerely committed to the religious tradition in question – who took that tradition's diagnosis and cure to fit their condition and meet their deepest religious need. There is no good reason to think it wicked of religious believers to hold the views these passages express. Sincere Marxists, Socialists, Feminists, Freudians, Supplyside Economists, Animal Rights Activists, Right to Choose Advocates, and Right to Life Advocates hold similar views regarding the inelegant consequences of those who reject their political and social programs. That is, they actually believe what they say and act on.

It is worth noting and emphasizing that these passages are not simply exceptions that do not deeply reflect the perspectives that we have been discussing. A religion typically offers an account of the conditions in which we exist, a conception of the religious problem that we face because of existing in those conditions, and a solution to that problem that is viewed as realistically facing and resolving that problem under those conditions. Different religions see those conditions differently. They hence describe the basic religious problem differently. They therefore offer different solutions. If you think that all religion is a crock, you will not take seriously those descriptions of the conditions in which we exist, and the problem that we thereby face; they will not describe live options for your acceptance. But you can still see that they are different and that the solutions offered are different. If you think that we are not in danger from fire or from flood, you will not think we need a fire extinguisher or an ark. But you can still see that the fire-fearers disagree with water-fearers in their analysis of our troubles and in their proposed remedies.

"Truth-claims"

Religions make what are sometimes called "truth-claims," though of course that is redundant since to make a claim in the sense of asserting something is to say that what is asserted is true. "Truth-claims" are just claims; there are *false* claims but there aren't any "falsity-claims." *Of course* religions make claims – if they asserted nothing, there would be no religions. Sometimes – particularly when a religious tradition is under rational scrutiny, or when a would-be believer recognizes that she thinks what she would like to be her religion is false and wants to keep it anyway – a religious tradition may be presented as claiming, and even may claim, that it makes no claim except that it makes no claims. But once the crisis is over, we are back to talking about God and sin and salvation, or Atman and Brahman and *moksha* and identity, or Jivas and *kevala* and enlightenment, or momentary states and nirvana and release from the Wheel. It is in the very nature of a religion to offer an account of our situation, our problem, and its solution. Not every problem can arise in every situation; not every problem has the same solution. The account of our problem depends on the account of our situation; the account of our salvation depends on what we are and what we need to be saved from. To accept a religion is to embrace some particular and connected account of the situation and problem and solution.

Two popular contemporary perspectives often keep people from seeing religious differences. One is a popular sort of academic quasi-religion that has as one of its doctrinal claims that religions do not differ. The other is the sort of popular religious perspective that supposes all religions to be down-deep identical; this sort of religion, of course, is different from those religions (most if not all others) that do not think that religions do not differ.[11] If you accept the claim that all religions are the same as part of your sacred or secular religion, you may have as much trouble in admitting that not all religions are the same as members of the Flat Earth Society have in admitting the earth is an oblate spheroid.[12]

The thing to note here[13] is that none of these sorts of views can be made compatible with any of the religious traditions we have been describing; they are not expositions of, and they are plainly incompatible with, those perspectives. This is highly relevant, since these views are often presented as compatible with, if not as expositions of, one or more of these traditions; they are not.

The question arises as to whether, in some significant sense, all religions are really the same. As we have seen, in various senses they are not. They teach different doctrines, and if some of those doctrines are true, then others are false. They appeal to experiences that differ in content and structure; if some of those experiences are reliable, then the others are not. They propose different diagnoses and cures, and if one of those diagnoses is true, then others are false and if one of those cures is genuine, then the others are not. So, in various senses of the same – making the same claims, appealing to the same experiences, proposing the same diagnoses, offering the same cures – it is emphatically false that all religions are the same. What other senses of "are the same" might there be?

Identity

Two kinds of identity: content identity and function identity

The question as to whether all religions are the same raises another: the same regarding what? Once we see this, we can see our question splitting in two: Do all religions have the same doctrinal content? Do they all serve the same psychological and/or social function? Do all religions have content-identity, and do they all have function-identity?

Low standards for identity: vagueness, generality, and trivial results

In spite of the partial descriptions we have offered of four religious traditions, it is possible to answer the question concerning content-identity affirmatively. So long as one makes the suggested criterion for identity of content vague and general, one can get the result that all of our religious traditions have identity of content. Thus one might suggest: all religious traditions (or at least those canvassed here) agree that a person's life does not consist in the abundance (or paucity) of material possessions; here is some identity of content. The same goes for identity of function. Thus one might suggest some such claim as *all religions provide meaning to life for their adherents*; to that extent, our religious traditions have identity of function.

In spite of the fact that the matters on which our traditions agree are neither obvious nor unimportant, there is a sense in which the result that one gets by using such vague and general criteria for identity of content or function is trivial. The result that all religions are the same regarding content and/or function is purchased at two prices. One price is that what each tradition regards as important is entirely left out. The other price is that the traditions themselves hardly make an appearance before they are judged identical and dismissed; most of the relevant information about the traditions is not used, and that seems just ridiculous. I suggest, therefore, that we use high standards for content-identity and function-identity among religions.

High standards for identity: clarity, specificity, and an interesting thesis

What these standards should be is not far to seek. Two religious traditions have identity of content if and only if they teach the same doctrines. Two religious traditions have identity of function if and only if they serve the same psychological or social function.

Some common themes

All of the religions described earlier agree on such claims as these: human life is not limited to three-score-and-ten years on this earth; nothing that we can lose is of ultimate value (this is one moral of the Jain story); pleasure is not the ultimate good; violence is not an end in itself; there is a correct description of our actual cosmic situation, our consequent basic religious problem, and its real and accessible solution; some actual religious tradition has the truth about these matters; it is foolish to live only for power or pleasure or wealth. These are not obvious or trivial truths; plenty of people would reject, say, more than three of these claims. Suppose that someone suggests that all religions have the same content if they all agree on some such claim as *a few years of life on earth under present conditions is not all there is* or *materialistic values are inadequate as a basis for living*. It plainly is worth noting that at least our four religious traditions – and many others as well – share these themes. Claiming, as I shall, that it is false that all religions are the same need not blind one to seeing that they agree on some things. But none of the things that they agree on are what the traditions themselves take to be the most important. I will argue that in fact the things they disagree about are the most important.

Two sorts of doctrine: metaphysical (cosmos and persons) and moral

If one looks at the accounts we have given of four religious traditions, it is clear that they include claims about at least two sorts of matter: what there is, or metaphysics, and what there ought to be, or ethics. I will briefly draw out some of the metaphysical, and some of the moral, claims that are constitutive of these religious traditions.

Some kinds of metaphysics

Arguably *the*, and certainly *a*, central sort of religious experience within the classical monotheisms, Christianity included, is what Rudolph Otto, in *The Idea of the Holy*, called 'numinous' experience (though there are problems with his second-order characterizations of it).[14] In such an experience, the subject of the experience at least seems to be aware of an awesome Being which is unapproachable save on its own terms, majestic, overpowering, independent, living, possessed of great energy, unique, compelling, both attractive and dangerous. Typical responses come in terms of awe, a sense of creaturehood and dependence, submission, worship, and guilt for one's sins. Plainly these experiences have a subject/consciousness/object structure; they at least seem to be encounters with something that exists quite distinct from and independent of the experiencing subject.

The relevance of this to our current topic is this: within the Christian tradition, experience and doctrine both emphasize the role of a Creator and Providence on whom all else depends. Between God and any human person there is a one-way dependence relationship; it is blasphemous to deny the Creator–creature distinction. For Advaita Vedanta, what seems to be creature really is not strictly the Creator, but at any rate underived Being. Creaturehood, sin, forgiveness, and the Divine Person as well, are illusory; all there is is qualityless and apersonal Brahman. Jainism ascribes to each person, as he or she really is as opposed as to how he or she seems to be, the independence of everything else that Christianity ascribes to God alone. It denies that there is any Creator, but denies as well that personal individuality is illusory or should or even can be lost in a sea of qualityless being. The Theravadin accepts neither God nor the Jain substantial soul, maintaining that all there is is transitory save for nirvana itself, the attaining of which involves not only the cessation of desire but apparently the cessation of individuality. In one sense, of course, setting aside the deep problems with such a notion, being identical to a qualityless and so apersonal Brahman and being absorbed into an apersonal state does not give one much to choose between, and some of his Vedantic critics accused Shankara of being a crypto-Buddhist.

However one should decide the question of the identity of the Advaita Vedanta Brahman and the Theravada nirvana, it is clear that at the least ultimate reality is conceived quite differently in Christianity and Jainism and Advaita Vedanta and Theravada. So are the nature and status of human beings. There is not identity of content here. It is false that all religions are doctrinally the same.

Some kinds of morality

The highest good for Advaita Vedanta is comprised by achieving *moksha;* the highest good for Jainism is comprised by achieving *kevala*; the highest good for Theravada is comprised by achieving nirvana. Our traditions recognize a distinction between experience had now that guarantees later escape from the Wheel, and post-mortem liberation itself. The highest good we can have in this life is achieving experiences that guarantee liberation at death. A key question in understanding how liberation is understood is this: is personal identity retained in enlightenment? The Advaita answer and the Theravada answer, for different reasons, are negative; the Jain answer is positive. All other values in these traditions serve as means to the end of enlightenment. In a tradition in which persons do not survive into enlightenment, persons cannot themselves have intrinsic value or inherent worth. So they lack such worth in Advaita Vedanta and Theravada, and possess it in Jainism. They possess it also in Christianity. In Jainism, persons owe none of their worth as persons to God; in Christianity persons owe all of their worth as persons to God. In these ways, differences in concepts of moral worth correspond to differences in metaphysics.

The argument here can be stated briefly as follows. Our four traditions deeply differ in their morality in the ways noted; they embrace different, and importantly incompatible, values. Two religious traditions are functionally identical only if their basic values – what they take to have inherently or intrinsic worth – are similar, for the lifestyles that religions sanction are functions of the intrinsic values they embrace. Hence our traditions are not functionally identical.

There is an objection to this argument that goes as follows. It is possible that a tradition embraces one set of values and that its adherents follow another. Thus the fact that two traditions sanction different values does not entail that they are not functionally identical, for their adherents may follow similar or identical values.

This objection embodies a popular mistake. The values a religion embraces are those its authoritative texts sanction; setting problems of relevant inconsistency aside (and if the relevant texts teach logically inconsistent values, then one cannot coherently speak of one set of values that a religion sanctions), if the adherents of a tradition do not embrace the values their own tradition sanctions, they are to that degree heretical or hypocritical, and nothing about the functional identity of religious traditions follows from their behavior or their value commitments. Attempts to evaluate religious traditions by looking at the behavior of its adherents is worthless as evidence regarding the tradition; what is evidentially relevant is what values the tradition's authoritative texts sanction.

Diversity

I would suggest, on the basis of what we have already said, that it is a plain fact that there is doctrinal diversity between religions; it simply is false that all religions are the same regarding content.

The agreement on the importance of doctrine undercuts the attempt both to represent the traditions and deny that doctrine matters

A matter on which our traditions do agree prevents anyone from successfully claiming to represent these traditions and go on to say that while there are doctrinal divergences these do not really matter. Those who try to do this may be contemporary secularists who do not care about religious matters or Religious Studies professors who think that tolerance for different opinions requires that the opinions not be different. They may be adherents of a religion that says that all religions are really the same even though in fact they are not. They may be adherents of one or another religious tradition who either do not know their own tradition very well or are just confused. But it is clear that, in their traditional forms, religious traditions take as essential to salvation precisely matters on which there is deep disagreement among religious traditions.

An argument sometimes is offered that two people who really respect one another cannot knowingly disagree on ultimate religious matters, and since we respect each other as persons we cannot really disagree on ultimate doctrines even though we may seem to. One of my two PhD advisors, who by the way did respect each other, was an orthodox rabbi and the other an atheist; both became my lifelong friends. I regret that I never saw anyone try to persuade my rabbi friend that he really did not disagree with Christianity or atheism or my atheist friend that he really believed in God; it would have been interesting. The reply to this argument is that since people plainly do manage both to differ knowingly on basic religious matters and yet respect one another, tolerance is compatible with known difference on ultimate religious matters.

The plain fact of functional diversity on high standards

I would suggest as well on the basis of what we have said that it simply is plain that there is not functional identity among religious traditions. They hold such divergent values that the ends they seek and the values they inculcate make it impossible for them to serve the same psychological ends or the same social functions, unless we describe these ends or functions with high generality. There may be some point to doing so sometimes; but if we ever want to look with any care at the religious phenomena we shall have to do so with far more specificity and clarity than will allow us to maintain cross-religious functional identity.

The doctrinal and functional diversity of religious traditions

Our original question was: are all religions really the same? This split into: Have they the same content? Have they the same function? On high standards that yield a significant conclusion rather than low standards that yield a trivial conclusion, the answers to our questions are: "No" and "No." What does it matter? The answer to this question depends on whether any of the traditions are true.

One's answer to "What difference does it make?" will depend on what view one takes of the religious traditions. If one supposes that all religious traditions are false, then the difference it makes is like the difference it makes as to whether one thinks that George Washington and Abraham Lincoln or Bruce Springsteen and Victoria Principal were the first and sixteenth US Presidents. One who made the latter choice would have a mistaken and skewed view of American history, and one who thought that all religions were the same would hold a mistaken and skewed view of religious traditions. It matters insofar as it is important to get your facts about religions straight, and not otherwise.

Suppose, however, one accepts one of the religious traditions. In one way, the answer is the same whichever of our traditions you accept. One of the traditions has the words of eternal life; if you embrace the right one and then read all the others as if they said the same thing, you will be wrong three times about what the other religions teach but you will have saved your soul (or whatever). If you accept a wrong one, and then read all the others as saying what that one says, then you hide from yourself the truth that you need by identifying it with the falsehood that you believe.

In another way, the answer to "What difference does it make?" will depend on what tradition one accepts. For in each case the conception of what believing and living the truth will bring is importantly different, as is the conception of what one gets when one believes and lives a falsehood.

There is a complicating factor that I mention in conclusion. Perhaps what most deeply motivates people to maintain that all religions are the same is that they cannot stand the idea that anyone be sincere and not be saved (or whatever). Sometimes this involves their thinking that no matter what anyone thinks, so long as they are sincere, they deserve heaven – even if all they sincerely believe in is pleasure-seeking or hatred and torture. But sometimes it involves believing that anyone who sincerely is seeking the truth and wants to do what is right must somehow make it home, religiously speaking. They think that since right belief is taken in religious traditions to be basic to being saved (or whatever), then if everyone who seeks salvation is to make it home, religiously speaking, all religious traditions must have the same beliefs. In some religious traditions at least, it is possible to respond with some degree of sympathy to this suggestion without denying the plain facts of the matter. Reincarnation traditions tend to talk here of other lives in other times and climes. The classical monotheisms talk of people being judged by their response to the truth that is available to them, and even of a "baptism of desire" in which genuine desire for the truth is taken as tantamount to possession of it. Exactly how this is developed will differ from tradition to tradition, and sub-tradition to sub-tradition, and doing this in any detail is not part of our task here. We merely point out that the connection between correct belief and being saved (or whatever) is by no means always taken in a wooden graceless way, particularly not within the classical monotheisms. But that is another story. Our story in this chapter ends when we have noted that it is false that all religions are the same regarding doctrine any more than they are the same regarding diagnosis and cure, or regarding the experiences they take to be essential to salvation or enlightenment.

Questions for reflection

1 What do the religious texts quoted at the beginning of this chapter say about the importance of having certain sorts of religious experiences? What do they say about the significance of correct belief?
2 Is the author right in claiming that those who accept what these texts say are not wicked by virtue of doing so? Can one be tolerant and accept the teachings of texts of this sort?
3 What importance, if any, is there to there being claims that are shared by most religions?
4 What importance, if any, is there to there being claims that are particular to each religion? What importance do the religions themselves attach to there being such claims?
5 What would a religion composed only of shared claims look like? How would particular religions look at such a composite religion?
6 Distinguish between functional sameness and substantial sameness. Which sort of sameness will seem the more important for the religions themselves?

Annotated reading

Carr, Brian and Mahalingham, Indira (1996) *Companion Encyclopedia of Asian Philosophy*, London: Routledge. Contains discussions of issues, views, and figures in Persian, Indian, Buddhist, Chinese, Japanese, and Islamic philosophy.
Frank, Daniel H. and Leaman, Oliver (1997) *History of Jewish Philosophy*, London: Routledge. A comprehensive volume on the nature and foundations of Jewish philosophy and its Medieval, Modern, and Contemporary representatives.
McGrath, Alister E. (1998) *Historical Theology*, Oxford: Blackwell. An historical presentation of the major figures and doctrines of Christian thought.
Nasr, S. H. and Leaman, Oliver (1996) *History of Islamic Philosophy*, London: Routledge. A very comprehensive presentation of Islamic philosophy: its history, context, representatives, fields, and issues.
Otto, Rudolph (1958) *The Idea of the Holy*, New York, Oxford University Press.
Quasten, Johannes (1996) *Patrology*, Allen, TX: Christian Classics Reprint. A standard reference work for the Church Fathers dealing with Patristic Literature from the Apostle's Creed to the "golden age" of their Greek and Latin writings.

CHAPTER 6
Religious pluralism

6
Religious pluralism

Religious plurality and religious pluralism

Religious plurality is simply a fact. There are religious traditions that differ deeply in terms of their doctrines, practices, institutions, scriptures, experiences, and hopes. Our concern is with religious pluralism – RP for short. RP is one interpretation of religious plurality. It comes in several varieties, among which one is in danger of becoming canonical. The nearly canonical version says that all nice religious traditions are "equally valid." Its longest expression is in Professor John Hick's 1989 *An Interpretation of Religion*.[1] The expression that makes the strongest effort to answer criticisms is Professor Hick's 1995 *A Christian Theology of Religions*.[2] We will focus on the 1995 expression, assessing RP as one finds it there.

The content of religious pluralism

At least much of the core of RP is captured by these claims.[3]

1 Each religion asks generically the same question: how do we get from our present lack to a better future?[4]
2 Each world religion is a response to the same thing.[5]
3 Each world religion has its own phenomenal reality.[6]
4 Since each world religion has its own phenomenal reality, the claims of one world religion do not conflict with those of another world religion.[7]
5 Responding to this phenomenal reality is, so far as we can tell, equally effective in each world religion.
6 Each world religion is equally valid.[8]

7 The sentences that apparently express the doctrines of the great world religions actually are mythological in the sense of telling a story which elicits behavior.
8 The mythology is true if the behavior is good. [9]
9 The reason for accepting religious pluralism is that it is the best explanation of central facts about religious plurality.

The general idea of RP goes like this. One begins by engaging in an act of abstraction. Particular diagnoses and cures are replaced by a vague question. Then appeal is made to the notion of phenomenal reality. The language of "phenomenal versus noumenal" is derived from the philosophy of Immanuel Kant. Its relevance to religious pluralism is that all the things that all religions think exist turn out to exist only phenomenally, not noumenally. Each religious phenomenal being is peculiar to one religious tradition. Each religious tradition makes claims about its own phenomenal being. Response to one phenomenal being in one religious tradition seems to produce people who are roughly as nice as response to another phenomenal being in another religious tradition.[10] Since this is so, one religious tradition is about equally effective in producing niceness as another. We can express this by saying that each is "equally valid." If we use "true" here we should mean "effective in producing nice people." We remove religious traditions further from considerations of truth if we claim that while they appear to make claims about what there is, religious traditions are myths or extended metaphors whose function is to elicit behavior. The reason for accepting this is that it better explains religious plurality than anything else.

Some religion-relevant consequences of RP

Here are some religion-relevant consequences of RP. First, each religious tradition is said to deal with phenomenal realities. According to RP, Jahweh and the Father and Allah and Brahman and Jivas and the Buddha-nature are all phenomenal realities. A phenomenal reality is something to which human cognitive capacities and the Real contribute. It is something that RP says arises when a human being responds to the Real in religious experience. It is how the Real appears to someone. Remove all human beings and you remove all phenomenal reality. One not immersed in the evasionary language of RP would simply say: phenomenal beings do not exist. After all, ghosts and leprechauns are describable as responses to something external to the one who claims to experience them. At best, the things that religious traditions think exist are like colors on the standard view in Modern Philosophy: they exist only in the sense that perceivers of colorless objects are affected by those objects. On this view, colors are subjective, mind-dependent contents of perceptual experiences that do not represent qualities in the things that cause them. RP, then, claims that Jahweh, the Father, Allah, etc. have an existence that depends on our minds and experiences. Put without evasion, RP has this to say to religious traditions: what you believe in simply does not exist. So far, it agrees with naturalism.

This comes out in another way when RP claims that religious traditions are really extended metaphors or myths that are, not true or false, but useful. I deny that there are roses if I say that there are no roses. I also deny that there are roses if I say that all talk of roses is an extended metaphor or a myth which is useful if it produces a certain sort of behavior. The same goes for parallel claims regarding God or nirvana.

Second, if RP is true, then no one has any of the problems that any religious tradition says they have. The one religious problem is that we are not morally nice. The one solution to that is to respond to something in such a way as to become nice. If things the traditions believe in do not exist, then the problems they think need solution do not actually plague anyone.

Third, evangelism is anathema to RP. Any member of any religious tradition who tries to convert someone is guilty of "treason against the peace and diversity of the human family."[11] Evangelism for RP of course comes under no such condemnation.

It is hardly obvious that, whatever the intent, one actually shows great respect for all religions by holding a view that denies that anything they think exists does exist and denying that what they take to be deep problems are problems at all. The same goes for holding a view that proposes replacing them by different claims that do not claim that any of the things they believe in exist or any of the problems they take seriously exist either. Further, RP itself looks suspiciously like an attempt at a new world religion which gives us a diagnosis of what it takes our deep problem to be really, though it has yet to propose a cure of its own.

There remains, then, the philosophical question to which everything said here thus far is preparatory: what reason, if any, is there to accept or reject RP?

A critical discussion of RP: Part one

It is on the face of it implausible to think that all religious experience is experience of the same thing. Neither the content nor the structure of such experience indicates that this suggestion is anything better than fanciful.[12] Thus there is a considerable hurdle over which RP must jump in order to have any initial promise. But set this aside.

Human concepts

What should be said about RP depends on which of various emphases one has in mind. RP makes various claims about restrictions on what one may properly say about Real. More than one account is given of these restrictions.

One account speaks of "human concepts."[13] A human concept is not a concept that applies to humans, but one that humans use. RP uses this claim, or one much like it, to deny that such concepts as *self-conscious being* and *non-self-conscious being* apply to the Real. The claim again comes in two steps:

(HC1) A human concept is any concept humans use.
(HC2) No human concept applies to the Real.

These two claims constitute what might be called Maximally Restrictive RP. In this mood one finds RP denying that even "exists" and "does not exist" can apply to the Real. RP denies that number concepts apply to the Real[14] though it also claims that there is only one item appropriately designated "the Real."[15] The result is that Maximally Restrictive RP is self-destructing. It says about the Real that nothing can be so said.

RP also insists that the Real is transcendent, a condition of our existence and our highest good,[16] and that to which religion and religious experience are responses.[17] But of course these too are human concepts, and the same filter that stops concepts used by actual religious traditions would also stop them in RP were RP not to cheat on its own behalf.[18] But on Maximally Restrictive RP it is also a mistake to ascribe transcendence, being a condition of our existence and wellbeing, and a contributor to religious experience to the Real.

Another account of the restrictions on what may properly be said about the Real is that only properties that are "generated" by logic alone may be ascribed to the Real. I take the notion to be this. Logic holds in all possible worlds. It applies to anything there possibly is, and hence to everything there actually is. To deny this is to embrace a self-contradictory claim. So far, so good.

The sorts of property logic "generates" are those properties that something must have if it is to be anything at all.[19] "Properties" here covers qualities and relations. Examples of such properties are *having properties, having only consistent properties, being self-identical, not being identical to anything different* and the like.[20] A letter home from a college student saying "I've met the most wonderful person – she *has properties* and *has only consistent properties*" will not communicate much about the student's new love interest. Mediumly Restrictive RP says that the only properties we can properly ascribe to the Real are properties that logic "generates."

The point is worth laboring. It has two parts as follows.

1 A property P is generated by logic if and only if *logic applies to X* entails *X has P*.
2 The only properties that can properly be ascribed to the Real are properties generated by logic.

This supposedly trivial admission has devastating consequences for RP.

Why the point is not trivial

First, note the properties that RP ascribes to the Real. It is transcendent.[21] There being the Real is a condition of our existence.[22] There being the Real is a condition of our wellbeing.[23] The Real is what all religious experience is a response to.[24] Talk of "the Real" with its various historical associations with features often spoken of with reference to God should not mislead us here. The Real is not personal, not conscious, and not God.

Second, note that none of these properties is generated by logic. It goes against a fundamental rule of Mediumly Restrictive RP to apply them to the Real. According to this RP doctrine, these properties cannot be ascribed to the Real. In case the point isn't clear, if RP is true, the Real cannot be said to be transcendent, a condition of our existence or our wellbeing, or what religious experience responds to. To ascribe such properties to the Real is to cheat at the RP game. No amount of talk about triviality alters the fact that this is so.[25]

Third, note that if none of these properties – *being transcendent, being a condition of our existence, being a condition of our wellbeing, being what religious experience is a response to* – can be ascribed to the Real, then the explanation that RP offers of religious plurality is impermissible. That explanation, stated consistently with RP, is this:

(RPE) There is something to which only such properties as *having properties, having only consistent properties*, and other logically generable properties can be ascribed, which is transcendent, a condition of our existence and wellbeing, and is what religious experience responds to.

Which entails:

(RPE*) There is something to which only logically generable properties may properly be ascribed and to which properties that are not logically generable may properly be ascribed.

Now (RPE*) is self-contradictory. Anything that entails a self-contradiction is itself self-contradictory. So (RPE) is self-contradictory. Self-contradictions are necessarily false. So (RPE) is necessarily false. But (RPE) is the very core of RP. So RP is necessarily false. It commits intellectual suicide of the worst sort. It has no possibly true explanation of religious plurality. Explanations that are not even possibly true are not genuine explanations. So it has no genuine explanation of religious plurality – none whatever.

We might ask if there is another way to restrict RP. This brings us to Minimally Restricted RP which says that properties to be ascribed to the Real so long as they are *either* properties generable from logic alone *or* what we might call *happy* properties – short for "properties an RP supporter could without inconsistency be happy to ascribe to the Real."[26] Then we need something like this:

(H) A property is *happy* if and only if it is (i) not generable from logic, (ii) the Real's having it is not incompatible with any doctrine that any religion accepts, (iii) there is no reason to think that the Real lacks this property, and (iv) the Real having this property would give content to the idea that there being such a thing as the Real might explain something RP is supposed to explain.

Whatever charm this idea has is at least matched by its vacuity. The Real being intelligent is one candidate for being a happy property. There are religious doctrines with which ascribing it to the Real are incompatible. So it will go for example after example. The implicit assumption of RP (in some passages, at least) is that we won't find any happy properties. This seems very plausible indeed. In fact, the existence of Advaita Vedanta and the absolutist brand of Mahayana Buddhism guarantee this result. Causal or dependence relations between what Advaita Vedanta or absolutist Mahayana Buddhism takes to exist and human persons are denied. RP's own attempt to be consistent with everything leads it to internal inconsistency. Any talk of the Real being what we respond to in religious experience, being transcendent in relation to our immanence as things that do exist, or being a condition of our existence and of our highest good distinguishes between us and ultimate reality in a way that Advaita Vedanta and absolutist Mahayana Buddhism (to take but two examples) deny. So Minimally Restrictive RP fails as well.

The importance to RP of (RPE)

According to RP, the Real is not anything described within any of the religious traditions – not Jahweh, the Father, Allah, the Buddha or the Buddha-nature, Brahman, Atman, Jiva, or whatever. It is supposed to be what is experienced as all these things, and more. Of course, *being experienced as Jahweh, the Father, Allah, the Buddha or the Buddha-nature, Brahman, Atman, Jiva, etc.* is also not a property – neither a quality nor a relation – generated by logic alone. Any such ascription to the Real – another ascription essential to RP – is bogus on RP terms.

This suggests the possibility that perhaps RP should simply drop the claim that only properties generated by logic can apply to the Real. After all, RP makes a career of violating the rule that only properties generated by logic may be ascribed to the Real. So one who accepts RP might as well abandon in theory what it habitually violates in practice. This suggestion ignores the crucial role that the claim that only properties that are generated by logic may properly be ascribed to the Real plays in RP. Professor Hick is aware of that role.

The gist of the reasoning behind the various RP restrictions is that if one does not limit RP-approved descriptions of the Real to properties generated by logic alone, one has no basis in RP for not doing one or the other of two RP-forbidden things:

1 One might ascribe to the Real either only the properties ascribed to Jahweh by Judaism, or to the Father by Christianity, or to Allah by Islam, or to the Buddha-nature by Mahayana Buddhism, etc. and then allow other ascriptions only if they are compatible with the favored ascription (this would treat one religion as true, the others as importantly false) or
2 One might try to ascribe to the Real all of the properties ascribed to Jahweh by Judaism, the Father by Christianity, Allah by Islam, the Buddha-nature by Mahayana Buddhism, etc. with the result that the

Real allegedly has a lot of logically inconsistent properties (this would treat all religions as true).

Even with the few examples given, and especially if one considers the long list of alternatives not mentioned, two things should be clear:

The only-one-religion-is-true line will require that much of very many religious traditions is false.

The all-religions-are-true line will yield one massive contradiction – indeed, a whole intellectual museum of contradictions.

The all-religions-are-true line is self-contradictory. The only-one-religion-is-true line is not self-contradictory, but it is anathema to RP. Reject the view that only properties generated from logic alone can be properly ascribed to the Real, and one has either the all-religions-are-true line or the only-one-religion-is-true line. So rejection of the view that only properties generated from logic can be properly ascribed to the Real leads to self-contradiction or to what RP finds despicable. So that view is one RP is reluctant to reject. Dropping it is as attractive to RP as beekeeping in swimwear is to those allergic to stings.

To put things bluntly, it is by appeal to the idea that the Real is both what religious experience is a response to and can be said to have no property not generable from logic alone that RP shifts religious traditions from being *either true or false, and largely incompatible* to *being useful, and non-competitive*. Drop either of those claims, and the shift is without basis in RP.

A critical discussion of RP: Part two

Various other attempts might be made to state a non-self-destructive and non-self-contradictory version of the restriction that RP so desperately needs. For example, one might consider two views about properties as follows.

Natures or essences

Consider the doctrine of *property universalism* which holds this:

(PU) For any item X and property Q, necessarily either X has Q or X does not have Q.

Contrast it to *restricted property universalism* which holds:

(RPU) For any item X and property Q, necessarily either X has Q or X does not have Q, unless X has a nature N such that *X has N* entails *X is not the sort of thing to have Q or not to have Q.*

Property universalism is a nice simple doctrine. It entails that, for any property Q, the Real – if there is any such thing – either has Q or lacks Q. Restricted property universalism entails the same claim minus those properties the Real cannot by its nature have. But according to RP one cannot ascribe *having a nature* to the Real.[27] So RP cannot appeal to restricted property universalism. If RP accepts unrestricted property realism, then for almost every property one can think of, it is *false* that the Real has that property. The importance of this entailment will become evident shortly.

In each of these ways – rejection of "human concepts" as applying to the Real, the denial that simple mathematics applies to the Real, the claim that only properties generable from logic apply to the Real, the denial of any nature ascribable to the Real – RP emphasizes its doctrine of the alleged inaccessibility of the Real to concepts. This simply underlines its own inconsistency in ascribing transcendence, necessity to existence and wellbeing, and contributing to religious experience[28] to the Real.

Maximally indeterminate beings

I suspect that talk of "the Real" gives RP the appearance of having more substance that it can possess on its own terms. Consider such properties as *having a property* and *having only consistent properties*. They are maximally indeterminate. Consider such properties as *being exactly an inch long* and *weighing one gram*. These are maximally determinate. In between are such properties as *being in space, being material, having length, having weight*. These are neither maximally determinate nor maximally indeterminate. Consider what we might call Maximally Indeterminate RP according to which the Real is maximally indeterminate in the sense that only maximally indeterminate properties can properly be ascribed to it. Given the history of philosophy, the term "the Real" has certain connotations. RP takes full advantage of these connotations in offering its theory. The Real, for example, is itself uncaused. The Real can cause other things. The Real has ultimate value. Highly positive itself, it has highly positive effects. There is a problem here. The problem is due to two facts:

1 According to Maximally Indeterminate RP, we can ascribe to the Real only maximally indeterminate properties.
2 Nothing to which we can ascribe only maximally indeterminate properties can consistently be conceived of as uncaused, cause of anything, of positive worth, or having positive effects.

The reason is simple: none of *being uncaused, being a cause, having positive worth, having positive effects* is a maximally indeterminate property. Given this simple pair of facts, devastating consequences follow for Maximally Indeterminate RP.

In order not to be led into conceptual sleight of hand, let's drop talk of "the Real" and replace it by an expression that is less lovely but free from traditional associations. Let's talk about a *maximally indeterminate being* – for short, a MIB. An MIB is not a being that *has* only maximally indeterminate properties. There cannot be anything like that. Anything has maximally indeterminate properties only by virtue of having more determinate properties, and at bottom fully determinate properties. Instead, an MIB is a being to whom for some reason we can only ascribe maximally indeterminate properties. If we ascribe even one property that is not maximally indeterminate to an MIB, we anger the MIB police who come out and dip us in colored dye. But even an MIB actually has fully determinate properties. There are some things that are just flagrantly obvious about an MIB.

To begin with, here are two facts about the properties that RP ascribes to the Real in order to have any explanation to offer or hypothesis to consider.

Fact 1: None of *being uncaused, being a cause, having positive worth, having positive effects* is a maximally indeterminate property. They are highly abstract, but they are not maximally indeterminate.

Fact 2: None of *being uncaused, being a cause, having positive worth, having positive effects* is a logical property – a property that logicians in their role as logicians ascribe to things.

It is obvious that by RP rules:

1 No MIB can be said to be uncaused, a cause, something of positive value, or something having positive effects.

It is obvious that:

2 Nothing that cannot be said to be a cause can be said to be a cause of religious experience.

It follows that:

3 No MIB can be said to be a cause of religious experience.

The same thing holds if we try to talk of "being what we respond to in religious experience" or the like. The idea such talk expresses is that the Real contributes something to religious experience and we contribute something to religious experience. But no MIB can be said to be something we respond to or something that is a co-contributor to experiences.

It is obvious that:

4 There is nothing that can be said about an MIB by virtue of which it is a cause of moral virtue in us.

5 There is nothing that can be said about an MIB that would make any response to it more appropriate to it as an MIB than any other.

6 There is as much to be said in favor of moral neutrality or moral viciousness being an appropriate response to an MIB as there is to moral virtuousness being an appropriate response to it.

An MIB cannot be said to have any relationship to any sort of moral character in any thing. So when we find RP saying that the Real is what lies beyond all religious experience, or what all religious experience is a response to, or the like, what it says is logically inconsistent with its doctrine of what can be said about the Real. No MIB can do what RP desperately needs it to do. This is important in understanding religious pluralism, since RP also desperately needs that the Real be an MIB in order for religious pluralism not to be plainly false. Here are some of the defusing strategies:

1 Talk about myth, not doctrine.

2 Use the word "true" to mean something other than "true."

3 Given 1 and 2, let a true myth be one that tends to produce behavior you approve of.

But such strategies do nothing to provide RP with content.

A critical discussion of RP: Part three

Besides the inconsistency, another basic problem arises. Suppose one posits that there being something X will explain there being something else Y. This is a candidate for being an explanation only if X is said to have some property such that X having that property would explain there being Y. Here are two specifications of this general point that use the "generable from logic alone" vocabulary introduced by RP:

1 If no properties beyond those generated by logic alone are properly ascribable to the Real, then it is no more reasonable or appropriate to think of the Real as transcendent than as not transcendent.
2 If no properties beyond those generated by logic are ascribable to the Real, no experience is better thought of as a response to (or as contributed to by) the Real than any other.

Further, RP allows no moral properties to be ascribed to the Real. But then:

3 If no moral properties are ascribable to the Real, then there being the Real no better explains moral niceness than it does moral degradation.

Presumably on RP no causal powers or properties are ascribable to the Real. But then:

4 If no causal properties are ascribable to the Real, then there being the Real no better explains our existence than it would the existence of a world without us or there being no world at all.

and:

5 There is no reason to think of only religious experience as a response to the Real; eating a Big Mac or kicking a can is *as* reasonably thought of as an experience of the Real.
6 Wishing one were torturing one's enemies, enjoying mugging a helpless victim, or happily kicking a dog is *as* reasonably viewed as an experience that is a response to (or as contributed to by) the Real. None of them is *at all* reasonably thought of in such terms, since no property that is properly ascribable to the Real would make it reasonable to make any such suggestion about response or contribution.

So there are two points here: (i) there is no such thing as an experience reasonably thought of as a response to, or as contributed to by, the Real; (ii) there is no reason at all to suppose that only nice religious and moral experiences are such responses or are contributed to by the Real.

The second basic point can be put again in two stages:

1 If one cannot in principle ascribe any property to X by virtue of which X can explain Y, then positing X as an explanation of Y is entirely vacuous – it offers a sham explanation.
2 RP cannot ascribe to the Real any property by virtue of which positing it might explain anything whatever.

But then RP is explanatorily vacuous. When it comes to unpack its cognitive content, its briefcase is empty.

One might offer this suggestion: when RP posits the Real, it is to be seen as itself a metaphor. It has no literal meaning and it is to be judged in terms of whether it is useful. Does encountering the RP-myth make people nicer? But then RP will offer no explanations of anything. It will not be an alternative to the one-religion-is-right line, the all-religions-are-right line, or any other actual account of religious plurality.

Questions for reflection

1 What is religious pluralism?
2 Does religious pluralism have the religious consequences ascribed to it in this chapter?
3 What (other?) religious consequences does religious pluralism have?
4 Explain and assess the claim that religious pluralism is self-contradictory.
5 Explain and assess the claim that religious pluralism's use of "the Real" suggests that we know more about the alleged source of religious experience than it says we do.
6 Suppose we can tell that some religious doctrine is false, or is even less reasonably believed than its alternatives. What implications would this have for religious pluralism?
7 Suppose we can tell that some religious doctrine is true, or is even more reasonably believed than its alternatives. What implications would this have for religious pluralism?

Annotated reading

In the list that follows, books that disagree with the view regarding doctrine defended in the preceding chapter are unmarked, books that argue for a view similar to the author's are marked with an asterisk, and those marked with a plus sign contain essays on both sides of the dispute.

*D'Costa, Gavin (1980) *Theology and Religious Pluralism*, Oxford: Basil Blackwell.
+Hewitt, Harold (1991) *Problems in the Philosophy of Religion*, New York: St Martin's Press.
Hick, John (1980) *God Has Many Names*, London: Macmillan.
Hick, John (1989) *An Interpretation of Religion*, New Haven: Yale University Press.
+Sharma, Arvind (1993) *God, Truth, and Reality*, New York: St Martin's Press.
Smith, Wilfred Cantwell (1979) *Faith and Belief*, Princeton, NJ: Princeton University Press.
Smith, Wilfred Cantwell (1981) *Towards a World Theology*, Philadelphia: Westminster Press.
*Wainwright, William J. (1984) "Wilfred Cantwell Smith on faith and belief," *Religious Studies* 20, 353–66.
*Yandell, Keith E. (1993) "Some varieties of religious Pluralism," in James Kellenberger (ed.), *Inter-religious Models and Criteria*, New York: St Martin's Press, pp. 187–211.

PART II

Religious conceptions of ultimate reality

CHAPTER 7
Monotheistic conceptions of ultimate reality

Generic philosophical monotheism

Greek monotheism

Semitic monotheism

Hindu monotheism

Monotheisms and atheisms

Questions for reflection

Annotated reading

7
Monotheistic conceptions of ultimate reality

Generic philosophical monotheism

For monotheism, God is ultimate reality.[1] We can call what is common between various types of monotheism *generic philosophical monotheism*, characterized as follows. The claim *X is God* is to be understood as entailing each of the following claims:

1. *X is necessarily ontologically independent* (i.e., X exists, and it is logically impossible that X depends for existence on anything).
2. *X is self-conscious* (i.e., is conscious and aware of himself or herself as such; thus X is a person).[2]
3. *X is transcendent* (i.e., X is not identical to the world and God does not depend on the world for existence or powers).
4. *X is the highest being* (i.e., the most valuable, greatest, or best).

One significant religious difference between diverse sorts of monotheism concerns whether, and to what extent, God acts in human history. We can say that God exercises *strong providence* if and only if God acts in such a way as to bring about particular public historical events, and does so not only by causing private revelations or events; God brings about both public events and private events, and does not do the former only by doing the latter. By contrast, God exercises *weak providence* if and only if, save for creation of the world, God acts in such a way as to bring about particular public historical events, but only by causing private revelations or events; God brings about both public events and private events, and does the former only by doing the latter. Alternatively, one might be monotheistic and not think of God as providentially active at all.

Greek monotheism

Greek,[3] understood as including generic, monotheism can be defined as follows:

1 The world has always existed.
2 God exercises neither strong nor weak providence.
3 The world does not exist because God wants it to.
4 Whatever is *everlastingly* true is *necessarily* true.
5 That God exists is necessarily true.
6 That the world exists is necessarily true.

Nonetheless, the world depends on God in two ways. First, God is viewed as immutable, unchanging, and perfect; the world is mutable, changing, and imperfect. *There being mutable things* is a state of affairs dependent on *there being an immutable thing*. There is one-way dependence but no creation, not merely in the sense that the world did not begin to exist but also in that *there being a world* is not something that God chose to be the case or could have prevented. Second, God is perfect, having no potential, the realization of which would bring about divine improvement or self-realization. By contrast, the world is imperfect; it has unrealized potential, the proper realization of which would improve the world. The things in the world are also imperfect, and they have unrealized potential, the proper realization of which would improve them. Anything that exists has a nature or essence, a set of properties that makes it the kind of thing that it is. The essence of a thing in turn determines the sorts of other properties a thing can have and hence the sorts of events in which it may participate. What something can be an effect of, or a cause of, is a function of what properties it has. Mutable things have essences. An essence defines a natural kind, and members of a natural kind can be better or worse exemplars of that kind. Some bananas and some beavers are better – better *as bananas* and *as beavers* – than others. Some bananas are bruised, fragile, overripe; some are not. Some beavers are crippled, ill, or brain-damaged; others are not. Any thing has potentialities, accessible ways of changing, realization of which will further or frustrate the degree to which it is a good example of its kind. Each mutable thing strives by nature to be the best something of its kind that it can be – to exemplify magnificently what something of its sort can be. In this respect, it is as if each thing tries to be as like God (viewed as the perfect member of the kind *unmoved mover* or *immovable cause of motion*) as it can be, given the sort of thing that it is.

This view has a curious result. On it, the world can depend for its existence on God, and seek its fullest realization as a thing of its sort, without God even knowing that there is a mutable world let alone knowing about any individual thing in the world. No providence occurs, no historical persons or events bear ultimate religious significance, and no worship or prayer has any point. This sort of monotheism is abstract; it will seem cold, if not dead, to any Semitic or Hindu monotheist. Yet many of the arguments offered within Judaism, Christianity, and Islam come historically from Greek monotheism. Hindu monotheism, perhaps untouched historically by Greek natural theology, nonetheless contains similar arguments.

There can be evil if Greek monotheism is true. There can be defective things, things that are poorly realized members of their kind that are incapable of becoming better-realized members. There can be wrong human choices, instances in which persons voluntarily go against their knowledge of what is right. But these evils cannot be evidence against the existence of God, as God is construed in Greek monotheism. This sort of deity, as we have noted, does not even know that particular persons exist. No truths that might have been false are objects of divine knowledge, and all historical claims, biological accounts, all descriptions of physical or psychological reality, have in common the feature that even if they are true, they might have been false. A Greek deity is not culpable for lacking such knowledge; it is logically impossible that the deity of Greek monotheism have any knowledge of what might not have been true. Nor can the God of Greek monotheism bring about occurrences in space or time; no divine action is possible. So while there can be natural evils ("monsters" or strongly defective members of species) and moral evils (wrong human actions), these evils cannot be evidence that Greek monotheism is false. This points to an interesting feature of monotheisms. A monotheism without any doctrine of creation or providence can offer neither God's help in salvation nor God's answer to prayer, God's forgiveness or God's aid, and neither is it possible for such a monotheism that the existence of evil be offered as any evidence against its truth. A monotheism with a doctrine of creation or providence can offer God's help in salvation or God's answer to prayer, God's forgiveness or God's aid, and it is possible that for such a monotheism the existence of evil be offered as evidence against its truth. Whether evil really is evidence against monotheism is another matter; the point is that only for certain sorts of monotheism does the question even arise.

There being things that might not have existed is something to be explained. There might not have been any human beings, any lions, any trees, any rocks, any atoms. There are all of these things. There being these things has an explanation. A common strategy, fine so far as it goes, explains the existence of larger things by reference to the existence of smaller things of which the larger things are made. But perhaps sooner or later one gets to things so small that they are not in turn made of still smaller things; call these things *simple units*. There might not have been any simple units, so their existence too has an explanation. But simple units cannot be explained by reference to the things they are composed of; they are simple, not composite. So their existence has to be explained in a different way. Alternatively, suppose that, so to speak, things are composite all the way down – everything is made up of some things that are also made up of some things, and so on for ever. Then the question arises as to why there is this dizzying series of composites of composites.[4] Either way, the idea is, we must appeal to something whose non-existence is not an option, something that *exists necessarily*. So if there is anything at all, something exists necessarily. It is obvious that things do exist; so something exists necessarily. This thought plays an important role in monotheism, with Greek monotheism offering one sort of explanation and Semitic and Hindu offering an explanation of a different sort.

What, then, is it for something to exist necessarily? It is at least this: something exists necessarily only if is not possible that it depends for existence on anything else. Further, on a Greek monotheistic notion of necessity, it will be impossible that it change; only immutable things can exist necessarily. The items in our immediate environment change; they gain some qualities and lose others. They also come to be and pass away. The class of things that change and come and cease belongs to *the realm of generation and corruption*. What exists in this realm depends for its existence on something that exists necessarily, but nothing that exists necessarily can be part of this realm.

Besides existing necessarily, the deity of Greek monotheism is self-conscious. He, she, or it is also omniscient relative to logically necessary truths. But he, she, or it has no feelings and no knowledge of logically contingent truths. Whatever might have been false lies beyond its range of thought. Indeed, the only thing of which it is aware is itself and the contents of its own mind. Thus the Greek deity does not create the world, or even

know that there is a world. The Greek deity does not know that you exist or that you have needs; it is not an appropriate target for prayer of any sort. There is no prayer that it could hear. Nor does the Greek deity bring about any events in history; there is no notion of providence in Greek monotheism.

Being a being that exists necessarily, is immutable, self-conscious, and knows all necessary truths is regarded as the best sort of thing to be. The Greek deity is thought of as being as magnificent, valuable, and glorious as it is possible to be. Other things have positive worth insofar as they resemble this deity and defective insofar as they lack such resemblance. God is the perfect paradigm, the standard of worth; in this sense, morality rests on God – God provides the criterion for positive worth. There can be evil in the world as Greek monotheism conceives it. That this is a religion, of course, is highly questionable. It is not easy to see what ceremonies, rituals, practices, or the like are appropriate to its core claims. Nonetheless, it is of interest here for two reasons. Understanding it provides a nice comparison and contrast to varieties of monotheism that plainly are religions; much of Semitic monotheism has tried to introduce much of Greek monotheism into its own perspective.

Semitic monotheism

Semitic monotheism – Judaism, and Christianity and Islam which build on Jewish foundations – also includes generic monotheism and in addition embraces the following claims.

1 The world has not always existed (it was created *in* time, or time was created *with* it).[5]
2 God exercises strong providence.
3 The world exists because God wants it to.
4 That the world exists is not necessarily true (i.e., it is false that it is impossible that the world not exist; remember here that *necessity* is *metaphysical,* having to do with what there is, not *epistemological,* having to do with what is known, so that what 4 asserts has to do with *what can be,* not with *what we know*).

Here, God could have chosen that there be no world. The world is not everlasting. Either God created time in the same act as that by which God created a world, or God created the world after a time when there was no world. God sustains the world in existence and at times brings it about that particular individuals are born or are chosen for specific religious roles and that specific events occur. A religious tradition with no Abraham, Sarah, Moses, David, Ruth, Isaiah, Micah, or any of the prophets, no exile in Egypt, no Passover, no era of judges or of prophecy, no Hebrew people chosen by God is not Judaism. If there have been none of these people and events, Judaism is false. If Jesus did not live, or died a peaceful death in his own bed, or remained in the grave, then Christianity is false. If Mohammed never existed, or was always an atheist, or was a wealthy merchant entirely uninterested in religion and never claimed to receive any revelation, then Islam is false. With room for debate about exactly the scope of the claims, the Semitic monotheisms have in common that their core doctrines refer to particular persons and particular events.

The deity of Greek monotheism cannot act, unless everlasting contemplation of necessary truths is acting. The deity of Semitic monotheism can act. The God of Semitic monotheism acts in history; it is unthinkable for Greek monotheism that the deity be able so to behave, and unthinkable for Semitic monotheism that the deity not be able so to behave. The deity of Greek monotheism is not the God of history; that would be beyond her power and beneath her dignity. The deity of Semitic monotheism is the God of history, not by necessity but by choice; this is not beyond his power or beneath his dignity.

Within Semitic monotheism, Jewish and Muslim monotheisms assert that God creates and providentially rules the world; God acts in history, ordains prophets, and gives revelations. Christian monotheism agrees, but also claims that God has become incarnate in the person of Jesus Christ. That God become incarnate, according to Jewish and Islamic monotheism, is beyond God's power and beneath God's dignity – that God be incarnate in a human being who is crucified is, if possible, even more impossible and even more against the divine status. Christian monotheism asserts that *becoming incarnate* is within the power of an omnicompetent God, and provides the supreme instance of God's wisdom and love.

Hindu monotheism

Hindu monotheism, in addition to accepting generic monotheism, accepts these claims.

1 The world has always existed.
2 God exercises weak providence.
3 The world exists because God wants it to.
4 It is not the case that whatever is *everlastingly* true is *necessarily* true.
5 That the world exists is not necessarily true.

Hindu monotheism embraces both a beginningless world and a doctrine of creation. Here, the idea that God (Brahman with qualities) creates the world teaches that while the world is everlasting toward the past, having no first moment of existence, it depends at each moment of its existence on the sustaining activity of God. God could cease sustaining the world in existence, at which point God would continue to exist but the world would not. There is an asymmetrical dependence relation between God and the world: the world depends for its existence on God's activity, but God's existence does not depend on there being a world.

The relationship between God and history, as seen by Hindu monotheism, is complex. Hindu monotheism is a religion of reincarnation and karma, with karma being viewed as under God's control. In response to a person's repentance and faith, God can remit punishment, cancelling negative karma. Escape from the reincarnation cycle comes by God's grace. There are incarnations of a sort – God causes theophanies or appearances. For example, Krishna is said to appear to a devotee and to instruct him or her to build a temple on the site where the appearance occurred. Temple traditions include stories that trace the temple's history back to such appearances. But Hindu monotheism does not include any claim to the effect that God is uniquely incarnate in any human being or provides a means for redemption in such a manner. God is capable of controlling the mind of a particular person in as extended a way and period as God wishes, and God is capable of causing whatever visions, auditory or visual, God wishes to bring about. Further, gods or goddesses, who exist dependent on God and under God's control, may take upon themselves human form. But nowhere is there a unique and definitive incarnation in which God is incarnate in order to redeem the world. If nothing else, this is precluded by the fact that Hindu monotheism is not trinitarian.

There are other possibilities. Neo-Platonism, for example, is a form of monotheism distinct in various ways from those sketched here. I make no pretense to being exhaustive. My claim is only that the considerations that apply to the sorts of monotheism we shall discuss apply as well to those we do not.

Monotheisms and atheisms

A different way of distinguishing monotheisms

Monotheisms can be distinguished on different criteria from those discussed above. Coming to grasp this requires learning some distinctions that will be useful, even crucial, to later discussions. Consider the difference between *(NG) It is a logically necessary truth that God exists* and *(CG) It is a logically contingent truth that God exists*. What (NG) says is (i) *God does not exist* is self-contradictory, (ii) there is *no* possible world in which God does not exist, (iii) there is *no* way things might have been such that God did not exist. What (CG) says is: (i*) *God does not exist* is *not* self-contradictory, (ii*) there *is* a possible world in which God does not exist, (iii*) there *is* a way things might have been such that God did not exist.

It may appear that a monotheist should much favor (NG) over (CG), and indeed some monotheists think this is so. But other monotheists do not think this; after all, what (ii*) and (iii*) do is just say what (i*) says, putting it in different terms. They are not *further* differences between the two sorts of monotheist beyond their difference regarding (i) versus (i*).[6]

A monotheist who accepts (CG) typically will also accept *(CG*) It is logically impossible that God depend for existence on anything else*. Since she thinks that *God exists* is true, she will think both that God exists and that God exists with perfect independence. The difference between types of monotheism – between a monotheism to which (NG) is essential and a monotheism to which (CG) is essential – is not unimportant. Here is why.

Suppose that Tim thinks that there are frogs and Tom thinks that there are not. Tom is wrong, and Tim is right. Suppose that Tex agrees that there are frogs, but also thinks that *Necessarily, there are frogs* is true. This is a remarkable belief on Tex's part. It entails that under any logically possible condition, there are frogs; frog extermination is logically impossible. Not even God could get rid of frogs. Tim thinks that there are frogs all right, but he denies that there would be frogs no matter what, that it is logically impossible that frogs be exterminated; he supposes that God could create a frogless world – all of which Tex denies.

Just as one or the other of Tim (who thinks there are frogs) and Tom (who thinks there are not) is right, so one or the other of Tim (who thinks there might not have been frogs) and Tex (who thinks it is logically impossible that there not have been frogs) is right. Again, of course, Tim wins. But notice the difference between the Tim/Tom and the Tex/Tim disagreements. We can represent them as follows:

Tim/Tom
Tim: There are frogs. [F]
Tom: There are no frogs. [not-F]
Tex/Tim
Tex: It is a logically necessary truth that there are frogs. [Necessarily, F]
Tim: It is not a logically necessary truth that there are frogs. [Not-(Necessarily, F)]

Tim and Tom hold contradictory beliefs. So do Tex and Tim. What Tex believes to be logically necessary, Tim believes not to be logically necessary. We can also put the dispute between Tex and Tim this way:

*Tex/Tim**
Tex: It is self-contradictory that there be no frogs. [Necessarily, not(not-F)]
Tim: It is not self-contradictory that there be no frogs. [Not-(Necessarily, not(not-F)]

Tex thinks something logically impossible that Tim thinks logically possible.

Logical necessity and *logical possibility* are modalities. We can put the difference between the disagreements in yet another way: the Tim/Tom disagreement is about the *truth* of *There are frogs*; the Tex/Tim dispute is about the *modality* of *There are frogs*. Disputes about whether there are frogs has, of course, no religious content. But the pretend disputes about frogs are paralleled by disputes about God.

The NN principle

A final point will place us in position to complete our discussion. A *modal* proposition is a second-order proposition[7] that says about some first-order proposition that it is necessarily true, necessarily false, or logically contingent. Here is a bit of the logic of modal propositions.[8] Where P is any proposition:

1 Necessarily, P (= It is not possible that P be false).
2 Necessarily, not-P (= It is not possible that P be true).
3 Contingent, P (= It is not impossible that P be true and it is not impossible that P be false)

express the possible modalities regarding P. They entail, respectively,

4 Possibly, P.
5 Not-(Possibly, P).
6 Possibly, P.

where "possibly" means not "maybe" but "it is logically possible that" or "P is not self-contradictory." A proposition of the form expressed in 1 through 6 is a second-order proposition; it says of a first-order proposition that it is necessary, contingent, or possible.

What the NN thesis tells us is this:

NN: *Every true modal proposition is necessarily true, and every false modal proposition is necessarily false; it is logically impossible that there be a contingently true or a contingently false modal proposition.*

This applies both to second-order and higher-order modal propositions.

Regarding kinds of monotheism and atheism

A little reflection suggests that, since a monotheist thinks that *God exists* is true, she can either take it to be a logically necessary truth or take it to be a logically contingent truth. She cannot remain a monotheist and think it false. Similarly, since an atheist thinks that *God exists* is false, she can take it to be a logically necessary falsehood or a logically contingent falsehood.

Thus there are exactly four alternatives here:

1 *(NG)*: it is a logically necessary truth that God exists.
2 *(CG)*: it is a logically contingent truth that God exists.
3 *N(not-G)*: it is a necessary truth that God does not exist.
4 *C(not-G)*: it is a logically contingent falsehood that God exists.

What (NG) amounts to is this: *Necessarily, it is true that God exists.* What (CG) amounts to is: *It is true that God exists, and it is false that Necessarily, it is true that God exists.* Hence one sort of monotheism – that which accepts (NG) or that which accepts (CG) – is false. Further, given the NN thesis, whichever sort is false is *necessarily* false. Similarly, either N(not-G) or C(not-G) is false, so one sort or the other of atheism is false. Further, whichever sort of atheism is false is *necessarily* false.

Ultimate reality, then, according to monotheism, consists in the existence of an omnipotent, omniscient, morally perfect self-conscious Being that cannot depend for its existence on anything else. This Being either is such that *Necessarily, God exists* is true or else such that *God exists is true, and it is logically necessary that God does not depend for existence on anything*. The difference between kinds of monotheism will come up again when we consider arguments, pro and con, regarding monotheism.[9,10]

There are, then, different varieties of monotheism, some of which we have described. There are different monotheistic notions regarding what has ultimate reality in the sense of depending for its existence on nothing else.

A few comments regarding monotheism and non-ultimate reality

Typically, monotheists have commonsensically held that there are persons and there are physical objects. Monotheism typically holds that *If there are persons then God created persons* and *If there are physical objects then God created physical objects*. The term "physical objects" here should be so understood as to include not only artifacts (cars, chairs, pens) but also natural objects (carrots, zebras, and galaxies). Monotheism typically adds that among the things created, those most like God are persons – self-conscious agents capable of acting rightly and wrongly, loving and hating, worshipping God and rebelling against God. There are different views within monotheism about even the broad details of how exactly to understand the relations between God and the world, some of which will come up later – in particular, those regarding determinism, freedom, and agency.

There are different views of what laws of nature are, and different accounts of how laws of nature are related to God. Roughly, a physical theory is a systematized attempt to explain observed physical phenomena. Such a theory will assume that certain sorts of things – say, *A-type things* – exist and behave[11] in certain ways, and that certain general statements (laws) are true, and that one can then explain the existence and behavior of other types of things given that there are A-type things and that the laws are true. Suppose simply for convenience that all the other natural sciences reduce to physics, and that somehow we have discovered the entirely correct physics. Then what the entirely correct physics included as basic laws would constitute the actual laws of nature. How should those laws be thought of?

On one account, they are abstract objects – propositions of some such form as (L1) *If A-type things exist and condition C obtains, then B-type things will exist* or (L2) *If A-type things behave in way W1, and condition C* holds, then B-type things will behave in way W2*. On this view, true statements of forms (L1) and (L2) will be necessary truths. God's role in creation will not be deciding what laws are true, but rather of deciding whether A-type and B-type things shall exist, and whether conditions C and C* will obtain. Thus if it is a law that *Water freezes at 32 degrees*[12] then, on the present account, *If there is water then it freezes at 32 degrees* is a necessary truth, and what is up to God is whether *There is water* and *It is 32 degrees where water exists* are ever true.

On what is sometimes thought of as another account, laws of nature are truths about the dispositions of natural objects. If water is what this glass contains, then – the idea is – it is an essential feature of the stuff in this glass that it freezes at 32 degrees.[13] Natural laws reflect the essential properties of natural objects and what happens to things with such properties in various environments. But on this account too *If there is water then it freezes at 32 degrees* is a necessary truth. If God creates water, God creates something which freezes at 32 degrees.

On either account, there might be considerable choice of what universe, if any, is created. The laws in question are expressed as *conditionals* or statements of the form *If A then C*. What holds that *A* place is the *antecedent* and what occupies the *C* place is the *consequent*. On the first view described, there might be various ways of putting individual laws together into logically consistent groupings such that a universe could be created containing the things referred to in the antecedents of these particular laws. There would be as many choices between orderly worlds as there were such sets of laws. On the second way of putting things, a similar result arises. The *essence* of some object is the set of properties necessary and sufficient for its existence as possessing a nature it cannot exist without and the existence of which in an object suffices to identify a kind.[14] Let an *essence description* be a description of a universe in which one or more logically compatible kinds of things co-existed. Every essence description would pick out a different world that God might create.

There are other conceptions of laws, or perhaps of conceptions on which there really aren't any laws. On another view, for example, what we call laws are only generalizations that we may discover to be strictly false though still fairly accurate, and that there is no more to a law than that – a typically accurate generalization which may well be false, and in any case is as explanatorily deep as things get. On this view, explaining why some generalizations are accurate and others are not is not going to be possible – not at any rate for the class of generalizations that have the widest scope.

There seems to be good reason to think that there are basic laws that are probabilistic – laws of the form (L1*) *If A-type things exist, and condition C obtains, then the probability of a B-type thing existing is .987* or (L2*) *If A-type things behave in way W1, and condition C* holds, then the probability of B-type things then behaving in way W2 is between .997 and .999.*

The philosophical interest of such matters, insofar as they relate to monotheism, has to do with how different notions of the relations between God and the world, and of God and laws of nature, relate to questions about creation, determinism, freedom, and responsibility – matters for later reflection.

Questions for reflection

1 What are the basic tenets of Greek monotheism? Does Greek monotheism serve as a sort of minimal monotheism, a possible philosophical position, with no religious importance, or is it a religion?
2 What are the basic tenets of Semitic monotheism? How do the different Semitic monotheisms differ? From the perspective of these traditions, how religiously important are the differences?
3 What are the basic tenets of Hindu monotheism?
4 Discuss what can be said for, and what can be said against, this claim: *Since Hindu monotheism makes no claim about historical persons or events religiously essential, it is as much like Greek monotheism as it is like Semitic monotheism.*

5 What is a modal proposition? Why must a modal proposition be a necessary truth if it is true, and a necessary falsehood if it is false?
6 Explain the following claim: there are two versions of monotheism, and two versions of atheism, and at least one version of each is necessarily false.

Annotated reading

Cohn-Sherbok, Daniel (1996) *Medieval Jewish Philosophy*, Surrey: Curzon. Brief, good discussion of perhaps the most flourishing period of Jewish philosophy.

Davidson, Herbert (1987) *Proofs for Eternity, Creation, and the Existence of God in Medieval Islamic and Jewish Philosophy*, Oxford: Oxford University Press. Detailed discussion of Jewish and Islamic medieval philosophers on arguments concerning the dependence and duration of the created world and arguments for God's existence, with some reference to Christian philosophers.

Davidson, Herbert (1992) *Alfarabi, Avicenna, and Averroes on Intellect*, Oxford: Oxford University Press. Fine discussion of theories of the mind held by three leading Islamic philosophers.

Kellner, Menachem (1986) *Dogma in Medieval Jewish Thought*, Oxford: Oxford University Press. Good discussion of the systems of Jewish thought that are more doctrinally oriented than others.

Kroner, Richard (1956) *Speculation in Pre-Christian Philosophy*, Philadelphia: Westminster Press. This book, and the next two, discuss the development of Christian thought in interaction with ancient, medieval, and modern philosophy.

Kroner, Richard (1959) *Speculation and Revelation in the Age of Christian Philosophy*, Philadelphia: Westminster Press. See previous reference.

Kroner, Richard (1961) *Speculation and Revelation in Modern Philosophy*, Philadelphia: Westminster Press. See Kroner (1956) comment.

Leaman, Oliver (1985) *An Introduction to Medieval Islamic Philosophy*, Cambridge: Cambridge University Press. Fairly brief, good discussion of perhaps the most flourishing period of Islamic philosophy.

Lipner, Julius (1986) *The Face of Truth*, Albany: SUNY Press. Fine explanation of the thought of the Hundu theologian–philosopher Ramanuja.

Lott, Eric (1976) *God and the Universe in the Vedantic Theology of Ramanuja*, Madras: Ramanuja Research Society. Another fine discussion of Ramanuja.

Lott, Eric (1980) *Vedantic Approaches to God*, London: Macmillan. Excellent discussion of the three major figures of Hindu Vedantic thought: Shankara, Ramanuja, Madhva.

McGrath, Alister (1994) *Christian Theology*, Oxford: Blackwell. Good historical discussion of the types and themes and Christian thought.

Watt, W. Montgomery (1973) *The Formative Period of Islamic Thought*, Edinburgh: Edinburgh University Press. Good discussion of early Islamic philosophy.

CHAPTER 8
Nonmonotheistic conceptions of ultimate reality

8
Nonmonotheistic conceptions of ultimate reality

Jainism has basically one account of ultimate reality; there are (and always have been) persons and there are (and always have been) the physical elements of which observable physical things are composed. There is no deity on which either depend for existence or arrangement. The Jain tradition is doctrinally homogeneous, so there is no need to say that it is this rather than that type of Jainism that is being described.

The Buddhist traditions range from the Theravada view, described here, through the Absolutism that is part of Mahayana and the at least nearly monotheistic perspective of Pure Land. For the moment, let us leave nirvana out of the account. Theravada Buddhism holds that (besides nirvana) what there is encompasses only momentary, dependent things. These things are[1] momentary states, some mental and some physical (some involving consciousness, some not). Much of later Buddhism accepts only mental states. These two claims[2] are as nearly orthodoxly Buddhist as anything; those who denied them were regarded as heretics. Everything is radically impermanent, transitory, fleeting; nothing exists independent of other things.

Advaita Vedanta Hinduism is itself a variety of Absolutism, which we will describe in contrast to the non-Absolutist views of two other varieties of Vedantic Hinduism. Advaita Absolutism holds that all that exists is qualityless Brahman. There is one thing, not many, and this one thing of course stands in no relation to any other thing. Nor does this one thing have any qualities whatever.

The task before us in this chapter, then, is to come to understand these three quite different, but all nonmonotheistic, accounts of what there is. Since Advaita Vedanta is perhaps best understood in contrast with the other varieties of Vedanta, which are monotheistic, beginning with it provides the easiest transition from the discussion of the previous chapter.

Advaita Vedanta Hinduism

Three major philosophers of Vedantic persuasion, with generally suggested dates, are Shankara (788–820CE), Ramanuja (1017–1137CE), and Madhva (1197–1276CE). Shankara holds to Advaita Vedanta or Unqualified Non-Dualism; Ramanuja holds to Vsistadvaita or Qualified Non-Dualism; Madhva holds to Dvaita or Unqualified Dualism.

It may be helpful to understand Shankara's views in contrast to those of Ramanuja and Madhva. Let *the world* be all bodies and all minds other than God. Ramanuja holds that God and the world are in a relationship of asymmetric dependence – the world depends on God but not God on the world. He then takes the world to be God's body in a somewhat technical sense of *body*. The world is God's body in the sense that God can affect any part of the world without having to do so by affecting some other part of it. One might think of one's own body as the part of the physical world that one can move without having to move anything else in order to move it; in order otherwise to affect the physical world, one has to move one's body. All dependent minds and bodies are related in this way to God; for any mind or any body, God can affect it without having to make use of some other mind or body in order to do so. Madhva rejects the notion that the world is God's body, thinking that this makes it sound as if God were dependent for existence and/or action on the world, whereas he holds that God exists independently and is capable of thought without needing any world for his self-conscious activities. Strictly, the disagreement between Ramanuja and Madhva here seems to lie in how one is to understand the notion of God's body; understood as Madhva takes it, Ramanuja too would reject the idea.

What Ramanuja and Madhva have in common – the notion that there exists an independent God and a dependent world – Shankara rejects. What exists for Shankara is *nirguna* or qualityless Brahman, though what *appears* to exist is a multiplicity of physical objects and persons and a personal God. Shankara sometimes explains his view by using analogies with sensory perception. For example, suppose it is the case that:

1 There is no man in the shadows.
2 Bimal (a typical perceiver) sincerely reports, based on his sensory experience, "I see a man in the shadows."
3 What really is in the shadows is only a coat hanging on a hook.

Then

4 There is something that Bimal sees.
5 What Bimal sees does not have the nature and properties that Bimal sees it as having.

The standard Indian examples are seeing a conch shell and mistaking it for silver and seeing a rope and mistaking it for a snake; each of these follows the (1) through (5) pattern. Analogously, then, the Advaita Vedantin claims, when one reports, based on one's sensory experience, that there is an experience-independent physical thing, it is nonetheless true that there exists nothing sensory. As there was no man who Bimal saw, but only a coat hanging on a hook, so there is no tree or table (or any other object) that anyone senses, but only qualityless Brahman. Strictly, the analogy does not work; *taking one thing for another* is very different from *sheer hallucination*. But the negative idea is clear – it is denied that there is a mind-independent physical world. This by itself would yield only idealism – the view that there are minds and experiences with sensory content, but no mind-independent objects of sensory experiences. Shankara's view is much more radical. He claims that there are neither minds nor experiences; there is only Brahman without qualities. All experience of physical objects or of self is illusory. It is not an illusion caused by Brahman; that would require that there be effects that were not identical to Brahman. Of course Brahman itself cannot be subject to illusion (that would be a limitation).

One should not suppose that Shankara is unaware of the very considerable difficulties of his view. Consider these passages by him:

1 To refute the self is impossible, for he who tries to refute it is the self.[3]
2 Only a deluded man could entertain the idea that he does not exist.[4]

The idea is that while it may be possible without self-refutation to deny that there are physical objects distinct from one's sensory experience, it is not possible without self-refutation to deny that one exists oneself.[5] Shankara then turns to the task of developing a perspective that he regards as fully consistent with certain central *Upanishadic* texts, particularly one that says simply "Thou art That" (the individual person is identical to Brahman). Taking this and other texts literally, Shankara opts for the view that *only* Brahman-without-qualities exists. He holds that if I exist, then – contrary to all sorts of powerful considerations – I am Brahman.

The *Vedas* and *Upanishads*, along with traditional commentaries on these documents, are the sacred texts of Hinduism. *Vedanta* means "end of the *Vedas*" – the tradition that faithfully follows the Vedic teachings. *Advaita* means "non-dual" and contrasts with *Dvaita* ("dual") and *Vsistadvaita* ("qualifiedly non-dual"), these being the three adjectives defining different Vedantic traditions. The core religious dispute among these three versions of Vedanta concerns the proper interpretation of the relevant authoritative texts concerning the nature of Brahman – that being whose existence does not depend on anything else. The Advaita reading is Absolutistic (non-dualist), the Dvaita and Vsistadvaita (dualist and qualifiedly dualist) readings are monotheistic.

At issue are various texts, some of which express the view that the soul or individual human person is literally identical to Brahman, others of which express the view that the human soul is more like Brahman than are other things. The core issue is which texts – the monotheistic or the Absolutistic – are to be read literally and which read non-literally.

Here is the monotheistic reading of such passages.

> Only on account of having for his essence qualities similar to those of Brahman is the soul spoken of as Brahman, as in the case of the all-wise Brahman. Since the essence, i.e. the very nature of the soul, consists only of wisdom, bliss, and other qualities similar [in some degree] to those of Brahman, there proceeds the statement that the soul is one with [like] Brahman; just as in the text, "All this is indeed Brahman."[6] Brahman is spoken of as "identical with all [the world] on account of there being qualities in Brahman which are predicated of the whole world." The following is in the *Bhavishyat Purana*: "The souls are separate, the perfect Lord is separate, still owing to the similarity of intelligent nature they are spoken of as Brahman in the various Scriptural disquisitions."[7]

In sum: like Brahman, who is a self-conscious Person, all-wise, filled with bliss, human persons also are self-conscious, capable of possessing some wisdom and some bliss. They are similar in ways that make both persons: one an Independent Person on whom everything else depends, one a dependent person who has sinned and thus both owes her existence to, and needs gracious forgiveness from, the One on whom she depends. This, again, is monotheism. Nonmonotheistic or Absolutist Advaita Vedanta rejects this reading of such passages.

Here is the nonmonotheistic reading.

> The difference between God and the individual soul is due to these differing limiting adjuncts [namely, the mind and the senses]. When these are absolutely negated . . . then there is no God and no individual, but there remains only the eternal, absolute, and pure Brahman . . . Scripture [*Upanishads*] says that the limiting adjuncts are accidental, and superimposed on Brahman; reasoning based on Scripture must negate them both.[8]

To thought and perception, there appear to be a multiplicity of persons and things. On an Advaita reading, the *Upanishads* deny this; so thought and perception must be "negated" in the sense that what appears to them to be so is rejected.

What exists, then, for Shankara is nirguna or qualityless Brahman, though what *appears* to exist is a multiplicity of physical objects and persons and a personal God. Until we get to the distinction between appearance and reality, he is a realist regarding objects, minds, and God; he holds that, "at the level of appearance," such things exist. Indeed, he argues strongly for their existence. But he also holds, on *Upanishadic* authority, that only qualityless Brahman exists "at the level of reality."

How are we to understand this claim? Plainly not in terms of the level of appearance being the set of things that exist dependently and Brahman being their independently existing Source. That is the position of Ramanuja and Madhva. The levels cannot be levels of reality distinguished by presence or absence of dependence. The levels presumably are in some manner levels of knowledge or belief, appearance being how things look and reality being how things are. How are we to understand this notion?

A two-theories account

Taking a cue from Spinoza, a favorite among Advaita Vedantins, one might try interpreting Advaita Vedanta along the lines of saying that there are two theories related in certain ways as follows. Suppose we have two theories, each of which has its own vocabulary; then we will have two theoretical languages, replete with their conceptual perspectives or world-views. Each, let us suppose, is exhaustive – it describes, or attempts to describe, all there is, not of course in concrete detail but in terms of general properties and kinds and the like. In each, whatever can be explained is explained. What one theory refers to is the same as what the other theory refers to, though of course each describes what it refers to very differently from that of the other. No descriptive term is common between or shared by both theories.[9] Thus, on the current account, there are two theories or theoretical languages that have parity of description and parity of explanatory power. The entities referred to in one language are identical to those of the other, and the explanatory connections alleged in the one will be paralleled by explanatory connections alleged in the other.

According to one of these theories, individual persons, physical objects, and a personal God exist. Since the Vedantic term for persons is *atman*, we can all this *the Atman theory* (AT). According to the other of these theories, all that exists is Brahman without qualities; we will call this *the Brahman theory* (BT). We then get something along these lines:

The Brahman Theory
1 Brahman exists and has no qualities at all.
2 Nothing but Brahman exists.
3 Every atman that exists is identical to Brahman.

The Atman Theory
1 There are individual atmans (dependent persons).
2 There is a personal Brahman and so Brahman has qualities.
3 No atman is Brahman.
4 Each atman has mental qualities.
5 There are physical objects.
6 Physical objects have physical qualities.

There are problems with this as an account of Advaita Vedanta. The Brahman Theory has almost no descriptive content, and no explanatory content. One cannot use terms from AT to shore up BT, since this mixes the theories; it would remove the alleged purity of the theoretical languages from being tainted by one another. The account requires descriptive and explanatory parity of two logically independent theories or theoretical languages. BT and AT lack such parity. Further, the account requires that the theories be equally justified. But according to Advaita Vedanta, BT and AT are not equally justified or equally accurate. Thus this does not seem a successful program for stating Advaita.

A causal theory of perception account

Perhaps one can approach matters in this way. Consider the sort of causal account of perception that John Locke offered.[10] On this view, a veridical perception of a tree is analyzed like this. Suppose it is true that *Manindra sees a tree*. What makes this true is there being a tree which causes certain images in Manindra's mind. These images represent, and in limited ways resemble, the tree. Perception occurs when a perceivable object has the right sort of causal impact on a perceiver.

Then whittle the account down. Locke himself held that, for example, color qualities were the product of interaction between object and perceiver; the tree itself has no color properties. But the tree itself does have shape properties, and the shape properties of the image must resemble the shape properties of the tree if Manindra, by virtue of having the images, is seeing the tree. But suppose one thinks that there is no tree, and indeed nothing with shape properties that caused Manindra's images. Suppose Manindra's images are caused by another mind or spirit. Then all of perception is illusory in the sense that there are no objects that cause our perceptual images. Now, one might suggest, this gives us what we might call a minimally informative causal theory of perception. It may be that this theory, while it has little to commend it philosophically, is the one to use in trying to explain Shankara's theory if we wish to use sensory analogies. Even this is dubious. On this account, which goes further than Locke's, *Manindra sees a green tree* will be true if and only if there is no green tree that Manindra sees. In fact, all analogy with perception has vanished. Further, in order to come to Shankara's view, one must somehow keep whittling away until neither Manindra's mind nor the mind that caused the images in Manindra's mind is thought of as having any properties. One wonders if one is then offering any account of anything. Further, Brahman is not construed as the cause of anything, and so is not conceived as the cause of perception. The most sensible procedure, then, would seem to be to leave perceptual analogies alone. In effect, this is what does happen when the Advaitin appeals to levels of being or to levels of truth or to the appearance/reality distinction construed in an Advaitin way.

Reductionism and eliminativism

Brahman accepts the claim, relative to each individual person or atman, that it is identical to Brahman. How is this to be understood? Consider a simple identity statement:

Ia Cicero is identical to Tully.

What this means is simply:[11]

Ia* "Cicero" designates the same person as "Tully" designates.

Shankara intends:

IIa The Atman is identical to Brahman.[12]

to entail:

IIa* "Atman" designates what "Brahman" designates.

But this tells us only a little. Idealism regarding physical objects contends that a physical object is identical to a collection of sensory images. This can be understood in either of two quite different ways as follows, using a cat named "Oscar" as our sample physical object:

III "Oscar" designates what "this collection of catty images"[13] designates.

So far, so good. Are we then to go on to IV or to V?:

IV All true statements about Oscar can be translated without remainder into (reduced to) statements about this collection of catty images.

V Statements about Oscar should[14] be dropped from our speech and replaced by sentences that speak only of this collection of catty images.[15]

What IV recommends is reduction; what V commends is replacement. It seems clear that the idealist, at least of Bishop Berkeley's sort, wants V. Berkeley takes statements about physical objects to be true only if there are exactly the sort of experience-independent extended objects it is the purpose of his theory to reject. Statements to the effect that there are such things, being in principle false, should be banned from our theories. The idea is that the truths cat sentences aim at and miss, collections of catty images sentences hit.

More formally, a statement A reduces without remainder to a statement B only if it is logically impossible that A and B differ in truth value. Statements about physical objects can differ in truth value from statements about collections of catty images. So IV recommends a logical impossibility. Further, given the conditions for reduction, if the recommended reduction could be carried out, it would import talk of objects into idealistic theory. Berkeleyian idealism is a replacement theory. It is eliminativist, not reductionist.

So is Advaita Vedanta, and for analogous reasons. Consider the difference between:

IV* All true statements about any Atman can be translated without remainder into (reduced to) statements about Brahman.

V* Statements about any Atman should be dropped from our speech and replaced by sentences that speak only of Brahman.[16]

Suppose that *This Atman is tired (i.e., I am tired)* is true. It has as truth conditions that I exist as the sort of being that can tire; if *Atman is Brahman* is treated as IV* requires, it will be true that *Brahman is tired*. Shankara rejects this. It is V* that his view requires. His view is eliminativist, not reductionist. It is in that context that we should understand his view that only Brahman without qualities exists.[17]

Advaita Vedanta will receive further description when we come later to ask what considerations have been offered on its behalf. In philosophy, understanding a view and understanding what can be said for and against it are not separate enterprises; they are intrinsically related, part of a single enterprise of understanding. What can be concluded thus far is that analogies to perception and theories of perception seem not helpful in coming to terms with the core of the philosophy of Advaita Vedanta.

Jainism and Buddhism

A radical substance-view (Jainism) and a non-substance-view (Theravada Buddhism) compared and contrasted

Jainism and Buddhism agree that our great need is to escape the circle of rebirths and achieve enlightenment and release. But they differ in what the enlightened person finds at the end of her search, and they disagree about what the nature of the searcher is. This difference is both religious and philosophical, and will be explained in both its religious and its philosophical contexts.

Jainism and persons: persons are substances[18]

For Jainism, consciousness is always someone's consciousness. There can no more be consciousness without persons than there can be triangles without angles.

A Jain text tells us the following:

> The distinctive characteristic of a substance is being. Being is a simultaneous possession of coming into existence, going out of existence, and permanence. Permanence means the indestructibility of the essence of the substance . . . substance is possessed of attributes and modifications . . . attributes depend upon sub-

> stratum and cannot be the substratum of another attribute. Modification is change of attribute.[19]

We are told that there are things (substances) that have qualities (attributes, properties) without themselves being qualities. These qualities are inherently first-order qualities (qualities of things that are not themselves qualities) and they begin and cease to be – they come into existence and go out of existence. For a quality to come into existence is for a thing that did not have it to come to have it; for a quality to go out of existence is for a thing that did have it to come to have it no longer (this is what it is for substances to undergo modifications). When things undergo modification (change of attribute) in the sense that they gain and lose qualities, they remain the same things (enjoy permanence) throughout the modifications that they undergo. Change presupposes that something is changed, and hence that something endures through the change. In sum: numerically identical things undergo change of qualities; change of one thing (quality) presupposes permanence of another thing (substance).

The same text adds that: "The self's essence is life . . The distinctive characteristic of self is attention . . Those with minds are knowers."[20] Among things or substances are some whose essence is *being alive and being capable of being liberated* or *being alive and being incapable of being liberated*.[21] Any such thing is conscious or capable of giving attention to objects of experience, and self-conscious or aware of itself as agent and as being affected by other things. These remarks serve as background to the religious point of the doctrines just noted:

> That which should be grasped by self-discrimination is "I" from the real point of view.[22] The soul has the nature of knowledge, and the realization of this nature is Nirvana; therefore one who is desirous of Nirvana must meditate on self-knowledge.[23]

According to Jainism, knowledge of the nature of the self or person is achievable through meditative self-awareness; such knowledge is constitutive of achieving enlightenment. The most desirable modification – namely, enlightenment – neither changes the nature of the self or person or *jiva* nor removes his capacity for awareness or his status as a knower:

> After the soul is released, there remain perfect right-belief, perfect right-knowledge, perfect perception, and the state of having accomplished all.[24]

Here, persons are enduring self-conscious substances, retaining numerical identity over time and retaining identity as individual persons in their enlightened state. Thus in the *Jaina Sutras*[25] one reads that when the Venerable Ascetic Mahavira had become enlightened, he was

> omniscient and comprehending all objects; he knew and saw all conditions of the world, of gods, men, and demons: whence they come, whither they go, whether they are born as men or animals .. or become gods or hell-beings .. the ideas, the thoughts of their minds, the food, doings, desires, the open and secret deeds of all living beings in the whole world; he the Arhat, for whom there is no secret, knew and saw all conditions of all living beings in the world, what they thought, spoke, or did at any moment.

Mahavira – founder of Jainism and achiever of enlightenment – is conceived as being the same person post-enlightenment as he was pre-enlightenment. Nor does post-mortem achievement of full and final enlightenment/nirvana alter this.

Buddhism and persons: persons as bundles[26]

A Buddhist text tells us that:

> Whether Buddhas arise, O priests, or whether Buddhas do not arise, it remains a fact and the fixed and necessary constitution of being that all its constituents are transitory. This fact a Buddha discovers and masters, and when he has discovered and mastered it, he announces, teaches, publishes, proclaims, discloses, minutely explains, and makes it clear that all the constituents of being are transitory . . . Whether Buddhas arise, O priests, or whether Buddhas do not arise, it remains a fact and the fixed and necessary constitution of being that all its elements are lacking in an ego [substantial, permanent self-nature]. This fact a Buddha discovers and masters, and when he has discovered and mastered it, he announces, teaches, publishes, proclaims, discloses, minutely explains, and makes it clear that all the elements of being are lacking in an ego.[27]

A longer and more familiar passage reads as follows:

> Just as the word "chariot" is but a mode of expression for axle, wheels, chariot-body, pole, and other constituent members, placed in a certain relation to each other, but when we come to examine the members one by one, we discover that in the

> absolute sense there is no chariot; and just as the word "house" is but a mode if expression for wood and other constituents of a house, surrounding space in a certain relation, but in the absolute sense there is no house; and just as the word "fist" is but a mode of expression for the fingers, the thumb, etc. in a certain relation; and the word "lute" for the body of the lute, strings, etc.; "army" for elephants, horses, etc.; "city" for fortifications, houses, gates, etc.; "tree" for trunk, branches, foliage, etc.; in a certain relation, but when we come to examine the parts one by one, we discover that in the absolute sense there is no tree; in exactly the same way words "living entity" and "ego" are but a mode of expression for the presence of the five attachment groups, but when we come to examine the elements of being one by one, we discover that in the absolute sense there is no living entity there to form a basis for such figments as "I am" or "I"; in other words, that in the absolute sense there is only name and form. The insight of him who perceives this is called knowledge of the truth.[28]

We are told here that there are constituents that are transitory. Further, there are collections of simultaneous constituents (call these simultaneous bundles) and there are collections of successive constituents (call these successions of bundles). Successions of bundles are made up of sequential simultaneous bundles and so-called physical objects are successions of bundles.[29] More importantly for our purposes, so-called persons are successions of bundles. There are no constituents that endure; each moment sees an entirely new constituent population. Successions of bundles are the only candidates for possessing numerical identity over time.

Review, comparison and contrast

1 Reincarnation and karma

The Jain and Buddhist traditions share belief in reincarnation and karma. Reincarnation doctrine teaches that each person beginninglessly lives one life after another, and will do so endlessly unless he becomes enlightened. Karma doctrine (in its nonmonotheistic version, which is the version relevant to Jainism and Buddhism) teaches that one inescapably receives the merit or demerit due; right or wrong actions not disinterestedly done yield weal or woe, and no one escapes their due recompense. Embedded in these doctrines is a *justice requirement*: the recipient of the recompense must be the doer of the deed for which recompense comes – she, and not another.

2 *Change*

On the Buddhist perspective described above, collections of simultaneous constituents are replaced by new collections of simultaneous constituents. No changes occur; replacement occurs.

A further Jain text reads:

> There cannot be a thing which is devoid of its modifications of birth and decay. On the other hand, modifications cannot exist without an abiding or eternal something – a permanent substance, for birth, decay, and stability (continuance) – these three constitute the characteristic of a substance or entity.[30]

"Birth and decay" refers to the comings and goings of qualities, "stability or continuance" to substances. Change requires permanence.[31]

3 *Simplicity*

Jain persons lack constituents. They have no elements and are incomposite. A Jain person at a time T is a self-conscious substance that exists at T. If she is embodied at T, her body is not *part* of her at T. Her thoughts at T are thoughts but not parts; her qualities at T are qualities but not parts. A person that exists at times T1 and T2 does not have a T1-part and a T2-part. One might say: *all of her exists at T1 and all of her exists at T2 – she is not temporally scattered*. She has a life, and that life (in some sense, at least) can have parts – say, one part where she is a student in Delhi and another part where she is a professor in Benares. Her life can have parts or segments; she cannot. She is an incomposite substance, a self-conscious mind. While *being alive* (not to be confused with *being embodied*) is essential to a person, a person is not identical to any particular life or series of lives. A person could have lived lives other than the one he did live, and he *has* a life, and a long series of lives, without *being* any or all of those lives (whatever exactly that might amount to).

Buddhist persons have constituents. They have elements and are composite. A Buddhist person at a time T is a simultaneous bundle that exists at T.[32] Her thoughts at T are thoughts that are parts of her at T; her qualities at T are qualities that are parts of her at T. A person that exists at times T1 and T2 does have a T1-part and a T2-part, the former being a bundle of elements-simultaneously-existing-at-T1 and the latter a bundle of elements-simultaneously-existing-at-T2. One might say: *at no moment of a person's existence does all of her exist at once – she is temporally scattered*. If a person could exist at just two moments, half of her would exist at each moment. If a life is composed of one simultaneous bundle followed by another followed by another, a person *is* a life, and that life has as many parts as there are moments at which some simultaneous bundle or other occurs in the life-series. While *being alive* (not to be confused with *being embodied*) is essential to a person, a person is identical to the particular series of lives that she lives.[33]

A basic difference between the Jain doctrine and the Buddhist doctrine of persons

The difference between the Jain and the Buddhist accounts of what it is to be a person is important but it can be difficult to grasp. Here is another way of putting it. Consider an atom of the sort that Isaac Newton believed in. In his physics, an atom in effect was a tiny pellet – a billiard ball shrunk to minuscule proportions. An atom was as small as anything can get, and was composed of no parts whatever. Homogeneous and ultimately tiny, atoms (Newton taught) are the things of which larger physical items are composed.

Suppose that at time T1 there is just one atom; call it Alice1. Suppose that at time T2 there is also just one atom; call it Alice2. Then ask: is Alice1 identical to Alice2? The answer is "Yes" provided Alice1 has stayed in existence from T1 through T2. Otherwise, Alice2 is a new atom.

Now suppose that instead of being a material atom, Alice1 is a person, a self-conscious immaterial mind, and the same for Alice2. Then ask: is Alice2 is identical to Alice1? The answer is "Yes" provided Alice1 has stayed in existence from T1 through T2. Otherwise, Alice2 is a new person.

Suppose Alice1 exists only at T1 and Alice2 exists only at T2; then they are not identical. This is the Buddhist answer to the identity of any incomposite thing over time. If there is such a thing as an Alice, it is simply a matter of there being a series composed of Alice1 at T1 and Alice2 at T2 (and perhaps Alice3 at T3, and so on). An Alice over time is a series of momentary Alices-at-one-time.

The difference, then, is that on a Jain account a person is one incomposite thing that exists over time – that endures through a series of times – whereas on a Buddhist account a person is a series of composite things no one of which exists over time.

The importance of the accounts of persons

To one trained in contemporary academic contexts, it may seem unlikely if not wildly implausible that issues in metaphysics, and disputes about such issues, be taken to be of central religious importance – to be viewed as matters centrally affecting salvation or enlightenment versus damnation or ignorance. But of course we do not get to decide these things; the indigenous authors and interpreters of normative texts, and the participants in the relevant rites and institutions related thereto, decide them. Thus on both Jain and Buddhist accounts of the matter, getting these metaphysical matters right[34] is central to becoming, and constitutive of being, enlightened. Further, from a Jain perspective, the Buddhist account ascribes too little (essentially, nothing) to *being a person* for any enlightenment to be possible, and from a Buddhist perspective the Jain account ascribes too much to *being a person* for enlightenment to be possible. One might say: the Buddhist thinks the Jain soul is too heavy to ride safely in the Great Vehicle and the Jain thinks the Buddhist (non-)soul too frail to get in the boat.

Some consequences

1 Action

Suppose that, as we would ordinarily say, Jamie fires three shots at Josie in order to scare her into revealing where her parents have hidden their life savings – shot 1 at time T1, shot 2 at time T2, shot 3 at time T3. On the bundle account, what fired shot 1 was a simultaneous bundle that exists only at T1; similarly for shot 2 and a simultaneous bundle that exists only at T2 as well as shot 3 and a simultaneous bundle that exists only at T3. One "element" fires shot 1, another fires shot 2, another fires shot 3. No simultaneous bundle fires all three shots. A succession of bundles fires shots only insofar as its simultaneous-bundle members fire shots; it *just is* those members. On a Jain account, a self-conscious substance fires the three shots – Jamie is numerically the same at T1, T2, and T3, and at each time he fires a shot.

2 Memory

Suppose that, as we would ordinarily say, Jamie is arrested for firing shots at Josie, and sadly remembers his wickedness toward her. On the Jain account, numerically the same self-conscious being who fired the shots thinks of himself as having done so. Memory[35] of performing an action involves numerically the same self-conscious substance who performed it thinking about himself having done so. On a Buddhist account, (reliable) memory is a matter of a later simultaneous bundle containing a state that represents an earlier simultaneous bundle acting in a certain manner, where it is true of the earlier simultaneous bundle that it did so act, and where the earlier and later simultaneous bundles are elements in the same succession of bundles.

As we have noted, the doctrines of reincarnation and karma require that appropriate recompense (weal or woe) come to each person for her own previous actions – actions not atypically in some lifetime prior to the life currently being lived.[36] Not only Mahavira but the Buddha is represented as remembering, upon becoming enlightened, all of his past reincarnational life.

The Jaina and Buddhist traditions, then, provide us with a sharply contrasting account of what a person is – a person *at* a time and a person *over* time. For the Jaina traditions, a person at a time is a self-conscious substance and over time is a self-conscious substance that exists continuously. For the Buddhist traditions, a person at a time is a bundle of momentary states and over time is a sequence of such bundles. So we have two quite different views of what a person is, and thus two quite different views of what it is for a person to be the same person at one time as at another.

Conclusion

Three nonmonotheistic views of ultimate reality have been described. For one, what exists is simply and only a qualityless being, *nirguna* Brahman.[37] For another, what exists are minds and physical elements. On both views, what is *ultimate* is *incomposite* (not made of parts) and *independent* (not depending for its existence on anything). For a third view, what is ultimate are physical and mental states, each momentary, transitory, and impermanent. Here *ultimate* bears the sense of *incomposite* but not of *independent*, as each state is conceived as existing dependently on other states. Nothing is thought to have existential independence.

Questions for reflection

1. Why, in the end, do analogies to perceptual experience, whether simple or complex, fail to communicate the core of Advaita Vedanta doctrine?
2. What does Advaita Vedanta doctrine affirm? What does it deny?
3. Explain the Jain account of persons, and its implications for action, memory, and personal identity.

4 Explain the Buddhist account of persons, and its implications for action, memory, and personal identity.

Annotated reading

Basham, A. L. (1951) *History and Doctrine of the Ajivikas*, London: Luzac Press. Good discussion of the doctrinal content and historical development of the Jain tradition.

Chatterjee, Satischandra and Datta, Dhirendramohan (1950) *An Introduction to Indian Philosophy*, Calcutta: University of Calcutta Press. A good general treatment of the various Indian philosophical systems; goes into more detail than a typical introduction.

Jaini, P. (1979) *The Jaina Path of Perfection*, Berkeley: University of California Press. A comprehensive account of Jain thought.

Mookerji, Satkari (1944) *The Jaina Philosophy of Non-Absolutism*, Calcutta: Bharati Mahavidyalaya. Good account of Jain doctrine with emphasis on one interpretation of Jain thought on which it sees claims as relative to perspectives; it is controversial as to whether this reading is correct.

Phillips, Steven (1995) *Classical Indian Metaphysics*, La Salle, IL: Open Court. Nice discussions of issues and systems.

Radhakrishnan, S. and Moore, C. A. (1952) *A Sourcebook in Indian Philosophy*, Princeton, NJ: Princeton University Press. While much of the material is philosophical only in a very loose sense, this is a useful anthology of some passages by Indian philosophers.

Rambachan, Anantanand (1991) *Accomplishing the Accomplished: The Vedas as a Source of Valid Knowledge in Sankara*, Honolulu: University of Hawaii Press. Good discussion of the view that Hindu Scripture, along with perception, inference, etc. is a source of genuine knowledge.

Warder, A. K. (1990) *A History of Indian Buddhism*, Honolulu: University of Hawaii Press. Standard history of Buddhism in the land of its origin.

Wood, Thomas (1990) *The Mandukya Upanishad and the Agama Sastra: An Investigation into the Meaning of the Vedanta*, (Honolulu: University of Hawaii Press, 1990). A lucid and excellent account of Advaita.

Wood, Thomas (1991) *Mind-Only*, Honolulu: University of Hawaii Press. An excellent account of Theravada doctrine, lucidly argued.

PART III

Arguments concerning monotheistic conceptions

CHAPTER 9
Arguments against monotheism

Three questions

The problem of evil

Failed escapes

The consistency issue

The evidential issue

Conclusion

Epilogue

Questions for reflection

Annotated reading

9
Arguments against monotheism

Three questions

A *theodicy* is an explanation of the role that evil plays in God's overall plan. A *defense regarding evil* is an argument that evil does not provide evidence that God does not exist. An *argument from evil* is an attempt to show that the existence of evil provides evidence that God does not exist. So there arise three questions regarding God and evil: Is there an adequate theodicy? Is there a successful defense regarding evil? Is there a successful argument from evil?

While the issues that come up in the attempt to develop a theodicy are of significant philosophical and religious interest, they typically occur within the context of a fairly detailed theology, and we will not try to develop one here. With one exception, we will set the first question aside.

Reincarnation, karma, and evil

The doctrine of reincarnation claims that each person is embodied in a newly born body, lives a human life for however long that body lives, and when that body dies the person who has been embodied in it becomes embodied in another newly born body.[1] This process is, for each person other than Brahman or God, beginningless and ends only if the person becomes enlightened or is saved. The doctrine of karma says that the physical, social, economic, political, etc. conditions under which a person is embodied and lives a given lifetime are the conditions rendered appropriate by the person's action in previous lifetimes. The two claims together yield a third: what evils occur to a person in a given lifetime are morally proper, being the appropriate consequences of what the person has previously done. God, of course, is not subject to reincarnation.

At least from some monotheistic standpoints, there is an attractiveness to this doctrine. All evils are just punishments. For example, if an infant is stillborn or has severe birth defects, these things happen, not to a person just coming to be, but to a person who has a long and intricate series of lifetimes in which he has behaved so viciously as to deserve this treatment.

Bad things happen to good people because they were not always good people. This view entails, then, that:

(EN) For any evil E that occurs to a person in lifetime N, E is the just consequence of wrong actions by that person in lifetime N or in her lifetimes prior to N.

Whether (EN) is true or not, it is logically consistent. Thus it is relevant to a use of the Consistency Strategy that we will consider shortly. Since there is little if any solid evidence in favor of the truth of the doctrines of reincarnation and karma,[2] it would be intellectually risky to offer them as part of a theodicy of which they formed an essential part, or a defense regarding evil.[3]

To begin by offering a defense regarding evil would be premature. One would need first to have reason to suppose that evil is evidence against the existence of God. Unless there is good reason to think this, there is no need for a defense regarding evil. While it is often assumed that the religious believer should provide evidence that God exists and also provide a defense regarding evil, the idea that the religious believer should always be the one who offers arguments is without justification. The place to start in considering God and evil is by asking whether there is any successful, or at least initially plausible, argument from evil. There is quite a variety of attempts to offer a successful argument from evil. It is time to consider some of them.

The problem of evil

What philosophers call *the problem of evil* concerns whether or not the existence of evil counts against the existence of God, makes belief that God exists unreasonable, or the like. The *pastoral* problem of evil – how one is to deal with the evil that one faces in one's own life and the lives of those one loves – is obviously important, but it is not the (philosophical) problem of evil. A *theodicy* is an account of why God allows, or even causes, evil – of the role evil plays in the great scheme of things, how it relates to divine providence, how God can bring good from evil, how God's love can triumph over evil, and the like. It is understandable that someone wants a theodicy. But offering a theodicy is not necessary in order to deal with the problem of evil, and it is a large topic all by itself. Here, the concern is with the problem of evil, itself quite enough to occupy one's attention.

The existence of evil is the most influential consideration against the existence of God. The fact is that there is evil in the world, and the fact is that this is at least initially puzzling if the world is created and providentially guided by a morally perfect and omnicompetent God. In this chapter, then, versions of this consideration are examined.[4]

It is often taken to be obvious that the existence of evil is at least evidence against the existence of God. Even if other, stronger considerations vote "Yes" regarding God's existence, it is claimed that evil obviously votes "No" in that election. I take this to be false. The existence of evil is evidence against the existence of God only if there is some sound and valid argument in which *There is evil* is an essential premise (one without which the argument is invalid) and *God does not exist*[5] is the conclusion. It is not obvious that there is any such argument. Anyone who claims there is such an argument may be challenged to produce it. This chapter considers various arguments that have been offered to meet this challenge.

Is the existence of evil evidence against the existence of God?

That there is evil seems to many a feature of the world that God would not have allowed. Thus they argue that since evil does exist, God does not. This inference is cogent if and only if *(E) There is evil* and *(G) God exists* are logically incompatible, or if *(E) plus some set S of discernible truths* is logically incompatible with *(G)*. Thus arguments from evil to the non-existence of God either claim that (*E*) and (*G*) are logically incompatible or seek some set *S* of discernible truths which, together with *(E)*, is incompatible with *(G)*. The claim is that (*E*) entails not-(G) or that a set *S* of discernible truths, together with *(E)*, *entails* not-*(G)*. It is possible to consider several arguments from *(E) is true* to *(G) is false* within a brief scope, thereby gaining a good sense of how likely to succeed this enterprise is.

Failed escapes

No typical version of monotheism can deny *(E)*. Semitic and Hindu monotheisms hold that our basic religious problem is sin from which we need forgiveness and deliverance. But to sin is to act in a way that is evil. Typical monotheisms are religions of redemption from evil. So they cannot deny that (*E*) is true.

Nor can monotheism consistently embrace the notion of a finite God – a deity who, for reasons of lack of knowledge, power, or goodness does not prevent evil. If a supposed deity is not perfectly good, it is not the deity of typical monotheism, so that route is closed. An omnicompetent but morally imperfect being would not be God.

Suppose, then, that a being is morally perfect but limited in either knowledge or power in such a way that, for certain evils at least, it would prevent them if it could but it cannot prevent them. This being also would not be God in any typical monotheistic sense. To see this, consider a being limited in knowledge; suppose that God lacks the knowledge to prevent evil, though God has the power to do so. Suppose also that I, walking alongside my friend Jon, know that if he does not stop walking now, he will be hit by a car. Then except under really extraordinary circumstances I am wicked if I do not stop him if I know how, and except under really extraordinary circumstances I will know a variety of ways to stop him. But, by the present hypothesis, God lacks that knowledge. So relative to preventing the evil of Jon's being hit by a car, I am smarter than God. But no being that I am smarter than, relative to preventing evil, is worthy of the name "God." Hence limiting divine knowledge to "solve" the problem of evil is no more successful than denying divine goodness.

Suppose instead that God's power is limited relative to preventing at least certain evils – God knows how to prevent them but lacks the ability to put that knowledge to work. I know that if Sharon is getting a migraine, the appropriate strength pain pill plus strong sweet tea will prevent it, and typically I have the power to provide both pill and tea. But, on the present hypothesis, God lacks the power so to act, because so acting would prevent evil. But no being that, relative to preventing an evil, has less power than I do is worthy of the name "God." Hence limiting divine power as a "solution" to the problem of evil is no more successful than is limiting divine knowledge.

We could follow a strategy of allowing that God can prevent any evils we can prevent but that God cannot prevent any evils we cannot prevent. Or we could deny that God could do any evil-prevention that required more knowledge than *K* or more power than *P*, where *K* represents some degree of knowledge way above what Einstein had but short of omniscience and *P* represents some degree of power way above that possessed by the world's strongest person but short of omnipotence. A condition of there being a point to attempting some such distinction is that we have some reason to think that God could be justified in allowing the evils that can be prevented by someone who has knowledge up to degree *K* or power up to degree *P* but not justified in allowing evils whose prevention would require more knowledge or power. So far as I know, no attempt has been made to do this, and there is no reason to think it a promising enterprise.

Summary regarding a finite deity and evil

The motivation to take refuge in the idea of a finite God – one limited in power and/or knowledge – can be motivated by this general assumption: the existence of an evil *E* is evidence against the existence of God unless it is the case that either (i) God lacks the power to prevent *E*, or (ii) God lacks the knowledge to prevent *E*. Considering all the evil there is, the consequent limitation on divine power, or divine knowledge, is enormous. No being so limited in power or knowledge is God.

It can also be motivated by a more nuanced assumption: the existence of an evil *E* is evidence against the existence of God unless it is the case that either (i) God lacks the power to prevent *E*, or (ii) God lacks the knowledge to prevent *E*, or (iii) God has a morally sufficient reason for allowing *E*. This assumption involves three claims. The actual evils that can be prevented by a being with power of degree *P* or degree of knowledge *K* are evils God has a morally sufficient reason for allowing. The actual evils that God has no morally sufficient reason for allowing are all evils whose prevention would require a degree of power beyond *P* and/or a degree of knowledge beyond *K*. God's power and knowledge end at *P* and *K*. The claims involved in this assumption are arbitrary. There is no reason to suppose that they correspond to any actual differences in evils, knowledge, and power.[6]

Denying that there is evil, or so restricting one's notion of God so that God is morally imperfect or so limited in power or knowledge that preventing evil exceeds divine capacities, all are dead ends for monotheism. These "answers" to the claim that evil is evidence against monotheisms are thinly disguised admissions to the charge. Monotheism has been right in firmly resisting these moves.

If the existence of evil is evidence against God's existence, this does not settle the issue as to whether God exists or as to whether it is reasonable to believe that God exists. There might, for example, be equally strong or stronger evidence in favor of God's existence. But the notion that the existence of evil actually is evidence against God's existence should not itself be accepted without careful examination. As we have noted, evil is evidence against there being a God only if (a) *(E) There is evil* and *(G) God exists* are logically incompatible, or (b) if *(E) plus some set S of discernible truths* is logically incompatible with *(G)*. But is either (a) or (b) true?

The consistency issue

Straightforward inconsistency

One might claim, as did my own Introduction to Philosophy teacher, that (*E*) and (*G*) are obviously logically incompatible. This claim is false. The Consistency Strategy tells us that if any three propositions A, B, and C are logically compatible, then any pair from that trio is also logically consistent provided none of A, B, or C is self-contradictory. Note that what a use of the Consistency Strategy can show is simply the logical compatibility of two propositions. A proper use of this strategy with regard to two propositions A and B will prove *Possibly, both A and B are true*. It will not, and is not intended to, prove that *A is true* or that *B is true*. With this limitation goes an advantage; *one using the strategy need not prove that any of A, B, or C is true*.

Consider, then, these propositions:

A1 God exists.
B1 If God allows an evil, then God has a morally sufficient reason for allowing it.
C1 There is evil.

None of A1, B1, or C1 appears to be self-contradictory. Nor does the trio A1, B1, C1 appear to be an inconsistent set. But if none of A1, B1, and C1 is self-contradictory, and if (A1, B1, C1) is a consistent trio, then no pair of propositions from that trio is logically incompatible. One such pair is (A1, C1). So A1 and C1 are not logically incompatible. But A1 is simply *(G) God exists* and C1 is simply *There is evil*. So *God exists* and *(E) There is evil* are not logically incompatible. Hence (a) is false. So if evil is evidence against God's existence, (b) must be true.

Another use of the Consistency Strategy goes like this. Consider these propositions:

(G) God exists.
(EN) For any evil E that occurs to a person in lifetime N, E is the just consequence of wrong actions by that person in lifetime N or in her lifetimes prior to N.
(E) There are evils.

What was true regarding the A1, B1, C1 trio seems also true of the G, EN, E trio, so it too seems to provide the basis for a successful use of the Consistency Strategy.

Problems with this use of the Consistency Strategy

There is a simple rule of logical inference that says this: *If a proposition A plus some necessary truth N entails proposition B, then A by itself entails B*. One who doubts the success of the use made of the Consistency Strategy in the preceding reasoning may try to find some necessary truth *N* that, *together with (E), entails the denial of (G)*. Finding such a necessary truth would show that (G) and (E) are logically incompatible after all. Various candidates are available. Here are two:

N1 Necessarily, if God creates at all, God will create the best possible world, and the best possible world will contain no evil.
N2 Necessarily, a perfectly good being prevents evil insofar as it can, and an omnipotent and omniscient being can prevent any evil.

Will either of these do? (N1) or (N2) will do only if it is a necessary truth. Is (N1) a necessary truth? Is (N2) a necessary truth?

(N1) uses the notion of a best possible world – a world that contains as much moral worth as it is logically possible that a world contain.[7] Several questions arise regarding (N1). First, is the notion of a best possible world itself consistent, or is it like the notion of a highest possible integer? *I think the highest possible integer should be named Charlie* sounds fine until one remembers it is a necessary truth that *For any integer I, there is an integer I* such that I* is higher than I*; it is logically impossible that there be a highest integer. Anyone appealing to (N1) owes us an account of "best possible world" on which it is logically possible that there be such a thing. One that would not do, for example, is this: *World W is the best possible world only if the number of good persons in that world is the same number as the highest possible integer*. Second, (N1) requires that a best possible world contain no evil; according to (N1), the presence of evil in a world will rule it out as being the best possible. It isn't at all obvious that this is right. Suppose, for example, that any world possessed of great moral value will have virtuous agents in it – agents who are honest, brave, compassionate, and the like. But necessarily virtue is earned; one becomes virtuous of character by acting rightly again and again. For some virtues, at least, the relevant occasions of acting rightly require conquering one or another evil. Bravery requires that one have fear that one conquers. Fortitude requires than one bear pain well, and hence that one bear pain. Compassion presupposes suffering, and various saints offer the experiential report that so does moral and religious maturity. Perhaps some virtues require conquering evil, and some do not. But perhaps also one who has a full quiver of virtues has among them the ones that require that they have conquered evil, and in the best possible world everyone's quiver of virtues will be filled with all virtue's varieties. So maybe the best possible world would contain evil after all.[8]

Third, suppose the best possible world will contain moral agents who act only freely and rightly, and that if an agent acts freely then that agent is not merely acting in the way God has built into her that she act. In the strictest sense, to *create* a world W is to *fiat* W – so to act that W obtains simply as a result of one's having so acted. But then the *free* actions of a created moral agent cannot themselves be created by God. If God *fiats* that Eve speaks truly, Eve does not *freely* speak truly. So, perhaps, even should there be some notion of a best possible world that is not self-contradictory, that world is one that God cannot fiat – cannot, strictly speaking, create – because it is logically impossible that this be done. But then it is false that, strictly speaking, *if God creates then God creates the best possible world*.

Fourth, there is an argument to the effect that there being a best possible world is not compatible with God being omnicompetent. The idea is that *God is omnicompetent* entails *No world God created would exhaust God's competence* or *For any world W that God created, God could create a world W* such that W* was better than W*. There is reason, then, to be dubious about the claim that (N1) *Necessarily, if God creates at all, God will create the best possible world, and the best possible world will contain no evil* is a necessary truth.

Perhaps things will go better if we appeal to

N2 Necessarily, a perfectly good being prevents evil insofar as it can, and an omnipotent and omniscient being can prevent any evil.

Reflection on (N2) brings us back to at least one of the considerations already raised regarding (N1). If a best possible world can contain evil, why think that a perfectly good and omnicompetent God would not permit evil?

There are other problems with (N2). Let the partial description of a possible person (a PDPP) be a description of a set of fully determinate properties such that, were God to, strictly speaking, create – i.e., fiat – something having those properties, God would have fiated a person. To each PDPP *X*, one might say, there will correspond a person if God chooses to follow the recipe that *X* contains. Suppose that for each PDPP *X* there is a truth about how the corresponding person would act if he was created. Whatever the truth is, if there is one, about whether there is any PDPP whose corresponding person would always freely act rightly, *that truth is not a necessary truth*. Suppose, finally, that the logically contingent fact of the matter is that there is no PDPP whose corresponding person, were she created, would always freely act rightly. A world possessing the highest possible moral worth, or any reasonable facsimile, will contain moral agents. If the truth is as assumed, then in creating moral agents to populate the best possible world, God is creating agents whose choices will introduce evil into that world. Since it is logically possible that the truth be as we have assumed, and logically necessary that the best possible world contain moral agents, it is logically possible that the best possible world contain agents who act wrongly, thereby introducing evil into that world. Hence it is not a logically necessary truth that the best possible world contains no evil. Nor is it a necessary truth that a morally perfect omnicompetent being cannot permit evil. But then neither (N1) nor (N2) is true; hence nor is the logically necessary truth that the critic sought to pair off with *(E) There is evil* for the purpose of deriving the denial of *(G) God exists*. Nor is either the basis for a successful challenge to the Consistency Strategy.

The evidential issue

Logical consistency with evidential conflict

It is not logically inconsistent of one to believe that almost no residents of Madison, Wisconsin would vote for Prince Charles as President of the United States, that Kim is a resident of Madison, and that Kim would vote for Prince Charles as President. But if one has no particular reason to think that Kim relevantly differs from her fellow Madisonians, one believes against the evidence when one picks her as a Prince Charles supporter. *Proposition A is logically consistent with proposition B* and *The truth of proposition A is evidence that proposition B is false* are not themselves logically incompatible claims. We have found no reason to think that the existence of evil is logically incompatible with God's existence. The remaining question concerns whether nonetheless the existence of evil is evidence against the existence of God. If there being evil counts against there being a God only if either (a) *(E) There is evil* and *(G) God exists* are logically incompatible, or (b) if *(E) plus some set S of discernible truths* is logically incompatible with *(G)*, and (a) is false, there remains (b). The discernible truths added to (E) need not be necessary truths; any old truths will do. Are there any?

Those who answer affirmatively take it that the existence of evil is something not to be expected if a morally perfect and omnicompetent God created the world. Suppose that Aunt Lucy is an exquisite housekeeper. Suppose too that one must choose whether she is staying in guest room 21 that is neat as a pin or in guest room 22 whose floor is invisible under dirty clothing. While it is logically possible that she is staying in 22, odds are Aunt Lucy is staying in 21. If God created the world, perhaps it is logically possible that there be evils in it; but odds are there won't be. So (roughly) the assumption goes. Is the assumption right?

There is at least this much to be said for the assumption: for typical monotheisms, the present state of the world is not such as to make God overly pleased. The prayer "Thy will be done, on earth as it is in heaven" has not exactly received a full answer yet. Critic and theist agree that things are not as a morally perfect and omnicompetent being would wish them to be. In Judeo-Christian terms, our world is a "fallen" world. The question remains whether the existence of evil is *evidence against* the existence of God.

Those who follow the strategy of seeking some set of non-necessary or logically contingent truths that, together with *(E) There is evil,* entail *not-(G) God does not exist* tend to appeal to claims about our knowledge and what is reasonable to accept in its light. The following argument provides a simple illustration. Let an evil whose purpose, if any, is unknown to us be an *apparently pointless* evil.

A simple argument

1 There are apparently pointless evils.
2 The Apparently Pointless Evil Claim: If there are apparently pointless evils, then God does not exist.[9]
3 God does not exist (from 1, 2).

The first premise is patently true. The conclusion follows from the premises. So the question is whether the second premise – The Apparently Pointless Evil Claim – is true. The idea behind this claim apparently is this:

2a The Actually Pointless Evil Claim: God would not allow actually pointless evils.
2b The We Would Know Claim: If an evil has a point, it will be apparent to us.

Then it follows that

2c God would not allow any evils that are apparently pointless.

And from 2c and 1 we can infer 3 – the claim that God does not exist. Suppose, then, that the truth of 2a and 2b is intended as the necessary and sufficient conditions of the truth of The Apparently Pointless Evil Claim. Suppose that 2a and 2b provide both background assumptions and presuppositions of that claim. Then if either 2a or 2b is false, 2 will be false. If we have no reason to think 2a (The Actually Pointless Evil Claim) is true, or no reason to think 2b (The We Would Know Claim) true, then we will have no reason to think The Apparently Pointless Evil Claim true.

In our discussion of these matters, we will focus almost entirely on The We Would Know Claim. The question as to whether God would allow actually pointless evils is very difficult to answer, and we will not argue either for or against it. The critic obviously needs it for his argument to succeed. We will suspend judgment here regarding its truth, and discuss its meaning only to the degree that this is helpful in getting clear about The We Would Know Claim.[10]

Let us begin, then, with The We Would Know Claim. Would we know it if an evil has a point? The purposes of an omnicompetent being might well be beyond our comprehension.[11] Hence there is no reason whatever to think that if God allows an evil E in the light of E's having a certain point P, we will know what P is. So there is no reason whatever to think The We Would Know Claim is true. Hence there is no reason whatever to suppose that The Apparently Pointless Evil Claim is true. Since we have no reason to accept The We Would Know Claim, we have no reason to think that The Apparently Pointless Evil Claim is true. Hence the Simple Argument fails. There is, however, a more sophisticated argument right next door.

A more sophisticated argument

It is true that, for lots of evils, we have no idea what their point, if any, actually is. What point does someone's having a migraine, a stomach ulcer, cancer, or the inability to speak have? Even if we are able to say *in general* what might serve as a rationale for a morally perfect omnicompetent being allowing evils, and even for allowing certain specific kinds of evils, we are not in a position to say things that would result from filling in sentences like this with the names of actual persons and actual evils: *The reason why person X experienced evil Y is that the point of evil Y is Z*. Doing so would presuppose a degree of knowledge we do not have. There are also evils regarding which it is hard to say what their point might be.

Suppose, then, we divide evils into two broad and admittedly ill-defined[12] classes: those kinds of evils for which we can at least imagine some point, and those for which we cannot. Call these very loosely defined classes of kind of evil, respectively, *imaginably pointful* and *unimaginably pointful*. Perhaps suffering that turns a miserably selfish person into a person of compassion falls into the former class; perhaps so does even a miserably selfish person being allowed to suffer as a way of providing her an opportunity to become compassionate. Perhaps an accident that renders irrevocably comatose a loving wife and mother whose community activities alleviated much suffering falls into the class of unimaginably pointful evils.[13]

The class of imaginably pointful evils can be further divided into those where nothing we know about a particular case renders it unavailable for being pointful in the imagined way, and cases where this is ruled out by what we know. Suppose two stingy hoarders face death by freezing and are discovered just in time to save their lives. The one becomes generous and charitable, but the other has been so completely conditioned to be mean about money that even his being rescued by Red Cross workers does not make him any more willing to be charitable. One might think of the suffering the first hoarder endured as having a point in its positive results on his character, but the latter hoarder was so set in his ways that changing was not an option, even if he nearly froze to death. Let the former sort of case be *imaginably and contextually pointful* and the latter sort of case be *imaginably, but not contextually, pointful*. A rough informal characterization of the sense of these terms is this: an *imaginably and contextually pointful* evil is one that, so far as we know, may occur to a person under conditions in which the evil serves some morally sufficient point – some point such that a perfectly good being who allowed the evil to occur in order that the point be served acted rightly in so doing.[14] An *imaginably, but not contextually, pointful* evil is one that might occur to a person under conditions in which the evil serves some morally sufficient point – some point such that a perfectly good being who allowed the evil to occur in order that the point be served acted rightly in so doing – but we know something about the circumstances in which the evil occurred that fully prevents them from being conditions of this sort. An evil is *unimaginably pointful* if after considerable effort we still cannot think of any condition under which the occurrence of that sort of evil might serve some morally sufficient point – some point such that a perfectly good being who allowed the evil to occur in order that the point be served acted rightly in so doing.[15]

A more formal characterization of these rough distinctions can be expressed along these lines:

D1 An evil E is *imaginably and contextually pointful* relative to person S if and only if (i) we can describe a condition C such that if S is in C and endures E, it is possible that her doing so will be a necessary condition of S coming to have property Q, where *S's having Q* is a sufficiently good state of affairs that one who allowed S to endure E for the sake of S coming to have Q would be morally justified in so doing, and (ii) *nothing* we know about S is incompatible with S's actually being in C when S endured E.[16]

D2 An evil E is *imaginably but not contextually pointful* relative to person S if and only if (i) we can a describe condition C such that if S is in C and endures E, it is possible that her doing so will be a necessary condition of S coming to have property Q, where *S's having Q* is a sufficiently good state of affairs that one who allowed S to endure E for the sake of S coming to have Q would be morally justified in so doing, and (ii) *something* we know about S is incompatible with S's actually being in C when S endured E.

By contrast:

D3 An evil E is *unimaginably pointful* relative to person S if and only if we *cannot* describe a condition C such that if S is in C and endures E, it is possible that her doing so will be a necessary condition of S coming to have property Q, where *S's having Q* is a sufficiently good state of affairs that one who allowed S to endure E for the sake of S coming to have Q would be morally justified in so doing.

Imaginably and contextually pointful evils are the least plausible candidates for use in an attempt to derive *not-(G) God does not exist* from *(E) There is evil.* Thus we will consider arguments that deal with the notions of the other sorts of evils. One might begin, then, with these reflections and offer either of the following arguments.

The *"imaginably but not contextually pointful"* argument

1* There are imaginably but not contextually pointful evils.
2* If there are imaginably but not contextually pointful evils then there are actually pointless evils.[17]
3* There are actually pointless evils (from 2*, 3*).
4* If there are actually pointless evils, then God does not exist.
5* God does not exist (from 3*, 4*).

The key premises in this argument are (2*) and (4*); we will first consider (2*). It is a restricted version of The We Would Know Claim. Even if, as we argued above, the unrestricted version is false, this restricted version might be true. Since it approves the inference from *There are imaginably but not contextually pointful evils* to *There are pointless evils,* what it says is tantamount to *Evils that are not contextually pointful are actually pointless.* Is that true?

The other, similar argument is the *"unimaginably pointful" argument.*

The *"unimaginably pointful"* argument

1** There are unimaginably pointful evils.
2** If there are unimaginably pointful evils then there are actually pointless evils.[18]
3* There are actually pointless evils. (from 1**, 2**)
4* If there are actually pointless evils, then God does not exist.
5* God does not exist (from 3*, 4*).

The key premises of this argument are (2**) and (4**); we will first consider (2**). It is a differently restricted version of The We Would Know Claim. Even if, as we argued above, the unrestricted version is false, this restricted version might be true. Since it approves the inference from *There are unimaginably pointful evils* to *There are pointless evils*, what it says is tantamount to *Evils that are unimaginably pointful are actually pointless*. Is that true?

Concerning premise 2* of the *"imaginably but not contextually pointful"* argument: evils that are not contextually pointful are actually pointless

Suppose, for the sake of the argument, that premise 1* is true. This helps the critic only if premise 2* is also true. Granting premise 1* grants this: there are evils that may have some point, but no point we can think of that they might have is compatible with what seems true about the circumstances in which they occur. What premise 2* says is that if there are evils that may have some point, but no point we can think of that they might have is compatible with what seems true about the circumstances in which they occur, then there is no point that they do serve.

Suppose a man wears a paper bag on his head. While either the man has a mustache, or he does not, so long as the bag is over his head it is neither apparent that he does nor apparent that he does not. We just can't see. Similarly, while either an evil has a point or it does not, it is possible that we cannot tell which is the case.[19] Competitive to premise 2*, then, is:

2a* If there are imaginably but not contextually pointful evils then there are evils regarding which we should suspend judgment as to whether or not they actually have a point.[20]

Where premise 2* counsels a specific conclusion (there are pointless evils), its competitor 2a* commends suspense of judgment regarding that conclusion. Not surprisingly, the same issue comes up again regarding the unimaginably pointful argument.

Concerning premise 2** of the "*unimaginably pointful*" argument: evils that are unimaginably pointful are actually pointless

Consider this argument:

2** If there are unimaginably pointful evils then there are actually pointless evils.

What this premise tells us is that if we cannot even imagine what point an evil of a certain kind might have, then it has no point. Competitive to 2** is:

2a** If there are unimaginably pointful evils then there are evils regarding which we should suspend judgment as to whether or not they actually have a point.

Whereas 2** counsels a specific conclusion (there are pointless evils), its competitor 2a* commends suspense of judgment regarding that conclusion.

An essential element in one influential attempt to move from *(E) There is evil* to *not-(G) God does not exist* is premise 2* (as against 2a*), premise 2** (as against 2a**), or some closely analogous claim. Is it 2* or 2**, rather than 2a* or 2a**, that are true? Perhaps the best way to decide is to consider the sort of case that makes premises like 2* and 2** plausible if anything does.

Animal suffering

Consider premises 2* *If there are imaginably but not contextually pointful evils then there are actually pointless evils* (= *Evils that are not contextually pointful are actually pointless*) and 2** *If there are unimaginably pointful evils then there are actually pointless evils* (= *Evils that are unimaginably pointful are actually pointless*) as applied to an example made famous by William Rowe.[21] Imagine a doe trapped in a forest fire and burned to death. On traditional views, the doe has no afterlife in which her suffering can somehow serve her. She has no capacity for moral character in which she could gain even momentary fortitude. Imagine also that no one knows or ever learns of her fate, so that no good comes to others from reflecting on her suffering. The point is that *even if* afterlife, moral character, or the sober reflections of others would obviously render her suffering less problematic, they do not apply here. In the case of non-human animals, exercise of responsible free will, the development of virtues, and future consequences for the sufferer, at least on traditional notions concerning the nature and status of such beings, do not arise. They do not arise even if the idea that the suffering of animals serves some human good is not itself morally problematic.

Strictly speaking, it seems false that animal suffering is an evil for we can conceive no possible point. Suppose that all animal suffering that occurred before human beings existed was caused by unembodied moral agents who exercised their freedom in ways that involved making innocent creatures suffer. They thereby went from being angels to being demons. Suppose further that there being moral agents whose exercises of freedom determine their moral character is itself, independent of how that character turns out, a highly good thing. Then even if some unembodied moral agents[22] cause animal suffering, it is not wrong that they have been allowed to do so. This seems a *conceivable* point for animal suffering. Given some ingenuity, it seems that we can find some conceivable point *for any evil we have any good reason to think has occurred.*

It does not follow that there is no evil whatever that God could not wrongly permit. Suppose God were to create seven persons who existed only for twelve years. At each moment they suffered as much agony as they were capable of experiencing while feeling a deep hatred of God and one another that inevitably arises from features built into them at creation. Then God annihilates each of them for ever. Suppose, finally, that these are the only things that God ever creates. Within the constraints of these assumptions, it seems that the evils these persons suffer can have no point.[23]

Rowe very plausibly believes that the sort of case he describes – commonly called "the Bambi case" – including various species of animals, have actually occurred in a time-span overlapping that of the human race. Further, most animal suffering occurred before there were any human beings. Consider propositions:

(K1) *Knowledge that there has been massive animal suffering, most of it occurring in particular cases not known by any human being, serves to cause in human beings a moral or religious state not otherwise obtainable save at comparable cost,*

and

(K2) *That state is sufficiently valuable to justify the suffering requisite to it.*

While (K1) and (K2) are not in any obvious manner self-contradictory, it is hard to see what the alleged moral or religious state might be, and there seems no reason whatever to think them true. This much of Rowe's case seems impeccable.

Animal suffering is a highly plausible candidate for an evil that is either imaginably but not contextually pointful or unimaginably pointful. Is it true regarding animal suffering that if it is imaginably but not contextually pointful, or unimaginably pointful, then animal suffering is actually pointless? The Rowean critic takes the answer to be affirmative. The monotheist is likely to disagree. Who is right?

The proper answer to the "Who is right?" question rests on the sort of connection it is reasonable to think holds between *an evil E being imaginably but not contextually pointful or else unimaginably pointful* and *E being actually pointless*. Are our relevant cognitive powers reliable enough, and our relevant knowledge great enough, for us to say that an evil's having the first of these properties is good evidence that it also has the second of these properties? The Rowean argument in favor of thinking that our cognitive powers are reliable, and our information sufficient, goes as follows.

We often have to make judgments in cases in which we would like more information. Nonetheless, our only choice is to follow the best reasoning we can find and accept the results. If it is true that:

1 For all we can tell, it is true that P;
2 We can find no evidence in favor of not-P,

it is proper to infer to

3 It is reasonable to believe that P, and unreasonable not to do so.

In accord with Professor Rowe's intention, we might call reasoning of the sort that 1–3 represents *Common Reasoning*. The relevant application of this reasoning is:

4 For all we can tell, it is true that animal suffering has no point.
5 We can find no evidence in favor of animal suffering having a point.[24]

So it is proper to infer to:

6 It is reasonable to believe that animal suffering has no point, and unreasonable not to do so.

Granted, either an evil has a point or it does not. Whether it does or not is independent of whether we think it does or not. There is no proposal that *evil E's having a point* and *our being aware of E's point* are related by entailment, natural law, or the like. But, the Rowean claims, the reasoning in 4–6 exemplifies the pattern exhibited by 1–3, and this pattern of reasoning is rightly of high repute and common use. Not to apply it to whether animal suffering has a point is tantamount to rejecting reasoning all of us apply all of the time. Such a strategy smacks of inconsistency, dishonesty, and special pleading, none of which is the way of true philosophy. So:

(2*) *If there are imaginably but not contextually pointful evils then there are actually pointless evils* (= *Evils that are not contextually pointful are actually pointless*)

and

(2**) *If there are unimaginably pointful evils then there are actually pointless evils* (= *Evils that are unimaginably pointful are actually pointless*)

triumph.

For all its apparent force, this argument fails. The question as to whether animal suffering has a point is the question as to whether God, if God exists, might have a morally sufficient reason for allowing it. Suppose the reasoning exhibited in 1–3[25] fits perfectly any such case as this:

4a For all we can tell, it is true that Bill's allowing his animals to suffer has no point.
5a We can find no evidence in favor of the view that Bill's allowing his animals to suffer has a point.[26]

So it is proper to infer to:

6a It is reasonable to believe that Bill's allowing his animals to suffer has no point, and unreasonable not to do so.

We can also argue:

4aa For all we can tell, Bill's animals are suffering.
5aa We can find no evidence that Bill's animals are not suffering.

So it is proper to infer to:

6aa It is reasonable to believe that Bill's animals are suffering, and unreasonable not to do so.

Such cases do not give reason for us to raise our intellectual eyebrows or think that the reasoner has exceeded proper limits. But it is not so clear that things continue to go well if we reason:

4* For all we can tell, God (if God exists) has no morally sufficient reason for allowing animal suffering.
5* We can find no evidence in favor of the view that God (if God exists) has a morally sufficient reason for allowing animal suffering.[27]

So it is proper to infer to

6* It is reasonable to believe that God (if God exists) has no morally sufficient reason for allowing animal suffering, and unreasonable not to do so.

Our ability to discern the truth about the situation concerning Bill intentions, motives, and consequences, and the truth about Bill's animals' suffering, presumably is quite reliable. The same is not so clear regarding the situation concerning God (if God exists) allowing animal suffering. To the degree that this is so:

(2*) *If there are imaginably but not contextually pointful evils then there are actually pointless evils* (= *Evils that are not contextually pointful are actually pointless*)

and

(2**) *If there are unimaginably pointful evils then there are actually pointless evils* (= *Evils that are unimaginably pointful are actually pointless*)

are in trouble.

Salient to God's situation regarding allowing animal suffering is this. Rowe's argument requires that it be true that *Necessarily, if God exists then there is no pointless evil*. Given that claim, any evidence we have for God's existence is evidence against there being pointless evil. (It need not be evidence against there simply being evil.) But no evidence regarding Bill's existence is automatically evidence against there being pointless evil. Further, Bill's capacities are like our own. His reasons for action, the range of his knowledge, the scope of his power are like ours. If after careful reflection we cannot see any good reason Bill might have for allowing his animals to suffer, this is some reason to think that he has no such reason. It is, at least, insofar as it is true that if Bill had some such reason, it would occur to us. Nonetheless, even with other human persons, observing their behavior and its consequences is often far easier than discerning their motives and intentions. Identifying any cases of divine behavior and its consequences is more difficult than doing the analogous thing regarding human behavior and its consequences. Drawing conclusions about any divine motives and intentions there may be is exquisitely difficult. This is very relevant to (2*) and (2**). It is important to take into full account in considering the principle of *Common Reasoning.*

Consider, then, these principles of reasoning:

(R) (For Roweanism) If a case in which one wishes to apply reasoning of the sort 1–3 exhibits – *Common Reasoning* – is one dealing with natural objects, artifacts, the means and ends of human persons, or the means and ends of a person whose cognitive capacities, moral goodness, and causal powers vastly exceed ours, then the results of applying it is reasonably believed to be reliable.

(R*) If a case in which one wishes to apply reasoning of the sort 1–3 exhibits – *Common Reasoning* – is one dealing with natural objects, artifacts, or other human persons, then applying it is reasonably believed to be reliable; if a case in which one wishes to apply reasoning of the sort 1–3 exhibits – *Common Reasoning* – is one dealing with a person whose cognitive capacities, moral goodness, and causal powers vastly exceed ours, it is reasonable to think that such reasoning is as likely to be unreliable as it is to be reliable.

The basic idea on which Rowe's position rests is that (R) is true, and that this gives a favorable presumption to:

(2*) *If there are imaginably but not contextually pointful evils then there are actually pointless evils* (= *Evils that are not contextually pointful are actually pointless*)

and

(2**) *If there are unimaginably pointful evils then there are actually pointless evils* (= *Evils that are unimaginably pointful are actually pointless*).

A Rowean needs (R); it is hard to see that (R) is correct as opposed to (R*). Let us look at matters a bit more fully. In doing so, we will need to consider The Actually Pointless Evil Claim that says:

2a God would not allow actually pointless evils.

Our concern, as noted above, will be with its meaning, not its truth – which the critic's argument requires and about which we here suspend judgment.

Actually (or metaphysically) pointless evils

We have talked about evils being imaginably or unimaginably pointless, and the like. These are *epistemological features* of evils, properties that they have in relation to us. They are relational properties that an evil may or may not have, but has if at all due to certain human cognitive states. *Being actually (or metaphysically) pointless,* like *having a point,* are properties an evil has, if at all, whether we know it has it or not.[28] But what, exactly, is a *pointless* evil? In considering this question, it seems best to start with what it might be for an evil to have a (metaphysical) point. Then we can, so to say, proceed by subtraction in defining an evil being without point. Here is one definition:

Definition 1: Evil E *has an actual (or metaphysical) point* if and only if there is some good G such that (i) E's obtaining is a logically necessary condition of G's obtaining,[29] and (ii) G's obtaining is of sufficient worth to justify E's being permitted in order to make G possible.

A pointless evil, on this account, is simply one for which there is no corresponding good of which both (i) and (ii) are true. Given this understanding of pointlessness, is

2a The Actually Pointless Evil Claim: God would not allow actually pointless evils

true?

The idea is not that under some circumstances, or given some conditions, God would not allow actually pointless evils, and those circumstances or conditions obtain. The idea is that 2a is a logically necessary truth – that (P) *It is logically impossible that a morally perfect and omnicompetent being allow any pointless evils.*[30] It is this assumption that her argument requires that makes it crucial for the critic to show that there are pointless evils. If (P) is false, the monotheist can simply say: maybe there are pointless evils – so what?

It is worth emphasizing that there are not two kinds of point, actual (or metaphysical) and epistemological (having to do with imaginability); there are simply actual points on the one hand, and our views about actual points on the other.

It also deserves emphasis that appeal to:

(R*) If a case in which one wishes to apply reasoning of the sort 1–3 exhibits – *Common Reasoning* – is one dealing with natural objects, artifacts, or other human persons, then applying it is reasonably believed to be reliable; if a case in which one wishes to apply reasoning of the sort 1–3 exhibits – *Common Reasoning* – is one dealing with a person whose cognitive capacities, moral goodness, and causal powers vastly exceed ours, it is reasonable to think that such reasoning is as likely to be unreliable as it is to be reliable.

over

(R) (For Roweanism) If a case in which one wishes to apply reasoning of the sort 1–3 exhibits – *Common Reasoning* – is one dealing with natural objects, artifacts, the means and ends of human persons, or the means and ends of a person whose cognitive capacities, moral goodness, and causal powers vastly exceed ours, then the results of applying it is reasonably believed to be reliable.

is not inconsistent with other claims we will make later. To prefer (R*) to (R) involves rejecting the principle of *Common Reasoning* as applied to God and evil. This is not inconsistent with offering arguments for the existence of God. It is not incompatible with claiming that religious experience is evidence for God's existence. It is easier to detect the existence of a human person, and to discover that she is self-conscious and possesses intelligence, than it is to discern her intentions, motives, and purposes. It is not inconsistent to hold that there is argument or evidence to the effect that God exists but that tracking God's reasons for allowing what God allows is often beyond us.

Chancey worlds

If (P) *It is logically impossible that a morally perfect and omnicompetent being allow any pointless evils* is true, it is a necessary truth. If (P) is a necessary truth then we cannot consistently describe any condition under which (P) is false. Here is an interesting attempt to offer such a description.[31] Consider a world W of this sort:[32] W is strongly random so that often the microevents in it constrain the macroevents that occur to a much less significant extent than presumably is the case in our world. For example, in W a car's being in a particular position at one moment may leave open where it will be a moment later in ways that far exceed considerations of what its driver may do or what would follow were there laws in that world like the laws that hold in our world. Call these events in which randomness is great *randomness cases*.[33] Suppose that in a randomness case, Sue crosses a street and is killed in an automobile accident which, given preceding conditions, might equally well never have happened. Chance plays a significant role in this world. The accident, strictly, has no cause if a cause is an event *A* such that, given *A* and all relevant laws, the accident's occurrence is more probable than not. In that very plausible sense of "cause," the accident was causeless, because it was as likely not to occur as to occur relative to what obtained independent of anyone's knowledge.

In a world where chance, or absence of cause, plays such an important role, it is false that such events as the accident are planned by anyone, human or divine. Indeed, this is true of all events that occur in randomness cases in this world. Even if God knows in advance that the accident would happen, God did not cause the accident (it had no cause). But if God did not cause the accident, then God did not plan the accident.

It is possible that God put constraints on this world so that, even by chance, no event can occur that God would be wrong in permitting. Suppose also that each person in W is under divine providence, so that while God permits Sue to be killed in the accident, God also preserves Sue in existence, reunites her with her family in the afterlife, and so on. In sum, one could complete the description of W in such a way that, even though there are evils in W for which God did not plan, nonetheless God brings good out of these evils for those who suffer them.

One thing that arises from such considerations is this: God presumably could know in advance what would happen even in a chancey world. An intrinsically omniscient God will not ever have to *infer* what will happen from something else God knows. So God would, even regarding chancey worlds, know what will occur and so create only a world in which there will randomly occur events that, if they are evils, have a point. In sum:

God's allowing an evil E to occur because it has a point does not entail *God caused or planned that E occur.*

Suppose (differently and dubiously) that God would not know what would happen in a chancey world until it happened. Still, God could set limits on what could happen in such a world so that no event that might take place within those boundaries was one God could not bring sufficient good out of to make it not morally wrong that the evil be allowed. This suggests a second definition of *having a point*:

Definition 2: Evil E *has an actual (or metaphysical) point* if and only if there is some good G such that (i) God can bring good G out of E's occurrence, and (ii) G's obtaining is of sufficient worth to justify E's being permitted, whether or not E is a logically necessary condition of G.

In one way it does not seem that the possibility of such a world as W changes much. In a chancey world, God is morally justified in allowing evils even though God did not cause them or plan them in any sense in which planning includes causing. It still may be that the evils in W are of a sort that the presence in W of evils of their sort has a point (in one or the other defined senses) though perhaps a point that might be served by other instances of their kind of evil or by instances of evils of some different kind. Let an evil be *divinely unjustified* if and only if God would be morally unjustified in allowing it to occur. It seems that the constraint that no divinely unjustified evils can be allowed applies to W as much as to any world God created. And it seems that the evils in W that are not planned are nonetheless permitted for morally sufficient reason, even if that reason is of a sort that could instead have applied to other specific evils, or to evils of some other kind, or been replaced by some other morally sufficient reason which would have applied had a different chance outcome arisen. What follows is that God can have a point in permitting an evil even if God did not plan the world in such a way that that evil occurred in it. It does not follow that God could allow an evil that was actually pointless. It does follow that even under conditions of randomness, where our ability to judge whether an evil has a point or not would be even less than whatever it is now, evils could have actual or metaphysical points. Not even the randomness of such a world would be forceful evidence of there being actually or metaphysically pointless evils – evils that were divinely unjustified.

Religious maturity

An important topic is relevant here about which the author claims no direct knowledge. In making it, it is assumed that a defensible monotheism cannot entail that any moral truth is not true, and that genuine religious values include rather than contradict moral values. Morality deals with what may not be done to, and what must be done for, people. What goes beyond this is supererogatory. Monotheistic theology is typically committed to the view that God is morally good. Thus God is conceived in such a manner as not to act against morality. But monotheism typically and very plausibly supposes that full moral maturity, however essential a part thereof, is not identical to full maturity as a person. Full maturity, it is held, goes beyond morality, partly by demanding what is morally supererogatory, partly by including features of character than are not purely and simply moral features. These matters are deep and complex, but a really nuanced discussion of the problem of evil cannot ignore them. Often ignored, they nonetheless fall within the range of what is relevant to the problem of evil.

Suppose that Susan can achieve a state of religious maturity – of relationship with and likeness to God, in such ways as are available to created persons – or to possess a degree of religious virtue or have a religious experience of an important sort, or the like, if Susan is allowed to experience a certain evil E. Call this state or disposition or experience that is of high religious value *saintliness* for lack of a better term. Suppose that evil E is not a logically necessary condition of anyone reaching saintliness. It is compatible with this that it is contingently true that Susan will not reach saintliness unless she does experience E. All of the ways by which one might reach this goal without enduring evil are ways Susan cannot take because of choices she might not have made, but has made, or might never make, but in fact would make. Finally, suppose that God allows Susan to undergo evil in order that she might reach saintliness. It seems logically possible that if Susan reaching saintliness is highly valuable, God's allowing her to find her way to it by means that include her suffering E is itself good, not evil. God's doing so would not be divinely unjustified.

We can now come to the point of this discussion. Consider its relevance to The Actually Pointless Evil Claim:

2a God would not allow actually pointless evils.

Add to it the definition:

Definition 1: Evil E *has an actual (or metaphysical) point* if and only if there is some good G such that (i) E's obtaining is a logically necessary condition of G's obtaining,[34] and (ii) G's obtaining is of sufficient worth to justify E's being permitted in order to make G possible.

If one takes this to be the proper definition of *has a point* then only evils that are logically necessary conditions of goods can have a point. The scenario offered concerning religious maturity seems logically consistent. If so, then this definition of *has a point* is too narrow. We need instead the more complex:

Definition 3: Evil E *has a point* if and only if (a) there is some good G such that (i) E's obtaining is a logically necessary condition of G's obtaining, and (ii) G's obtaining is of sufficient worth to justify E's being permitted in order to make G possible *or* (b) there is some good G such that (iii) God can bring good G out of E's occurrence, and (iv) G's obtaining is of sufficient worth to justify E's being permitted, whether or not E is a logically necessary condition of G.

It would be helpful here, no doubt, to offer plausible, fleshed-out examples of what sort of state, virtue, or experience *saintliness* might amount to, or at least sketchily described description, perhaps in terms of a durable disposition toward self-giving love, a tranquil and charitable character expressed in improving people's lives, or a continuing sense of the presence of God. For a Jew, the suffering of the Jewish people no doubt is relevant here, and for a Christian the suffering of Christ. But conceptually and empirically, these are beyond this author. I simply note the relevance of such matters to a nuanced account of the problem of evil. I also note that the occurrence of the sort of saintliness roughly characterized here is of great importance to the monotheistic religious traditions. It is the sort of character that genuine faith, worship, and monotheistic religious experience is supposed to bring the believer to, if only in the long run.

One misplaced criticism should be noted. The discussion here does not assume, contrary to the critic's own beliefs, that there are such states or experiences in the offing, with God ready to supply them. The point is simply that when one is considering propositions that are, if true, then necessarily true – such as The Actually Pointless Evil Claim (that God would not allow pointless evil) – one is not only entitled but required to consider what the possibilities are. If there are possibilities that would not be possible if a proposition P were a necessary truth, then P is not a necessary truth (and if P is, if true, then a necessary truth, then P is, if false, necessarily false). If it appears that X is a possibility, and X is not a possibility if P is true, then the apparent possibility of X is evidence against P's truth. The argument here is that the logical possibility of the saintliness scenario is evidence against The Actually Pointless Evil Claim (that God would not allow pointless evil) if it limits *having a point* to Definition 1. What is required, if The Actually Pointless Evil Claim is to be true, is that it be construed along lines as least as broad as:

Definition 3: Evil E *has a point* if and only if (a) there is some good G such that (i) E's obtaining is a logically necessary condition of G's obtaining, and (ii) G's obtaining is of sufficient worth to justify E's being permitted in order to make G possible *or* (b) there is some good G such that (iii) God can bring good G out of E's occurrence, and (iv) G's obtaining is of sufficient worth to justify E's being permitted, whether or not E is a logically necessary condition of G.

Common Reasoning, however reliable relative to the scope of natural objects, artifacts, the means and ends of human persons, it does not follow that it is reliable concerning the means and ends used by a person whose cognitive capacities, moral goodness, and causal powers vastly exceed our own.

One thing that makes deciding between:

(R) (For Roweanism) If a case in which one wishes to apply reasoning of the sort 1–3 exhibits – *Common Reasoning* – is one dealing with natural objects, artifacts, the means and ends of human persons, or the means and ends of a person whose cognitive capacities, moral goodness, and causal powers vastly exceed ours, then the result of applying it is reasonably believed to be reliable.

and

(R*) If a case in which one wishes to apply reasoning of the sort 1–3 exhibits – *Common Reasoning* – is one dealing with natural objects, artifacts, or other human persons, then applying it is reasonably believed to be reliable; if a case in which one wishes to apply reasoning of the sort 1–3 exhibits – *Common Reasoning* – is one dealing with a person whose cognitive capacities, moral goodness, and causal powers vastly exceed ours, it is reasonable to think that such reasoning is as likely to be unreliable as it is to be reliable.

is that reflection about a monotheistic conception of God is a going enterprise; it is not impossible to draw any justified conclusions in the philosophy of monotheistic religion. It is easy to take an all-or-nothing stance here: either we can come to a reasonable decision regarding the truth or falsity of every proposition of interest to philosophy of monotheistic religion, or we can come to a reasonable decision regarding none. But this stance is mistaken. It is false that, if God exists and each evil God allows has an actual point, we can reasonably expect to judge with confidence that we have discerned, for every type of evil, what that point is. That simply is not something we could reasonably expect. This being so, it is (R*), not (R), that is true. It is not cause for surprise if there are types of evil for which no one can suggest plausible candidates for the point, if any, they may serve. Nor is it evidence that they serve no point.

The Actually Pointless Evil Claim (that God would not allow pointless evil) and Definition 3

The relevance of Definition 3, and the discussion that led to it, can be simply stated. It is this: our ability to tell whether or not an actual evil has a point in the sense defined by Definition 3 is even more restricted than our ability to tell whether an evil has a point in the sense defined by the earlier definitions. It serves to increase awareness of the sorts of point an evil might serve, points not incompatible with, but also not limited to, morality. It thus renders Roweanism – acceptance of (R) as a correct characterization of reasonable confidence concerning *Common Reasoning* – less plausible by pointing out further sorts of points evils might have. Deciding whether an evil could have any point of this sort is even more demanding than whether it could serve any point that falls within the scope of morality.[35]

Evil and moral acceptability

One might suggest this as a rough criterion for the moral acceptability of a person being allowed to suffer evil:

C1 Kim's suffering evil E is morally acceptable if and only if Kim, relevantly informed about E, and insofar as rational, accepts E without moral protest.

For purposes of considering this notion, we can include under the notion of moral acceptability the occurrence of evils that serve to promote religious personal maturity in the rough sense characterized above. Kim's being relevantly informed regarding an evil is a matter of her knowing whatever is relevant to making a rational assessment of the moral justifiability of Kim suffering it – its effect on Kim, on others, what it makes available that would otherwise not be, and the like. The sort of ideal rationality required might be easier to achieve after an evil was undergone, even if undergoing it was not morally problematic. Perhaps C1 is true; even if it is, however, it is not easy to see how to apply it in any useful manner, since no one is likely to have much reason to think they are in the ideal situation C1 requires.

Succinct Roweanism

Roweanism, in one version at least, argues as follows. Let an evil E be *Rowean* if and only if (i) we have good reason to think it occurred; (ii) either we can think of no conceivable morally sufficient reason R that God might have for allowing it, or we can think of such an R but know[36] that the context in which the evil occurred rules out R applying, or we know that R would apply only if sorts of things exist that we know not to exist. Then the basic argument is:

R1 There are Rowean evils.
R2 If there are Rowean evils, then there are[37] actually pointless evils.

So

R3 There are actually pointless evils.

Behind premise R2 lies some such principle of inference as:

P1 If we can think of no conceivable morally sufficient reason R that God might have for allowing it, or we can think of such an R but know[38] that the context in which the evil occurred rules out R applying, or we know that R would apply only if sorts of things exist that we know not to exist, then we know that E is pointless.

Competitive to principle P1 is principle:

P2 Even if either we can think of no conceivable morally sufficient reason R that God might have for allowing it, or we can think of such an R but know[39] that the context in which the evil occurred rules out R applying or we know that R would apply only if sorts of things exist that we know not to exist, it is reasonable to suspend judgment as to whether there are actually pointless evils.

A reply to succinct Roweanism

Here is a brief argument in reply:

1 Roweanism is correct only if it is more rational to accept P1 than it is to accept P2.
2 It is at least as rational to accept P2 as it is to accept P1.
3 If it is at least as rational to accept P2 as it is to accept P1 then it is not more rational to accept P1 than it is to accept P2.
4 It is not more rational to accept P1 than it is to accept P2 (from 2, 3).
5 Succinct Roweanism is not correct.

If this argument succeeds, succinct Roweanism fails. The crucial premise is 2; if it is true, then the rest of the argument is in order. Thus Roweanism requires that 2 be false. But there seems to be no good reason provided for thinking it false. So succinct Roweanism fails. (It is worth remarking here that the same rules apply in arguing against a claim as apply in arguing for it. The position offering the argument is supposed to provide the justifications.)

Evil and ecology

Most discussions of the problem of evil leave aside reference to such matters as the disappearance of species. This is understandable – environmental ethics is a complex and controversial field and any discussion of anything relevant to it is bound to make controversial claims. So it is safer to avoid such matters altogether unless one can devote an entire book to them. Perhaps unwisely, I will not follow this practice here. While various claims made may be even more controversial than philosophical claims usually are,[40] perhaps what follows may at least elicit some careful reflection about the alleged problem of ecological evil. (The use of "alleged" here is not intended to deny that there is ecological evil, but to be neutral at the outset as to whether the existence of such evil is evidence that God does not exist.)

Considering the problem of evil from a different angle may be helpful. There are at least two sorts of consideration that relate evil and ecology. One has to do with the suffering of non-human animals. The other is the disappearance of species. Connected with the second consideration is the fact that the history of the natural world is very far from presenting a picture of neatness and efficiency. These are two rather different sorts of issue, divisible along the lines of what we might call *the disappearing species problem* and *the animal suffering problem*.[41] Either could arise without the other, and it seems fairly clear that a solution to the one need not be any solution at all regarding the other. In any case, the animal suffering issue has already been addressed. It is a particularly thorny issue for theodicy, but it does not follow that it is somehow equally difficult regarding the problem of evil, which is the concern here. The comments that follow focus on the matter of disappearing species and the connected matter of inefficiency.

Inefficiency

Inefficiency issues hardly arise concerning an omnicompetent being. It is false that:

(N) *Necessarily, if a being B can achieve end E by means of causing process Q1 or by causing process Q2, where Q1 is simpler* than Q2, then it is a defect in B if B elects to achieve E by causing Q2.*[42]

Perhaps one can refine (N) by way of reference to scarcity of material, energy, time, or the like – but then an omnicompetent being won't be working under any variety of inherent scarcity. One might think of (N) as somehow defining, or following from, *rationality*, but artistic profusion is not inherently less rational than mathematical elegance. Presumably there is no rational need that the rhinoceros be among the inhabitants of our earth, but a rhinoceros is a fascinating creature. It is no less so if an efficiency expert would have removed him from the list of things to be produced. Whatever force remains to the inefficiency issue concerns the total disappearance of species.

It was argued above that our having no clear idea as to how to explain Bambi's suffering (or animal suffering in general) is no evidence whatever that such suffering is gratuitous. An exactly analogous argument holds regarding the disappearance of species, if that is an evil. There is no need to develop that argument here, since it is obvious how it would go. Other matters deserve fuller attention.

The disappearance of species

Let's say that some item X has *purely extrinsic value* if and only if X has worth for the sake of what it contributes to Y, and no other value whatever. Of course something may have both intrinsic and extrinsic worth; then it won't have purely extrinsic value. Let us say an item X has *purely intrinsic value* if and only if X has value and all of the value that X has lies entirely in X and not at all in anything that X contributes to anything else.

(Aristotle's Unmoved Mover might be such a thing, or an enlightened Jain person in her isolated enlightened state.) God, minus creation, will have very high purely intrinsic value; once God creates, God keeps high intrinsic value but presumably also has extrinsic value – if God creates John, then God contributes a lot to John, having brought John into being and sustaining John and so on.[43]

Value by association is a variety of extrinsic value. Suppose the President gives you a cactus. In charge of your cactus while you vacation, your friend Susan overwaters, and thereby kills, it. Even if Susan replaces it by a qualitatively identical cactus, the new cactus isn't the one the President gave you. It hasn't the same value to you, since it hasn't the same associations, and you find the associations significant.

One question is whether things below a certain level of complexity or capacity have any value or worth, or any beyond purely extrinsic value. Would there be any worth or value, say, in a world in which the most complex thing was a pile of sand and nothing had any capacities beyond those possessed by such a pile and its members? Value in this context is conceived in terms of natural value – the sort of thing that is expressed in the tradition that the existence itself of something X (that is, *there being an X*) has value. This question concerns whether not *living members of species* but *non-living members of natural kinds* have natural value.[44] It is not obvious that they do. Suppose that God executed a plan on which a universe of isolated electrons exists for, say, a trillion years and then goes *poof*. It is hard to see that this would be *wrong* of God to do. Nonetheless, since the objection being considered has more potential force if the pile-of-sand, or the isolated electrons, world has some natural value, assume for the sake of the argument that it does, and take the pile-of-sand world as a representative world of non-living things.

That this assumption is correct can be argued in at least two ways. Perhaps sand grains, electrons, and quantities of matter have purely extrinsic value, so the pile-of-sand world will have a purely extrinsic value sort of natural value. This argument fails, since there is nothing in the pile-of-sand world, considered as containing only extrinsic worth, to generate that worth. There is nothing of intrinsic value for the alleged extrinsic value to serve. The other is that such items have some intrinsic worth just by virtue of their existing at all. Then the idea is that even a pile-of-sand world has intrinsic value of some sort K. It still does not follow that it would be morally wrong that God obliterate something that has intrinsic worth of sort K. Even if it is true that something's existence has natural worth, it does not follow that causing or allowing it to cease to exist is wrong. Even if it would be wrong unless one had a morally sufficient reason for doing so, what follows is that doing so is something one should have a sufficient reason for doing. It may be that simply by virtue of having created a grain of sand or a mountain "from nothing" – that is, not out of pre-existing material – God has the right to do as God likes with the grain or the mountain.

In any case, it is living, or living-and-conscious, species that typically are the cause for greatest concern among those troubled by the disappearance of natural kinds; not, say, electrons but species of living things. Regarding living things that are not persons – plants and animals – there are again the two alternatives: that even plant and animal life has only pure extrinsic value or that it has intrinsic value of some sort K*. The argument that we should not so act as to cause species to go out of existence because we may discover that some feature of some plant, insect, or animal may provide the cure for some dread disease, insofar as that is the whole argument, is based on a pure extrinsic value view of the plants, insects, and animals concerned. Those who claim it is an evil that plant and animal species are allowed to become extinct typically take this to be so because they take plants and animals to have pure intrinsic worth. Otherwise, as above, their ceasing to exist is not an evil unless persons who have pure intrinsic value also exist or cessation of plants and animals will prevent the existence of persons. Suppose, then, that plants and animals are held to have pure intrinsic worth.

That something has intrinsic natural worth does not by itself entail that it would be wrong to cause or allow it to cease to exist. Even if it would be wrong to allow it to cease to exist without sufficient reason for doing so, what follows is that in order to do so blamelessly one must have such a reason. The sheer fact of species disappearance – and of course an enormous number of species have gone extinct – seems by itself no evidence of anything gone morally awry.[45]

It is clear that various species of living and of living-and-conscious, beings have become extinct. The ecological argument from evil goes:

E1 There being non-extinct species of living, and/or living-and-conscious, beings has natural worth.
E2 Species of such beings that were once not extinct now are extinct.
E3 It is wrong to permit species of beings that have natural worth to become extinct unless one has sufficient moral justification for doing so.
E4 If God exists then God has permitted species of beings that have natural worth to become extinct, and this was wrong unless God has sufficient moral justification for doing so[46] (from E1–E3).
E5 There is no moral justification that God could have for permitting species that have natural worth to become extinct.[47]
E6 God does not exist (from E4, E5).

It is not clear that E4 is true. Nor is it clear that E5 is true. Suppose, simply for the sake of the argument, that E4 is true, and focus on E5. If God were to have the sort of reason E5 says God could not have, what might it be?

Dinosaurs were living and conscious. There now aren't any. Assume that their presence was a natural good. Is their absence an evil which God could have no good reason for allowing? Presumably the following is true:

(GN) For any number N of types of living and conscious things a world W contained, there is a possible world W* such that W* contains N + 1 types of living and conscious things.

Ecological or systemic considerations might make sheer addition impossible in certain worlds at certain points, but there is nothing in (GN) that requires that W* be produced, so to say, from W by adding some new species. If (GN) is true, then for any number of non-extinct species containing living, or living-and-conscious, beings, there could be yet another. Hence whatever world God creates, God is "guilty" of not having produced as much natural value as there might be, and such "guilt" is vacuous.[48]

One might claim that while it is true that God could also have created living-and-conscious things that God did not in fact create, still it is wrong that God in fact did create living-and-conscious things and then let them cease to exist. This claim has two versions, one concerning individuals and one concerning species, as follows:

(P) For any item X, if X is a particular, actual living-and-conscious thing then it is wrong of God to allow X to cease to exist.

(S) For any species X, if X is a species whose particular, actual members are living-and-conscious things, and there are particular members of X, then it is wrong of God to allow there to cease to be members of X.

The idea that individual members of animal species have intrinsic worth seems to enjoy little popularity among ecologists, whereas the idea that species have such worth enjoys high ratings. If there is any plausible reason, as opposed to sheer fashion and taste, behind preferring (S) to (P), presumably it is (or is closely related to) this: where *X* ranges over natural kinds of living-and-conscious things, that *there being Xs* is a good thing but it does not matter which Xs there are. The worth of a duck lies not in *being the duck it is* but in its *being some duck or other*. For any biological species Q, if there are no things that belong to Q, then there is no Q; those who talk about species having vanished take exactly this view though they also talk about the value of the species, not the value of its members. They agree that when there are no more ducks (and no duck eggs or DNA) there is no duck species either. They seem typically to think that all the value lies, not in the particular deer that is now feeding on the salt lick that one put out last night, but in *there being some deer or other, who cares which?* Nonetheless, there cannot be intrinsic value in there being deer without there being intrinsic value in the deer that is now feeding on the salt lick. To put the relevant point positively, it is a necessary truth that:

(C) For any class C, if *C's having members* has intrinsic worth, then for any item X that belongs to C, X has intrinsic worth.

But then the death of any given deer involves the loss of something that has intrinsic natural worth.[49] If there is something requiring moral justification in a species becoming extinct, there is also something requiring moral justification in the demise of one of that species' members.

Monotheism typically contends that creation was a matter of grace. God created things that might never have been, not only freely but also without obligation. It was (so to say) morally permissible for God not to have created at all, as well as morally permissible for God to have created as God did create, or to have created in lots of ways in which God did not create, but might have created. Monotheists also hold that, at least in the case of things not strictly created in God's image – in the case of things not persons – *being X's creator* entails *being permitted to cease to sustain X in existence without needing moral justification.* If this is so, the E1–E5 argument fails. It is then false that

(E*) If X has intrinsic worth, and God permits X to cease to exist without having some morally sufficient justification for so doing, then God acts wrongly.

In sum: the critic who bases her case on alleged ecological evil needs (E*) or something like it, and strong arguments for (E*) are scarce at best.

Exchangeable intrinsic natural worth

Still, there remains the question as to what morally sufficient reason for allowing a species whose members possessed intrinsic natural worth to go extinct might amount to whether or not God would need such a reason. Suppose that:

(C) For any class C, if *C's having members* has intrinsic worth, then for any item X that belongs to C, X has intrinsic worth.

or something much like it is true. Perhaps we should distinguish between *exchangeable intrinsic worth* and *unexchangeable intrinsic worth*. Having exchangeable intrinsic worth is a matter of having intrinsic worth but its not being wrong of an agent to eliminate it by causing there to be something else that also has intrinsic worth. If cacti have intrinsic worth, it is of the former sort. Extrinsic worth (including value by association) aside, if Jim drives over Ron's bush but apologizes and replaces it with another that is relevantly similar, then Ron owes Jim no more. If Jim does not care whether the bush is of the same sort, or whether the replacement item is a bush rather than a tree, if Jim apologizes and replaces the original bush by one of a different sort or by a tree, once again Ron owes Jim no more. But if Ruth is babysitting for Rita's child, loses her, and replaces her with another of the same age, gender, weight, IQ, and the like, it is false that it is only value by association that remains as a basis for Rita's agonizing protest. Those who accept (S) typically ascribe exchangeable intrinsic worth, not unexchangeable intrinsic worth, to dinosaurs and the members of other species. They need not deny (C) – the claim that *For any class C, if C's having members has intrinsic worth, then for any item X that belongs to C, X has intrinsic worth*; they need only to take the members of the relevant species to have exchangeable intrinsic worth. The monotheist can also grant that dinosaurs have exchangeable intrinsic worth.

Even if God would need a morally sufficient reason to allow a species whose members have exchangeable intrinsic natural worth to cease to exist – even if it is true, for example, that

(D) *God needs a morally sufficient reason for there once having been dinosaurs and there not now being any.*

– it also seems plain that God has one if it is the case that God replaced dinosaurs by things of comparable exchangeable intrinsic worth (post-dinosaurean mammals). On the other hand, if (D) is false, it is hard to see why one should accept anything along the lines of:

(D*) *God's goodness is called into question by there once having been N number of species and there now being N-minus-M number of species around now or ever again.*

It is worth noting that there is nothing in the notion of exchangeable intrinsic value that requires that the replacements be of the same kind, or in the same quantity, as what they replace.

Consider two sorts of exchange as follows:

(EX) Y is permissibly interchangeable for X, where X has exchangeable intrinsic worth, only if Y is of the same species as X.

(EY) Y is permissibly interchangeable for X, where X has exchangeable intrinsic worth, only if Y is of the same species as X, or if Y is of a different species than X, where there being things of the species that Y belongs to is of at least as much intrinsic natural value as there being things of the species to which X belongs.

The idea, of course, is that (EX) allows only within-species substitutions whereas (EY) allows between-species replacements. It seems plain that if anything in the neighborhood of (EX) and (EY) is true, it is (EY). If (EY) is true, then even if it would be wrong of God to create something of exchangeable intrinsic worth and then let it go out of existence without replacing it with something of equal worth, God could allow any number of species to go out of existence so long as there were appropriate replacements. And (EY) does not forbid that there be one replacement that belongs to one species that replaces the members of a number of other species so long as the one is valuable enough. The sort of replacement that is relevant here might be, for example, something of high intrinsic worth for things of lower, or something of unexchangeable intrinsic worth for things of only exchangeable intrinsic worth.[50]

Two things should be noticed here. There is nothing in the notion of exchangeable intrinsic natural worth that requires, or that forbids, that if something X that has it, and is replaced by something Y, that X's having existed was somehow necessary for Y's coming to exist, whether Y has exchangeable intrinsic natural worth or unexchangeable intrinsic natural worth. Further, as noted earlier, for any world whose members have any degree of either exchangeable or unexchangeable intrinsic natural worth, God could create a world possessed of a higher degree.

Unexchangeable natural intrinsic worth

Traditional claims to the effect that something has unexchangeable intrinsic worth (though not using this language) have found the exchangeable intrinsic natural worth versus unexchangeable natural worth distinction to be based on the former lacking, and the latter having, moral worth. This claim, or one much like it, is at the basis of a respect for persons ethic. This distinction provides a clear and defensible answer to an otherwise baffling question: how can one rationally ground any such distinction?

The answer expresses a view sometimes called *speciesism,* which means "unjustifiably favoring one's own species." This is an evaluative term, and it is either accompanied by an argument defending the allegation of unjustifiability or it is a mere term of abuse. It may be true, as those who use the term sometimes say, that hippos would assign ultimate value to their own kind if they could. Those who hold a respect for persons ethic agree that were hippos capable of holding such positions, they would be persons – self-conscious minds embodied in hippo bodies – and as persons they would be correct in ascribing ultimate value to persons.

Consider the notion of *baseline natural intrinsic worth* where X has baseline intrinsic worth if and only if the proposition *It is wrong to use X for the sake of something else in a way that reduces X's intrinsic worth, and wrong to destroy X.* The notion of baseline natural intrinsic worth is the notion of unexchangeable natural intrinsic worth writ in a different script. Monotheists frequently, perhaps typically,[51] have taken *being a person* to include having unexchangeable intrinsic natural worth, or baseline natural intrinsic worth. (This is one reason why the typical monotheistic doctrine that persons survive the death of their bodies is not an arbitrary addition to monotheism.) Were God, then, to obliterate one person and fiat another, simply for the sake of changing the population content, this would be wrong. One standard basis for this view is that persons are agents, possessing rationality, freedom, responsibility, and the capacity to love God and others. Having baseline intrinsic natural worth, on this account, is inherently associated with having moral worth – with being capable of moral agency.[52]

The monotheist, then, can hold that while God has allowed a great many sorts of things that possessed exchangeable intrinsic natural worth to come and go, God has also has supplemented or replaced them with a species whose members have unexchangeable intrinsic natural worth.[53] So if God must have a morally sufficient reason for allowing things with exchangeable intrinsic natural worth to cease to exist, both in the sense of individuals dying and of species becoming extinct, it is possible that God has such reason. Thus E5 *There is no moral justification that God could have for permitting species that have natural worth to become extinct,* an essential premise in the critic's argument, is false. Hence, even if we, as it were, make a present to the critic of premise E4 *If God exists then God has permitted species of beings that have natural worth to become extinct, and this was wrong unless God has sufficient moral justification for doing so,* another essential premise in that argument, the argument fails; and of course E4 is itself hardly an evident truth.[54]

Conclusion

Of course there are other attempts – some made, some waiting discovery – to move from (E) *There is evil* through some set of further premises to *not-(G) God does not exist*. The enterprise of constructing such arguments is endless. The arguments so constructed infer from the existence of evil to the non-existence of God either claim that (a) *(E)* and *(G)* are logically incompatible or (b) seek some set *S* of discernible truths which, together with *(E)*, is incompatible with *(G)* – or, if you prefer, a set *S* of discernible truths that, together with *(E)*, entail the denial of *(G)*. It turns out that (a) is false, and none of the versions of (b) considered above are successful. These attempts are typical ones – a fair sampling of such efforts. It is, then, dubious that the existence of evil is in fact evidence against the existence of God.[55] If there is a genuine problem of evil only if there is some such argument, it is dubious that there is any genuine problem of evil.

Epilogue

Another angle on Rowean arguments

We have called any evil that God could have no point in allowing a *divinely unjustifiable* evil. A follower of Rowe's argument need not suppose that there are actual evils that are divinely unjustifiable. She need only claim something weaker. Suppose an evil that we have good reason to suppose real has this feature: we can conceive of no point that this evil might serve which does not involve our positing the existence of things we have no reason to think exist. Call such evils *inexplicable evils*. An evil whose only conceivable purpose was to make trolls better people would be, in the relevant sense, inexplicable. Then the idea behind a Rowean argument will be:

1*** An evil that is inexplicable is actually pointless.
2*** God would not allow actually pointless evils.
3*** There are inexplicable evils.
4*** There are actually pointless evils (from 1*** and 3***).
5 God does not exist (from 2*** and 4***).

The justification of 1*** is that an inexplicable evil – one for which we cannot think of any possible point without positing things which we have no reason to suppose exist – is an evil we *may justifiably claim has no point*. Roweanism presumably reasons as follows: on the evidence we actually have, an inexplicable evil has no discernible point. Maybe nonetheless it has a point; maybe, too, there are no pigs and Rhode Island is a desert. But on the evidence we possess, there are pigs, Rhode Island is not a desert, and there are pointless evils. It is reasonable to believe what is properly inferred from or based on our best evidence. So we are justified in accepting premise 1***. Since 3*** is obviously true, and 1*** and 3*** entail 4***, we are justified in accepting 4***. So, if we are also justified in accepting 2***, we are justified in concluding that there is no God. If *Necessarily, God allows no actually pointless evils* is true, then – the Rowean claims – the newest Rowean argument wins the day. Thus reads the present version of Roweanism.

Here, then, the critic appeals to some such consideration as this:

(E*) If upon careful reflection an evil is inexplicable, the reasonable conclusion is that it has no actual point.

If (E*) or its near kin is true, then the argument succeeds provided its second premise is also true. The question regarding (E*) is why we should prefer it as opposed to:

(E**) Even if upon careful reflection an evil is inexplicable, it is reasonable to suspend judgment as to whether it has no actual point, since we are not possessed of sufficient information and cognitive power to be able reasonably to claim that were an evil to have a point, then that evil would not be inexplicable to us.

Deciding whether an inexplicable evil is actually pointless is not something we must do for practical reasons – not something we must take a position on in the interests of world peace or better economic conditions or the like. So while sometimes we must make a judgment concerning some very tricky moral issue since no decision is worse than being wrong, a decision between (E*) and (E**) is not one of these cases. Nor will the attractiveness of (E*) as a rule for when we must decide give it any force for cases when we do not.

Unless one has good reason to accept (E*) over (E**), a Rowean argument will not work. What can be said in favor of (E*) over (E**) has to do with the claim that it is (E*) that we follow in cases other than deciding whether inexplicable evils are actually pointless, and we are inconsistent if we do not follow (E*) here. But it is utterly unclear that we do follow (E*) in *relevantly similar cases* or even whether there are any relevantly similar cases. The idea that we are inconsistent if we do not use (E*) in a Rowean manner requires some such claim as this:

(EE) If we follow (E*) in cases where we are not inferring from an evil being inexplicable to our being justified in claiming that it actually has no point, we should follow (E*) in that case as well.

The critic is assuming this: (N) *Necessarily, if God has a morally sufficient reason for allowing E, then E has an actual point,* because the critic infers from *Some evil has no actual point* to *God does not exist* via the claims that *If an evil exists which God would have no morally sufficient reason for allowing, then (since God would allow no evil without having a morally sufficient reason) God does not exist.* Thus, on the critic's view, (EE) is identical to:

(EE*) If we follow (E*) in cases where we are not inferring from an evil being inexplicable to our being justified in claiming that God has no morally sufficient reason for allowing it, we should follow (E*) in that case as well.

Whether something like (EE) or (EE*) is true depends on whether there is some relevant difference between cases in which it is reasonable[56] to follow them and the case in which we infer from an evil's inexplicability to (our being justified in) thinking it has no point. In applying (EE) or (EE*), we are taking ourselves to be in a position to infer that an omnicompetent being has no morally sufficient reason to allow an evil from the fact that we cannot think of what such a reason might be. It hardly seems unreasonable at least to suspend judgment about the applicability of (EE) or (EE*) to this sort of case, however wedded we are to its applicability in cases involving no such considerations. There seems, then, no reason to think it rationally inappropriate at least to suspend judgment regarding the applicability of (EE) and (EE*) to the sort of cases that a Rowean argument requires us to apply it. If this is so, we've no reason as yet to accept the conclusion of that argument.

A slightly different Rowean attempt goes like this. Consider this definition:

> Evil E has a *rationale* if and only if God brings about, or permits, E to obtain in the light of some morally sufficient reason that God has for so doing.

Then we can form the Rowean argument:

Ra There are many evils whose rationale, if any, is unknown to us even after our most careful reflections.
Rb If the rationale of an evil is unknown to us even after our most careful reflections, then it has no rationale.[57]
Rc There are many evils that have no rationale (from Ra, Rb).
Rd If God exists, then all evils have a rationale.
Re God does not exist (from Rc, Rd).

And while Ra is very plausible, Rb relies again on its being Principle P1 rather than Principle P2 that is the proper principle to apply to propositions like Ra.

Questions for reflection

1 Are *God exists* and *There is evil* logically incompatible propositions? How is the *Consistency Strategy* related to this question?
2 Does it solve whatever evidential problem the existence of evil may pose for monotheism if the monotheist says that God is very powerful but not omnipotent, knows a lot but is not omniscient, or is very good but not morally perfect?
3 Discuss the notion of a *best possible world*. What is contained in this notion? Is it logically possible that there be such a world?
4 Can even an omnipotent God create persons who are free and morally responsible for their actions but guaranteed always to act rightly?
5 What is it for an evil to *have a point* ? Can a morally perfect God allow an evil that has no point?
6 Does Rowe's "Bambi argument" prove its point?
7 Discuss this argument: real evil exists only if persons have intrinsic worth; that persons have intrinsic worth is more plausible if monotheism is true than if any alternative is true; hence it is more plausible that there is real evil if monotheism is true than if any alternative is true; if it is more plausible that there is real evil if monotheism is true than if any alternative is true, then there being real evil is not an objection to monotheism; hence there being real evil is not an objection to monotheism. Is this argument, or some close cousin, sound and valid?

Annotated reading

Griffiths, Paul (1983) "Notes toward a critique of Buddhist karmic theory," *Religious studies* 18, 3 pp. 277–91. Argues that Buddhist karmic doctrine is incompatible with what we learn from contemporary physics.

Herman, Arthur (1976) *The Problem of Evil in Indian Thought,* Delhi: Motilal Barnasidas. A consideration of the idea that karmic theory allows one to solve the alleged problem of evil.

Leaman, Oliver (1995) *Evil and Suffering in Jewish Philosophy,* Cambridge: Cambridge University Press. A fine discussion of Jewish approaches to the alleged problem of evil.

Mackie, J. L. (1982) *The Miracle of Theism,* Oxford: Clarendon Press. A clear general critique of monotheism; the "miracle" is that anyone is a theist.

Ormsby, Eric (1984) *Theodicy in Islamic Thought,* Princeton: Princeton University Press. A fine discussion of Islamic approaches to the alleged problem of evil.

Pike, Nelson (ed.) (1964) *God and Evil,* Englewood Cliffs, N.J.: Prentice Hall. A good collection of articles that helped frame contemporary discussions.

Plantinga, Alvin (1977) *God, Freedom, and Evil,* Grand Rapids, MI: Eerdmans; reprint of 1974 edition. A detailed clear discussion of the relevance of human freedom to the alleged problem of evil.

Reichenback, Bruce (1990) *The Law of Karma,* Honolulu, HI: University of Hawaii Press. An account and critique of the doctrine of karma.

CHAPTER 10
Arguments for monotheism

10
Arguments for monotheism

Proof

Proof is a complex notion. In simplest terms, a proof is a valid argument with true premises. This is the standard notion of *proof* in logic. An argument consists of premises intended to provide support for a conclusion. An argument is valid if it is logically impossible that the premises be true and the conclusion be false.[1] Any argument of the form *If A then B, A; therefore B,* for example, will be valid.

Given this basic notion of a proof, the contemporary philosopher George Mavrodes has noted that one of the following arguments is a proof and the other is not:[2]

Argument A
1. Either God exists or nothing exists.
2. Something exists.
So: 3. God exists.

Argument B
1*. Either God does not exist or nothing exists.
2. Something exists.
So: 3*. God does not exist.[3]

Note that:

(i) Premises 1 and 1* are disjunctions. They have the forms, respectively, *Either G or N* and *Either not-G or N*.
(ii) It is false that nothing exists. So the *N* disjunct is false.
(iii) Necessarily, either God exists or God does not exist; either *G* is true or else *not-G* is true.
(iv) A disjunction is true so long as at least one of its members is true. So either 1 is true or else 1* is true.
(v) Premise 2, which appears in both arguments, is true.
(vi) Both arguments are valid.
(vii) Argument A has the form: *1. Either G or N; 2. Not-N; so 3.G.*

(viii) Argument B has the form: *1*. Not-G or N; 2. Not-N; so 3*. Not-G.*
(ix) Thus either Argument A is valid and has only true premises or Argument B is valid and has only true premises.
(x) Exactly one of these arguments is a proof in the sense of *proof in logic*: one of these argument not only is valid but also has only true premises.

Unless we know, independently of these arguments, whether God exists or not we cannot tell which argument is a proof. The simple notion of a *proof in logic* is perfectly proper for some purposes. But having a proof in that, and no stronger, sense for some conclusion C is of no help in deciding whether C is true. Mavrodes notes that we need a notion of *a proof that extends our knowledge*. Perhaps something along these lines will do.

Argument A is an argument that extends our knowledge relative to its conclusion C only if:

(i) *A* is a proof in logic;
(ii) we know that *A* is valid (that its premises entail its conclusion);
(iii) we know that *A* is sound (that its premises are true);
(iv) for each premise P of *A*, we can know whether or not P is true without having to know whether C is true (our knowledge of each of the argument's premises is independent of our knowing whether the argument's conclusion is true);
(v) for the conjunct of all of the premises of *A* (premise one *and* premise two *and* premise three, etc.) we can know whether or not that conjunct is true without having to know whether C is true (our knowledge of all of the argument's premises together is independent of our knowing whether the argument's conclusion is true);
(vi) for each premise P of *A*, our knowledge of P is better founded than our knowledge of C;
(vii) for the conjunct of all of the premises of *A* (premise one *and* premise two *and* premise three, etc.), our knowledge of that conjunct is better founded than our knowledge of C.

This, or something much like it, is the sense of "proof" in which we seek proofs that religious beliefs are true. In what follows, we will consider some of the more interesting of the many attempts to provide such proofs.

Types of propositions

Something *has truth value* if and only if it is *either true or false*. Anything that has truth value is a *proposition*. Declarative sentences, typically used, *express* propositions; the same proposition can be expressed by various sentences in the same language or by various sentences in different languages. Thus "The man is old and asleep, and the woman is reading" and "The old man is asleep, and the woman is reading" are different sentences that typically express the same proposition. A proposition is either:

1 *necessarily true* (P is a necessary truth if and only if not-P is a contradiction – e.g., *Nothing has logically incompatible properties* is a necessary truth.)
2 *necessarily false* (P is necessarily false if and only if P is a contradiction – e.g., *Bill Russell is exactly 6′9″ tall, and is not exactly 6′9″ tall* is a necessary truth.)[4]
3 *logically contingent* (P is logically contingent if and only if it is neither necessarily true nor necessarily false; a logically contingent proposition may be true or it may be false – e.g., *Bill Russell is exactly 6′9″ tall* is a logically contingent proposition.)

Further:

4 A proposition P is *possibly true* if and only if P is not a necessary falsehood – every necessary truth, and every logically contingent proposition, is possibly true.

Logical necessity

There are different views about logical necessity, and different meaning assigned to the words "logically necessary proposition." A brief explanation is in order as to how logical necessity is understood here.[5]

Logical necessity is a feature of propositions, not sentences. It is not an artifact of our language or thought. Coming to see that a proposition is necessarily true is a discovery, not an invention or a discovery about our inventions. The reason for this is that necessary truths are not possibly false. Anything whose truth depends on our language or our conventions is possibly false, for our language and our conventions might never have existed at all. So neither the necessity nor the truth of necessary truths depends on our language or our conventions. Such truths are true under all conditions, and hence true in all possible worlds and across all possible cultures.

The prime example of a necessary truth in the history of philosophy is the principle of non-contradiction, which, as Aristotle said, is a principle both of thought and of things. It can be expressed as *Necessarily, no proposition is both true and false* or as *Necessarily, no thing can have logically incompatible properties*. These ways of putting the principle are mutually entailing. If something could have incompatible properties, then propositions could be both true and false. If propositions could be both true and false, then the proposition that a thing had incompatible properties could be true and so a thing could have incompatible properties.

Many contemporary philosophers, using the language of some medieval philosophers, distinguish between *necessity de dicto* and *necessity de re* – necessity in speech and necessity in things. Suppose that Tony is a local barber and consider two sentences about him:

A Necessarily, Tony is a person.
B Tony is necessarily a person.

These sentences express different propositions. What A says is this:

A1 Tony is a person, and it is logically impossible that Tony not be a person.

This entails:

A2 Necessarily, Tony exists.

Of course A2 is false; however much he and his skills might be missed, Tony does not enjoy logically necessary existence. There are possible conditions in which, or possible worlds in which, Tony would not exist. No doubt for a very long time our own world was Tonyless.

What B says is:

B1 Tony is a person, and anything that is a person is a person so long as it exists at all; *being a person* entails *being a person necessarily* because *being a person* (unlike *being a Democrat* or *having false teeth*) is an essential property of anything that has it.

To embrace the idea that there are *necessities de re* one must think that there are essential properties or essences. B1, and hence B, is true if this idea is true; if there are essential properties or essences, *being a person* is among them.

Unfortunately (something its users do not intend) the language that contrasts *de dicto* (of speech) and *de re* necessity can easily suggest that there is one thing – say, logical necessity – and another thing – say, metaphysical necessity – and that the former is relative to language and the latter, if it exists at all, is a human-mind–independent thing. In fact, those philosophers who favor the view that there are both *necessities de dicto* and *necessities de re* view things very differently. To speak of the necessity of a dictum is to speak of the necessity not of an asserted declarative sentence but of what is asserted by that sentence – of a proposition. Necessarily true propositions, on their view, are human-mind-independently necessary and human-mind-independently true. They no more depend for their necessity or their truth on us than do *necessities de re*. There are *necessities de re* only if there are essences.

One can summarily put the point like this: there are necessarily true propositions, and if there are essences, some of those necessarily true propositions will be necessarily true about essences, including some conditional necessary truths about things that have those essences to the effect that they necessarily have them if they have them at all. For example, it is true of Tony that:

B Tony is necessarily a person.

and that:

A* If Tony is necessarily a person, then the proposition *If Tony exists then Tony is a person* is a necessary truth.

Proposition B expresses a *de re* necessity. Proposition A* expresses a *de dicto* necessity.

If something X lacks logically necessary existence, then even if it has an essence E, it is not a logically necessary truth that X has E, because it is not a logically necessary truth that X exists. What is necessarily true, if thing X has essence E, is that X has E *if X exists*.

Assuming they exist at all, *necessity de dicto* is no less metaphysical than *necessity de re* – no less language-and-convention independent, no less human-mind–independent. There being *necessities de dicto* does not require that there are essences; there are *necessities de re* only if there are essences. If they exist at all, *de re* necessities are logical necessities among things – things including but not limited to propositions. If they exist at all, *de dicto* necessities are logical necessities only among things that are propositions.

A final point on this topic. Suppose that *Water is essentially* H_2O is true. Then *Necessarily, water (if it exists) is* H_2O is true. To each *necessity de re* there corresponds a *necessity de dicto* expressible in a corresponding conditional statement. If things have essences, then insofar as our concepts of things are accurate regarding their essences, those concepts will enable us to see *de dicto* as well as *de re* necessities.

This account of necessity is controversial and a defense of it would be lengthy and complex,[6] and though I think it is also successful the purpose of presenting it is simply to explain what is meant here by logical necessity. It is an appropriate meaning for use in discussing the ontological argument.

Purely conceptual proofs and the Ontological Argument

A purely conceptual proof of God's existence is an argument that is valid, has only necessary truths as premises, and has *God exists* as its conclusion. Such a proof that extends our knowledge – which of course is what is sought – will satisfy (at least something like) the other conditions noted above.

The most famous attempts to provide such a proof constitute various varieties of the *Ontological Argument* – an argument offered (among many others) by St Anselm in medieval times, Descartes in the modern period, and Alvin Plantinga in contemporary philosophy. In coming to understand this sort of argument, we begin with two definitions:

Definition 1: *X is a logically necessary being* = *X exists* is necessarily true (*X does not exist* is self-contradictory).

Definition 2: *X is a causally necessary being* = *X exists* is true and logically contingent, and *X is caused to exist* is self-contradictory.

A logically necessary being has not causally but logically necessary existence – it exists and it is not possible that it not exist.

Four objections to the notion of logically necessary existence

There are various objections to the very idea of logically necessary existence. Here are four of the most common:

1 All necessary propositions are conditional – they have a structure properly expressed in an *If A then B* form.

2 No necessary propositions are existential – none entails that anything actually exists.
3 All necessary propositions are tautological – they have a sense property expressed in an *All A is A* or *All AB is B* form.
4 No necessary statements provide genuine information.

We can take these objections in pairs. Objection 1 tells us that all necessary statements are of the form "if A then B" which neither asserts that A exists nor that B exists. Objection 2 tells us that no necessary statement asserts that anything exists. Both 1 and 2 are false, since *There are prime numbers larger than 17* and *There is a successor to two* obviously are necessary truths but do assert that something exists. Objection 3 tells us that all necessary statements are true by virtue of the meanings of the words they contain, like "All uncles are uncles" and "Any aunt has a niece or nephew." (It is allowed that there be a rule to the effect that "A" means "B or C" so that a proposition expressible in the form *All A is A* also is expressible in the form *All A is B or C*.) Objection 4 tells us that necessary truths provide no genuine information. But both *If proposition P is necessarily true, then it is necessarily true that P is necessarily true* and *If proposition P is necessarily false, then it is necessarily true that P is necessarily false* are necessary truths, and they are not tautological and they do provide genuine information. So both 3 and 4 are false.[7] None of these common objections shows that the notion of logically necessary existence is incoherent.

The Ontological Argument

The Ontological Argument is an attempt to state a series of necessarily true propositions which serve as premises that entail the conclusion *God exists*. A successful argument of this sort would prove its conclusion to be necessarily true – it would show that God has logically necessary existence. Were any of the four objections just discussed to have succeeded, it would have undermined the ontological argument.

In constructing perhaps the most interesting version of the ontological argument,[8] we need some further definitions as follows:

Definition 3: Proposition P *entails* proposition Q if and only if *P, but not Q* is a contradiction.
Definition 4: Proposition P is a *maximal proposition* if and only if, for any proposition Q, either P entails Q or P entails not-Q
Definition 5: Each maximal proposition defines an entire *possible world*.[9]

Definition 6: A being has *maximal excellence* if and only if it is omnipotent, omniscient, and omnibenevolent in some possible world.
Definition 7: A being has *maximal greatness* if and only if it has maximal excellence in every possible world.
Definition 8: A proposition is *true in all possible worlds* if and only if it is necessarily true.[10]

There are various versions of the Ontological Argument. Here is one:

A God is a perfect being.
B A perfect being has all perfections.
C *Having logically necessary existence* is a perfection.
D God has *logically necessary existence* (from A, B, C).
E If God has *logically necessary existence* then *God exists* is necessarily true.
F *God exists* is necessarily true (from D, E).

While it has played a significant role in the history of philosophy, it remains true that the notion of perfection is hard to define with any precision. If the argument can be stated without appeal to this notion, so much the better. In fact, it can be so stated, and if the argument stated without the notion of a perfection fails, then so does the argument stated with that notion.

The Ontological Argument without the notion of perfection

Here is a formulation that makes no appeal to the notion of a perfection, though it does include certain central concepts that express what the tradition plausibly thinks are qualities that a perfect being would have.

1 *God has maximal greatness (has maximal excellence in every possible world)* is true unless it is self-contradictory.
2 *God has maximal greatness* is not self-contradictory. So:
3 *God has maximal greatness* is true.
4 If *God has maximal greatness* is true then God exists. So:
5 God exists.

The argument is plainly valid. Its form is:

1 P unless necessarily not-P.
2 Not necessarily not-P. So:

3 P.
4 If P then G. So:
5 G.

and that form is logically impeccable. If there are any problems with the argument, then, it is that one or more of its premises are false.

Premise 1 is true. *Having maximal greatness* is a matter of *having maximal excellence in every possible world; having maximal excellence in every possible world* is tantamount to *necessarily having maximal excellence*. It is not hard to see this provided we keep in mind what the notion of maximal greatness involves, namely having *being omnicompetent in all possible worlds*. For any quality Q, to say that something has Q in all possible worlds is to say that it is logically necessary that it has Q. This claim is, as premise 1 says, true unless it is a necessary falsehood. Any proposition of the form *Necessarily, P* is necessarily true if true and necessarily false if false. *Necessarily, God has maximal greatness* is either true or false; so it is necessarily true or necessarily false. Thus, if it is not necessarily false (i.e., self-contradictory), then it is necessarily true; that is what premise 1 claims.

Premise 3 follows from premises 1 and 2; since God cannot have maximal greatness without existing, premise 4 is true; premises 3 and 4 entail premise 5. Everything depends, then, on whether premise 2 is true. Is it true?

In considering this question, it is helpful to consider some arguments that are analogous to the current version of the Ontological Argument.

The X argument

1x *Necessarily, God does not exist* is true unless it is self-contradictory.
2x *Necessarily, God does not exist* is not self-contradictory. So:
3x *Necessarily, God does not exist* is true.
4x If *Necessarily, God does not exist* is true then God does not exist. So:
5x God does not exist.

This argument is also valid, and premise 1x is true for reasons exactly analogous to those noted regarding premise 1. Premise 4x is obviously true. So if premise 2x is true, then the argument is a proof. Is premise 2x true?

The Y argument

1y *God exists is logically contingent* is true unless it is self-contradictory.
2y *God exists is logically contingent* is not self-contradictory. So:

3y *God exists is logically contingent* is true.
4y If *God exists is logically contingent* is true then *Necessarily, God exists* is false.
5y *Necessarily, God exists* is false.

This argument is also valid. Premise 1y is true for reasons exactly analogous to those that favor 1 and 1x. If it is true that *God exists is logically contingent* then *God exists is logically necessary* is false. (So then is *God has maximal excellence,* which entails *God exists is logically necessary.*) So if *God exists is logically contingent* is true, then *God has maximal excellence* is false, and that is what premise 4y says. So if premise 2y is true, then the Y argument is sound and valid, and thus its conclusion is true. Is 2y true?

The Z argument

1z *God does not exist is logically contingent* is true unless it is self-contradictory.
2z *God does not exist is logically contingent* is not self-contradictory. So:
3z *God does not exist is logically contingent* is true.
4z If *God does not exist is logically contingent* is true then *Necessarily, God exists* is false.
5z *Necessarily, God exists* is false.

This argument is also valid. Premise 1z is true for reasons exactly analogous to those that favor 1, 1x, and 1y. If it is true that *God does not exist is logically contingent* then *God exists is logically necessary* is false. (So then is *God has maximal excellence,* which entails *God exists is logically necessary.*) So if *God does not exist is logically contingent* is true, then *Necessarily, God exists* is false, and that is what premise 4z says. So if premise 2z is true, the Z argument is sound and valid, and its conclusion is true. Is 2z true?

Summary regarding the Ontological Argument (version 1) and the X, Y, and Z arguments

A Each argument is logically valid.
B In each argument, the first premise is true.
C In each argument, the fourth premise is true.
D In each argument, only the first, second, and fourth premises are independent; the first and second entail the third, and the third and fourth entail the conclusion.

E In each argument, if the second premise is true, the argument is sound.
F Premise 2y is true if and only if premise 2z is true, so we need concern ourselves only with one of them; we will use 2y.
G It is logically impossible that *more* than one (or that *less* than one) of these three premises be true: premise 2 of the Ontological Argument, premise 2x, premise 2y.

What is crucial in evaluating the Ontological Argument is that this argument does not establish which of these three premises is true. It leaves that issue completely open. Hence the Ontological Argument fails as a proof that extends our knowledge. Given the discussion thus far, the point can be put succinctly as follows. Consider:

0 Either *God exists* is (a) necessarily true, (b) necessarily false, (c) logically contingent and true, or (d) logically contingent and false.

The Ontological Argument requires that (a) be the right alternative. But that argument contains the thesis that (a) is the right alternative – that is what premise 2 of the argument says. No argument is given to the effect that (a) is the right alternative. Granted, (a) does not seem self-contradictory; but nor do any of (b), (c), or (d), each of which is incompatible with (a). So we are left without any reason for picking (a) as the truth.

Another look at the Ontological Argument

1 It is logically possible that God has maximal excellence if the concept of God is not contradictory.
2 The concept of God is not contradictory. So:
3 It is logically possible that God has maximal excellence.
4 If it is logically possible that God has maximal excellence, then God has maximal excellence. So:
5 God has maximal excellence.
6 If God has maximal excellence, then God exists in all possible worlds. So:
7 God exists in all possible worlds.
8 If God exists in all possible worlds, then necessarily God exists. So:
9 Necessarily, God exists.

Exposition of the Ontological Argument

From 3 on, the argument is correct. You might object to 4, but what 4 says is this: *Possibly, God has maximal excellence* entails *God has maximal excellence*. What you need to keep in mind is that *God has maximal excellence* entails *God exists in all possible worlds* (= *Necessarily, God exists*). Thus *God has maximal excellence* ascribes the modality necessarily true to the proposition *God has maximal greatness*. Thus, given that necessary truths are necessarily necessarily true and necessary falsehoods are necessarily necessarily false, it follows that *God has maximal excellence* is either necessarily true, or else is a contradiction.

Further discussion of Ontological Argument

There is a problem with the argument, and it starts earlier. It lies exactly in premise 1 (in contrast to version 1, where the problem arises with premise 2). Suppose what is true is *The proposition that God exists is logically contingent*. Then the following things are true: (i) *God exists* is not a contradiction; (ii) *God does not exist* is not a contradiction; and (iii) *Necessarily, God exists* is a contradiction, and (iv) *Necessarily, God does not exist* is a contradiction. If (iii) is true, then premise 1 of the Ontological Argument is false. Thus if it is true that *The proposition that God exists is logically contingent is true*, premise 1 of the argument is false. Nothing in the argument shows that *The proposition that God exists is logically contingent* is not true. So the argument fails.

A proof that something has logically necessary existence

Consider this brief argument:

1 Necessarily, if it is possible that something has logically necessary existence, then something has logically necessary existence.
2 It is possible that something has logically necessary existence. So:
3 Something has logically necessary existence.

In other terms:

1* Necessarily, (Possibly, something has logically necessary existence) entails (Something has logically necessary existence.)
2* (Possibly, something has logically necessary existence). So:
3* (Something has logically necessary existence.)

The reasoning here is simple: 1 and 1* are necessary truths. Premises 2 and 2*, being modal claims, are either necessarily false or necessarily true. Neither 2 nor 2* is necessarily false. So 2 and 2* are necessarily true. The inferences *1 and 2, hence 3* and *1* and 2*, hence 3** are obviously valid. Hence conclusions 3 and 3*, being entailed by necessary truths, are themselves necessary truths. Something has logically necessary existence.

If the ontological argument is sound and valid, then this argument must be sound and valid; its soundness and validity are a necessary, but not a sufficient, condition of the soundness and validity of the Ontological Argument. The simple argument is powerful; perhaps it is a proof that extends our knowledge. But even if this is so, the Ontological Argument itself is not a proof that extends our knowledge.

Empirical proofs, argument strategies, and principles of sufficient reason[11]

In contrast to a purely conceptual proof of God's existence, an empirical proof of God's existence is an argument that is valid, has at least one logically contingent truth among its premises, has only true premises, and has *God exists* as its conclusion. Such a proof that extends our knowledge – which of course is what is sought – will satisfy the other conditions noted above. There are various starting points for such arguments, and various strategies for going on from the beginning. For example, one might begin with the fact that there is a universe, though it is logically possible that there might not have been, or that there is some particular thing (say, oneself), though it is logically possible that there may not have been that particular thing, or the fact that the universe is intelligible (science is possible), though it is logically possible that there be a universe that is not intelligible. Suppose one begins with the fact that there is a universe, though it is logically possible that there may not have been. Then there are at least these strategies for continuing.

1 The *everlasting world* strategy: prove that the world is everlasting and dependent, then infer to a necessarily independent being on which the dependent everlasting world depends.
2 The *world-has-a-beginning* strategy: prove that the world is not everlasting past, then infer to a cause of the world beginning to exist.
3 The *inclusive* strategy: prove it the case that the world is everlasting and dependent *or* that the world is not everlasting past; then infer to there being either a necessarily independent being on which the dependent everlasting world depends or a necessarily independent cause of the world beginning to exist.

Which strategy a philosopher chooses may, but need not, depend on what her religious beliefs are. A Christian, like Augustine, who believes that God created time and the universe together (that God's creating a universe is both necessary and sufficient for there being time) will suppose that the universe is everlasting in one sense – there is no time at which there was no universe – but will also suppose that it is impossible that there be a time T1 at which the universe was not created and then another later time T2 at which the universe was created. We might call this *universe-time-together creation* view. In another sense, in holding this view, she will deny that the world is everlasting; on her view, there will have been a first time – time will go back so far, and no further. But a Jewish, Christian, or Muslim monotheist might perfectly well hold that time has no beginning and that God created the world at some time prior to which time flowed but no universe existed. We can call this the *creation in time* view. A monotheist might even hold that the universe has always existed, and the doctrine that God created the universe entails that the universe always depends on God for its existence, has always done so, and will do so as long as it exists at all. We can call this the *beginningless creation* view. On this view, *God created the universe* entails *The universe has always existed in such a way that it depends on God, God does not depend for God's existence on there being a universe, and were God to cease sustaining the universe in existence, it would not exist but God would still exist*. But there being a first time, or a first moment at which the universe began to exist, will not be entailed. A monotheist can accept any of these alternatives. Typically Jewish, Christian, and Muslim monotheists have accepted either a universe-time-together or a creation in time perspective. Hindu monotheism, by contrast, holds to a beginningless creation perspective. This has largely to do with their interpretations of their religious texts.

A philosopher might think that one could not decide between these alternatives by appeal to anything other than Scripture, and wish to base his arguments only on what he thought was philosophically accessible. In this case, the third strategy may well seem attractive.[12] In any case, each strategy will require its own version of the general thesis that whatever can be explained has an explanation – its own formulation of the Principle of Sufficient Reason (PSR).

Principles of Sufficient Reason

1 The Everlasting World Strategy requires something like this: (PSR1) *If it is logically possible that something depends for its existence on something else, then it does depend for its existence on something else*

or *What can depend for its existence on something else does depend for its existence on something else.*

2 The World Has A Beginning Strategy requires something like this: (PSR2) *What begins to exist must have a cause of existence* or *Nothing can simply begin to exist without being caused to do so.*

3 The Inclusive Strategy requires something like this: *(PSR1) and (PSR2).*

Crucial premises

The different strategies will also require somewhat different premises along these lines.

1 The Everlasting World Strategy requires some such premise as this: *It is logically impossible that everything that exists exists dependently.*

2 The World Has A Beginning Strategy requires some such premise as this: *It is logically impossible that everything that exists has had a beginning of existence.*

3 The Inclusive Strategy requires something like this: *(a) It is logically impossible that everything that exists exists dependently and (b) it is logically impossible that everything that exists has had a beginning of existence.*

The idea is that if the world is beginningless past, it does not exist independently (because of the truth of (a)) and if the world has a beginning it does not exist independently (because of the truth of (b)).

The inclusive strategy is safer with respect to one of its basic premises which is a weaker claim than its analogues – one who uses it need not care whether the world ever began to exist or not. But it is riskier with respect to its version of the Principle of Sufficient Reason (it requires both PSR1 and PSR2).

Differences in conclusions

The strategies, of course, will also yield somewhat different conclusions. Aristotle wants to infer from the world's existence to God's existence in a way that does not require that God have made any choices or performed any actions. Semitic and Hindu monotheists want to infer from the world's existence to God's existence in a way that does require that God has chosen to create and that God created (the choice and the act may be the same). Even if a monotheist does not think that you can successfully infer from the world's existence to God's existence, she typically will have a view about how the world is related to God. Ramanuja, for example, rejects any inference from the world's existence to God's existence, but holds that the world is everlastingly dependent for its existence on God. Among the most famous and influential of arguments for monotheism are Aquinas's Five Ways.

Arguments by Thomas Aquinas

Aquinas's arguments are of considerable historical interest. For our present purposes, however, three questions matter: (i) do any of his arguments prove their intended conclusion?; (ii) if not, can one learn from them how to frame a more powerful argument for their intended conclusion or something much like it?; (iii) do his arguments suggest some other approach to the question of the truth or falsity of monotheism? Questions (i) and (ii) are considered in this chapter; the third receives attention in the later chapter on Faith and Reason.

Aquinas asks whether the existence of God can be proved and answers in the affirmative. He then offers five arguments for God's existence followed by an argument that the being referred to in the conclusion of the first argument is the same as that referred to in the conclusion of each of the other arguments. Here, too, beginning with a few definitions will enable us to state complex arguments with much greater simplicity than we could without them.

Reflexive and irreflexive relations

Aquinas's arguments deal with certain relationships he takes to hold between one thing in the world and another thing in the world, or between the world and God. Here are some fundamental features of relations:[13]

Definition 1: Relation R, holding between X and Y, is *reflexive* if *X has R to Y* entails *Y has R to X*.

If Jack is the same height as Jill, then Jill is the same height as Jack; *being the same height as* is a reflexive relation.

Definition 2: Relation R, holding between X and Y, is *irreflexive* if *X has R to Y* entails *Y does not have R to X*.

If Tim is Tom's father, then Tom is not Tim's father; *being a father, being a mother, being a parent* are irreflexive relations.

It will be useful to have two further ways of talking about relations. Let us say that if *X has R to Y* then X has R *forwardly* to Y, and that Y has R *backwardly* to X. Reflexive relations between X and Y are had both forwardly and backwardly by both X and Y. Irreflexive relations between X and Y are had only forwardly by X and only backwardly by Y.

General structure

The general structure – the logical skeleton, as it were – of Aquinas's arguments, typically called the "Five Ways," as we will see, can be expressed either as:

1 There is an X and a Y such that X bears relation R to Y.
2 Either (a) there is an infinite series of items such that each member has R both forwardly to something and backwardly to something, or (b) there is some item that has R only forwardly.
3 Not-(a). So:
4 (b).

or as

1 There is an X and a Y such that X has R to Y.
2 Either (a) there is an infinite series of items such that each member has R both forwardly to something and backwardly to something, or (b) there is some item that has Y only forwardly.
3 If (a) then (b).
4 If not-(a) then (b). So:
5 (b).

Chronological versus concurrent causes

If we are to understand Aquinas, it is important to distinguish between what we will call chronological versus concurrent causes.

Definition 3: X is a *chronological* cause of Y if and only if X's doing something or having some quality at some time *before* T is necessary for Y at T.

Putting the water over the fire, causing it to boil; turning the key in the ignition, causing the car to start; throwing the ball, causing the window to break, are chronological causes.

Definition 4: X is a *concurrent* cause of Y if and only if X doing something or having some quality *at* T is a necessary condition of Y at T.

Holding a door to keep it open; holding one's breath to keep one's lungs full; pushing the bell to keep the bell ringing are cases of concurrent causation. It is typically cases of concurrent, not chronological, causation that Aquinas has in mind in offering his arguments. Thus criticisms based on the assumption that he has chronological causation in mind will be off target.

Each of Aquinas's five arguments concerns a different relationship as follows.

Argument 1: something moving/changing something else.
Argument 2: something causing something to come to exist.
Argument 3: X can cease to exist by becoming Y.
Argument 4: things having different degrees of worth.
Argument 5: something behaving at least as if it were seeking a goal.

Domains, forwardness, and backwardness

A finite domain is a collection having a finite number of members; a pile of forty rocks, a flock of seventy geese, a galaxy of a million stars are finite domains. Suppose that we have a domain of three things – Al, Bob, and Carl. Suppose that an irreflexive relationship – say, *being a father* – relates Al and Bob, and Bob and Carl. Within this domain, Al stands in the relation *being a father* only forwardly, Carl stands in the relation *being a father* only backwardly, and Bob stands in the relation *being a father* forwardly toward Carl and backwardly toward Al. If this domain is all there is, Al has no father and Carl has no children. This domain is *ordered by* an irreflexive relationship. Each member of the domain is related to every other by an instance of the same irreflexive relationship – in the case just described, by *being a father*.

Consider a different domain – a domain defined in terms of its members being ordered by a particular sort of dependence relationship. The sort of dependence in question is *non-reciprocal dependence* where *B non-reciprocally depends for existence on A if and only if B depends for its existence on A and A does not depend for its existence on B*. Suppose, then, that there exists a domain of things each of which stands in a non-reciprocal dependence relation to something, and that this domain is finite. Then it follows that some member of this domain stands in the relationship of non-reciprocal dependence only forwardly. The only alternatives are that the domain is infinite (which we have stipulated is not so) or that there is a circle of non-reciprocal dependence, which is impossible. If B non-reciprocally depends on A, and C non-reciprocally depends on B, and A non-reciprocally depends on C, then the relationship between A and B is *reciprocal* dependence, not non-reciprocal. A circle of non-reciprocal relationships is logically impossible. So some member of the domain must stand in the relationship of non-reciprocal dependence only forwardly[14] – i.e., must exist independently of the other members of the domain ordered by the irreflexive relationship of non-reciprocal dependence.

Aquinas takes this relationship of non-reciprocal dependence to be one involving concurrent causation – if the existence of A fully explains the existence of B, then so long as B exists it must be the case that A is causing it to exist.

It is not obvious that the world of physical things and nondivine minds is a finitely large domain of things ordered by the relationship of non-reflexive dependence. But that it is such a domain is something that at least the first three of Aquinas's arguments require.

Change, potentiality, actuality[15]

Aquinas defines *change* in a way reminiscent of Aristotle's philosophy.

Definition 5: X is in actuality with respect to some property Q if and only if X has Q.

Definition 6: X is in potentiality with respect to some property Q if and only if (i) X does not have Q, but (ii) X is the sort of thing capable of having Q.

Elk cannot be prime numbers, eggs cannot run faster than hares, and pigs cannot fly; so these things are not in potentiality with regard to these properties. Elk can be dyed pink, eggs can be swallowed whole, and pigs can be dressed in tuxedos, so they are in potentiality with respect to these properties. Elk have legs, eggs have shells, and pigs have ears, so they are in actuality with regard to these properties.

Definition 7: X changes with respect to property Q if and only if X moves from potentiality to actuality, or from actuality to potentiality, with respect to Q.[16]

Definition 8: Y causes X to change with respect to property Q if and only if Y causes X to move from potentiality to actuality, or from actuality to potentiality, with respect to Q.

The First Way

The First Way concerns things being caused to move, in the usual sense of going from one place to another but also in the more general sense of simply changing, in position or some other way. It is assumed that *X changing Y with respect to Q* is a relationship that is non-reciprocal – is analogous to *non-reciprocal dependence*. Thus the idea is that it cannot be the case that *X's changing Y with respect to Q* causes *Y's becoming Q* only if *Y's becoming Q* causes *Y's causing Z to become Q* and *Z's becoming Q* causes *X's causing Y to become Q*. The argument goes as follows.

1 Some things change.
2 If X changes at time T then there is something Y that changes X at T (understood as that Y is something different from X).
3 Either (a) there is an infinite series of changed and changing beings (i.e., a series each member of which is both a changed and a changing thing) or (b) there is some being that is a changing being (a cause of motion/change) but is *not* a changed being (something that changes).
4 Not-(a). So:
5 (b).

Aquinas offers a subsidiary argument for premise 2:

2a For all times T, and all X, X is in actuality with respect to moving at T or X is in potentiality regarding motion at T.
2b If X is in potentiality regarding motion at T, then X is not moving at T.
2c If X is not moving at T, then X cannot cause motion at T.
2d Nothing can cause its own motion at T (since in order to do so it would have to both be in actuality regarding motion at T and in potentiality regarding motion at T, and that is impossible).
2e No motion can be uncaused.

Hence:

2 If X changes at time T then there is something Y that changes X at T (understood as that that Y is something different from X).

The issue of whether there can be self-moving or self-changing things was hotly disputed in the medieval period. Scotus, for example, offered powerful arguments against Aquinas in this regard. But there is to be a replacement for premise 2 that restricts its basic idea to cases of which it is true, and we will follow this strategy.

Self-change

The First Way, if successful, would establish the existence of a cause of change that did not change.[17] Premise 2 – the denial of self-motion – is apparently problematic. There seem to be cases of self-movement – one's walking to the store, for example – and of self-caused change that does not involve movement from place to place – deliberately stopping thinking about one thing in order to reflect on another. But there are lots of changes in which something is caused to change by something else, and the best strategy for defending Aquinas here seems to be this: argue that, with respect to the sorts of qualities with which the arguments are concerned, self-change is not an option. Something depending for existence on itself – a physical object or a human mind, for example, having some feature by virtue of which it existed independently of anything else – is not a promising notion. Perhaps the simplest defense of Aquinas here is to argue as follows: we know that every physical thing, and that every human mind,[18] in fact depends for its existence on the existence of other things. But *being dependent* is an essential property of everything that has it; *X is dependent for existence on something else* entails *Necessarily, X is dependent for existence on something else*. Further, *Nothing can cause its own existence* is a necessary truth; in order for something to cause its own existence, it must do so at some time T. Then, at some time T, something that causes its own existence must both not exist in order to be caused and exist in order to do the causing – a feat that is logically impossible to perform.

Even if one provides this line of reasoning on Aquinas's behalf, however – even if one grants that a version of, or replacement for, premise 2 that is restricted to some such quality as *non-reciprocally causing change* will serve his purposes even if some instances of self-change are possible – his case is not made. Consider this pair of claims:

T1: For any time T1, everything that exists at T1 depends for its existence on something else that exists at T1.

T2: For any time T2, everything that exists at T2 was caused to come into existence at T2 by something that existed at T1.

The sort of dependence that T2 describes is non-reciprocal and consecutive. The sort of dependence that T1 describes is reciprocal and concurrent. The First Way requires that there be a sort of dependence that is non-reciprocal and concurrent. Suppose that T1 and T2 are true and describe the only sorts of dependence there are. Then the First Way fails. Nothing in the First Way proves that T1 and T2 are not true and descriptive of the only sorts of dependence that there are. So the First Way is not a proof that extends our knowledge. Perhaps there is the sort of non-reciprocal dependence that Aquinas requires, but we have no proof of it here.

Infinite series[19]

It is not obvious why there cannot be an infinite series of changed and changing things, whether we have chronological or concurrent cases of causation in mind. We have seen why premise 4 – the rejection of an infinite series of things changing one another regarding quality Q – is needed. Aware of this, Aquinas offers a subsidiary argument for premise 4:

4a An infinite series has no first (earliest?) member.
4b If a series has no first (earlier?) members, it has no later or succeeding members
4c If a series has neither earlier nor later members, it has no members.
4d No series can have no members. So:
4 Not-(a) – there is *not* an infinite series of changed and changing beings (i.e., a series each member of which is both a changed and a changing thing).

Aquinas[20] admits that there can be a temporally beginningless causal series; so presumably it is concurrent, not chronological, causality that Aquinas has in mind in this argument (and elsewhere in the Five Ways). The argument for the fourth premise is puzzling. There were sharp disputes among medieval philosophers as to whether an infinite series was possible. Perhaps the sub-proof rests on the idea that, in constructing a series, one has to begin somewhere, and if one does not start with a first thing one will never construct even a two-member, let alone an infinitely membered, series. Then the argument is correct but irrelevant, since those who contend that there are series that are infinite does not contend that we have to construct them. One can reply that any actual series must be one that could in principle be constructed by someone, and an infinitely membered series could not be. But then we need another argument that any infinite series must be one that could in principle be constructed, and another to show that an infinitely membered series does not fit this description. Plainly nothing in the argument of the First Way, in either its main or its subsidiary lines of reasoning, provides anything like this. Thus the First Way seems not to be a proof of its conclusion.

The Second Way

Again we begin with a couple of definitions.

Definition 9: X is in motion *per accidens* if and only if X moves only because X is part of or is located in Y and X moves only because Y moves.

The car moves *per se*. A cup of coffee set in the cup holder of a moving car moves *per accidens*.

Definition 10: X moves *per se* if and only if X moves and X does not move *per accidens*.

The Second Way runs as follows; it takes *coming to be* or *coming to exist* as a change.

1 If X comes to be at T then X's coming to be at T is caused.
2 Nothing can cause its own coming to exist (it would have both to exist to do the causing and not exist to be caused to come to be).
3 If X comes to be at T then X is caused to come to be at T by something other than X.
4 Either (a) there is an infinite series of beings that come to be and are caused to come to be by other beings that were caused to come to be, or (b) there is a being that causes other things to come to be but is not itself caused to come to be.
5 Not-(a). So:
6 (b)

Aquinas argues for premise 5 in this manner:

5a An infinite series has no first member.
5b If a series has no first member, then it has no later members.
5c A series having neither a first nor later members has no members; a series without members cannot exist. So:

5 There is not an infinite series of beings that come to be and are caused to come to be by other beings that were caused to come to be.

The argument for premise 5 here is identical to the argument for premise 4 of the First Way, and hence has exactly the same problems. Further, coming to exist is not a change in the thing which comes to exist; assuming the definition of change offered above, it is not a change – non-existent things have neither potentiality nor actuality. *It is possible that X, which does not exist at time T, comes to exist at time T1* does not entail *X, which does not exist, has the potentiality to exist; X has some potentiality or other* entails *X exists*. So the Second Way is not a proof.

The Third Way

Two simple definitions are helpful here.

Definition 11: X is *generable* if and only if X can be caused to come to be.

Definition 12: X is *corruptible* if and only if X can be caused to change and can be caused to cease to exist.

Aristotle and Aquinas seem to assume *X can be caused to change* entails *X can be caused to cease to exist*, and conversely, so that necessarily anything that meets one of the conditions of being generable also meets the other. It is not at all obvious that this is so. In any case, the Third Way goes like this:

1 If X is generable and corruptible then X's non-existence is possible.
2 There are corruptible and generable things. So:
3 There are things whose non-existence is possible (from 1 and 2).
4 Assume for the sake of showing it to be false that: For all X, X's non-existence is possible.[21]
5 If for all X, X's non-existence is possible, then there is some time T such that nothing exists at T.
6 There is some time T such that nothing exists at T (from 4 and 5).
7 It is impossible that anything comes to exist without its being caused to do so by something that already exists.
8 If there is some time T such that nothing exists at T, then for any time T* later than T, nothing exists at T*.
9 Nothing exists at T* (from 5 through 8).
10 If there is some time T such that nothing exists at T, T has already occurred. So:

11 T has already occurred.
12 If T has already occurred, then nothing exists now. So:
13 Nothing exists now (from 10 through 12).
14 If for all X, X's non-existence is possible, then nothing exists now (from 4 through 12).
15 It is false that nothing exists now. So:
16 It is false that for all X, X's non-existence is possible.
17 If it is false that for all X, X's non-existence is possible, then something exists whose non-existence is impossible. So:
18 Something exists whose non-existence is impossible (from 16 and 17).

Aquinas's Third Way is read in different ways. Aquinas is read as saying either:

(a) It is impossible that all generable things exist at every single time. (= Necessarily, every generable thing at some time or other does not exist.)

or:

(b) It is impossible that, at every time whatever, some generable thing exists. (Necessarily, at some time or other, no generable thing exists.)

Compare *Necessarily, every elk passes on sooner or later*; this is analogous to (a). Consider *Necessarily, at some time, there are no elk at all*; this is analogous to (b). What Aquinas needs is (b), (a) will not help him. Aquinas also needs:

(c) It is impossible that everything that exists is a generable being.

This indication of what he requires is relevant to two fallacious inferences he is often charged with making in the Third Way; either would, of course, invalidate the argument.

Inference one: from A to B

Consider:

A For all X, it is possible that X corrupt.
B It is possible that everything (simultaneously) corrupt.

A world W of which A is true might be one of which it was also true that:

C It is not possible that W be entirely unpopulated.

But a world of which B was true is a world of which C could not be true. Hence inferring from A to B is fallacious.[22] Inferring from (a) to (b) is tantamout to inferring from A to B. If Aquinas either inferred from (a) to (b), or simply did not adequately distinguish between them, the argument fails.

Inference two: from D to E

D Everything at some time fails to exist.
E Sometime, everything fails to exist.[23]

Everything is green at some time or other does not entail *At some time or other, everything is green*. Similarly, D does not entail E. Again, the inference from (a) to (b) is tantamount to inferring from D to E. If Aquinas either inferred from (a) to (b), or simply did not adequately distinguish between them, the argument fails.

The gist of these criticisms is that even if at some time or other, each thing that exists will pass out of existence, it does not follow that they will all pass out of existence at the same time, and so long as earlier members can generate later ones, things will go on. If Aquinas is not entitled to infer from (a) to (b), then even if he is entitled to infer from (b) to (c) this will not help, since he has no legitimate way to get to (b).

Aquinas is also criticized for claiming that the alleged time at which everything would simultaneously pass away would already have occurred; why not regard the proof (if it did succeed) as proving that at some future time there will not be any generable things? His answer is that if there have been generable things for only a finite time past, then there had to be a cause of there coming to be generable things and so there is something that is not itself a generable thing, and if there have always been generable things, then an infinite time has passed and in any infinite time we would have reached the time at which everything has passed away. We can afford not to enter into this controversy.[24]

The first three of Aquinas's Five Ways begin by reference to the fact that things exist that might not have existed and that depend for their existence on something else, and that things change. They then require some such claim as *What can depend for its existence on something else does depend for its existence on something else* and *What changes is changed by something else*, as well as such claims as *If there are things that exist that depend for their existence on something else, then there is something that exists independent of anything else* and *If things are caused to change by something else, then there is something that causes change without itself ever changing*. In part for reasons given as we explained these arguments, none of them constitutes a proof that extends our knowledge. Thus the results of examining these arguments has not been very positive; none seems even close to a proof that God exists. But rearrangement and revision of the materials these arguments contain provide something stronger.

Some further definitions

If these materials do yield a stronger – even a successful – argument, perhaps they do so via the following argument. Once again, some definitions will make it possible to state the argument less complexly than otherwise. Further, the way the premises are stated is intended to keep them from being open to various standard objections. Note that nothing in the following argument requires that there not be various sorts of self-motion or self-change and it requires no assumptions about whether there is an infinite series of anything.

By way of reminder:

Definition 1: P is a *logically contingent proposition* = neither P nor not-P is self-contradictory.
Definition 2: P is a *logically necessary proposition* = not-P is self-contradictory.

Further:

Definition 3: P is an *existential proposition* = P entails a proposition of the form *X exists*.
Definition 4: It is *logically possible that P's truth be explained* = There is some proposition Q such that *Q's truth explains P's truth* is not self-contradictory.

To give an analysis: if it is logically possible that the existence of something X be explained, then it is logically possible that X *not* exist, and if it is logically possible that the truth of a proposition P be explained, it is logically possible that it *not* be true.

Given these definitions, we can state another version of the Cosmological Argument.

Cosmological Argument, stage one

1 If it is logically possible that the truth of a logically contingent existential proposition be explained, then there actually is an explanation of its truth (whether we know what it is or not).

Premise 1 is a version of the Principle of Sufficient Reason.

2 *There exist things whose existence it is logically possible to explain* is a true logically contingent existential proposition.

There are rose bushes, there might not have been rose bushes, and there is an explanation of there being rose bushes; hence premise 2 is true.

3 There is an explanation of the truth of *There exist things whose existence it is logically possible to explain* (from 1, 2).

Premise 3 obviously follows from premises 1 and 2. So if they are true, so is it. The success of stage one depends on what is true regarding the first premise.

Cosmological Argument, stage two

4 The truth of *There exist things whose existence it is logically possible to explain* cannot be explained by there being things whose existence it is logically possible to explain (the existence of *those* things is just what is to be explained).

Suppose that Pat wants to know why there now are golden retriever puppies. She is told that there are golden retriever parents. She asks why there are golden retriever parents. She is told about golden retriever grandparents. Pat then wants to know why there are any golden retrievers at all. She cannot now be told about golden retriever parents, grandparents, great grandparents, or the like; these will all be things she wants to know about – why have any golden retrievers at all existed? Here, one either refuses to answer, claims that there being golden retrievers is just a fundamental feature of the world, or explains that there were non-golden retrievers that caused there to be golden retrievers.

If Pat asks why there have ever been any possibly explicable things at all that exist though they might not have existed, she cannot properly be told about there being possibly explicable things that exist but might not have existed; those are the things she asks about. So one can refuse to answer, claim that there being possibly explicable things that exist but might not have existed is a fundamental feature of the universe, or refer to something that is *not* such as to exist and be possibly explicable though it might not have existed. This line of thought is correct, and is what premise 4 says.

5 That a logically contingent existential proposition is true can only be explained by some other existential proposition being true.

If, in the relevant sense of explanation, P's truth entails Q's truth, then P entails Q. No existential proposition is entailed by a set of propositions that does not contain any existential propositions.

6 If an existential proposition does not concern something whose existence it is logically possible to explain, it concerns something whose existence is logically impossible to explain.

These exhaust the possibilities.

7 The truth of *There exist things whose existence it is logically possible to explain* can only be explained by a true existential proposition concerning something whose existence it is logically impossible to explain (from 4, 5, 6).
8 Some existential proposition concerning something whose existence it is logically impossible to explain, and whose existence can explain the existence of things whose existence it is logically possible to explain, is true (from 3, 7).

Premise 4 is plainly true; whatever Xs are, *there being Xs* cannot explain *there being Xs*. Nor can the existence of something that might not have existed be explained other than by reference to things that exist; the existence of contingent things can only be explained by reference to something that exists, not by reference to something that doesn't exist. So premise 5 is true. Necessarily, for anything X that exists, either it is logically possible that X's existence be explained or it isn't; that is what premise 6 says. If (i) X's existence can be explained, and (ii) can be explained only by the truth of a type A proposition or by the truth of a type B proposition, and (iii) cannot be explained by the truth of a type A proposition, then it follows that (iv) X's existence can be explained by the truth of a type B proposition. Premise 7 applies this reasoning to the notions of propositions concerning the existence of things whose existence can be explained and propositions concerning the existence of things whose existence cannot be explained. Premises 4, 5, 6 entail 7 and 3 and 7 entail 8; if they are true (and they are) so is it. Hence stage two is successful.

Cosmological argument, stage three

9 If some existential proposition concerning something whose existence it is logically impossible to explain, and whose existence can explain the existence of things whose existence it is logically possible to explain, is true, then something exists whose existence it is logically impossible to explain and whose existence can explain the existence of things whose existence it is logically possible to explain.
10 Something exists whose existence it is logically impossible to explain and whose existence can explain the existence of things whose existence it is logically possible to explain (from 8, 9).

Premises 8 and 9 entail step 10, and premise 9 is, I take it, a necessary truth. So stage three succeeds. The conclusion thus far – *Something exists whose existence it is logically impossible to explain and whose existence can explain the existence of things whose existence it is logically possible to explain* – is interesting all by itself. The crucial premise is the first:

> If it is logically possible that the truth of a logically contingent existential proposition be explained, then there actually is an explanation of its truth (whether we know what it is or not).

Premise 1 is a version of the Principle of Sufficient Reason. Call it PSR*.

Suppose one claims the truth of every logically contingent proposition has an explanation, and that it cannot be the case that the truth of every logically contingent proposition is explicable by reference to the truth of other logically contingent propositions. Then one will be claiming that there is some logically contingent proposition whose truth is explicable by reference to some true but not logically contingent proposition – some logically necessary truth. If *P's truth explains Q's truth* entails *P entails Q*, then one is claiming that a necessary truth entails a logically contingent truth. This is necessarily false – if Q is a logically contingent proposition, it is possibly false. No necessary truth is possibly false. Were a necessary truth to entail a logically contingent proposition, then it would be possibly false. Hence no necessary truth can entail a logically contingent proposition. If there are any true logically contingent propositions – and there plainly are – then either every one of them is explicably true by reference to some other, whose truth is explicable by reference to some other, and so on, or some among them are true but their truth cannot be explained. PSR* is compatible with all this. It requires no attempt to explain contingent propositions only by reference to necessary truths, and it is compatible with there being an infinite number of contingent truths, each explained by some other contingent proposition. It is also compatible with the fact that, if there are any logically contingent propositions – and there plainly are – then some must be true: if Q is a logically contingent proposition, so is not-Q, and of (Q and not-Q) one must be true.

What it does require is that *there being logically contingent true existential statements* is possibly explicable – as it is – and hence that it has an actual explanation. If it does have an explanation, it seems that the Cosmological Argument has the right sort of explanation. Obviously no necessary truth will explain it, and no possibly explicable contingent proposition will explain it, and no non-existential statement will explain it. What is left, since necessary falsehoods and contingent falsehoods explain nothing, is a logically contingent existential statement whose truth is necessarily inexplicable. While it is true that of any pair composed of a logically contingent existential statement and its denial, one must be true, it might always be that it was the denial that was true. So it is not a logical necessity that there be true logically contingent existential statements. There remains, then, this question: is it contingently inexplicable that there are true logically contingent existential statements? That there are such statements is possibly explicable, so if there is no explanation of there being such, there is a perfectly intelligible question – *Why are there true logically contingent existential propositions?* – that might perfectly well have had an answer, but that in fact has none. What PSR* denies is that this is possible – the possibly explicable is actually explicable.

Is PSR* true? There does not seem to be anything more obviously true than PSR* from which it follows. PSR* does not seem to be contradictory, and if it is true, it is necessarily true. So it is, if not contradictory, then necessarily true. But (I) *It is contingently inexplicable that there are logically contingent true existential statements* is not obviously contradictory, and it is, if true, then necessarily true. So if it is not contradictory, then it is necessarily true. Nothing in the Cosmological Argument shows that it is PSR* rather than (I) that is true. So the Cosmological Argument is not a proof that extends our knowledge.

There is a bit more to be said regarding PSR*. A standard objection to weaker formulations of the Cosmological Argument is that if one infers from the world to God, and it is logically possible that God not exist, then one might as well have stopped with the world. A Cosmological Argument with PSR* as an essential premise, assuming the remainder to be crafted in line with PSR*'s content, will be subject to no such objection. Further, if one rejects PSR* one is left with an ultimate mystery, an intelligible and basic question to which there might have been an answer, but is not. Reject PSR* and mystery lies on your side of the fence, not on the monotheists' side.

Cosmological Argument, stage four

It is at least not unreasonable to accept PSR*, and it is worth seeing how the argument that requires it continues. A few additional definitions will serve the familiar service of simplifying the statement of the argument.

D4 Being X has necessary existential security = X exists, and *X is caused to exist or depends for its existence on something else* is self-contradictory.
D5 Q is a basic property of X = X has Q, and X has no property Q* such that *X has Q** explains the truth of *X has Q*.
D6 Q is a non-basic property of X = X has Q, and X has some property Q* such that *X has Q** explains the truth of *X has Q*.
D7 X has logically necessary existence = X exists, our concept of X is accurate relative to X's existence and *X does not exist* is self-contradictory.
D8 X has logically contingent existence = X exists, our concept of X is accurate relative to X's existence, and neither *X exists* nor *X does not exist* is self-contradictory.

Note that:

(i) *X has necessary existential security* does not entail *X has logically necessary existence*;
(ii) *X has logically necessary existence* does entail *X has necessary existential security*;
(iii) whatever exists has either logically necessary or logically contingent existence;
(iv) while if it is logically possible that the existence of something be explained, it follows that it is logically possible that the thing *not* exist, it is not true that if it is logically possible that it *not* exist, then it is logically possible that its existence be explained;
(v) while it is true that if it is logically possible that the truth of a proposition be explained, it is logically possible that the proposition *not* be true, it does not follow that if it is logically possible that a proposition *not* be true, then it is logically possible its truth be explained.

Now we can begin stage four.

11 *X's existence is logically impossible to explain and its existence can explain the existence of things whose existence it is logically possible to explain* is true only if *X has necessary existential security* is true.

12 If something exists whose existence it is logically impossible to explain and whose existence can explain the existence of things whose existence it is logically possible to explain, something has necessary existential security.

13 Something has necessary existential security.

14 Both *explaining the existence of things whose existence it is logically possible to explain* and *having necessary existential security* are non-basic properties of anything that has them.

15 If *having necessary existential security* is a non-basic property of anything that has it, then the something that has necessary existential security has some other property whose possession explains its *having necessary existential security.*

16 The something that has necessary existential security has some other property whose possession explains its *having necessary existential security.*

17 The only properties that something might have that would explain its *having necessary existential security* are A: *having logically necessary existence* or B: *being omnipotent, omniscient, and morally perfect.*

18 Something has A or B.

19 The concept of something that has A but lacks B is the concept of an abstract object, and since abstract objects lack causal powers they cannot explain the existence of anything whose existence it is logically possible to explain; thus *having A* will not explain anything having the property *explaining the existence of things whose existence it is not logically impossible to explain.*

20 The concept of a being that has B but lacks A is the concept of a being that has causal powers and whose existence can explain the existence of anything whose existence it is logically possible to explain; thus *having B* will explain anything having the property *explaining the existence of things whose existence it is logically possible to explain.*

21 The concept of a being that has B and also has A is also the concept of a being that has causal powers and whose existence can explain the existence of anything whose existence it is logically possible to explain; thus *having A and B* will explain anything having the property *explaining the existence of things whose existence it is logically possible to explain.*

22 Something exists that has B.

23 The concept of something that has B is the concept of God, conceived either as having logically necessary existence or as having logically contingent existence, but in either case as possessing necessary existential security and causal powers that can explain the existence of anything whose existence it is logically possible to explain.

24 God exists.

Suppose that God exists, and is omnipotent and omniscient. Then God will lack no power, and no knowledge, failure to have which would allow some enemy to do God in. God's existence is utterly safe; it is logically impossible that this being be destroyed from without. Suppose God is also perfectly good. A perfectly good being won't commit suicide or deicide. There are no conditions under which a perfectly good being who is omnipotent and omniscient will ever decide that destruction of itself would be a good thing for it to do. It is logically impossible that such a being, while remaining perfectly good, will cause itself to implode. Were it ever to do so, or act in some other wrong way, then it would always know it would do so. A being that always knew that it would act wrongly, and never did anything about it, would never be morally perfect after all.[25]

God's moral perfection is conceived by monotheists in two different ways. On one account, what is true is *Necessarily, God is morally perfect*; on the other, what is logically contingent and true is *God is morally perfect*.[26] On the former account, it is logically impossible that God commit deicide. On the latter account, it is not logically impossible that God commit deicide, though one may properly trust God not to do so. On neither account of divine moral perfection is it logically possible that God depend on anything for God's existence.

Two points relevant to the Cosmological Argument

Consider two claims:

1 *Possibly, X is contingent* entails *X is contingent* if *contingent* means *logically contingent* (=neither necessarily true nor necessarily false).
2 *Possibly, X is contingent* does not entail *X is contingent* if *contingent* means *depends for existence on something distinct from itself*.

The Cosmological Argument requires that both of these claims be true.

Argument for 1

A proposition has its modality necessarily; thus whatever modality a proposition lacks, it lacks necessarily; logical contingency is a modality; hence whatever has it has it necessarily, and whatever lacks it lacks it necessarily; hence if it is possible that a proposition is contingent, then it is.

Argument for 2

It is not logically impossible that X have logically contingent existence and yet it be false that X depends for existence on something else – a logically contingent and necessarily independent being would fit this description, for example.

Hence both 1 and 2 are true.

Conclusion

Besides requiring PSR*, this version of the Cosmological Argument is strongest if it can be shown that *Necessarily, God exists* is false. Only then (if at all) can one infer to the cause of possibly explicable logically contingent beings having the properties that a logically contingent being must have if its existence is to be necessarily inexplicable.

A supplementary argument

An argument distinct from the Cosmological Argument that nonetheless dwells in the same conceptual neighborhood is the following:

10a It is logically possible that an omnicompetent being exists.
10b If it is logically possible that an omnicompetent being exists, then it is logically possible that an omnicompetent being destroy everything material. So:
10c It is logically possible that an omnicompetent being destroy everything material. (from 10, 10b)
10d If it is logically possible that an omnicompetent being destroy everything material, then nothing material has necessary existential security. So:
10e Nothing material has necessary existential security. (from 10c, 10d)

Thus far, the argument is obviously valid and the independent (non-inferred) premises seem to be true. If this is correct, it is a useful supplement to the Cosmological Argument. A natural off-shoot is this argument:

10e1 If nothing material has necessary existential security, then something exists that is not material. So:
10e2 Something exists that is not material.
10e3 If something exists that is not material, then materialism is false. So:
10e4 Materialism is false.

The truth of 10e1 requires the conclusion of stage three of the Cosmological Argument, i.e., premise 10, and is exactly as secure as that premise is.

Aquinas's Fifth Way

The Fifth Way is one version of the argument from design. To say that something *seeks its own end* is to say that *it seeks its own flourishing as a member of its kind*. The following characterization of the Fifth Way reads it as asserting that each generable body seeks its own end, not that all generable bodies together seek some *universal* end or some end that characterizes the universe as a whole (e.g., universal orderliness).[27, 28]

1 We observe generable bodies that lack awareness typically seek their own flourishing.
2 What happens typically does not happen accidentally. So:
3 Generable bodies typically seeking their own flourishing does not happen accidentally. (from 1 and 2)
4 Generable bodies typically seeking their own flourishing, if it does not happen accidentally, occurs only because they are caused to do so by an agent that intends that this occur. So:
5 Generable bodies typically seeking their own flourishing occurs only because they are caused to do so by an agent that intends that this occur. (from 3 and 4)
6 If they are caused to do so by an agent that intends that this occur, then there is an agent that intends that this occur. So:
7 There is an agent that intends that this occur. (from 5 and 6)

A different way of putting the argument invokes the distinction, but also the similarity, between artifacts and natural objects. Artifacts are made by humans; their parts are made and organized so as to produce some end or other. They are made to do something, and insofar as they are well made, they do that thing. Call the feature of having parts that were made to be organized so as to produce specific results *being operationally functional*. Then the argument goes:

1 Artifacts are operationally functional things.
2 Natural objects are operationally functional things.
3 Operational functionality in artifacts is adequately explicable only by reference to intelligence.
4 If artifacts are operationally functional things, natural objects are operationally functional things, and operational functionality in

artifacts is adequately explicable only by reference to (human) intelligence, then operational functionality in natural objects is adequately explained only by reference to intelligence. So:

5 Operational functionality in natural objects is adequately explained only by reference to intelligence. (from 1–4)

6 Operational functionality in natural objects is not caused by human intelligence.

7 What is caused by intelligence other than human is caused by non-human intelligence.

8 If operational functionality in natural objects is adequately explained only by reference to intelligence, and operational functionality in natural objects is not caused by human intelligence, and what is caused by intelligence other than human is caused by non-human intelligence, then operational functionality in natural objects is adequately explained only by reference to non-human intelligence.

9 Operational functionality in natural objects is adequately explained only by reference to non-human intelligence. (from 5–8)

10 If operational functionality in natural objects is adequately explained only by reference to non-human intelligence, then there is strong evidence that there is non-human intelligence.

11 There is strong evidence that there is non-human intelligence. (from 9, 10)

The conclusion is neither uninteresting (a newspaper editor convinced of its truth would put it in her headlines) nor as strong as *Monotheism is true*. Its religious relevance becomes obvious if one thinks what sorts of powers a being would have to have in order to cause operational functionality in natural objects.

The Hindu monotheist Ramanuja offers the following objections to the argument from design. Reacting to Indian versions of the argument from design he says:

> (1) There is no proof to show that the earth, oceans, etc., although things produced, were created at one time by one creator. Nor can it be pleaded in favor of such a conclusion that all those things have one uniform character of being effects, and thus are analogous to one single jar, for we observe that various effects are distinguished by difference of time of production, and difference of producers . . . for experience does not exhibit to us one agent capable of producing everything.[29]

That is, if we take our experience with artifacts as the clue to operational functionality in natural objects, often various humans cooperate in the production of an artifact, or make changes in it; the evidence cited by the argument from design suggests a committee as much as it does a single intelligence. A standard response is that one is justified in positing no more intelligences than is necessary to explain the data.

> (2) Experience further teaches that earthen pots and similar things are produced by intelligent agents possessing material bodies, using implements, not endowed with the power of a Supreme Lord, limited in knowledge, and so on; the quality of being an effect therefore supplies a reason for inferring an intelligent agent of the kind described only.[30]

That is, if we take our experience with artifacts as the clue to operational functionality in nature, its intelligent causes are embodied[31] and possess limited intelligence and power.

> (3) Consider the following point also. Does the Lord produce His effect with His body or apart from His body? Not the latter, for we do not observe causal agency on the part of any bodyless being; nor is the former alternative admissible, for in that case the Lord's body would be permanent or impermanent. The former would imply that something made up of parts is eternal; and if we say this we may as well admit that the world itself is eternal, and then there is no reason to infer a Lord. And the latter alternative is inadmissible because in that case there would be no cause of the body different from it (which would account for the origination of the body). Nor could the Lord Himself be assumed as the cause of the body, since a bodyless being cannot be assumed as the cause of a body. Nor could it be maintained that the Lord can be assumed to be "embodied" by means of some other body; for this leads us into a regress in infinitum.[32]

Here, the reply is more complex. Suppose that God, like human artificers, must have a body in order for God to produce operational functionality in anything. Then God, able to produce operational functionality only through use of a body that is already is operationally functional, did not produce operational functionality in *that* body. God's own body, construed on the analogy with human artificers, has an operational functionality not produced by God. But then why not simply view all bodies as having some such intrinsic not-produced-by-God operational functionality? Ramanuja, then, concludes that

> the inference of a creative Lord which claims to be in agreement with observation is refuted by reasoning which itself is in agreement with observation, and we hence conclude that Scripture is the only source of knowledge with regard to a supreme soul that is the Lord of all and constitutes a highest Brahman.[33]

David Hume, in his famous *Dialogues Concerning Natural Religion*, offers criticisms similar to those of Ramanuja.[34] He views the argument from design as an inductive argument. The property relevant to the inductive inference is something like *orderliness* or *behaving in specifiable, predictable ways always or for the most part*. The things relevant to the inference are artifacts, like clocks, and natural objects, like apples or sheep. One is invited to infer from a sample class of which one has had experience (artifacts having been produced by an observable designer by an observable process) to a reference class of which one has had only partial relevant experience (one has observed natural objects though one has not observed them being caused to possess *orderliness* by a non-human intelligence). So the premises concern there being artifacts and natural objects, and both having orderliness. The conclusion is that natural objects are caused to have orderliness by a non-human intelligence.

The connecting premises point to the cause of orderliness in artifacts, namely human intelligence. The core idea is that inferring that orderliness in natural objects should be taken to have the same sort of cause – an intelligent mind – and obviously human minds do not cause orderliness in apples and goats.[35]

Hume makes these objections among others:

> (a) there are other explanations of orderliness in natural objects than that they were designed – for example, natural objects might have a sort of intrinsic order, being by nature organisms or natural machines produced by natural processes;
> (b) we cannot in principle observe natural objects being caused to have orderliness by non-human intelligence nor can we in principle observe natural objects being caused to have orderliness by something else; observing an apple grow or a goat give birth are examples of orderliness, not explanations of orderliness of the sort disputers regarding the argument from design are concerned with;
> (c) there is no lawlike connection that we can know of between *natural objects possessing orderliness* and *natural objects being caused to have orderliness by X*, whether "X" is filled in by

> reference to intelligence, natural processes, or anything else, and legitimate inductive inferences ride the rails of natural laws.

The argument from design is, in effect, an argument to the best explanation – an argument that is intended to establish that, if we follow the sorts of procedures we typically follow in making probabilistic inference, we shall come to the conclusion that there is a designer. But there obviously are other explanations of operative functionality in natural objects – for example, that material particles evolved over a long period in such a manner as to produce such items. All that is required, the proposal is, is particles of the right sorts, laws, and time. This sort of explanation of operative functionality in natural objects is intended as well to explain there being human intelligence capable of causing operative functionality in artifacts. Thus most of the philosophically interesting issues raised by arguments from design have to do with how to decide which, among a group of explanations, is best, and how exactly to understand the relevant data and formulate the theories relevant to explaining them. This sort of issue comes up again in the final chapter on Faith and Reason.

The Teleological Argument

Another argument in the same family as the argument from design, but different in what it begins with – the intelligibility of nature or the possibility of science – and its straightforwardness as an argument to the best explanation – is the Teleological Argument. As construed here, it is a supplement to the Cosmological Argument. Here is one more objection to the Cosmological Argument: what the conclusion of the Cosmological Argument does (roughly) is to say that the universe of dependent things is caused by the act of an intelligent divine agent; it says that God, who might not have created anything, acted to create dependent things. But then God's action of creating might not have occurred. So we are left, not with a being that might not have existed but whose existence is really impossible to explain, but with an action that might not have occurred; what's the gain? – either way we stop our explanation arbitrarily. One way of construing the Teleological Argument – is not as an independent argument but rather as an answer to this objection to the Cosmological Argument.

The Teleological Argument is often stated as an independent argument. As stated here, it is a continuation of the Cosmological Argument, and offers an answer to the present objection to that argument. Again, some beginning definitions simplify the overall presentation.

D1 R is S's *sufficient reason* for doing A = S does A for reason R, there is no better reason for doing A than R, there is nothing better that S might do than A, and S's doing A is right (note that *being right* does not entail *being obligatory*; if there is more than one right way of acting in a given circumstance, one's obligations in that circumstance are simply to act in one of those ways).

D2 R is S's *proper ultimate reason* for doing A = R is S's sufficient reason for doing A, there is no true moral proposition from which R follows in any way that justifies R, R is true, and S knows that R is true (every proposition follows from other propositions – any proposition P follows from [(Q or P) and not-Q] – but not every proposition follows from others in a way that proves it true; if we cannot have some knowledge without proving it, we cannot prove anything).

D3 S is *completely rational* in doing A = S has a proper ultimate reason for doing A.

D4 E is an *ultimate existence explanation* = E explains the truth of a logically contingent existence proposition by reference to the truth of an existence proposition whose truth it is logically impossible to explain.

Statement of the Teleological Argument

1 If an ultimate existence explanation has a teleological explanation as an essential component, then the agent referred to in that teleological explanation is completely rational in acting as that explanation says she acts.

2 If an agent is completely rational in acting in a certain way, then there can be no further teleological explanation of her acting in that way.

3 If there can be no further teleological explanation of an agent's acting in a certain way, then unless the existence of that agent can be explained, there is nothing relevant that is left unexplained.

4 If God created the world, God was completely rational in doing so.

According (roughly) to the conclusion of the Cosmological Argument:

5 God created the world.

Hence, from 4 and 5:

6 God was completely rational in doing so.

Hence, from 2 and 6:

7 There can be no further explanation of God's creating the world.

But:

8 It is not possible to explain the existence of God.

Hence, from 3, 7, and 8:

9 There is nothing relevant that is left unexplained.

Hence the objection fails. One is not left with something explicable that is unexplained.

Conclusion

The combination of the Cosmological and Teleological Arguments considered above is one of the stronger versions of one sort at least of natural theology – the effort to present arguments that are plainly valid, have premises that are discernibly necessarily true or contingently true propositions, and infer to the existence of God. Even it, however, does not yield a proof that extends our knowledge.

Questions for reflection

1 What sort of proof extends our knowledge?
2 Explain the distinction between a necessarily true proposition and a contingently true proposition.
3 Is there a successful purely conceptual proof that God exists?
4 Does the existence of apparent design provide reason to think that God exists?
5 Discuss the inference from *Something that might not have existed does exist and it is possible that its existence be explained* to *There is something that exists whose existence cannot be explained*. If this inference is justified, how close does its conclusion get to monotheism?
6 Suppose there is no proof that God exists. Does anything else of philosophical interest follow?

Annotated reading

Burrell, Donald (ed.) (1967) *Cosmological Arguments*, Garden City, NY: Anchor Books. An excellent collection of historical and recent discussions of the argument.

Flew, Anthony (1966) *God and Philosophy*, London: Hutchinson. Philosophy of religion done on the presumption of atheism.

Hick, John and McGill, Arthur (eds) (1967) *The Many-faced Argument*, New York: Macmillan. An excellent collection of historical and recent discussions of the ontological argument.

Haldane, J. J. and Smart, J. J. C. (1996) *Theism and Atheism*, Oxford: Blackwell. An atheist and a Catholic theist argue their cases.

Plantinga, Alvin (ed.) (1974) *The Ontological Argument*, New York: Harper and Row. An excellent collection of traditional, and some recent, treatments of the argument.

Rowe, William (1975) *The Cosmological Argument*, Princeton, NJ: Princeton University Press. Probably the best discussion of the argument.

Swinburne, Richard (1979) *The Existence of God*, Oxford. Clarendon Press. Argues for the existence of God from a perspective in which the controversial idea of *a priori* simplicity is important.

CHAPTER 11
Monotheism and religious experience

11 Monotheism and religious experience

Phenomenologically thick experiences

A phenomenological description of an experience is a description that tells us how the things appear to a person who has it. Consider these sentences, each of which uses the word "seems" in a different sense:

1 Kim seems less capable than she is. (Here, "seems" contrasts appearance to reality.)
2 It seems to Kim that she left the oven on. (Here, "seems" reports a shaky belief on Kim's part.)
3 There seems to Kim to be a chair in front of her. (Here, "seems" expresses how Kim is "appeared to;" whether there is a chair there or not, it remains true that *if things are as they perceptually appear to Kim, a chair is in front of her.*)

So there are at least three senses of "seems" – a contrastive sense (in 1), an opinionative or belief-expressive sense (in 2), and an experiential and perceptual sense (in 3). Our concern is with the experiential, perceptual sense.

Suppose Kim is in a room that she knows was set up by some majors in psychology and physics. There seem to be twice as many chairs in the room as there are – half of the "chairs" are in fact holograms of chairs. Not having been in the room before, but knowing that half of what seem to be chairs are not, Kim nonetheless properly says:

4 It seems to me that there is a chair in front of me, though I have no idea whether I am seeing a chair or a hologram of a chair.

The "seems" here is experiential and perceptual; it is also *phenomenological* – it describes how things perceptually seem, whether they are that way or not. Using phenomenological descriptions, an atheist and a theist can agree that experiences occur in which it at least seems to the subject that she is perceiving a powerful, holy being[1] distinct from herself. They disagree over whether there is such a being that she perceives.

Thin description versus thick description

Members of monotheistic religious traditions report what they describe as experience of God. Sometimes the phenomenologies of these experiences are vanishingly thin, simply a matter of feeling forgiven or a sense that they ought to perform some action. Only if one reasonably already takes monotheism to be true, and even then only with various qualifications, might one also reasonably take these experiences actually to be experiences of God – at any rate *reasonably* in any sense in which it was not equally reasonable not so to take them.

Other experiences described as experiences of God are, as it were, phenomenologically thicker – the subjects report an awareness of a being of majestic power, profound holiness, overwhelming purity, and deep love. Such experiences are reported in various formal and informal mystical traditions in Catholic, Orthodox, and Protestant contexts, in all of the Semitic monotheisms, and in Hindu monotheism. Similar reports are given by persons not associated with any mystical tradition, sometimes by persons not religious by any monotheistic standard. Sometimes these experiences are sought and sometimes they simply occur. An earlier chapter lists a few descriptions of such experiences.[2] The present question is whether the occurrence of these phenomenologically richer experiences provide any evidence that God exists. This question can be answered with any care only if we ask and answer some other questions first. Here is a series of relevant questions and answers. Throughout these questions and answers, but not elsewhere, "religious experience" will simply mean "experiences that, given their phenomenology, are, if reliable, experiences of God."

Experience as direct evidence

Question 1: what sort of experience are we asking about?

The relevant experiences are subject/consciousness/object in structure; they involve a person having an experience which, providing that the experience is reliable, involves being aware of something or someone that is not dependent for its existence on being experienced. In that respect, such experiences resemble experiences of shrubs and worms (these being typically reliable, and shrubs and worms existing independent of one's experiencing them) or of ghosts (if experiences of ghosts were reliable, then ghosts would have experience-independent existence). They have the sort of content described above in the first part of our series of descriptions of religious experiences. They are also experiences in which the at least apparent object is not oneself, one's body, or one's mental states; they are (if reliable) experiences of something other than oneself or one's body or one's states – a being that exists distinct from and independent of oneself.

Question 2: can any experience be evidence for just any old claim?

Distinguish between direct evidence and indirect evidence. An experience is direct evidence for a claim that something exists only if it is true that the experience in question, if reliable, just is an experience of that thing. We take it that we have exactly that sort of experience of cats and computers. An experience is indirect evidence for the existence of something only if it is, if reliable, experience of something else, where if the something else exists, then the thing in question exists. Suppose that Ralph and Mabel are hosting Mabel's sloppy brother Jim, whom they know to be the only person in the world who eats peanut butter and mustard sandwiches. Arriving home, Ralph is hopeful that his brother-in-law may have ended his visit, but is chagrined to find on the kitchen table two peanut butter and mustard sandwiches waiting to be devoured; he infers that Jim is still around, and will soon be having a snack. Seeing the sandwiches provides direct evidence of their existence, and indirect evidence of Jim's continued presence. Our concern in this chapter will be with direct evidence only, and our concern with it focuses on the conditions under which experience provides direct evidence for the existence of something.

Not every experience can be direct evidence for the existence of just anything. Its at least seeming to Mary that there is tea in her cup, bread on her table, and music coming over the radio will not provide her with direct evidence that the Alps are still around, there are trolls, or that God exists. Mountains, trolls, and God are not among the things she even seems to experience. An experience is direct evidence only for what exists provided that experience is reliable – provided things are as that experience represents them as being. How an experience represents things as being is a function of its phenomenological content. Our concern here is with, and only with, experience as potential evidence for claims to the effect that things are as the experiences that are potential direct evidence for them represent things as being[3] – with the cases of experiences and claims where the claims match up with the phenomenological content of the experiences. Experiences will not be direct evidence for any other claims.

A principle of experiential evidence

Question 3: how do we tell what an experience can be direct evidence for the existence of?

Suppose that Mary reports at least seeming to see a tiger in her garden; having this experience provides her with reason for concern or delight (depending on her views about having a tiger in her garden that she previously lacked). She has some evidence that *There is a tiger in Mary's garden* is true. There may not be: it is logically possible that she seems to see a tiger and there is none there. But even if tigers do not typically roam in her garden, her at least seeming to see a tiger in her garden provides her with hitherto absent evidence that there is one there now. The basic idea, then, is this: if Mary has an experience which, if reliable, is a matter of seeing a tiger in her garden, then she has experiential evidence that there is a tiger there. More formally:

(P) If a person S has an experience E which, if reliable, is a matter of being aware of an experience-independently existing item X, then S's having E gives S evidence that X exists.

Alternatively, suppose that Max has an experience, the phenomenological content of which justifies Max in saying *If this experience is reliable, then I am experiencing something that fits description D*, where D simply says what features it at least experientially seems to Max that something has. Then Max's experience is evidence that *Something fitting D exists*. If there ever is experiential evidence for anything that exists independent of our experience, (P) or some close cousin is true. What an experience can be evidence for is a function of what its phenomenology is; its phenomenology constrains what an experience can be evidence for. Further, *at least seeming to see a tiger* correctly describes only a very small range of possible phenomenologies or phenomenological contents. If an experience is correctly described as *at least seeming to hear Beethoven's Fifth Symphony, at least seeming to smell coffee brewing, at least tasting like peppermint, at least seeming to see a large elephantly shaped thing, at least seeming to see a battleship*, or the like, it will not have the proper phenomenological features to be direct evidence for *at least seeming to see a tiger*. In sum: an experience is evidence that there is an experience independently existing X only if having the experience is a matter of at least seeming to be aware of an X.

Question 4: can't such experiences go wrong in various ways?

Yes. If Mary is drinking a special Tiger Tea that always produces tiger-in-the-garden hallucinations, it will appear to her that there is a tiger in her garden whether there is one or not. This circumstance, let us say, will *cancel* the evidential force of the experience relative to there being a tiger in the garden. So we need to revise (P) via:

(P1) If a person S has an experience E which, if reliable, is a matter of being aware of an experience-independently existing item X, and E is not *canceled*, then S's having E gives S evidence that X exists.

If Mary knows that the tea she has been drinking has this feature, she is justified in taking her evidence to have been cancelled.

Suppose that Mary has imbibed not the Tiger Tea that produces as-if-a-tiger-in-the-garden perceptions, but Sometime Tiger Tea that produces such perceptions on a more complex schedule. It never works if there is a tiger in the garden. But if there is no tiger in the garden then it causes as-if-tiger-in-the-garden perceptions a little more than half of the time. Once in a while, let us assume, there is a tiger in a garden. Sometime Tiger Tea produces tiger hallucinations exactly enough more than half so that the net result is that, taking into account genuine perceptions, half of the time if one drinks Sometime Tiger Tea one has an as-if-tiger-in-the-garden perception which corresponds to no tiger. Then the situation is that Mary, in having her as-if-tiger-in-the-garden experience, is exactly as likely as not to be seeing a real tiger, i.e., exactly as likely as not not to be seeing a real tiger. Then she has no more experiential evidence in favor of *There is a tiger in the garden* than there is against it. If she knows that her tea has this effect, she is justified in drawing no inference from her at least seeming to see a tiger to there being a tiger in the garden. Let us say that being in these circumstances has the effect of *counterbalancing* the evidential force of Mary's experience, and revise (P1) accordingly:

(P2) If a person S has an experience E which, if reliable, is a matter of being aware of an experience-independently existing item X, and E is not canceled *or counterbalanced*, then S's having E gives S evidence that X exists.

If Mary knows that her experience of at least seeming to see a tiger is counterbalanced, then she is justified in not taking it to be evidence that there is a tiger that she sees.

Suppose that just prior to Mary's experience she undergoes a strange change regarding her perceptions that are, or seem to be, of a tiger – a change that others do not undergo. The change is this: she can never perceptually confirm *There is not a tiger in the garden* (or anywhere else). For whatever reason, she is perceptually incapable of noting the absence of tigers. Suppose, further, that it is true that:

(E) If it is not possible for anyone to experientially disconfirm existential claim P, then it is not possible for anyone to experientially confirm P

and that applied to Mary (E) yields this truth:

(E-Mary) If it is not possible for Mary to experientially disconfirm existential claim P, then it is not possible for Mary to experientially confirm P.

Since, by hypothesis, *Tigers exist* is not experientially disconfirmable by Mary, it is, by (E-Mary), not experientially confirmable by Mary either. In such a circumstance, let us say that Mary's as-if-a-tiger-in-the-garden experience is *compromised* relative to *There is a tiger in the garden*. So we replace (P2) by:

(P3) If a person S has an experience E which, if reliable, is a matter of being aware of an experience-independently existing item X, and E is not canceled or counterbalanced *or compromised*, then S's having E gives S evidence that X exists.

If Mary discovers that she has changed in the way described, and that (E) is true, she is justified in not taking her experience to be evidence of the presence of tigers.

Again, suppose someone discovers a proof that shows that there cannot be any tigers (the notion of a tiger contains a hidden inconsistency) or there cannot be any tigers in our world (what we know about initial physical conditions and laws of nature precludes the development of tigers). If our world cannot contain tigers, either because no world can or because of particular features of our world, then as-if-there-is-a-tiger experiences will all be unreliable. Under these conditions, let us say, Mary's as-if-there-is-a-tiger-in-the-garden experience is *contradicted*. Hence goodbye to (P3) and hello to:

(P4) If a person S has an experience E which, if reliable, is a matter of being aware of an experience-independently existing item X, and E is not canceled or counterbalanced or compromised *or contradicted*, then S's having E gives S evidence that X exists.

If Mary knows of the proof or the physical conditions and laws, she is justified in not taking her experience to be evidence that she sees a real tiger.

Yet again, suppose that someone proves, or gives us superb reason for believing, that there is a Tiger Deceiver who has complete power relative to the production of as-if-there-is-a-tiger perceptions and causes them only when there are no tigers. Thus, while we do not know whether there are tigers or not, we do know that all our experiences that seem to tell us that there are tigers are fakes. Under these conditions, let us say, Mary's as-if-there-is-a-tiger-in-the-garden experience is *confuted*. Thus (P4) yields pride of place to:

(P5) If a person S has an experience E which, if reliable, is a matter of being aware of an experience-independently existing item X, and E is not canceled or counterbalanced or compromised or contradicted *or confuted*, then S's having E gives S evidence that X exists.

If Mary has good reason for thinking that there is a Tiger Deceiver, she is justified in not taking her experience as evidence that she sees a tiger.

The notion of a Tiger Deceiver is one way of expressing the idea that what we call perceptions of tigers are *universally illusory*. This idea is distinct from the fact that it is logically possible that all perceptions of tigers are deceptive – that there never is a tiger when one seems to perceive one. That is a fact, just as it is a fact that it is logically possible that no perceptions of tigers are deceptive – that there always is a tiger that one sees when one seems to perceive one. The logical possibility of universal correctness, and the logical possibility of universal incorrectness, of tiger perceptions are not in dispute; neither idea is what the Tiger Deceiver idea concerns. That idea concerns the actual universal incorrectness of perceptions of tigers.

Finally, consider the neither lucid nor empty notion of a *kind* of experience. Let all sensory experiences be of the same kind, all introspective experiences be of the same kind, all moral experiences be of the same kind, all aesthetic experiences be of the same kind, presumably with various sub-kinds within each kind. Consider claims:

(K) If it is logically possible that an experience E of kind K provide evidence in favor of existential proposition P, then it is logically possible that an experience E* of kind K provide evidence against P.

(K1) If it is empirically possible that an experience E of kind K provide evidence in favor of existential proposition P, then it is empirically possible that an experience E* of kind K provide evidence against P.

The notion of *empirical possibility* does not really introduce a new notion of possibility; it simply amounts to *logical consistency with natural laws and actual conditions*. Suppose there were a natural law to the effect that (i) *If an elephant is within ten yards of a peanut, the elephant cries*. This, plus the truth of (ii) *Here is an elephant within ten yards of a peanut,* entails (iii) *Here is an elephant that is crying*. It is logically impossible that (i) and (ii) be true and (iii) be false. Since (i) is a natural law, and (ii) an empirical truth, (iii) is also an empirical truth.

Now suppose we have a natural law of the form (i*) *If A then B does not obtain,* and suppose that (ii*) *A obtains* is something that is always true in our world but is not a necessary truth – something like *There is energy* which might have been false, is true, and presumably is always true so long as our physical world exists at all. Then (iii*) *B does not obtain* follows; it is logically impossible that (i*) and (ii*) be true and (iii*) be false. The truth of not-(iii*) *B obtains* is logically inconsistent with the truth of (i*) – a natural law – and (ii*) – an always prevailing empirical condition. Then, we shall say, *B's obtaining is empirically inconsistent*.

Suppose that:

(K) If it is logically possible that an experience E of kind K provide evidence in favor of existential proposition P, then it is logically possible that an experience E* of kind K provide evidence against P

is true. Suppose that it were logically impossible that there be experiential evidence against (T) *There is a tiger in the garden*. Then, if (K) is true, Mary could in principle have no sensory experience that provided evidence against (T) *There is a tiger in the garden*. Then, given (K), her as-if-a-tiger-is-in-the-garden experience would not provide evidence *for* that claim. If such conditions held, let us say that the evidential force of Mary's experience would be *logically consumed*.

Suppose that:

(K1) If it is empirically possible that an experience E of kind K provide evidence in favor of existential proposition P, then it is empirically possible that an experience E* of kind K provide evidence against P.

It might be that while it was not logically impossible that sensory experience that provided evidence against (T) occur, certain features in our world might serve always to prevent the occurrence of experiential evidence against (T) – experiential evidence against (T) might be empirically impossible. Then, if (K1) is true, Mary could *in fact* have no sensory experience that provided evidence against (T) *There is a tiger in the garden* and then her as-if-a-tiger-is-in-the-garden experience would not provide evidence *for* that claim. Under that condition, let us say that her apparent experiential evidence was *empirically consumed.* (Here, as opposed to the discussion that led to (P3), *everyone* is in the state that we assumed there that only Mary was in.) Of course (P5) is now to be replaced by:

(P*) If a person S has an experience E which, if reliable, is a matter of being aware of an experience-independently existing item X, and E is not canceled or counterbalanced or compromised or contradicted or confuted *or logically consumed or empirically consumed,* then S's having E is evidence that X exists.

There is something further to be noted about our application of (P*) here. Our interest is in experiential evidence regarding the existence of things other than ourselves and our states. So our application of (P*) will be to experiences that, if reliable, are experiences of things other than ourselves and our states – not because of any inherent limits in (P*) but because it is experiences that at least seem to be of things other than ourselves and our states that interest us here. Experiences that at least seem to be of ourselves and our states will come up in the next chapter.

Question 5: are all of these qualifications to (P) necessary?

Perhaps so, perhaps not; exactly what is appropriate to add to something like (P) is controversial. Some philosophers who have discussed a principle very similar to (P) have thought it too strong. If it is, that is no problem for our argument. Suppose religious experience is evidence if it passes the test of applying (P*) to it. Suppose also what is true is not (P*) but rather (P*)-minus-*X*, where X is what makes (P*) stronger than it should be. Any experience that passes the test of having (P*) applied to it and still being evidence will also pass the test of having (P*)-minus-*X* applied to it and still being evidence.[4] It should be clear that any experience that was not disqualified as evidence by (P*) will also not be disqualified as evidence by any of the preceding principles. Our basic question, then, now becomes: assuming that (P*) is at least a sufficiently strong principle of experiential evidence – at least a powerful enough criterion to eliminate the mere pretenders among the candidates for experiences that provide evidence – are at least apparent experiences of God evidence that God exists?

Question 6: are all the necessary qualifications to (P) included in (P*)?

It is hard to tell; if additional qualifications are suggested, they can be looked at one by one. A proof that all of the necessary qualifications are included is hard to imagine – what, exactly, would such a proof look like? What one can do is to add all the qualifications one can think of that are defensible, even if this gives one more than is required.

Question 7: what about the claim that God is ineffable, or that religious experience is ineffable?

To say of something X that it is seriously and literally ineffable is to say that (I) *For any concept C, C does not apply to X*. Since the concept of ineffability is a concept, to make the claim that anything is seriously and literally ineffable is to assert something that is necessarily false. So neither God nor religious experience can be literally ineffable. It is possible to revise the thesis and say something like (Ia) *For any concept C save the concept of ineffability, C does not apply to X*. But *X is ineffable* entails *X exists*, so the concept of existence applies to X and thus (Ia) is false. One can then try (Ib) *For any concept C save the concepts of ineffability and existence, C does not apply to X*. But *X exists and X has no properties* is also necessarily false. One can then try (Ic) *For any concept C save the concepts of ineffability, existence, and having properties, C does not apply to X*. If the concept *having properties* applies to X, then so does the concept *having only consistent properties, not being both prime and not prime, being either good or not,* and so on. By the time one has finally reached a non-contradictory thesis, serious and literal ineffability has been left far behind. It is only serious and literal ineffability that would raise a problem for our argument.

Question 8: isn't the sort of criticism just made merely literary, superficial, intellectual cleverness without substance, and so worthless?

No. If one claims that nothing said in English can be true, what one says cannot be true. If one says that all sentences of more than four words are gibberish, if what one said were true, one would have said nothing. If one claims that the state of Washington is a prime number, one asserts that a concrete object is identical to an abstract object, that something spatially located is identical with something that cannot be spatially located, that something that might never have existed is identical to something which (if it exists at all) has logically necessary existence. All of these claims are discernibly intellectually disreputable in the light of what they entail. The same goes for the claim that something is ineffable.

The claim that something is ineffable, while it is (like all claims) made by the use of language, is not about language – it is about God, or religious experience, or whatever is said to be ineffable. Any claim that God, religious experience, or anything else is ineffable, as it turns out, is necessarily false. If one claims instead that God cannot be described *in physical terms* or that we cannot completely describe God,[5] these claims are true. But they have nothing to do with ineffability.

Question 9: can't we always "explain away" any religious experience without any reference to God?[6]

Consider some person Tom and some experience E that Tom has. To give a social science explanation of Tom's having E is to refer to some science phenomenon SSP – some institution, practice, community membership, phobia, desire, economic status, political role or perspective, social standing, unconscious motivations, or whatever – and to claim that Tom's having SSP is the cause of Tom's experience E. Suppose some such explanation is true. Does it disqualify E from being reliable? Suppose E is a conceptual experience – Tom's belief that social science is not simply a superstition that unscrupulous academics have developed in order to bilk money from students and government agencies. Is that conceptual experience of Tom's rendered unreliable, or at least somehow evidentially neutralized, by its being social science explicable? Suppose instead Tom's experience is that of appreciating the love of his family, respecting the environment, hoping studying hard will enable him to pass his social science course, or being shocked at the number of conspiracy theories people accept. If there are social science explanations, as there seem to be, these experiences are going to be explained by them in whatever sense social science explanations do explain anything. But their being social science explicable in no way discredits the evidential value of such experiences, if they have any in the first place. After all, the development of the social sciences themselves, their procedures of inquiry and standards of research and methods of theory testing are all themselves social science explicable. If being social science renders unreliable what is explained, social science itself is a crock.

Two things are necessary for what might be called social science debunking. The first is that the thing – the experience, belief, practice, or whatever – has been shown to be unreliable, false, unsuccessful, or otherwise defective. Then some social science explanation is appealed to in order to explain how anybody could accept an unreliable experience, a false belief, an unsuccessful practice. But all of the critical intellectual work involved in the debunking has already been done by the time social science is appealed to. Of course what typically happens is that opponents of a view simply offer the social science explanation without bothering about offering actual arguments and evidence against what they oppose, and then claim to have debunked the view they dislike, hoping that no one will notice that their own view is also social science explicable and that they haven't actually refuted anything.

Question 10: aren't there crucial differences between, say, sensory experience and religious experience?

There certainly are differences. They are crucial for some matters, and not crucial for others. Let such experiences as *seeing that identity is transitive, recognizing that no contradiction can be true, discerning that arguments of the form (P or Q, and not-Q; therefore P) are valid but arguments of the form (P or Q, and Q; therefore P) are invalid* be *conceptual experiences*. There are crucial differences between sensory experiences and conceptual experiences; that fact casts no aspersions on either sort of experience and gives no reason to suppose that either is evidentially suspect.

Suppose that Tara and Todd sit beside one another at morning worship. Tara and Todd both at least appear to see a stained-glass window and Tara has a religious experience whereas Todd does not. If Tara were to seem to see a window and Todd were not, given that both are sighted and looking in the same place, either Tara is window-hallucinating or Todd is window-blind. But Todd's not having a religious experience does not call into question Tara's having one, nor does it raise doubts about the religious experience that Tara has. This difference sometimes is put by saying that sensory experience is *public* in a way that religious experience is not. Further, if one wants to see the window, simple procedures will allow this, whereas experiences of God are not producible by following a procedure. Sensory experiences typically are *controllable* where religious experiences are not. Further still, if one sees the window, one can predict that if one reaches out, one will touch it; if one raps it gently, one will hear a sound; if one tastes it, one will get a cold, smooth sensation; were one to strike it sharply with a hammer, it would break, and so on. Sensory experiences typically ground *predictions* and are *testable by comparison with experiences from other sensory modalities*. Typically, religious experiences do not ground predictions nor do there seem to be multiple religious modalities.[7]

These differences are crucial only if they underlie this difference: it is possible to cross-check sensory experiences but it is not possible to cross-check religious experiences. Since this is not so, these differences are not crucial relative to the question of whether religious experience provides evidence that God exists.

Question 11: how can one check religious experiences?

In exactly the ways one might expect. First, any experience that satisfies (P*) is evidence by virtue of that fact. There isn't any point in checking, say, one sensory experience against another unless each such experience has some presumptive evidential force. If it looks like my computer screen has turned solid gold, there is no point in checking unless my looking again has some evidential punch all on its own; but then the first look has evidential punch too. If there isn't any conflict among one's sensory experiences, as there very often is not, then comparison will have no negative results regarding their reliability. The same typically holds for at least apparent experiences of God. Second, one appeals to other things one knows or reasonably believes in sorting out what experiential conflicts one finds in sensory experience. If an experience is reliable only if something is false that we have good reason to believe, its reliability is properly questioned. The same holds for religious experiences. Third, if religious experiences occur, as they do, in various cultures, at various times, to people in various sorts of social, economic, political, and psychological situations, that is all to the good – it broadens the base of possible comparison of experience with experience, removes concern that religious experience is somehow tied to one culture or another, and the like.

Being evidence versus providing evidence

If (P*) is true, any experience not disqualified by it *is* evidence. It does not follow that any such experience is taken as evidence by one. Perhaps no one even considers whether the experience is evidence or takes it to be such; perhaps everyone falsely believes that it is not evidence. *Being evidence* is a necessary but not sufficient condition for *providing evidence*. What else is required? One obvious thing is this: in order for an experience to provide evidence to one, one must believe it to be evidence, and it must be evidence. But what else?

An honorable tradition tells us this. It is logically possible that there is a Terrible Tiger Deceiver who produces as-if-there-is-a-tiger experiences only when there is not a tiger; therefore whether there are tigers or not, all of our as-if-there-is-a-tiger experiences are unreliable. If Mary has no reason to think the Terrible Tiger Deceiver hypothesis false, Mary cannot properly claim to have experiential evidence that there is a tiger in the garden. Since Mary will have a hard time refuting that hypothesis, it seems that Mary's experience provides her no tiger-favoring evidence.

Another, and opposite, perspective says that Mary only need (non-culpably) to have no reason to think that the Terrible Tiger hypothesis is true. The notion of non-culpably having no reason is complex, but we need here only a brief characterization. If a matter is of enough importance, and there are considerations relative to whether an experience is reliable, and these considerations are accessible, then one basing a belief on the evidence that his experience seems to provide should see if it does so in the light of those considerations. If he does not do so, his belief is arguably unreasonable; he has not checked out what he should. The various notions involved here – *matter of enough importance, relevant considerations, accessibility* – are hardly lucid. For our purposes, only two things need be noted: (i) since our concern is centrally with whether religious experiences *are* evidence, and so *can provide evidence*, for religious belief, we need not enter deeply into a discussion as to exactly when a particular person is reasonable in accepting them as evidence, and (ii) if an experience does not run afoul of any of the canceling factors mentioned in our principle of experiential evidence, or there isn't any good reason to think that it does, that greatly reduces the plausibility of claiming that one who takes them to provide evidence is unreasonable in virtue of doing so.

Since Mary will have a hard time finding much of substance to say on behalf of the Terrible Tiger hypothesis – there being no reason to think it true – it seems that her as-if-there-is-a-tiger experience is evidentially in order.

It is easy to reason: the former standard seems higher and safer, so perhaps it is the one to accept. This is deceptive. The solid philosophical core of the honorable tradition is the truth of these propositions:

(LP1) It is logically possible that, for *any* person S and sensory experience E that S has, E is unreliable.

It is always logically possible that, say, one seems to see a glass and there is no glass there.

(LP2) It is logically possible that, for *every* person S and sensory experience E that S has, E is unreliable.

While (LP2) does not follow from (LP1), both are true (indeed, necessarily true).

But consider these claims:

(LP3) It is logically possible that, for *any* person S and sensory experience E that S has, E is reliable.

It is always logically possible that, say, one seems to see a glass and there is a glass there.

(LP4) It is logically possible that, for *every* person S and sensory experience E that S has, E is reliable.

While (LP4) does not follow from (LP3), both are true (indeed, necessarily true). So far as logical possibilities go, each of these four is as much a possibility as any other. No amount of reflection on these possibilities will tell us whether Mary's experience is tiger-favoring evidence. So the truth of (LP1) and (LP2) provides no support for its claims about what Mary must know if her experience is evidentially in order.

To the Terrible Tiger Deceiver hypothesis there corresponds the Terrific Tiger Promoter hypothesis that tells us of a being who produces as-if-there-is-a-tiger experiences only when there is a tiger, so that all as-if-there-is-a-tiger experiences are reliable. Mary has just as much reason to accept the Terrific Tiger Promoter hypothesis as she has to embrace the Terrible Tiger Deceiver hypothesis, namely none whatever. In sum, taken as a way of highlighting the truth of (LP1) and (LP2), the Terrible Tiger hypothesis simply reduces to (LP1) and (LP2), which along with (LP3) and (LP4) are both true and of no help in deciding when Mary's experience provides her with evidence. Taken as a literal thesis about what there is, it is competitive to (for example) the Terrific Tiger Promoter hypothesis, and there is no reason at all to think it, or its competitor, true. Further, both are irrelevant to what Mary must know or believe in order for her experience to be evidence.

If what the honorable tradition proposes as decisive is in fact irrelevant, there remains the other suggestion, which is the one pursued here. Whatever the correct principle of experiential evidence is, in order for Mary's experience to provide her with evidence, it must be evidence, she must take it as such, and she must (non-culpably) have no reason to think that what the correct principle of experiential evidence says would render her experience non-evidential actually does so. In terms of the principle of experiential (P*), she must (non-culpably) have no reason to think that her experience is canceled or counterbalanced or compromised or contradicted or confuted or logically consumed or empirically consumed. Then her experience provides evidence that there is a tiger in the garden. Thus:

(P**) If a person S has an experience E which, if reliable, is a matter of being aware of an experience-independently existing item X, and S (non-culpably) has no reason to think that E is canceled or counterbalanced or compromised or contradicted or confuted or logically consumed or empirically consumed, and S takes E as evidence that X exists, then in having E, S has evidence that X exists.

The evidential argument from religious experience

One might argue in this manner: religious experiences are at least apparently experiences of God; the best explanation of the occurrence of these experiences is that God causes them; so it is more reasonable than not to believe that God causes them; if God causes them, then God exists; so it is more reasonable than not to believe that God exists. This is an *inferential* argument from religious experience. It is compatible with the argument offered here that this inferential argument succeeds. But the argument here is not an inferential argument from religious experience.

An *evidential* argument from religious experience has a different shape. It goes like this: experiences occur which at least seem to be experiences of God; if these satisfy a correct principle of experiential evidence, they are reasonably taken to be reliable; they do satisfy a correct principle of experiential evidence; they are hence reasonably taken to be reliable; if they are reasonably taken to be reliable, then they provide evidence that God exists; hence they provide evidence that God exists. The argument presented here is an *evidential* argument from religious experience, not an inferential argument from religious experience.[8]

Here is a basic version of the evidential argument from religious experience:

1 Experiences occur which are a matter of their subjects at least seeming to experience God.
2 If the subjects of experiences of this sort (non-culpably) have no reason to think that these experiences are canceled or counterbalanced or compromised or contradicted or confuted or logically consumed or empirically consumed, then their occurrence gives them evidence that God exists.
3 The subjects of experiences of this sort typically have no reason to think that these experiences are canceled or counterbalanced or compromised or contradicted or confuted or logically consumed or empirically consumed. Hence:
4 These experiences give them evidence that God exists. (from 1–3)

The principle of experiential evidence applied

The first premise is an empirical truth. The argument of course also requires that premise 2 is true. Here is an argument for that premise. Premise 2 says that religious experience is not disqualified by any of the considerations included in:

(P*) If a person S has an experience E which, if reliable, is a matter of being aware of an experience-independently existing item X, and S (non-culpably) has no reason to think that E is canceled or counterbalanced or compromised or contradicted or confuted or logically consumed or empirically consumed, then S's having E is evidence that X exists.

Suppose, then, that Mary has what is an at least apparent experience of God. The first two relevant terms in (P*) are defined, relative to an experience providing evidence, as follows:

1 Mary's experience is *canceled* as evidence if she has reason to think that she would seem to experience God whether or not God exists.
2 Mary's experience is *counterbalanced* as evidence if she has reason to believe that it is just as likely that she seem to experience God if God does not exist as it is if God does exist.

Suppose, then, that Mary has a religious experience in which she at least appears to encounter a majestic, holy, powerful, loving being – an experience similar to those described earlier as central to monotheistic traditions. It is very likely that Mary will have no reason whatever to think that she would seem to experience this being even if it did not exist. This is particularly likely if she has not been taking drugs that might cause such an experience. If (as was argued earlier) social science explanations do not typically "explain away" religious experience, Mary's experiential evidence is not canceled. She is also unlikely to have any reason to think that it is just as likely that she have the experience if the being in question does not exist as it is that she have it if that being does exist. In the light of the truth of the basic idea of our principle of experiential evidence – that one's at least seeming to experience *X* is evidence that *X* exists unless we have some good reason to think otherwise, one claiming that Mary's experience is counterbalanced owes us some particular reason for thinking so. An argument that God does not exist, even if it had some force, would provide evidence one way; this would not entail that Mary's experience did not provide evidence the other way. It is hard to make a good case that Mary's experience, and all others like it, suffer the fate of being counterbalanced.

The remaining relevant terms from (P*) are defined in this manner:

3 Mary's experience is *compromised* as evidence if Mary has reason to believe that it is not logically possible that *God exists* be experientially disconfirmed.
4 Mary's experience is *contradicted* as evidence if Mary has reason to believe that it is logically impossible that God exist, or to believe that the existence of the initial physical conditions we have reason to think obtain plus the laws of nature are incompatible with God existing.
5 Mary's experience is *confuted* as evidence if Mary has reason to believe that there is a being that is not God but produces what appear to be experiences of God.
6 Mary's experience is *logically or in fact consumed* as evidence if it is logically impossible, or inconsistent with the existence of the initial physical conditions we have reason to think obtain, plus the laws of nature, that there be experiences of the same kind as Mary's experience which provide evidence against *God exists*.

Condition 4 will apply only if Mary has reason to think that any concept of God adequate to the monotheistic traditions is logically inconsistent or if there being a world with the physical characteristics of our world is logically inconsistent with God existing. There seem to be no good reasons to think either of these things.

Condition 5 will raise a problem for Mary's experience being reliable only if it is logically or empirically impossible that there be experiential evidence against the claim that God exists. Suppose, then, as is logically possible and consistent with what we know about initial conditions and laws of nature, that these two sorts of experience were to occur.

Sort 1: everyone, upon dying, were to go to a place where everyone was exquisitely happy, civilized, and glad to be alive, or to a place where everyone was devastatingly unhappy, crude and violent, and devoutly wishing for their annihilation; those in the happy habitat are without exception those who have opposed the idea of God, been atheists or at least agnostics, been hostile to monotheism of any kind, and enjoyed nothing so much as committing blasphemy; those in the miserable habitat are without exception those who have, as they thought, worshipped and served God, been sincere monotheists, prayed, sung hymns, and tried to live lives in accord with monotheistic morality; societies for psychical research communicate with both habitats and receive convincing evidence that this is indeed how things are in the after-life; scientists working in the happy habitat discover that there are fundamental laws of nature that will keep those in the happy habitat there, and those in the miserable habitat there, for ever.

Sort 2: most apparent experiences of a non-human intelligence were of a powerful being who enjoys wickedness, encourages rape and murder and torture. Excruciating suffering accompanies all such experiences and those who have them become exceedingly violent and dangerous, and the only remaining religious experiences are those in which the subjects are first given experiences with phenomenologies like those of monotheistic experiences and then followed by phenomenologies in which it is explained that monotheistic experiences were given to religious fools to deceive them.

Were experiences of Sort 1 to occur, we would have experiential evidence against the existence of God, perhaps of the same kind as are Mary's own experience and possibly not. (Given the looseness of the notion of a *kind* of experience, one could dispute the claim that they would be of the same kind. If Sort 1 experiences are not of the same kind as Mary's at least apparent experience of God, it may also be the case that the requirement that they be of the same kind is too unclear to give any force to the idea that relevant possibly confirming and possibly disconfirming experience be of the same kind.) Were experiences of Sort 2 to occur, we would have experiences more clearly of the same kind as Mary's – experiences at least apparently of a powerful, overwhelming non-human being who was, not holy and loving, but wicked and hateful; these experiences would be experiential evidence against *God exists*. It is logically possible, and in fact possible, that such experiences occur. So it is not logically, or in fact, impossible that there be experiential evidence against God's existence, both not of the same sort as Mary's and of that sort. Mary is likely to have no reason to think that such experiences are logically impossible, and she would be mistaken to think that they were. So Conditions 3 and 6 raise no barrier to Mary's experience being evidence. Nor is Mary likely to have any reason to think that her experience is caused by someone or something other than God. So Condition 5 raises no difficulties. For many, probably most, experiences like Mary's, (P*) is indeed satisfied. Hence premise 2 is true.

Evidence only for the experiential subjects?

Suppose one learns that explorers in northern Minnesota have discovered thick-furred black squirrels, hitherto thought to inhabit only the East with their center on the Princeton University campus, that thrive on pine cones and fish as well as nuts and weigh as much as forty pounds. The explorers' squirrel-spotting and squirrel-weighing experiences satisfy (P*), and so are evidence for there being the squirrel giants. They also satisfy (P**) and so provide the explorers with evidence for their conclusions. There is nothing to prevent one from learning from all this that northern Minnesota is blessed with giant black squirrels without oneself making a trip there. Similarly, if religious experiences occur that satisfy (P*), and so are evidence, and satisfy (P**) relative to their subjects who accept the experiences as evidence, they provide evidence for the claim that God exists. There is no reason why one cannot learn of the occurrence of such experiences, consider (P*) and (P**) relative to one's own situation, and conclude that these experience, had by others, provide one with evidence that God exists. Indeed, there would be nothing unreasonable in taking them to be such evidence, even if their subjects did not, provided one had no reason to think that those subjects were anything other than mistaken in whatever reasons they might have for not accepting their own experiences as evidence that God exists.[9]

Questions for reflection

1 Explain what is meant by a "phenomenological description" and why they are useful in the philosophy of religion.
2 What is the difference between an experience providing direct evidence for a claim that something exists and an experience providing indirect evidence for a claim that something exists? Give examples.
3 What is a principle of experiential evidence? What considerations are relevant when one constructs one?
4 State and assess a direct argument from at least apparent experience of God to God's existence.
5 What sorts of experiences can be shown not to be evidence by applying a principle of experiential evidence to them?
6 Can one person's religious experience provide evidence for another person?

Annotated reading

Alston, William (1991) *Perceiving God*, Ithaca, NY: Cornell University Press. Argues that the practice of belief-formation within which Christians claim to experience God is reliable; considers a host of epistemological views.

Broad, C. D. (1953) *Religion, Philosophy, and Psychical Research*, London: Routledge and Kegan Paul. Contains a standard, rather favorable discussion of religious experience by an agnostic.

Davis, Carolyn Franks (1989) *The Evidential Force of Religious Experience*, Oxford: Clarendon Press. Argues that religious experience provides evidence for God's existence. Strength is its detailed discussion of social science theories; supposes that there is only one kind of religious experience.

Hardy, Alister (1979) *The Spiritual Nature of Man: A Study of Contemporary Religious Experience*, Oxford: Clarendon Press. Presents reports of religious experiences by "ordinary people."

Martin, C. B. (1989) *Religious Experience*, Ithaca, NY: Cornell University Press. Argues that religious experience does not provide evidence that God exists.

Rowe, W. L. (1982) "Religious experience and the principle of credulity," *International Journal for the Philosophy of Religion* 13, pp. 85–92. Argues that religious experience does not provide evidence for religious belief.

Yandell, Keith E. (1993) *The Epistemology of Religious Experience*, Cambridge: Cambridge University Press. Full-dress presentation of the argument of this chapter.

PART IV

Arguments concerning nonmonotheistic conceptions

CHAPTER 12
Arguments concerning nonmonotheistic conceptions (1)

12
Arguments concerning nonmonotheistic conceptions (1)

Appeals to argument and appeals to experience

Three views are relevant here: Advaita Vedanta's claim that (i) only Brahman without qualities exists, Jainism's contention that (ii) persons are inherently immortal and independently existing beings, and the typical Buddhist view that (iii) persons are composite entities, made up of other things that are not persons and that comprise the basic constituents of the universe. These are obviously logically incompatible claims; all could be false, but not more than one could be true. If only qualityless Brahman exists, persons and nonperson constituents of persons, which have qualities if they exist, do not exist – if (i) is true, (ii) and (iii) are false. If persons are not composed of nonperson constituents, then they have properties, and so are not identical to Brahman – if (ii) is true, then (i) and (iii) are false. If persons are made up of nonperson constituents, then these constituents have properties and persons are composite and so dependent – if (iii) is true, then (i) and (ii) are false.

These claims are defended and attacked by appeal to argument and appeal to experience. By *appeal to argument* is meant *use of arguments whose premises do not contain reports of nonconceptual experiences people have or are alleged to have had;* by *appeal to experience* is meant *use of arguments that do contain reports of nonconceptual experiences people have, or are alleged to have had, or simple appeal to those reports.* A *conceptual* experience is one in which, without appeal to sensory or introspective experience, one comes to see the meaning, and perhaps the truth value, of some proposition; seeing that nothing can have incompatible properties, noticing that it cannot be known that no one knows anything, seeing if there are tables then there are physical objects, are examples of conceptual experiences. Highly undervalued, and often ignored, such experiences *are* experiences without whose possession ordinary life, let alone philosophy, would be impossible. Yet empiricists have officially treated them as trivial. The present chapter will be concerned with appeal to argument; the next chapter will deal with appeal to experience.

Advaita Vedanta

It looks as if Advaita wants to hold all of a set of logically inconsistent theses. In particular, it begins with the claim that something exists but altogether lacks properties, and that something that altogether lacks properties can be identical to a variety of things that have properties and are distinct from one another. The dodge that *nirguna* Brahman is ineffable has its own enormous problems, and in any case if we have no idea what properties Brahman has, and can form no concept of them, how could we possibly know that Brahman is qualityless or with what Brahman was or was not identical?

Ramanuja,[1] for example, held that it was contradictory to hold that *There is an X such that for any property P, X lacks P.* (Or, if existence itself is a property, *There is an X such that for any property P other than existence, X lacks P.*) Thus to claim that Brahman, or anything else, is qualityless is to claim that it exists and deny an entailment of that very claim. Hence Advaita Vedanta metaphysics is not even possibly true. Ramanuja's critique seems decisive, and there is no point in lingering over logical impossibilities.

Jainism and Buddhism on persons

The philosophical context: three exclusive but non-exhaustive alternatives[2]

Three alternatives regarding the nature of mind and body are idealism, materialism, and dualism. Idealism holds that *having a mental property* is kind-defining relative to the only kind of substances there are; materialism gives that status to *having a physical property*; dualism holds that *having a mental property* and *having a physical property* are kind-defining relative to two distinct kinds of substances.[3] Thus each of these views is *substantival* and *essentialist*: each holds that there are substances that belong to a kind and hence have essences. Among mind–body dualists, some suppose minds or souls to exist without depending on anything else whatever, and so as inherently immortal; others take souls to exist dependent upon God, and as immortal only in the sense that God alone could annihilate them by simply ceasing to cause them to exist. Jainism embraces the former, more radical, dualism on which it is impossible that a soul cease to exist; Christianity, insofar as it accepts dualism, holds to the less radical version.

Property dualism versus substance dualism

Jain dualism is one version of mind–body dualism. Insofar as religious traditions are dualistic concerning mind and body, they tend to a dualism of substances, not merely a dualism of properties. Property dualism concerning mental and physical properties holds that *being a mental property* defines one kind of property and *being a physical property* defines another kind of property, and it is logically impossible that any property belong to both kinds. A property Q is a mental property if and only if *X has Q* entails *X is self-conscious*. Not every non-mental property is a physical property; *being prime* is not a physical property, nor is *having only consistent properties*. Without pretense of precision, let us refer to such properties as "abstract properties" and then suggest that property Q* is a physical property, if and only if Q* is neither mental nor abstract. There are more concrete definitions of *being a physical property*; for example, one can say that Q* is a physical property if and only if *X has Q** entails *X is spatially located* or *X is a property referred to by some predicative term used in some contemporary theory in natural science or some similar successor*. But the more concrete examples raise problems; it is not clear that there is any univocal sense in which both chairs and elementary particles are "spatially located" and "similar" in "similar successor" means "physicalistic" (or something less clear).[4]

Philosophical timidity will, in the current academic climate, suggest to even the most convinced property dualist, of which there are many, that they should not go further and embrace substance dualism. A substance dualist concerning mind and body holds that not only are *being mental* and *being physical* definitive of different kinds of properties, but each is a kind-defining property relative to a sort of substance – *being mental* constitutes one kind or essence and *being physical* constitutes another kind or essence, it being logically impossible that any one substance belong to both kinds. Something is a substance if and only if it has properties, is not itself merely a bundle of properties, and (if it is temporal) can remain the same over time and through change of non-essential properties. For a substance dualist, persons are mental substances. Typically, human beings are persons embodied in genetically *homo sapiens* bodies.

Substance dualism, and its associated view of persons, has a highly distinguished history. Plato, Augustine, Anselm, Descartes, Samuel Clarke, and Thomas Reid all held it. It also has some distinguished contemporary advocates.[5] Its popularity currently is at low tide, this arguably (if a pun be allowed) being more a matter of fashion than of substance.

Identity

Symmetry and transitivity of identity

The proposition *A is identical to B* entails the proposition *B is identical to A*. The proposition *A is identical to B and B is identical to C* entails the proposition *A is identical to C*. These two simple facts about identity are expressed by logicians by saying that identity is *reflexive* and *transitive*. Whether A, B, and C are wombats, kumquats, tuxedos, numbers, angels, or galaxies, identity among them is reflexive and transitory. To deny this is to deny that there is any such thing as identity as applied to them, which is the same as denying that there are any such things.

Numerical versus qualitative identity

In considering competing views of persons, and of personal identity, it is crucial to keep firmly in mind the distinction between numerical identity and the quite different matter of qualitative (so-called) identity or resemblance. Suppose Tim has a penny in each hand, each minted in Philadelphia in 1998, both bright and unscratched. He names the one in his left hand "Cop" and the one in his right hand "Per." Cupping his hands together, he shakes the pennies and then again grasps one in one hand and one in the other. Neither he nor we were able to keep track of either penny during the shaking. In these simple circumstances, we know that Cop is still in Tim's left hand or else Cop is now in Tim's right hand, and that either Per is still in Tim's right hand or else Per is now in Tim's left hand. But we do not know which.

This simple example illustrates various important concepts. Both Cop and Per retain numerical identity over time. Since we do not know which penny Cop is, Cop's having numerical identity over time is a fact about it independent of our knowledge of it. Cop and Per are qualitatively identical; that is why we cannot, at the end of the shaking, tell which penny is which. These basic notions can be formally characterized as follows:

Full Qualitative Identity: X is fully qualitatively identical to Y if and only if for any quality Q, X has Q if and only if Y has Q (here "Q" ranges over spatial and temporal qualities as well as other qualities).

Nearly Full Qualitative Identity: X is nearly fully qualitatively identical to Y if and only if for any quality Q, if Q is not a spatial or a temporal quality, X has Q if and only if Y has Q (here "Q" does not range over temporal or spatial qualities).

The pennies Cop and Per are not fully qualitatively identical; they occupy different places. But they are nearly fully qualitatively identical, hence our inability to tell one from the other after they are shaken.[6]

Any substance is self-identical, identical to itself at each moment of its existence; identity in this sense is *numerical* identity. If substance X exists at time T1 and continues to exist at the next moment T2, then the X that exists at T2 is identical to the X that existed at T1; here, too, identity is numerical identity.

Numerical identity, strictly speaking, is identity; qualitative identity is a matter, not of identity, but of resemblance. For a dualist, personal identity is numerical identity of a person – a self-conscious substance: identity to itself at a time, and to its continuingly existing self over each of various times.[7]

Temporal endurance of a simple substance is sufficient for its continuing numerical identity. For a simple substance X to endure from T through T* is for it to be the case that at each time from T through T*, and for any property Q such that *Q is essential to X*, X has Q at each moment from T through T*. The *closest thing to*[8] temporal endurance of a simple substance X from T through T* is for a certain sort of series of things to exist – a series that contains X at T (and then X ceases to exist), and at each moment from T1 through T* one or another substance Y that is nearly fully qualitatively identical to X at T exists. Such a series will exist if either (i) at each moment from T through T*, a different simple substance exists that is nearly fully qualitatively identical to each other in the series, or (ii) at each moment after T through T*, there is one simple substance that is nearly fully qualitatively identical to X, or (iii) something between (i) and (ii).[9] But that (i) be satisfied is not sufficient for there being a single simple substance from T through T*. The same holds for (ii) and (iii). If the closest thing to temporal endurance of a simple substance enduring from T through T* is not sufficient for there being a single substance that exists from T through T*, then those conditions being satisfied is not the same as there being a simple substance that endures from T through T*.

Personal identity

General criteria for theories of personal identity

A theory of personal identity should consist of elements, none of which is itself self-contradictory, which are also logically consistent with one another, each of which coheres with the others in such a way as to yield a plausible account of what it is to be a person, which account is compatible with and explanatory of the things we know about persons.

An exhaustive and exclusive disjunction

These are two basic sorts of views held regarding persons: persons are simple or complex. If they are simple, they are substances.[10] If they are complex, they are composed of substances or qualities or states or whatever. If they are substances, they are either mental or physical. If they are not substances, they are complex and composed of mental and/or physical qualities or states or whatever. It is logically impossible that both views be true. There are various substantival views about persons other than the Jain view (for example, that persons are material substances, that persons are mental substances whose essence differs from that proposed by Jainism). There are other non-substantival views about persons other than the Theravada view (for example, that rather than states or qualities, it is events, processes, or the like that make up persons).[11] But the claims *Persons are simple substances*, essential to Jainism, and *Persons are not simple substances*, essential to Buddhism, are exhaustive as well as exclusive. Thus one or the other is true, and the remaining view is false. Can we tell which is true?

Bundle theory

A non-substantival view of persons

A *complexity account of persons* holds that (i) *a person may be made of elements that are not themselves persons*, (ii) *these elements, whatever they are, exist only momentarily*, and (iii) *what makes a bundle of elements that comprises a person at one time (part of) the same person as another bundle at a later time is some relation R that holds between the bundles*. There is a constraint on what relation R can be. *It cannot be numerical identity over time*, since R is supposed to *explain* – to state the sufficient conditions for – numerical identity of persons over time.

The idea, then, is that a *person at a time* is a bundle *B1* of momentary apersonal elements, that *a person at another time* is another bundle *B2* of momentary elements. No element in one bundle can be identical to an element in another bundle. *Over time, a person is a series of bundles*. Our concern here is with the *structure* of this type of view, not with its content. There are different accounts of what the alleged elements are that make up a person at a time; they may be viewed as physical, as mental, or as some of each. There are different notions of what relation R allegedly relates bundles over time into one person: perfect or imperfect resemblance, temporal continuity, memory, causality, a combination of these, and so on. If the critique offered here is correct, then questions of content and relationship become moot; no such view can succeed if the critique is correct. One thing the Complexity View cannot allow is that a person is a substance – a simple thing that endures over time. It is precisely that substantival view (whether the substance be viewed as mental or as physical) that the Complexity View is intended to supersede. We will consider arguments for the view that persons are bundles in the next chapter in connection will appeals to experience; these have been historically the most influential arguments for the view. In this chapter, we will consider arguments against the view.

Jainism, Buddhism, and the justice requirement

One can put the Buddhist view this way. There are persons(1) and persons(2):

1 Tom is a person(1) if and only if Tom is a one-or-more-membered bundle of conscious states at time T and Tom exists at no time other than T.
2 Tom* is a person(2) if and only if Tom* is a more-than-one-membered series of persons(1).

Let the notion of a *constituent* be defined as follows: A is a constituent of B if and only if (i) B is composite or has parts, and (ii) A is a part of B. Given the Buddhist account of person(2), a person(2) can have a constituent. Further, since even momentary bundles can be complex, persons(1) can have constituents.[12] On the Jain account of persons, persons can have no constituents. At a time, on the Buddhist account, a person simply is a bundle of conscious states. This is all there is to any person – say, Amy – at a given time. For Amy to perform some action at time T is for the bundle – the person(1) – that is Amy at time T to act. The karmic effects of Amy's action at T do not all occur at T; it is false that the effects that Buddhist doctrine regards as karmic all occur then and if they did all occur at T then, contrary to Buddhist doctrine, karmic effects would not lead to reincarnation. Karmic credit or debit would be instantaneously paid in or out. After T, there is no such person(1) that is identical to Amy-at-T. Hence no effects shall accrue to that person(1). The Buddhist idea is that the justice requirement be met as follows: a person(1) other than Amy-at-T will receive the relevant karmic effects, and this person(1) must be a part of the person(2) to which Amy-at-T belongs. On a Jain account, the justice requirement is fulfilled only if the same self-conscious substance as performed the deed receives the consequences.

An external critique of the view that persons are bundles[13]

There are external criticisms of Buddhist-type views – criticisms that appeal to claims that are not part of a Buddhist-type account of persons or otherwise elements in a Buddhist perspective. There is nothing intrinsically philosophically problematic in the notion of such a critique or in various of its instances. If I forward the hypothesis that Mahavira was a Buddhist, I am not thereby licensed to dismiss appeals to the contrary historical evidence by noting that such evidence is not part of *my* perspective; in fact, the evidence should be. There is no more reason to despise external philosophical criticism than to despise external historical criticism. If I maintain that *A rule of inference is valid if and only if everyone who is asked about it accepts it*, thereby proposing to turn logic into a sort of sociology, I cannot reply to the objection that I assume a mutual implication not analyzable in my own terms without evacuating my claim of its intended content by saying something like *Since I don't agree, that doesn't refute me*. It does, whether I accept it or not. Consider, then, this argument:

1 I exist now.
2 If I exist now, it is logically possible that I exist now. (If a proposition P is true, then of course it is possible that it is true.)
3 It is logically possible that I exist now. (from 1 and 2)
4 If it is logically possible that I exist now, it is logically possible that I exist a moment from now.
5 It is logically possible that I exist a moment from now. (from 3 and 4)
6 If it is logically possible that I exist a moment from now, it is not logically possible that the existence a moment from now of something just like me would prevent me from existing a moment from now.

7 It is not logically possible that the existence a moment from now of something just like me would prevent me from existing a moment from now. (from 5 and 6)
8 If a Buddhist-type view of persons is true, then the existence a moment from now of something just like me would prevent me from existing a moment from now.[14]
9 If the existence a moment from now of something just like me would prevent me from existing a moment from now, then it is logically possible that the existence a moment from now of something just like me would prevent me from existing a moment from now. (See comment after 2.)
10 If a Buddhist-type view of persons is true, then it is logically possible that the existence a moment from now of something just like me would prevent me from existing a moment from now. (from 8 and 9)
11 A Buddhist-type view of persons is not true. (from 7 and 10)

The truth of the first premise, I take it, is not in question.[15] The second premise invokes the unexceptionable principle *If X is actual, then X is possible*. The fourth premise notes that if *my existing at all* is logically possible, and *my existing at time T1* is logically possible, there is nothing logically impossible about *my existing at T2*. Given the truth of premise 4, for any time T* you like, it is logically possible that I exist at T* and that there is something else just like me[16] that also exists at T* that is neither identical to me at T* nor identical to what was me at T*-minus-one; this is what premise 6 says. The remainder of the premises either simply state what is true about a Buddhist-type view or are entailed by premises already noted. This seems a powerful, indeed successful, external critique.

An internal critique of the view that persons are bundles

Internal critiques of the sort relevant here come in two brands: an argument to the effect that the Buddhist-type account is internally inconsistent, or an argument to the effect that a Buddhist-type account is inconsistent with other Buddhist claims. Jain and Buddhist doctrines now diverge on two further points. In order to express them precisely, let us adopt a bit of technical terminology, but in order to express them clearly, let it be only a tiny bit. The Jain view of persons, we have noted, entails that for any person Lucy, all of Lucy exists at each moment at which Lucy exists. Lucy contains no elements; she is incomposite; she enjoys numerical identity over time. She is, then, a *noncomposite endurer*. On the

Buddhist view, there are no noncomposite endurers. Instead, there are *noncomposite nonendurers*. These are single momentary constituents. There are *composite nonendurers*. These are bundles of noncomposite nonendurers. There are *composite endurers*. These are successions of composite nonendurers.

Certain claims regarding recompense[17] and memory naturally arise from a Jain account of persons. The claims are these:

(J1*) *If Lucy at T1 receives recompense for something A done by a person at time T, then Lucy at T1 is a noncomposite endurer who is numerically identical to the person (the noncomposite endurer) who did A at T.*

(J2*) *If Lucy at time T1 remembers performing action A at time T, then Lucy is a noncomposite endurer who is numerically identical at T and T1.*

It is necessarily true that no Buddhist person/recompense pair ever satisfy (J1*) and that no Buddhist person/memory pair ever satisfy (J2*).[18]

The Buddhist replacements for (J1*) and (J2*) will be something along the lines of:

(B1*) *If Lucy at T1 receives recompense for something A done by a person at time T, then Lucy at T1 is a composite nonendurer who is a member of (an element of or a constituent in) a composite endurer in which the composite nonendurer that did A at T is an earlier member.*[19]

(B2*) *If Lucy at time T1 remembers performing action A at time T, then Lucy at T1 is a composite nonendurer who is a member of (an element of or a constituent in) a composite endurer in which the composite nonendurer that did A at T is an earlier member.*

If you like, (the right sort of) composite nonendurer is a Buddhist person(1) and (the right sort) of composite endurer is a Buddhist person(2). Recompense and memory require that the recompense and the rememberer be persons(1) within the same person(2).

The doctrines cited in (J1*) and (J2*) require that there be noncomposite endurers; that among the denizens of the actual world such things are to be found. Consider these replacements for (J1*) and (J2*):

(B1*a) *If Lucy at T1 receives recompense for something A done by a person at time T, then Lucy at T1 is a composite nonendurer who is identical to a composite nonendurer which did A at T.*[20]

(B2*a) *If Lucy at time T1 remembers performing action A at time T, then Lucy at T1 is a composite nonendurer who is identical to the composite endurer that did A at T.*

Of course, it is logically impossible that anyone ever satisfy the conditions laid down in (B1*a) or (B2*a). Thus there is strong pressure for a Buddhist to avoid them. Unless there are composite endurers who are things in addition to composite nonendurers (and who are persons), there will be no such thing as reincarnation, recompense, or memories. But it seems that, on the Buddhist-type account, there cannot be any such thing as composite endurers save in the insipid sense in which "composite endurers" refers to one composite nonendurer and then to another and then to another, which of course is *not* a sense of *there being composite endurers in addition to there being composite nonendurers.*

Consistency[21]

While there are various problems in the neighborhood,[22] one looms over the rest. On the Buddhist-type account of persons, all there is to a composite endurer at time T is its single composite nonendurer constituent that exists only at T. All there is to a composite endurer at time T1 is its single composite nonendurer constituent that exists only at T1. Reference to a composite endurer that exists at both T and T1 is only verbally distinct from reference to a composite nonendurer at T and another composite nonendurer at T1; terms multiply, but entities do not increase.

Consider this argument:[23]

1 If *W* is *all* that *X* is at time T, then *X* is identical to *W* at time T.
2 For every composite endurer *E* that exists at time T, there is a composite nonendurer *E** that exists at time T such that *E** is all there is of *E* at T.
3 For every composite endurer *E* that exists at time T, there is a composite nonendurer *E** that exists at time T such that *E** is identical to *E* (from 1 and 2).
4 If composite nonendurer *E** is identical to *E*, then *E* cannot outlast *E**.
5 For every composite endurer *E* that exists at time T, *E* does not exist other than at T.
6 It is logically impossible that anything that does not exist other than at time T be a composite *endurer*.
7 It is logically impossible that there be composite *endurers*.

Put it this way: let *E1* and *E2* be composite nonendurers that exist, respectively, at T1 and T2. Let *E* be a proposed composite endurer whose only elements are *E1* and *E2*. Then:

1* At T1, *E1* is all there is of *E*.
2* At T2, *E2* is all there is of *E*.
3* If 1 is true, then *E1* is identical to *E*.
4* If 2 is true, then *E2* is identical to *E*.
5 *E1* is identical to *E*. (from 1 and 3)
6 *E2* is identical to *E*. (from 2 and 4)
7 *E1* is not identical to *E2*.[24]

But the set of propositions (5, 6, 7) is inconsistent. Thus a succession of bundles is not anything more than the bundles in the succession. No doctrine not applicable to the latter can be true of the former.[25] There *cannot be* any composite endurers if these are construed as items that inhabit the world *in addition to* composite nonendurers. No composite nonendurer can be justly recompensed for, or remember performing, the deeds of an earlier composite nonendurer. So no recompensation or remembering can occur. So there is no reincarnation-and-karma cycle and no Buddha remembers past lives. The strategy of saying "What recompense really is . . ." or "What memory really is . . ." and filling it in a manner compatible with there only being composite nonendurers is like answering, when one has shown you to have offered an invalid argument of the form *If A then B; B; therefore A*, that what you mean by "valid argument" is any argument that you offer. Any victory so purchased is entirely empty. If that is all there is to recompense or memory, there is no recompense or memory for there to be anything to.

Copiers and annihilators

Another argument against complexity accounts of persons

Scenario one

The present critique involves four very simple thought experiments. The participants in these experiments are Edward, a very ordinary accountant, Tedward (who may or may not be identical to Edward), and Nedward (who may or not be identical to Edward or Tedward).

These experiments also involve a voting-booth-sized machine – the Digitator – that comes in four varieties, one for each scenario. Our first scenario has Edward entering into a Digitator 101. The Digitator 101 annihilates the person who enters it and produces an exact copy; Edward enters at time T1 and the Digitator 101 works instantly, annihilating what entered it and producing a copy. Let relation R be whatever relation the Complexity Account says makes successive bundles so related to be parts of the same person. The copy bears that relation R to the person who was annihilated. The popular terms for a Digitator 101 is "Copy-Annihilator" (see Figure 1) but the firm's advertising department insists on using the more formal name. What the Digitator 101 makes as it annihilates Edward we will call "Tedward" and the question that arises is: Is Tedward identical to Edward? Since Tedward bears relation R to Edward, the answer that a Complexity Account of Persons must give is affirmative; Tedward is identical to Edward.

Scenario two

Our second scenario has Edward entering a Digitator 101X. Sales of the 101 model have been slow; people have been uncommonly shy about using the ones that have been sold. The 101X model is popularly simply called the Copier model (see Figure 2). When Edward enters it, it does not annihilate Edward. Instead, it produces an exact copy of Edward, whom we will also call Tedward. Thus Edward enters at time T1, and at time T2 the machine has produced a being who bears to the Edward that entered the machine relation R, as does of course Edward at T2. Here, two questions arise: Is Edward at T2 identical to Edward at T1? Is Tedward identical to Edward? Since both Edward at T2 and Tedward bear relation R to Edward at T1, a Complexity Account of Persons must answer both questions in the affirmative. Edward at T2 is identical to Edward at T1. Tedward is identical to Edward. This, of course, raises a problem. Edward at T2 is not identical

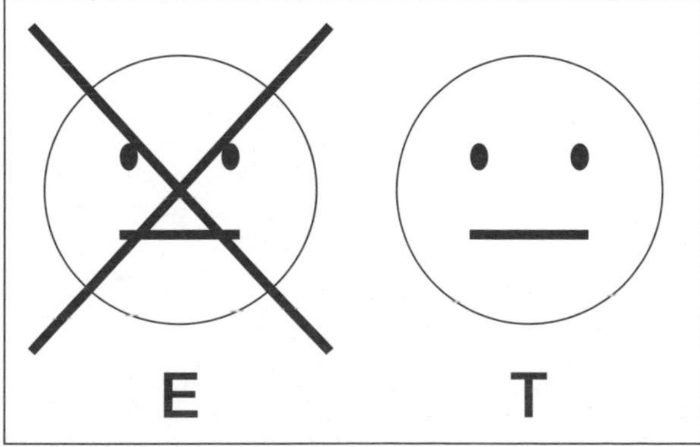

Figure 1 Digitator 101

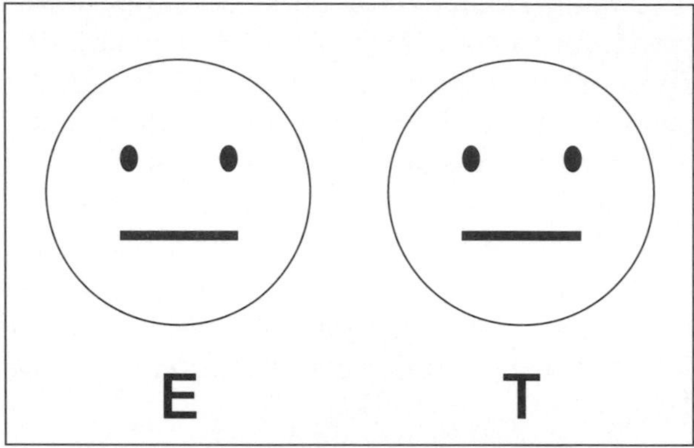

Figure 2 Digitator 101X

to Tedward. So either Edward at T2 is not identical to Edward at T1 or Tedward is not identical to Edward. Identity is reflexive and transitory. The fact, then, is that *bearing relation R to one another* cannot be sufficient to make two items the same person. For any Complexity Account of Persons, R is sufficient. Hence all of the Complexity Accounts of Persons are false.

Scenario three

Our third scenario has Edward entering a Digitator 201 (see Figure 3). This machine is popularly called the Double Copier-Annihilator. Its improvement over the 101 version is that it annihilates the person who enters it but produces two copies, whom we will call Tedward and Nedward. Each copy, of course, bears relation R to Edward. Two questions arise. Is Tedward identical to Edward? Is Nedward identical to Edward?

Figure 3 Digitator 201

Since each bears relation R to Edward, any Complexity Account of Persons must answer affirmatively. Tedward is identical to Edward. Nedward is identical to Edward. But Tedward and Nedward are not identical to one another. Identity is reflexive and transitive. So they cannot both be identical to Edward, and any view that says they are is false because it says that.

Scenario four

Our final scenario has Edward entering a Digitator 201X, popularly called a Double Copier (see Figure 4). When Edward enters it at time T1, the machine at time T2 produces two copies of Edward – Tedward and Nedward – without annihilating Edward. But now Edward at T2, and Tedward, and Nedward all bear R to Edward at T1. So on any Complexity Account of Persons, all are identical to Edward at T1; each is the same person at T2 that Edward was at T1. But identity is reflexive and transitive. So Edward at T2, Tedward, and Nedward cannot be identical to one another. But then not more than one of them can be identical to – be the same person as – Edward at T1. So *bearing R to one another* cannot be sufficient for *being the same person over time.*

Reflections on the scenarios: the different results problem

It is striking that, then, on a Complexity View, one gets quite different results in scenario two from what one gets in scenario one, and again in scenario four from what one gets in scenario three. Given the Complexity View, in scenario one one would expect that Tedward would be Edward; in scenario two, one would not – that honor would be expected to go to the later Edward. In scenario four, one would also expect the later Edward to be

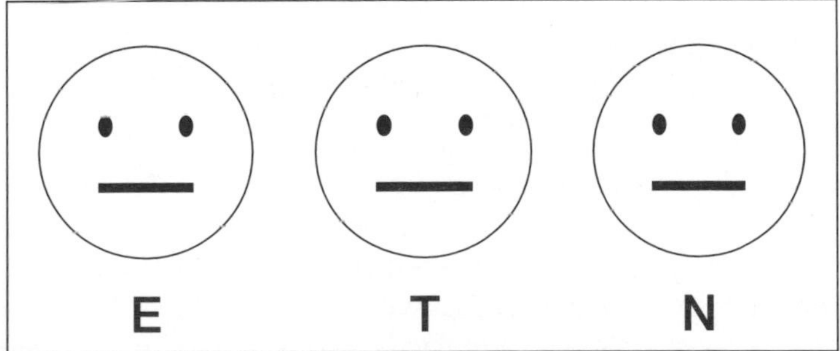

Figure 4 Digitator 201X

identical to the earlier, whereas in scenario three there is no later Edward for the honor to go to (or else there are too many).

The *different results problem* has to do with the entailments of the Complexity View being different from what, intuitively, we would expect. What matters is not this fact, but what lies behind it. We now turn to that.

Reflections on the scenarios: the problem concerning logical impossibility

In scenarios one and two, the Complexity View requires that Tedward be identical to Edward, and in the second that both Tedward and the later Edward are identical to the earlier. But it is logically impossible that the earlier Edward be identical both to the later Edward and to Tedward. So the Complexity View requires that something contradictory be true. No contradiction can be true. So the Complexity View is false. While it is convenient to put the second scenario in terms of "(the later) Edward and Tedward" this is *only* a convenience. The point is that whichever of the beings that walk out of Double Copier we call "Edward" (or whatever we call them), there are *two* of them. Hence they are not identical to one another. On the Complexity View, both should be the same person as the Edward who stepped into the Double Copier. That is logically impossible. So the Complexity View is false. It should be remembered here, and throughout the discussion, that it is metaphysical, not epistemological, identity conditions that are relevant here.

Similarly, the Complexity View requires that in scenario three Edward is identical with both Tedward and Nedward, which is logically impossible since Tedward and Nedward are distinct. Again, while it is a convenience to give names to the beings who emerge from the Double Copier-Annihilator, whatever name one uses (and whether one uses any names or not), the Complexity View entails that both the beings who emerge are identical to the Edward who entered, and they cannot be. Similar comments hold regarding scenario four with the Double Copier; the Edward who entered the machine, given the Complexity View, is identical with three distinct persons, whatever they are (or are not) called. Again, what entails the logical possibility of the logically impossible is false.[26]

Reflections on the scenarios: the perfect resemblance mistake

There is another way of looking at the difficulty. What lies behind these different results is this: given a Complexity View, the sheer fact that there would exist at a given time a person perfectly resembling me prevents me from existing at that time. But while there are lots of things on which my continuing to exist a moment from now depends, one of those things is not whether a moment from now there could or will be someone perfectly resembling me. I can exist a moment from now, and whether I do so or not is not dependent on whether a twin pops up. But on a Complexity View, I exist a moment from now only if no twin does pop up. That contention is false. Whatever entails a false contention is itself false. Hence the Complexity View is false. (Both twins would have to bear R to me.)

The argument here is this: the Complexity View entails that, for any person S at time T, S will exist at time T-plus-1 only if, at time T-plus-1, there are not two persons who (spatio-temporal properties aside) are perfectly resembling. My existing a moment from now is compatible with God creating my perfectly resembling twin a moment from now while not annihilating me. If my existing a moment from now is compatible with God creating my perfectly resembling twin a moment from now while not annihilating me, then it is false I will exist a moment from now only if there does not then also exist another person who perfectly resembles me. Hence, it is false that I will exist a moment from now only if there does not then also exist another person who perfectly resembles me. If it is false that I will exist a moment from now only if there does not then also exist another person who perfectly resembles me then the Complexity View is false. So the Complexity View is false. Indeed, since it entails things that are not even possibly true, it is not even possibly true; it is necessarily false.

The relevance of all this to Jainism and Buddhism

The relevance of these arguments to the dispute between Jainism and Buddhism is this: Theravada Buddhism holds a Complexity View of persons. The Jain tradition holds a Substantival View. The Complexity View is false. Hence the Theravada view is false. If there is only the Substantival View and the Complexity View, then the Substantival View is true.[27] It does not follow that it is true in the Jain version thereof.[28] But at the very least, the Jain view of what a person is will be closer to right than the Theravada Buddhist view.

On there being a fact of the matter

There is a reply to the criticisms that goes as follows: suppose that there is a person – Sam, let's say – at time T. Then at time T1 there come to be two persons – Sam1 and Sam2 – each of whom bears R (whatever relation the complexity theory takes to constitute *being the same person*) to Sam.

Then we can say what we like – that Sam 1 is identical to Sam, that Sam2 is identical to Sam, that Sam has ceased to exist and been replaced by Sam1 and Sam2, that Sam1 is identical to Sam on even numbered days and Sam2 is identical to Sam on odd numbered days, or whatever. The claim is that there would be no fact of the matter about whether Sam continues to exist if Sam is followed by Sam1 and Sam2. What we say, if anything, in answer to *Is either Sam1 or Sam2 identical to Sam?* is conventional, arbitrary or at most pragmatic; there is no true answer.

The reply faces two problems. One is that there are contradictory answers to the question, and the Complexity View – as we have seen – entails them. What entails a contradiction is necessarily false. This critique is not something that can be successfully responded to by saying, "Well, I accept the Complexity View but when it comes to what it entails I just dismiss those entailments that are false." The question is not about what someone who holds the Complexity View feels comfortable about doing, but about whether the theory is true, and if it entails falsehoods, it isn't true.

The other problem becomes clear when one examines the denial that there would be a fact of the matter if Sam1 and Sam2 bear R (the alleged person-constituting relation) to Sam. The fact is that, on the Complexity View, there is no fact of the matter whether Sam1 and Sam2 come along or not.

One way of seeing this is by going back to, and reflecting on, the argument that has among its premises *If I exist now, then it is logically possible that I exist a moment from now*. This argument contends that (i) plainly, there is a fact of the matter about whether I exist now or not, and (ii) if (i) is true then for any time there is a fact of the matter about whether or not I exist then.

But here is another way of seeing the problem. Consider Sam and the way things ordinarily go – Sam exists at time T and Sam exists at time T1 and no Sam1 and Sam2 crop up. If Sam-at-T is identical to – is the same person as – Sam-at-T1, then necessarily Sam-at-T is identical to – is the same person as – Sam-at-T1. Metaphysical identity – e.g., the numerical identity of anything – is necessary if it obtains at all.[29]

The argument for this can be put quite simply. Consider two possible worlds W1 and W2. Deny that identity is necessary. Suppose that A, B, and C all exist in possible worlds W1 and W2. Suppose also, as is possible if identity is contingent rather than necessary, that in W1, A is identical to B, and C is distinct from A and B. Suppose also, as is possible if identity is contingent rather than necessary, that in W2 A is identical to C, and B is distinct from A and C. If identity is contingent rather than necessary, W1 and W2 are possible as described. Now A-in-W1 is identical to A-in-W2, B-in-W1 is identical to B-in-W2, and C-in-W1 is identical to C-in-W2.

But A-in-W1 W1 is distinct from C-in-W1 and A-in-W2 is identical to C-in-W2; since C-in-W1 is identical to C-in-W2, it follows that A-in-W2 is identical to C-in-W1. Since A-in-W1 is identical to A-in-W2, it follows that "both" A-in-W1 and A-in-W2 are, and also are not, identical to "both" C-in-W1 and C-in-W2.

Now the second reply can be put simply. The Complexity View entails that Personal Identity View over time is logically contingent, and that view is self-contradictory. Thus on a Complexity View, there is no such thing as personal identity – were personal identity what a Complexity View says it is, there would be no such things. There would be a fact of the matter about Sam-at-T and Sam-at-T1 being the same person; he would not be, because there would be no such thing as being the same person over time.

Put differently, on the Complexity View, with or without Sam1-and-Sam2-type scenarios, there aren't any persons – talk of persons is "conventional" is a sense in which talking about persons is a way of speaking to which nothing that is a person corresponds. This, of course, is not an account of what persons are. It is a denial that there are any persons.

Substance theory

Jain dualism

There is a variety of arguments for mind–body dualism of the sort Jainism embraces. Some of them are clear failures. Epistemological arguments for mind–body dualism infer from something about *the way in which we know* minds and bodies to the conclusion that the mind is distinct from the body. Let X = *my mind's existing* or *that my mind exists*, as grammatical structure dictates; let Y = *my body's existing* or *that my body exists*, as grammatical structure dictates.

Argument 1: I can think of X without thinking of Y; *If I can think of X without thinking of Y, then not(X =* Y), so: not(X = Y).

Argument 2: I cannot be mistaken with respect to X but I can be mistaken with respect to Y; *If I cannot be mistaken with respect to X but I can be mistaken with respect to Y, then not(X =* Y), so: not(X = Y).

Argument 3: I cannot doubt X but I can doubt Y; *If I cannot doubt X but I can doubt Y then not(X =* Y), so: not(X = Y).

Argument 4: I can be directly aware of X but I cannot be directly aware of Y; *If I can be directly aware of X but I cannot be directly aware of Y then not(X =* Y), so: not(X = Y).

The problem with this sort of argument is that, in each case, the italicized middle premise is false. "Can" here means "it is logically possible that." Consider these objections:

Reply To Argument 1: I can (It is logically possible that I) think of the cat Socks without thinking of the Clintons' favorite cat, because it is logically possible that Socks is not the Clintons' favorite cat. But it does not follow from this that Socks is not the Clintons' favorite cat.
Reply To Argument 2: I cannot be mistaken if I think that two is greater than one, and I can be mistaken if I think that your favorite number is greater than one, but it does not follow that your favorite number is not two.
Reply To Argument 3: I cannot doubt that I exist but I can doubt that I am the one who is supposed to take out the garbage, but it does not follow that I am not the one who is supposed to take out the garbage.
Reply To Argument 4: I can be directly aware of my being in pain and I cannot be directly aware of my feeling worse than ever before, but it does not follow that my being in pain is not my feeling worse than ever before.

Epistemological arguments such as these fail to prove their conclusions. The question remains as to whether other sorts of arguments are better.

Arguments for Jain dualism

Philosophers James W. Cornman and Keith Lehrer remark that

> mind–body dualism seems to be essential to most religions. The body will disintegrate after death, but according to the doctrines of many religions, the soul, the immaterial part of us which is quite distinct and different from the body, will live on eternally . . . The primary philosophical problem is to find out whether dualistic interactionism or some other position is the most plausible view about the nature of a person.[30]

This remark fits at least Jainism. Consider this argument:

1 It is logically possible that Manindra is self-conscious and Manindra has no bodily states.
2 If it is logically possible that Manindra is self-conscious and Manindra

has no bodily states then Manindra's being self-conscious is not identical to Manindra's having bodily states. So:

3 Manindra's being self-conscious is not identical to Manindra's having bodily states.

This argument assumes some such claim as:

(N) If Manindra's being self-conscious is identical to Manindra's having bodily states, then necessarily, Manindra's being self-conscious is identical to Manindra's having bodily states.

The argument is plainly valid, and if (N) is true then premise 2 is true. (N) expresses the doctrine of the necessity of metaphysical identity, for which an argument was presented earlier. If – as appears the case – that argument is a proof that extends our knowledge, and premise 1 is plainly true, then the conclusion is true.

One way of continuing is to note regarding *being self-conscious* that anything that has it would be radically different if it irretrievably lost it; its causal powers would be greatly diminished and its causal potencies would be significantly altered. *Being self-conscious* is a very plausible property for *being a kind-defining property* or *being an essential property* of anything that has it.[31] This reflection leads naturally to this continuation of the argument:

4 It is logically possible for Manindra to exist as a self-conscious being and for Manindra to have no body.

5 If it is logically possible for Manindra to exist as a self-conscious being and for Manindra to have no body then Manindra existing as a self-conscious being is not identical to Manindra's having a body. So:

6 Manindra's existing as a self-conscious being is not identical to Manindra's having a body.

This brief argument is powerful and controversial.

In spite of the fact that mind–body dualism seems not subject to the sorts of critique to which complexity accounts of persons are subject, it is widely rejected and often despised in contemporary academic studies. What is favored instead is materialism, the view that there are material substances but not substances of any other kind.[32] The materialism/dualism controversy is complex and fascinating. There do not seem to be such powerful arguments for materialism that dualism should be ruled out as a viable position.

Arguments against dualism

There are widely accepted arguments against dualism. One such argument contends that materialism is simpler, positing less kinds of substance, though why having two sorts of material substance, one capable of self-consciousness and one not, is in any significant way simpler is as unclear as why appeal to simplicity of kinds of substances should carry the day (or favor materialism, since idealism is simpler than dualism in the same sense as that in which materialism is). The most frequent criticism is that the only version of dualism that is plausible is interactionism, the position that mental events cause physical events and physical events cause mental events. But mind–body interaction, we are told, is impossible – how could such different things as an immaterial substance and a material substance interact? This is perhaps the only time in contemporary philosophy in which the *causal likeness principle* is invoked – the claim that in order for X to affect Y with respect to some property Q, X must have Q or something like Q. There is neither criterion for what degree of similarity is required nor reason to accept the principle. Dualists find it unclear why color experience being caused by non-colored things, colds and flu by bacteria and viruses, pain by unfeeling things, and the like somehow are unproblematic whereas mind–body interaction is problematic.

It seems that the basic reason for the rejection of dualism as a live option in much of contemporary academia has to do with what might be called *the mapping problem*: how does one relate the description of the physical world, insofar as we can provide this, to the descriptions true of everyday choices and actions? Roughly, how does one map our descriptions of the mental world onto our descriptions of the physical world?

It is tempting to deny that there is a mapping problem by suggesting that our descriptions of the physical world, cast in natural science terms, and our descriptions of persons and their freedom of thought and action, are incommensurable in the sense that they do not bear logical relations to one another – that they do enter into relations of consistency, inconsistency, entailment, and the like. The problem is that the suggestion is false; given that a description of the physical world is true, there are hosts of actions not available that would be available were the physical world otherwise. For example, if the correct description D1 of the physical places an orange at place P at time T, then at T it is not possible to bring the orange to P – it is already there. If the correct description included the information that the orange was elsewhere than P, bringing it to P would (given other features of things) be possible. In such ways, and much more complex ones, what makes a particular description of the physical world at a given time true also constrains what can be done in that world at and after that time.[33]

Eliminative materialism, which denies that there are any mental properties, dismisses the mapping problem by denying that there is anything that mental descriptions describe. It thereby dismisses the possibility of distinguishing between good science and bad, and between science and superstition. Those who claim that the distinction between the mental and the physical captures, not substances or properties, but ways of talking, both fail to solve the mapping problem and give no account of the phenomenological and explanatory differences between the mental and the material. Property dualists grant that there are both mental and physical properties, but are no better at dealing with the mapping problem than are substance dualists. Insofar as its roots are intellectual, the current disposition to dismiss dualism seems to lie in the hope that if one embraces property dualism, one can grant the phenomenological and explanatory differences between the mental and the physical and have the best chance, some day, of solving the mapping problem. If, as argued earlier, *being self-conscious* has strong credentials as a kind-defining property, property dualism is a longer step toward substance dualism than most property dualists would like.

Mounting a full-scale defense of a substantivalist and dualist view of persons would require more space than is available here. What has been done is this: we have argued that while epistemological arguments for dualism fail, there are metaphysical arguments of much more power in its favor, and the objections against it have much less force than is usually assumed. What follows is that, insofar as Cornman and Lehrer are right about what (monotheistic) religions take to be true about persons, their perspective is far more defensible than it currently is usually thought to be.

Questions for reflection

1 What is the difference between an appeal to argument and an appeal to experience?
2 Offer a reasoned assessment of the core claims made by Advaita Vedanta.
3 Explain and argue for or against the Complexity View of persons.
4 Explain and argue for or against the view that persons are self-conscious substances or souls.
5 Is the doctrine of metaphysical identity true?
6 Explain, and argue for or against, the view that if one person claims *There are persons,* and someone else denies this, they dispute over a merely conventional matter.

Annotated reading

Donagan, Alan (1987) *Choice: The Essential Element in Human Action*, London: Routledge and Kegan Paul. Argues for a view of persons as enduring free agents.

Hoffman, Joshua and Rosenkrantz, Gary S. (1994) *Substance Among Other Categories*, Cambridge: Cambridge University Press. Discusses various views of what a substance is, objections to these views, and arguments for them.

Hoffman, Joshua and Rosenkrantz, Gary S. (1997) *Substance: Its Nature and Existence*, London: Routledge. See previous reference.

Lowe, E. J. (1989) *Kinds of Being*, Oxford: Basil Blackwell. Discusses substance theories and competing theories, arguments for and against each.

Lowe, E. J. (1996) *Subjects of Experience*, Cambridge: Cambridge University Press. See previous reference.

Parfit, Derek (1984) *Reasons and Persons*, Oxford: Oxford University Press. Defends a Buddhist-type account of persons.

CHAPTER 13
Arguments concerning nonmonotheistic conceptions (2)

Appeals to enlightenment experience

Self-authentication

Advaita appeal to enlightenment experience

Jain-type appeals to experience

Buddhist-type appeals to experience

The contrasting arguments

Questions for reflection

Annotated reading

13
Arguments concerning nonmonotheistic conceptions (2)

Appeals to enlightenment experience

Appeals to religious experience as evidence for religious belief are not, of course, limited to consideration of experiences that are taken by their subjects to be experiences of God. Appeals are made to enlightenment experiences as well. While, as noted earlier, the psychological features (detachment, calm, bliss, and the like) of Advaita, Jain, and Buddhist enlightenment experiences are very similar, their reported structure and their proposed doctrinal significance are quite different. Enlightenment experiences are not viewed by religious traditions in which they are prized as a sort of cosmic Prozac; they are not primarily prized for their psychological features. They are believed to cure, not remove symptoms, and the ills they are said to cure are not depression, but the basic illness common to us all, as each particular religious tradition perceives it. If a devotee of Advaita Vedanta appeals to Advaita enlightenment experience as evidence for religious belief, it will be Advaita beliefs that are said to be supported by the experience. Analogously, of course, for Jain or Buddhist appeals to Jain or Buddhist enlightenment experiences.

The exact nature of the appeals to experiential evidence

An appeal to experience as evidence typically involves, as we have seen, referring to a description of the experience and explicitly or implicitly assuming some conceptual connection between the occurrence of an experience that fits that description and the proposition for whose truth that occurrence is said to provide evidence. The core idea is:

1 An experience that fits description D has occurred.
2 If an experience that fits description D has occurred, that fact is evidence that proposition P is true. So:
3 That fact is evidence that P is true.

One who wishes to make a claim like 3 regarding some religious doctrine requires that some claims like 1 and 2 are true when one replaces "D" by a relevant description and "P" by a statement of a relevant doctrine. The role of the connecting premise may be implicit, necessary for the appeal to experience but unstated. Like versions of the principle of experiential evidence, the connecting premises are typically assumed but not asserted; indeed, the connecting premise typically will simply be an assumed principle of experiential evidence.

Advaita, Jain, and Buddhist enlightenment experiences are called, respectively, *moksha*, *kevala*, and *nirvana* experiences. We can expect, then, appeals to experience of the following sort.

Experiential evidence and enlightenment experiences

Our question concerning enlightenment experience is the same as the one raised regarding numinous experience: is it direct evidence (evidence not mediated through theory) for religious belief? If it is such evidence, one will be able to argue successfully as follows.

Advaita Vedanta

A1 *Moksha* experiences (in which one realizes one's identity with qualityless Brahman) have occurred.
A2 If *moksha* experiences have occurred, that fact is evidence that *We are identical to qualityless Braham* is true. So:
A3 That fact is evidence that *We are identical to qualityless Brahman* is true.

Jainism

J1 *Kevala* experiences (in which one realizes one's existential independence or ontological security and one's omniscience) have occurred.
J2 If *kevala* experiences have occurred, that fact is evidence that *We have existential independence or ontological security and are omniscient* is true. So:
J3 The fact is evidence that *We have existential independence or ontological security and are omniscient* is true.

Theravada Buddhism

T1 *Nirvana* experiences (in which one realizes one's nature as composed at a time of momentary elements and over time of a series of bundles of such elements) have occurred.
T2 If *nirvana* experiences have occurred, that fact is evidence that *We are*

composed at a time of momentary elements and over time of bundles of such elements is true. So:

T3 That fact is evidence that *We are composed at a time of momentary elements and over time of bundles of such elements* is true.[1]

Further, in treating these appeals to experience in the same sort of way as we treated appeals to numinous experience, the first premise of each triad must be read phenomenologically; thus we will have:

A1* *Moksha* experiences (in which one *at least appears to* realize one's identity with qualityless Brahman) have occurred.

J1* *Kevala* experiences (in which one *at least appears to* realize one's existential independence or ontological security and one's omniscience) have occurred.

T1* *Nirvana* experiences (in which one *at least appears to* realize one's nature as composed at a time of momentary elements and over time of a series of bundles of such elements) have occurred.

These will replace A1, J1, and T1, and the beginning (the antecedent) of A2, J2, and T2 will be modified accordingly. The central question then is whether it is true that:

A2* If *moksha* experiences (in which one *at least appears to* realize one's identity with qualityless Brahman) have occurred, this is evidence that one is identical to qualityless Brahman.

J2* If *kevala* experiences (in which one *at least appears to* realize one's existential independence or ontological security and one's omniscience) have occurred, then this is evidence that one is existentially independent or has ontological security and one is omniscient.

T2* If *nirvana* experiences (in which one *at least appears to* realize one's nature as composed at a time of momentary elements and over time of a series of bundles of such elements) have occurred then this is evidence that one is composed at a time of momentary elements and over time of a series of bundles of such elements.

If one or more of these is true, then there is some principle of experiential evidence that plays the same role relevant to A2*, J2*, and T2* as our earlier principles do relative to similar claims concerning numinous experience. Is there any such principle?

Two counterbalancing considerations

It is sometimes suggested that those who have had religious experiences are the real experts as to what those experiences show – as to what they are evidence for. This claim is often made regarding enlightenment experiences. While perhaps, just by virtue of having them, persons who have enlightenment experiences are experts about what it is like to have the sort of religious experience they have had, this does not tell us anything about whether such experiences are self-authenticating relative to any religious claims based on such experiences, or whether these experiences provide evidence for the beliefs based on them.

If some have claimed that religious experiencers – those who have had religious experiences – are thereby experts about the reliability or veridicality of those experiences (about whether or not they correctly represent the world), it should be noted that others have claimed that religious experiencers are the last people one should expect to have any such expertise. They have argued that the very having of such experiences – experiences that are often emotionally very powerful and that sometimes result in instantaneous conversions or redirections of a life – renders them in no position to evaluate the cognitive significance of such experiences objectively. Further, particularly in the traditions that center on enlightenment experience, the investment in having such experiences is great. One walks for years in a loin cloth from one end of India to the other, begging one's bread. Or one spends years learning the meanings of ancient arcane texts under the relentless guidance of demanding gurus. Or one spends a near lifetime on good works, in each case instead of devoting oneself to seeking pleasure, wealth, and power. Also the status given to those who attain the goal is high (being elevated to a semi-divine status where others bow in your presence or dare not even look you in the face). The investment and rewards are just too great for anyone who claims to have had any such experience to be trusted to be at all rational in his reasoning or judgment regarding its cognitive significance.

Whatever weight either sort of consideration has is balanced by the other sort, and neither sort justifies concluding either that religious experiencers are the experts regarding what their experiences evidentially justify or that if those experiences serve as evidence they can only do so for those who have them.

Self-authentication

Religious experiences are often said to be self-authenticating or self-guaranteeing, so that appeal to them gives one a uniquely secure source of experiential confirmation. If this is so, it is obviously an important fact about religious experiences. It would be particularly relevant to their status as evidence for religious beliefs. What exactly, then, is it for some experience to be self-authenticating? *Self-authentication* is a three-term relation; there is a person to whom an experience authenticates, an experience that does the authenticating, and a belief or proposition that is authenticated. Further, the idea is, the belief or proposition in question is evidenced or authenticated in a particularly strong way – in such a way, in fact, that the person cannot be mistaken in accepting that belief or in believing that proposition. Formally, the idea can be put in this fashion:

> Chandra's experience E is *self-authenticating* regarding proposition P if and only if Chandra has experience E, it is logically impossible that Chandra have E and proposition P be false, and Chandra rests his acceptance of P on his having had E.[2, 3]

If there are experiences that satisfy these conditions regarding persons and beliefs, the most obvious examples do not concern religious beliefs. Suppose that Wendy, perhaps feeling philosophical, reflects that, in contrast to Santa Claus and unicorns but like salamanders and her dog, she exists. Reflection is, after all, a kind of experience, and if Wendy reflects at time T that she exists at T (a reflection that, she notes, includes her believing that she exists), then she is fully justified if she also notes that her reflecting that she exists is impossible unless she does exist; Wendy's experience of believingly reflecting on the fact of her existence is such that it is logically impossible that she do so and her belief be false. So if she rests her belief that she exists at T on the experience of believingly reflecting that she exists at T, her experience of believingly reflecting that she exists at T can be self-authenticating regarding her belief that she exists at T. If we ask, then, what sorts of beliefs there are that can receive self-authentication from experience, it seems clear that among them are: one's belief that one now exists, that one is now conscious, that one now has at least one belief, and the like. Perhaps if one believes that one is now in pain, then it is true that one is now in pain (though one can be wrong about the pain's cause and its location). These sorts of experiences and beliefs represent the least controversial cases of self-authentication.

Consider claims central to Advaita Vedanta, Jainism, and Theravada Buddhism:

AV *We are identical to qualityless Brahman.*
J *We have existential independence or ontological security and are omniscient.*
TB *We are composed at a time of momentary elements and over time of bundles of such elements.*[4]

Each of these claims, if they are true at all, are – as their adherents insist – true whether we know them to be true, and true independent of anyone having any enlightenment experience.[5] Further, each tradition holds that one can believe two of these three claims, and have the experience that the tradition that accepts this claim alleges confirms that claim, without that claim being true. It seems plain that it is logically possible that one believe any of *We are identical to qualityless Brahman, We have existential independence or ontological security and are omniscient,* or *We are composed at a time of a bundle of momentary elements and over time of a series of bundles of such elements* and believe falsely, just as it is logically possible that one believe oneself to be more courageous than one is, or free from illness while a disease silently takes its toll, or devoid of pride while enamored of one's humility. It may well also be that in all three cases, one can have the relevant enlightenment experience, believe the corresponding doctrine, think the experience confirms the doctrine, and be mistaken on all counts. Each tradition holds views that entail that the members of the other two traditions are in exactly this position.

None of this is denied by even the strongest proponents of the self-authenticating character of enlightenment experiences.[6] What is claimed is not that it is logically impossible that one believe the preferred doctrine and that doctrine nonetheless be false, but that (i) it is logically impossible that anyone have an enlightenment experience that self-authenticates a doctrine and the doctrine nonetheless be false, and (ii) enlightenment experiences (of the right kind) are self-authenticating regarding (the right) doctrine. While (i) is true by definition of "self-authentication," (ii) is a substantial claim that we will explore.

Descriptions

In exploring it, we begin with this question: What sort of descriptions will be true of an enlightenment experience that is self-authenticating regarding, say, a Jain religious doctrine? To put the same question in a different way, what sort of phenomenology or observable features must such an experience have? Since what is said to be self-authenticated is *We have existential independence or ontological security and are omniscient*, it must have a phenomenology appropriate to confirming that claim. The simplest description will be something like *at least apparently recognizing one's existential independence or ontological security and one's omniscience*. There are various problems with offering this as the description relevant for the appeal to experience as evidence.

Suppose that you and I are looking at an ancient coin. You claim it is Roman, and I claim it is Greek. I say *I see it is Greek* and regard the case as closed. You claim *I see it is Roman* and regard the case as closed. But at least one of us is wrong, and neither of us has provided any evidence by describing the experience in a way that simply assumes that our claim is true. It is not that I express my evidence by saying *I see it is Greek*; I do not thereby recite any evidence whatever. I merely repeat my claim. If your experience is to be evidence that the coin is Roman,[7] it must be the case that there are features that the coin at least seems to have such that, if the coin has those features, it is at least probably Roman. So to speak, the phenomenology of your coin-experience must be Romanesque. For example, it may bear the likeness of a Roman emperor rather than a Greek statesman. If I am to have evidence, the coin must at least appear to me to have some feature such that, if the coin has that feature, that fact supports its Greekness. For example, it may bear the likeness of a Greek statesman rather than a Roman emperor.

The case of enlightenment experience is analogous. Simply to assert, for some religious claim C, that one has an experience in which one recognizes or realizes its truth, with no specification of what it is about the experience that confirms C, is pointless so far as evidence is concerned.

Evidence about what?

Enlightenment experience is supposed to teach one about one's nature – about what one is. This is obvious in the cases of Advaita Vedanta (*identity with qualityless Brahman*) and Jainism (*being an indestructible, all-knowing self-conscious substance*). It is typical of Buddhist traditions to deny that anything has a "same-nature" or essence. Nonetheless, it is also typical of Buddhist traditions to hold that every item that we commonsensically regard as an enduring thing is really composed at a time of a bundle of momentary elements and over time of a series of momentary bundles of elements. Whether or not one calls this a doctrine of the nature of persons,[8] the idea is that this is what persons really are. For each of these traditions, the goal is the truth about oneself.

If, however, any of these claims is true, it is true about everyone, not just about oneself; the idea is that if anyone then everyone is identical to qualityless Brahman or is an indestructible enduring mind or is composed only of momentary elements. Further, these claims can be true only if various other things are false. For example, if monotheism is true, God is ultimate and has qualities (so there is no qualityless Brahman), persons are created and endure by divine courtesy (they are not indestructible), and God is neither transient nor composed of transient elements (it is false that everything is impermanent).

Particular experiences, universal claims

The various doctrines about persons are universal in scope; the experiences occur to particular individuals. When we ask whether these particular experiences provide evidence for claims that are universal in their scope, we get different results depending on the case. Suppose that enlightenment experience provides evidence that one is identical to qualityless Brahman. Will this also provide evidence that everyone else is? The question is peculiar in a way that arises from the doctrine itself. If A is identical to B and C is identical to B, then A is identical to C. So if you are identical to qualityless Brahman and I am too, we are identical to one another; so there isn't "anyone else." If there is anyone else, the doctrine is false.

Suppose that enlightenment experience provides evidence that one is an indestructible mind or is composed of momentary elements. Will this also provide evidence that everyone else is? It will do so in the presence of a doctrine to the effect that the subject of the experience is a person and what makes her a person is the same as what makes everyone else a person, assuming that one is justified in taking these additional claims to be true. Discussing these issues in any detail would take us too far away from our basic concerns here. Thus we simply note that it is widely assumed that these sorts of additional claim are true.[9]

Phenomenologies that fit the claims

The right sort of phenomenology seems to be of this sort: for Advaita enlightenment experience, *appearing or seeming to be identical with qualityless Brahman*; for Jainism, *appearing or seeming to be an indestructible and highly knowledgeable mind*; for Buddhism, *appearing or seeming to be only a bundle of transitory states*. One might question whether these are, strictly speaking, possible phenomenological features of an experience. They seem, like *being a Roman coin*, to be features something could have only by virtue of other features also had by that thing. In the case of a Roman coin, *bearing the image of an emperor* is one such feature. In the enlightenment cases, presumably the relevant further features are such qualities as *having no sense of possessing qualities, feeling indestructible, and being aware only of states of mind.* It is, however, logically possible that one possesses qualities that one has no sense of having, feels indestructible while being dependent for existence on something else, and is aware of nothing but one's current mental states without being identical to those states even at the time at which one has them. Further, that one has no sense of having qualities is possible only if one does have qualities – to have no qualities at all is simply not to exist at all, and not existing gets very much in the way of having experiences. Having a sense of being indestructible is perfectly compatible with not being indestructible, and having a sense of being momentary is perfectly compatible with being an enduring thing.

One way of putting the problems with the notion that enlightenment experiences are self-authenticating with regard to Advaita, Jain, or Buddhist doctrinal claims is this:

(i) the claims are, if true of one at all, true of one so long as one exists, whereas in the least controversial cases of self-authentication the claims that are authenticated have to do with one's existence right now or one's current, momentary states of awareness; the claims in cases where claims to self-authentication is plausible are about a time span that corresponds, and is limited, to the time during which the authenticating experience occurs;
(ii) the quality or state ascribed to oneself by the claim is an observable quality – like being in pain – or is entailed by any quality anything has – like existing.

By contrast, the Advaita, Jain, and Buddhist claims concern times not limited to the duration of the enlightenment experience and qualities neither observable nor entailed by simply possessing any quality at all. Further, such states as *seeming to oneself to be qualityless, seeming to be indestructible, seeming to be momentary* are states that can easily be mistaken – one may seem to oneself to be qualityless, indestructible, or momentary without these things being in fact true.

It is important to remember here that we are not asking what sort of phenomenological features an experience might have were one's having it to lead them to accept a particular religious doctrine, especially if one had it in a context in which it was expected that such experiences might occur – for example, within a meditative tradition the very purpose of which was the preparation for having such experiences whose interpretation was built into the institutional context within which the meditative practice occurred. We are not seeking to give a psychological explanation of enlightenment experiences, but asking whether these experiences provide self-authentication for certain religious beliefs.

What follows from our discussion is that they do not. The argument is not that Advaita Vedanta, Jainism, and Theravada Buddhism can all claim self-authentication for logically incompatible beliefs so that at least two of the traditions will be mistaken, though that is the case. The argument is that none of the enlightenment experiences possesses a phenomenology which self-authenticates the beliefs in question. It is not logically impossible that one have an enlightenment experience – whether Advaita Vedanta, Jain, or Buddhist – that possesses the relevant phenomenological features and it also is the case that the corresponding Advaita, Jain, or Buddhist doctrine is false. So enlightenment experiences do not self-authenticate doctrines based on them. The argument showing this can be made fully explicit as follows:

1 One's enlightenment experience is *self-authenticating* regarding a proposition that expresses the core Advaita, Jain, or Buddhist doctrinal claim if and only if:
   (i) one seems (respectively) to be qualityless, indestructible, or momentary,
   (ii) it is logically impossible that one seems to oneself to be qualityless, indestructible, or momentary, and one is not qualityless, indestructible, or momentary, and
   (iii) one rests one's acceptance of core Advaita, Jain, or Buddhist doctrine on one's having seemed to oneself to be qualityless, indestructible, or momentary.
2 It is not logically impossible that one seem to oneself to be qualityless, indestructible, or momentary and one not be so. Hence:
3 One's enlightenment experience is not self-authenticating relative to Advaita, Jain, or Buddhist doctrine.

We have argued that enlightenment experiences are not self-authenticating regarding these claims. That they are not self-authenticating regarding the religious claims often based on them does not entail that these experiences are not evidence for those claims. Evidence need not be self-authenticating. So the next question is: Do enlightenment experiences provide evidence for religious beliefs?

Previous principles of experiential evidence

We have explained and defended some principles of experiential evidence. They are examples of claims that can provide support for premises like the second steps of the brief three-step arguments sketched early in this chapter. These principles can be expressed as follows:

(P*) If a person S has an experience E which, if reliable, is a matter of being aware of an experience-independently existing item X, and E is not canceled or counterbalanced or compromised or contradicted or confuted or logically consumed or empirically consumed, then S's having E is evidence that X exists.

and

(P**) If a person S has an experience E which, if reliable, is a matter of being aware of an experience-independently existing item X, and S (non-culpably) has no reason to think that E is canceled or counterbalanced or compromised or contradicted or confuted or logically consumed or empirically consumed, then S's having E provides S evidence that X exists.

Some experiences, we have noted, are matters of someone's at least seeming to perceive something which, *if it exists at all,* exists independent of its being experienced. These have a particular structure – subject/consciousness/object. Other experiences are matters of someone's feeling a certain way. These also have a particular structure – subject/content. Seeing an apple tree is of the former sort; so is merely seeming to see an apple tree. Feeling nauseous or dizzy, and experiencing generalized anxiety or euphoria, are examples of the latter sort. It is important to keep in mind the differences between experiences that are subject/consciousness/object in structure and experiences that are subject/content in structure.

Subject/content experience and a principle of experiential evidence

Treating subject/content experience as evidence requires, implicitly if not explicitly, a principle of experiential evidence different from (P*) and (P**) which refer to evidence for the existence of experience-independent things and apply to subject/consciousness/object experiences. Where we allow *being in a state* to be broadly construed (so as to cover things like *having a quality, being an event,* and the like), consider:

(P***) If a person S has an experience E which, if reliable, is a matter of S being aware of an experience-dependently existing quality or state X of S, then S's having E is evidence that S is in state, or has quality, X.

Experiencing pain, euphoria, or anxiety is evidence that one is in a state of pain, euphoria, or anxiety.[10] Religious claims do not typically concern such private, momentary psychological states, and no religion bases its core doctrines on their occurrence. Being identical to Brahman or being qualityless, being indestructible or a soul that exists independently, and being a momentary being or a being whose constituents are momentary are not features or qualities or states that are experience-dependent. If someone has any of them, she has them whether she experiences herself as having them or not. Thus the principle

(P***) If a person S has an experience E which, if reliable, is a matter of S being aware of an experience-dependently existing quality or state X of S, then S's having E is evidence that S is in state, or has quality X

is not the proper principle of enlightenment experiences. The qualities the relevant religious beliefs ascribe to people are not experience-dependent properties.

One might try instead:

(P****) If a person S has an experience E which, if reliable, is a matter of S being introspectively aware of being in an experience-*in*dependently existing state X of S, then S's having E is evidence that S is in state X.

This principle raises the question of whether it is possible to be *introspectively* aware of an experience-independent property. The notion of introspection is not lucid. It is not obvious what the range of introspection is – not clear what is and is not a possibly introspected quality or state. One's cognitive states – e.g., one's thinking about squares or wondering where to look for a new blowfish – are known by introspection. So are one's psychological states – being depressed about the demise of one's old blowfish but relieved that one's guppy is healthy again. Whether or not one is in pain is learned by introspection. If one wants "introspection" to refer to a particularly reliable state, then one will count *feeling cold* and *feeling in love* to be introspective states, but not *being cold* or *being in love*, since one can feel cold though one's body is warm or feel like one is in love when one but suffers a short-lived infatuation that vanishes at the first sign of inconvenience. Thus, in keeping with the idea of so characterizing introspection that it is a particularly reliable sort of experience, let us restrict the scope of introspection as follows:

> Person S is introspectively aware of state or quality Q only if S being in or possessing Q depends on S's being aware of being in or possessing Q.

One can introspectively *seem* to oneself to be qualityless, indestructible, or momentary in the sense that one can *believe* this to be so. Nothing could make it true that one was qualityless. Even if one had an experience in which one seemed to one to have no qualities, this would not show, or even be evidence that, one was without qualities. In fact, having qualities would be a condition of having any such experience. Being indestructible would not prevent one from having a sense that was indestructible – believing that one is indestructible is not incompatible with one's being so. But having such a sense or belief would not by itself be evidence that one was indestructible. Suppose a momentary being could believe or feel it was momentary. This would not show, or even be evidence, that it was indestructible or momentary. Actually being indestructible or actually being momentary would be a non-introspectible property. Nor is the sort of property such that, even if one has it, it would be open to introspective awareness. Nor are any of *being qualityless, being indestructible, being composed of momentary items* features or qualities or states such that, if one has or is in them, one necessarily would know it, or one would more likely know it rather than not know it, or more likely know it about oneself than would someone else. Like such features or qualities or states as *being the brightest person in the class, having a good chance to be elected to the Senate, possessing a more misleading view of oneself than most people, being identical to the future spouse of the most attractive person in the class*, and a great many others, one could believe oneself to have these features or qualities even when one did not. One could have these features or qualities and not believe that one did. Being mistaken in these ways is not only possible; it would not even be surprising. Behind these facts lies the more basic fact noted above: *being qualityless, being indestructible, being composed of momentary items* are not introspectible properties; even if one has them, one cannot be introspectively aware of having them. Further, there is no introspective feature that one can be aware of that entails one has them.

Since *being qualityless, being indestructible, being composed of momentary items*, unlike *being in pain, feeling anxious, being euphoric*, are not introspectively accessible or observable states, Principle (P****), which makes essential reference to introspectibly accessible states, does not apply to them. Thus the principle

(P****) If a person S has an experience E which, if reliable, is a matter of S being introspectively aware of being in an experience-*in*dependently existing state or quality X of S, then S's having E is evidence that S is in state, or has quality, X

will not do. Experience-independently existing states or qualities, on the construal of introspection on which it is particularly reliable, are not possible objects of introspection.

One might instead suggest something like:

(P*****) If a person S has an experience E which, if reliable, is a matter of S being non-introspectively aware of being in an experience-*in*dependently existing state or having an experience-*in*dependently possessed quality X of S, then S's having E is evidence that S is in state, or possesses quality, X.

The question that (P*****) raises is whether a subject/content experience can be non-introspective and yet be direct evidence for someone being in an experience-independent state or having some experience-independent quality. Sensory experience and monotheistic religious experience are subject/consciousness/object, not subject/content.[11] The requisite sort of experience would be direct evidence that one was in an experience-independent state or had an experience-independent quality and yet be a subject/content experience.

An experience of the kinesthetic sort in which one is aware that one is moving or of the position of one's body is not subject/content – it is awareness of one's body moving or being in a certain position. Feeling a tingling in one's fingers is also subject/consciousness/object. These sorts of experiences, like sensory experience of physical objects other than one's body and introspective experience, won't provide an analogy for the sort of experience that would provide evidence for the religious beliefs of enlightenment traditions.

One who holds that enlightenment experiences provide such evidence will contend that such experiences are unique in kind. Thus the failure to find similar experiences is not surprising or problematic. The idea is that enlightenment experiences just are awareness of *one's being qualityless, one's being indestructible,* or *one's being momentary or composed of momentary constituents*. The problem with this suggestion is that these states or qualities are not directly observable. Nothing can be qualityless; that would effectively get in the way of its existing. One could discern the momentariness of something else, but one would have to outlast it in order to do so. A person could be indestructible just as a person could be stronger or smarter than any other person. A person who was indestructible or strongest or smartest could learn that he had this exalted status. But the ways of learning this would not include directly experiencing those qualities in oneself. Regarding being strongest, one could discover that one could lift heavier weights, or throw heavy objects farther, than anyone else could. Regarding being smartest, one could find that one's intelligence test results were above anyone else's or that one has made discoveries in vastly different areas that no one else had thought of.

Discovering that one was indestructible would be harder. No one claims the indestructibility of one's body. Those who have held to the inherent indestructibility of the person have identified the person with the mind or soul. They have then argued that the mind or soul is immaterial and not subject to anything analogous to erosion or decomposition. Plato's *Phaedo* is a classic example. Jain texts at least contain the raw materials for such an argument. But unlike *being in pain, being indestructible* is something one would seem to have to learn one had by inference. Even if one had some sort of series of experiences in which one had reason to believe that, if one's mind or soul destructible, it would by now have been destroyed, this would still be knowledge by inference, not by direct awareness.

The problem, then, is that the relevant states or qualities – the ones that we would have to have awareness of in order for enlightenment experience to be evidence for religious beliefs – are not possible objects of awareness. If this is so, then there will not be any principle of experiential evidence by virtue of which being aware of such states or qualities is evidence for religious belief, because there will be no such awareness to be evidence. The principle

(P*****) If a person S has an experience E which, if reliable, is a matter of S being non-introspectively aware of being in an experience-*in*dependently existing state or having an experience-*in*dependently possessed quality X of S, then S's having E is evidence that S is in state, or possesses quality, X

will not help because it will not apply to enlightenment experiences.

The fact of the matter is that there seems to be no principle of experiential evidence on which enlightenment experience provides evidence for religious belief.

The argument stated specifically regarding our three enlightenment traditions[12]

Consider our three cases.

Advaita

Appearing to be qualityless not only is not evidence that one is qualityless but is sufficient evidence for possession of qualities; it is logically impossible that one have any experience at all and not exist, and logically impossible that one exist without having qualities. Indian critics of Advaita Vedanta, the most famous of whom is Ramanuja, have pressed this decisive objection with great force and clarity.

Jainism and Buddhism

Appearing to oneself to be indestructible is not evidence that one is indestructible. Claims of indestructibility, of course, are not made regarding the body; Jain philosophers know as well as anyone that the human body is not indestructible. What they claim, along with Plato and Platonists, is that the mind or soul or person is indestructible in principle. The point remains, however, that the mind or soul or person having an experience in which it seems to itself to be indestructible in principle is not evidence that it is indestructible in principle. Not only is it logically possible that one have an experience in which it seems to them that they are indestructible though in fact they are not; it is also that having such an experience is not any evidence that one is indestructible, any more than having an experience in which one seems to oneself to be destructible is evidence that one is destructible. Similarly, a sense of one's existence as momentary, or as composed of momentary items is one thing, and one's being in momentary existence or being composed of things that exist only for an instant is another, and having a sense of one's momentariness is not evidence that one is merely momentary or that one is composed of momentary constituents.

The argument restated

The argument can be stated along the following lines. Consider three claims, each of which is true:

1 There are states, like being in pain, feeling happy, worrying about one's health, and the like, where one's having the sense that one is

in pain, happy, or worried, justifies one's belief that one is in pain, happy, or worried – such states involve phenomenological awareness of the actual state that one ascribes to oneself and one's being aware of being in such a state is evidence that one is in it.[13]

2 There are other states, like thinking that one can wave one's arms and fly, that one has grown a lion's head, or that one's head is made of glass, where one's having the sense that one can fly, has grown a lion's head, or one's head is made of glass does not involve a phenomenological awareness of one's actually flying, actually having a lion's head, or actually having a head made of glass, and one's having such a sense is not evidence that one is in the state that one ascribes to oneself.

When one believes on the basis of introspection that one is in one of the sorts of states that 1 describes, one typically is right. When one believes on the basis of introspection that one is in one of the sorts of states that 2 describes, one typically is wrong. Consider:

3 There are still other states, like thinking that one is the brightest member of one's class, the most talented actor in one's school, an immortal soul, someone who will die today, and the like, where one's having the sense that one is brightest, most talented, immortal, or will die today does not involve a phenomenological awareness of one's actually being brightest, most talented, immortal, or dying today, and one's having such a sense is not evidence that one is in the state that one ascribes to oneself.

In these cases, in contrast to those described in 2 it is not just obvious that one is not in the state mentioned. But the cases are similar in this respect: the state in question, unlike those mentioned in 1, is not a state that is introspectively accessible or discernible. One cannot, so to speak, read off one's introspective awareness that one is in the sort of states described in 2 and 3. Nor is there any entailment between *seeming to be in the state* and *being in the state* or any relation such that *seeming to be in the state* renders it more likely than not that one is in the state.

Consider, then, this way of putting the argument:

A Enlightenment experiences are senses of being in a certain state and they fall into either class 2 or class 3.

B Senses of being in a certain state that fall into either class 2 or class 3 are not evidence that the person who has that sense is in that state.

Thus:

C Enlightenment experiences are not evidence that the person who has them is in the state she thinks she is in.

Hence appeal to enlightenment experience will not confirm Advaita, Jain, or Buddhist doctrine.

Conclusion

If the arguments just considered are correct, what has been established is the following. Consider the crucial steps in the reasoning that must be correct if enlightenment experience provides evidence for religious belief. As we noted earlier, they are:

A2* If *moksha* experiences (in which one *at least appears to* realize one's identity with qualityless Brahman) have occurred, this is evidence that one is identical to qualityless Brahman.

J2* If *kevala* experiences (in which one *at least appears to* realize one's existential independence or ontological security and one's omniscience) have occurred, then this is evidence that one is existentially independent or has ontological security and one is omniscient.

T2* If *nirvana* experiences (in which one *at least appears to* realize one's nature as composed at a time of momentary elements and over time of a series of bundles of such elements) have occurred, then this is evidence that one is composed at a time of momentary elements and over time of a series of bundles of such elements.

If the arguments just considered are correct, then there is no such thing as one's experientially appearing to be qualityless, indestructible, or momentary. What there is are experiences in which one "has a feeling of being qualityless or indestructible or momentary" – believes oneself to be such where one's belief is associated with certain feelings. This is quite distinct from a case in which one is aware of having a particular quality or being in a particular state that is not a belief-state or a feeling-state. That one is in an enlightenment belief-state or feeling-state is not the same as being aware of being in the state that the associated religious tradition says that you are in or having the quality that the associated religious tradition says that you have. Nor is being in such a belief-state or feeling-state itself any evidence that one is in the state that the associated religious tradition says that you are in or having the quality that the associated religious tradition says that you have.

A caveat

While the arguments presented thus far have a certain force, and are eminently defensible, they do not discuss the actual contexts in which one finds the other side presented. In discussing these matters still further, it will be useful to consider first the Advaita Vedanta appeal to experience as evidence, and then the Jain and the Buddhist appeals. The critique of the Advaita appeal that one finds readymade in Indian thought is straightforward and decisive. The latter two appeals in particular are very like positions taken outside of any religious context, and are best seen in a cross-cultural context.

Advaita appeal to enlightenment experience

Shankara rightly held that we do know that we exist and that we have certain properties. Chandra can know that he now exists, and that he is conscious now – and thus he can know that *For all X, if X lacks properties, then X is not me*. Further, Chandra can know that there are things that he does not know, and if there cannot be things that Brahman does not know (and this is supposed to be a necessary truth – at least it is supposed to be a necessary truth that "not knowing something" cannot be properly ascribed to Brahman), then Chandra can know that he is not identical to Brahman. If one knows both *I exist, and have P* and *There is an item – namely, X – that (if it exists) lacks P*, then one can properly infer to *I am not X*. Hence the Advaita Vedanta claim – its reading of the *Upanishadic* passage "Thou art That" – is not true. Similarly, on Shankara's own view, if Chandra sees an elephant, Chandra sees a mind-independently existing large grey or albino mammal, so there are mind-independently existing large grey or albino mammals. But Brahman is not any sort of mammal at all, and so even if Brahman exists, Brahman does not exist alone.

Shankara is of course aware of such objections, and while Ramanuja, Madhva, and other Vedantins make them because they believe that Shankara has no adequate answer, the answer that he has should be noted. The answer[14] is that enlightenment experience trumps or "sublates" all other sorts of experience, and enlightenment experience is self-authenticating. Further, each sensory or introspective experience is self-defeating, because it is either subject/consciousness/object or else subject/content in structure – it includes "the making of distinctions" – and any such experience is (it is claimed) inherently unreliable. Such later critics as Ramanuja and Vadarija turn the latter claim against its author. In *moksha* or enlightenment experience, one is supposed to learn that one is identical to qualityless Brahman. While this is not viewed as being like learning that seven and five are twelve, or that Alaska and Hawaii are US states – it is an experience said to be life-changing, transforming, accompanied with calm and bliss and freedom from desire, and the like – still it is a matter of coming to see some alleged truth. Enlightenment experience is supposed to confirm core Advaita doctrine. Suppose it does so; then it is a matter of someone learning something – a subject/consciousness/object or else a subject/content experience. If all experiences with such structures are unreliable, so is enlightenment experience. On the other hand, if enlightenment experience is reliable, then other experiences possessing a similar structure can be reliable, and all sensory and introspective experience provides evidence against the claim that only qualityless Brahman exists. Should it be replied that enlightenment experience has no object and no content, then it cannot be the case that it confirms some doctrine rather than some other. "Contentless and objectless experience" describes no possible experience, and if it did describe any experience, such an experience would not be evidence for Advaita versus Jain, Buddhist, monotheistic, or other religious claims.

Jain-type appeals to experience

Both Jain and Buddhist traditions appeal to introspective experience as evidence for, or confirmation of, their particular doctrines of what a person is. From a Jain perspective, "introspective experience" here means "self-awareness" or "awareness of one's mental states," irrespective of how those states are elicited or understood. Jain enlightenment experience is taken to have the same structure, and to reveal the same substantival being, that is encountered in ordinary everyday self-consciousness. The Buddhist tradition typically takes ordinary self-awareness to be deceptive and restricts its appeal to enlightenment experiences and experiences that occur to those trained in meditative traditions. Philosophers – of whom David Hume is the most famous – claim that the most ordinary of introspective experiences confirm the same view as that which the Buddhist derives from esoteric experiences. In what follows, then, we will simply speak of introspective experiences, not limiting ourselves to those which are meditative or religious. As the dispute is cross-cultural, we may as well see it in that context, quoting both European and Indian representatives of both positions. One position is propounded by Descartes, various Jain texts, and Ramanuja, and the other asserted by David Hume and various Theravada Buddhist texts.

The dispute here concerns, then, whether or not persons are self-conscious and enduring substances. This matter, at least, Descartes, Ramanuja, Jainism, Buddhism, and Hume think can be settled by appeal to introspection. They disagree as to what the introspective evidence confirms. We begin with the position that claims that introspection and enlightenment experience clearly and incontrovertibly shows that persons are enduring mental substances, and follow with the position that introspection and/or enlightenment experience clearly and incontrovertibly shows that persons at a time are but bundles of momentary states, so that over time a person can be nothing more substantial than a series of such bundles.

The duration problem

It is impossible for one to tell by immediate awareness at time T that one is, or is not, something that does, or does not, endure beyond T. Descartes emphasizes this: he knows by immediate awareness that he exists *now* – that "*I am, I exist,* is . . . true each time that I pronounce it, or that I mentally conceive it." Appeal to memory is required. There are obvious problems in appealing to memory to establish one's own lack of endurance, but for present purposes we shall simply set aside reference to duration and lack of duration and consider only the idea that either the Jain sort of appeal to experience can establish that persons are mental substances or the Buddhist sort of appeal to experience can confirm that persons are individual states.[15]

Descartes

Descartes writes:

> of a surety I myself did exist since I persuaded myself of something (or merely because I thought of something). But there is some deceiver or other, very powerful and very cunning, who ever employs his ingenuity in deceiving me. Then without doubt I exist also if he deceives me, and let him deceive me as much as he will, he can never cause me to be nothing so long as

> I think that I am something, so that after having reflected well and carefully examined all things, we must come to the definite conclusion that this proposition: *I am, I exist*, is necessarily true each time that I pronounce it, or that I mentally conceive it.[16]

The claim is that *Necessarily, the fact that I think includes the fact of my existence* and that I can know without danger of error that I am a thinking being and that I exist. Descartes does not make the false claim that *Descartes exists* is, if true, then necessarily true. In his investigations of self-consciousness he "was merely investigating these properties of which I was able to attain to sure and evident knowledge"[17] – in particular such properties as pertain to the nature of Descartes as a sample person. He claims that he, as a person, is a self-conscious substance, and that this is introspectively evident. It is logically impossible that he exist without being a self-conscious being, and hence being a self-conscious being is at least part of his essence. He adds that since this is true of him as a representative person, what it is to be a person is to be an enduring self-conscious substance.

Two sorts of claims are represented here. One sort is introspective, strictly speaking; Descartes is aware of his thinking of the nature of persons rather than reflecting about triangularity, logical necessity, the nature of matter, or the prospects of his completing a letter to Elizabeth. Discerning what one is thinking about is a matter of being aware of one's thoughts – a matter of introspection. Another sort is conceptual and metaphysical – he is considering the nature of persons rather than wondering how his mother is doing or considering what to have for dinner, and by doing such conceptual thinking he can discern the nature of persons – just as, in thinking about triangles, he can discern their essence. In this special case, he holds, he has (as anyone can have) a unique advantage – what he considers the essence of is also an object of direct awareness and thus the concept of essence can be compared with something that has the essence the concept expresses. Thus his claim is that these two sorts of thinking – introspective and conceptual – to some degree coalesce in the case of his deliberate use of self-awareness as a source of knowledge regarding his nature as a person. He observes in himself not only his thinking and his existence but also a necessary connection between the property *Descartes thinking now* and the property *Descartes existing now* that eliminates any need for inference from the fact that he has the one property to the fact that he has the other (though of course that inference is proper). He is able to reflect that he exists only if he is a self-conscious thing – permanent loss of self-consciousness is also cessation of his existence; and he is directly aware of himself as a self-conscious substance.

Put differently, Descartes is often aware of his being in certain introspective states. Some of these states are states of abstract thought, and among these are reflections concerning the nature of persons. When he thinks of triangles, bluebirds, or waffles, Descartes is thinking of kinds of things to which he does not himself belong. Not so when he thinks of persons. When he thinks about the nature of a triangle – what it is to be one, or of a bluebird or a waffle, he does not think about his own nature; not so when he thinks of what it is to be a person. His view is that he can learn what it is to be a person by (i) noting what sorts of properties he himself has – something introspectively accessible to him, and (ii) reflecting about what properties he could exist without having and what properties he could not exist without having – something conceptually accessible to him.

Explaining his position in reply to an objection, Descartes says:

> Everything in which there resides immediately, as in a subject, or by means of which there exists anything that we perceive, i.e. any property, quality, or attribute, of which we have a real idea, is called a Substance.[18]

Since he is aware of himself as having various qualities and being in various states, he is introspectively aware of being a substance. Since allegedly he knows that it is his essence to be self-conscious – he could survive without any other features not identical to or entailed by self-consciousness; without self-consciousness,[19] he does not exist – he concludes that it is his nature as a person (and hence the nature of persons) to be a self-conscious substance.

Jainism

A Jain text tells us the following:

> The distinctive characteristic of a substance is being. Being is a simultaneous possession of coming into existence, going out of existence, and permanence. Permanence means the indestructibility of the essence of the substance . . . substance is possessed of attributes and modifications. . . . attributes depend upon substratum and cannot be the substratum of another attribute. Modification is change of attribute.[20]

A substance, we are told, has attributes – properties or qualities, if you please. No attribute can exist that is not the attribute of some substance.

Things come into existence in the sense that substances come to have qualities they did not have and to lose qualities they did have; through such changes, substances continue to exist and of course retain their essential qualities. Further:

> The self's essence is life . . . The distinctive characteristic of self is attention . . . Those with minds are knowers.[21]

"Selves are substances"[22] and their definitive characteristic or essence is described as "life" and "attention." Further:

> That which should be grasped by self-discrimination is "from the real point of view."[23] "The soul has the nature of knowledge, and the realization of this nature is Nirvana; therefore one who is desirous of Nirvana must meditate on self-knowledge."[24]

Jainism sometimes uses *nirvana* rather than *kevala* to refer to enlightenment experience. Self-realization involves self-knowledge, and it "has the nature of knowledge." This obviously comes very close at least to Descartes's view of the person, mind, or soul as being a self-conscious substance. In both introspective and enlightenment experience, one appears to oneself as a thinking thing, a substance that possesses cognitive mental qualities.

Ramanuja

In a passage that expresses the same sort of view as that of Descartes and Jainism, the Hindu monotheist Ramanuja writes:

> The judgment "I am conscious" reveals an "I" distinguished by consciousness; and to declare that it refers only to a state of consciousness – which is a mere attribute – is no better than to say of the judgment "Devadatta carries a stick" is about the stick only.[25]

He adds:

> Consciousness is the illuminating, in the present moment, to its own substrate, by its own existence alone . . . Or else, it is the establishing of its own subject by its own existence alone . . . A conscious act is the illumination of a particular object to its own

> substrate by its own existence alone . . . The nature of consciousness is to make something into an object of experience of its own substrate through its own being alone.[26]

According to Ramanuja, a person can be directly aware of herself as the subject of her experiences, including an awareness of herself. Seeing a lamp, one can be aware of oneself as so seeing. One need not infer from *Someone is seeing a lamp* to *I am someone* or *I am seeing a lamp*. The same experience yields the information that both of these sentences express, and it is *Someone is seeing a lamp* that requires inference if anything does, for it abstractly expresses a consequence of one's concrete first-person experience.

Ramanuja makes his allegiance to a Cartesian doctrine of the person plain when he writes:

> Now the permanence of the producer [of conscious acts], and the origination, duration, and cessation, as for pleasure and pain, of what is known as the conscious act, which is an attribute of the producer, are directly perceived. The permanence of the producer is established by recognition from such judgments as *This is the very same thing previously known by me*.[27]

The first sentence of this passage appeals to direct perception. Only in the second sentence is there appeal to argument, and the argument infers from reliable memory to the endurance of oneself as a substance.[28]

Nor, in Ramanuja's view, is this nature as a self-conscious being lost in enlightenment. Ramanuja waxes eloquent on the point:

> To maintain that the consciousness of the "I" does not persist in the state of final release is again altogether inappropriate. It, in fact, amounts to the doctrine – only expressed in somewhat different words – that final release is the annihilation of the self. The "I" is not a mere attribute of the self so that even after its destruction the essential nature of the self might persist – as it persists on the cessation of ignorance; but it constitutes the very nature of the self. Such judgments as: "I know," "Knowledge has arisen in me," show, on the other hand, that we are conscious of knowledge as a mere attribute of the self. – Moreover, a man who, suffering pain, mental or of other kind – whether such pain be real or due to error only – puts himself in relation to pain – "I am suffering pain" – naturally begins to reflect how he may once for all free himself from all these manifold afflictions and enjoy a state of untroubled ease; the desire of final

> release thus having arisen in him he at once sets to work to accomplish it. If, on the other hand, he were to realize that the effect of such activity would be the loss of personal existence, he surely would turn away as soon as somebody began to tell him about "release" . . . Nor must you maintain against this that even in the state of release there persists pure consciousness; . . . No sensible person exerts himself under the influence of the idea that after he himself has perished there will remain some entity termed "pure light"! – What constitutes the "inward" self thus is the "I," the knowing subject.[29]

A similar theme is expressed in this passage:

> "May I, freeing myself from all pain, enter on free possession of endless delight?" This is the thought which prompts the man desirous of release to apply himself to the study of the sacred texts. Were it a settled matter that release consists in the annihilation of the "I," the man would move away as soon as release were only hinted at. "When I myself have perished, there persists some consciousness different from me," to bring this about nobody truly will exert himself.[30]

The "permanence" referred to here, like that of the Jain and unlike that of the Cartesian doctrine, is everlasting; like the Cartesian doctrine, and unlike the Jain, Ramanuja holds the permanence to be possessed only by divine courtesy and dependent on divine grace. In addition to an insistence on the distinctness, endurance, and value of the individual person or self, Ramanuja refers us to the nature of conscious experience as a basis for the view that a person is a mental substance in yet another passage:

> Some things – e.g., staffs and bracelets – appear sometimes as having a separate, independent existence of their own; at other times they present themselves as distinguishing attributes of other things or beings (i.e., of the persons carrying staffs or wearing bracelets). Other entities – e.g., the generic character of cows – have a being only insofar as they constitute the form of substances, and thus always present themselves as distinguishing attributes of those substances . . . The assertion, therefore, that the difference of things is refuted by immediate consciousness is based on the plain denial of a certain form of consciousness, the one namely – admitted by every one – which is expressed by the judgment "This thing is such and such."[31]

The gist of this passage is that experiences that we all have are properly reported by statements of the form *I experience an X that has Q* where "X" refers to some thing and "Q" to some quality.

Indestructibility aside, then, Descartes, Jainism, and Ramanuja – a French Catholic, an atheistic religious tradition, and a Hindu Vsistadvaita Vedanta monotheist – hold that introspective (and for Jainism and Ramanuja, enlightenment) experience confirms that persons are self-conscious substances that endure through time. In briefest scope, the idea is this: *I am what I appear to be in introspective and enlightenment experience; what I appear to be in introspective and enlightenment experience is this: a mental substance; hence I am a mental substance.*

Buddhist-type appeals to experience

David Hume

David Hume writes concerning "all of our particular perceptions" that:

> All these are different, and distinguishable, and separable from each other, and may be separately consider'd, and may exist separately, and have no need of any thing to support their existence. After what manner, therefore, do they belong to self; and how are they connected with it? For my part, when I enter most intimately into what I call myself, I always stumble on some particular perception or other, or heat or cold, light or shade, love or hatred, pain or pleasure. I never can catch myself at any time without a perception, and never can observe any thing but the perception. When my perceptions are remov'd for any time, as by sound sleep; so long am I insensible of myself, and may truly be said not to exist. And were all my perceptions remov'd by death, and cou'd I neither think, nor feel, nor see, nor love, nor hate after the dissolution of my body, I shou'd be entirely annihilated, nor do I conceive what is farther requisite to make me a perfect non-entity. If any one upon serious and unprejudic'd reflexion, thinks he has a different notion of himself, I must confess I can reason no longer with him. All I can allow him is, that he may be in the right as well as I, and that we are essentially different in this particular. He may, perhaps, perceive something simple and continuous, which he calls himself; tho' I am certain there is no such principle in me.[32]

Hume's claim is that all his introspection yields is awareness of independent states – say, a state of being in pain and a state of wondering where the aspirin went. At another later time, introspection may reveal, say, a desire for fish and wine and a regret that one forgot to buy either. What there are, so far as persons go, are such states, and nothing else. In briefest scope, his line of reasoning goes: *I am what I appear to be in introspective experience; what I appear to be in introspective experience is this: individual states; hence I am individual states.*

Theravada Buddhism

It is well known that this Humean view is shared by various Buddhist perspectives. A Buddhist text tells us that:

> Whether Buddhas arise, O priests, or whether Buddhas do not arise, it remains a fact and the fixed and necessary constitution of being that all its constituents are transitory. This fact a Buddha discovers and masters, and when he has discovered and mastered it, he announces, teaches, publishes, proclaims, discloses, minutely explains, and makes it clear, that all the constituents of being are transitory . . . Whether Buddhas arise, O priests, or whether Buddhas do not arise, it remains a fact and the fixed and necessary constitution of being, that all its elements are lacking in an ego [substantial, permanent self-nature]. This fact a Buddha discovers and masters, and when he has discovered and mastered it, he announces, teaches, publishes, proclaims, discloses, minutely explains, and makes it clear, that all the elements of being are lacking in an ego.[33]

A longer and more familiar passage reads as follows:

> Just as the word "chariot" is but a mode of expression for axle, wheels, chariot-body, pole, and other constituent members, placed in a certain relation to each other, but when we come to examine the members one by one, we discover that in the absolute sense there is not chariot; and just as the word "house" is but a mode of expression for wood and other constituents of a house, surrounding space in a certain relation, but in the absolute sense there is no house; and just as the word "fist" is but a mode of expression for the fingers, the thumb, etc. in a certain relation; and the word "lute" for the body of the lute, strings, etc.; "army" for elephants, horses, etc.; "city" for fortifications,

> houses, gates, etc.; "tree" for trunk, branches, foliage, etc.; in a certain relation, but when we come to examine the parts one by one, we discover that in the absolute sense there is no tree; in exactly the same way words "living entity" and "ego" are but a mode of expression for the presence of the five attachment groups, but when we come to examine the elements of being one by one, we discover that in the absolute sense there is no living entity there to form a basis for such figments as "I am" or "I"; in other words, that in the absolute sense there is only name and form. The insight of him who perceives this is called knowledge of the truth.[34]

In brief, the line of reasoning is this: *I am what I appear to be in enlightenment experience; what I appear to be in enlightenment experience is this: individual states; hence I am individual states.*

These Buddhist passages express the doctrine that Hume claims to derive from introspective experience and that Theravada (and other) Buddhist traditions believe to be confirmed in meditative and enlightenment experience. The gist of the passages is put more succinctly via the terse claim "Consciousness is soulless."[35] Hume takes each mental state – each perception, or impression and idea, as he says – to exist independent of every other. The Buddhist traditions hold that each mental state depends for its existence on other states. But this difference aside, they agree – persons at a time are bundles of momentary states, over time are a series of such bundles, and introspective and/or enlightenment experience teaches us this sort of view.

The contrasting arguments

The enduring-mental-substance view and the bundle-of-momentary-states view do agree on an important and controversial claim, namely that what we appear to be in introspective, meditative, or enlightenment experience is what we are. It is not obvious that this is so. John Locke, in Book Two of his *Essay Concerning Human Understanding*, offers an interesting third view. He agrees with Hume and Buddhism that what we are aware of is momentary states. He holds that momentary states can exist only as states of enduring substances. So he accepts the description of introspective data given by the momentary-mental-state theorist and the conclusion held by the enduring-mental-substance theorist, and there is at least nothing obviously incoherent about this view. It is incoherent if one thinks that what we are is exactly what introspection (etc.) reveals; but

Locke does not hold that. Further, of course the view that we are simply what appears to, or in, our introspective, meditative, or enlightenment experience is not something that is introspectively (etc.) confirmable. Further, if one denies that we are only what appears to, or in, our introspective (etc.) experience one does not embrace a self-contradictory doctrine. Still further, we have lots of tendencies, habits, dispositions, and properties that are not introspectively (etc.) available to us – some (like our ability to make logical inferences) are not always introspectively accessible, since we are not always making inferences; some, like either our being indestructible or our not being indestructible, are not ever introspectively available. Since the view that we are what we introspectively seem to be is common to both sides of the dispute, and an important part of their appeal to experience, both are – to that important degree at any rate – mistaken. That assumption is false.

One might revise the claim regarding introspection (etc.) to claim merely that whatever structure the self seemed to introspection (etc.) to have, or whatever fundamental sort it seemed to introspection to belong, was the structure it had or the kind to which it belonged. But *belonging to a kind* is not the sort of property that is introspectively discernible; if persons are *essentially self-conscious*, and *to be self–conscious* is the nature of persons, it still does not follow that *self-consciousness being the nature of persons* is somehow introspectively accessible. Similarly, if one has a triangular image before the mind's eye, and *being closed and three-sided* is essential to a triangle, it does not follow that *being closed and three-sided is essential to a triangle* are part of one's image. Neither *self-consciousness being the nature of persons* nor *being closed and three-sided is the nature of triangles* is an introspectively (etc.) accessible quality.

It is crucial here that Descartes used both introspective report and conceptual consideration. So did Locke: so also do Ramanuja, Hume, and the Jain and Buddhist traditions. The substantivalists – Descartes, Ramanuja, and the Jain tradition – take it to be true that it is logically impossible that there be mental states that are not the states of some person in the sense of being states of some mental substance. Here Locke, who describes his experience in Humean and Buddhist terms, agrees with Descartes, Ramanuja, and the Jains. For Jainism, Descartes, and Ramanuja, what introspection yields is not a pain, but *one's being in pain*; not a (or the) thought that Abraham Lincoln was once US President, but *one's thinking that Lincoln was President*; not hunger, but *one's being hungry*. It is *oneself-in-some-state* that is introspected. The Buddhist tradition typically takes this to be a correct account of ordinary introspection, and to that extent agrees with the substantivalists against Hume. Hence their appeal to meditative and enlightenment experience which they take to be different.

Hume takes persons to be, at a time, merely bundles of states. He takes introspection to reveal this, whereas the Buddhist tradition agrees with Hume's doctrine while taking his description of introspection to be true only of meditative and enlightenment experiences. These experiences have been, on the Buddhist view, purified from mistaken notions and, from the Jain view, rendered evidentially worthless by importation of Buddhist assumptions and made unnatural and non-representative of reliable human experience.

It is tempting to offer this explanation of the differences. Each perspective offers its reports of what experience teaches on report forms constructed in their own shops, substantival forms from the Jain shop and non-substantival forms from the Buddhist shop. What makes this possible regarding introspective experience and the dispute at hand is a variety of things we have noted already – the dispute is not a dispute about introspectively accessible properties or states, and it is a dispute inherently involving contrary philosophical theses. The Buddhist tradition is unwilling to rest the case on appeal to introspective or sensory experience because it thinks that this would refute its own position. It thus appeals to experiences that occur in meditative and enlightenment contexts of the right sort – e.g., not of the Jain sort. This involves a move not unlike the Advaita appeal to *moksha* experience as trumping others, unless Hume is right about introspective experience after all.

The problem with both the appeal-to-experience of the substantivalists and of the non-substantivalists is this: it marks out the dispute on ground that cannot offer evidence regarding it. The problem is not merely that there is no neutral way of describing introspective experience to which one can appeal for evidence that is of any use – though that is true. The problem is that the sorts of properties or states, experience of which would be evidence, are not accessible to introspective experience. *Being a substance* and *being a bundle of states* are not more properties or features that are introspectively accessible than are *being indestructible* or *being destructible*; both sorts of features differ in that regard from *being fatigued or worried or elated.*

If appeal to introspectibly accessible features are relevant to the dispute, as of course they are, they are relevant by virtue of their connection to competing theories of the self or person. The dispute then switches to the competing theories themselves – to the internal consistency, the coherence, the explanatory power, and so on, of substantival versus non-substantival theories of persons. But that is a different matter from appeal to introspective, meditative, or enlightenment experience as evidence for religious belief. It is a matter of which theory – substantivalist or non-substantivalist – can explain memory, responsibility, self-consciousness, and the like.[36] It is not a matter of direct experiential evidence.

Questions for reflection

1 Construct and assess an argument for the claim *Numinous experience is not self-authenticating regarding the claim that God exists* analogous to the one offered above regarding the claim that enlightenment experience is not self-authenticating regarding religious belief.
2 Give the best argument you can for the claim *Kevala experience provides evidence for Jain belief* and then subject it to the best critique that you can offer. What is the result?
3 Give the best argument you can for the claim *Moksha experience provides evidence for Advaita belief* and then subject it to the best critique that you can offer. What is the result?
4 Give the best argument you can for the claim *Nirvana experience provides evidence for Theravada belief* and then subject it to the best critique that you can offer. What is the result?
5 Give the best argument you can for the claim *Numinous experience provides evidence for monotheistic belief* and then subject it to the best critique that you can offer. What is the result?
6 Give the best argument you can for the claim *Sensory experience provides evidence for belief in the existence of physical objects* and then subject it to the best critique that you can offer. What is the result?

Annotated reading

Braddon-Mitchell, David and Jackson, Frank (eds) (1996) *Philosophy of Mind and Cognition*, Oxford: Blackwell. A good survey of contemporary philosophy of mind.
Chisholm, Roderick (1976) *Person and Object*, LaSalle, IL: Open Court. Defends a substance account of persons.
Loux, Michael (1997) *Metaphysics*, London: Routledge. Contains a good discussion of substance-theories and bundle-theories.
Yandell, Keith E. (1990) *Hume's "Inexplicable Mystery,"* Philadelphia: Temple University Press. Contains a detailed discussion of Hume's views.

PART V

Religion, morality, faith, and reason

CHAPTER 14
Religion and morality

14
Religion and morality

Religious values and moral values

Nonmonotheistic traditions

Religious traditions sanction religious values. Advaita Vedanta, Theravada Buddhism, and Jainism find the highest value in the attainment of release from reincarnation and the achieving of enlightenment – first a pre-enlightenment experience in this life which guarantees a later and final enlightenment upon death.

There are various logically possible relationships between moral and religious values. At one extreme, one might hold that the only way to salvation was by trampling moral values under foot or, at the other, that the only way of being morally mature was by way of rejecting all religious values as unworthy. Pursuing either line of reasoning would require a general discussion of the nature of morality. Here a more modest route is taken. Our concern is with what views of morality are available within the religious perspectives already outlined.

A key question to ask in this regard is whether moral values, as conceived by a religious tradition, are taken up into its ultimate religious value. What is of ultimate religious value for a tradition is gaining the proffered cure to its diagnosed illness, or attaining salvation or enlightenment. For Advaita Vedanta, then, however important moral values are at the level of appearance, and however stressed it is in practice that only the morally pure can achieve enlightenment, since morality has no place or purchase on a qualityless Brahman, the ultimate religious value – realization of identity with qualityless Brahman, recognition of an identity alleged always to have held – has no moral content. Moral virtue is at best a means to the achievement of an amoral religious condition.

Theravada Buddhism construes the achievement of nirvana either as annihilation altogether or at least as involving the loss of anything that would involve the continued existence of an individual person. On this perspective, there is comparatively little to a person at a time, or over time, and it appears that this notion of what individuality amounts to is preparatory to an account on which all individuality is lost.

Here, too, then, final enlightenment has no moral content – indeed, perhaps, no content period. Thus, however nice individual or typical Theravada Buddhists, or Advaita Vedantins, may be, and whatever the morally relevant effects of their respective traditions in the cultures that they influence, it seems true that ultimate religious value has, for these traditions, no place for any sort of intrinsic moral value.

Jainism is more complex in this regard. In Jain enlightenment, personal identity is retained, and there is no reason to deny that what sort of person, morally speaking, one has been may enter into one's status in final enlightenment – may, so to say, flavor the enlightenment experience in one way or another. Thus while following a strict code is required here, as in Theravada and Advaita, in order to achieve enlightenment, in Jainism alone of these alternatives is it possible to contend that one's moral character now somehow carries over into one's condition in enlightenment, for only in Jainism is there anything in the condition of enlightenment to which moral properties might belong or which might possess moral character.

Monotheistic traditions

If God is conceived as a moral agent, as is frequent but not universal among monotheists, then God's existence is the highest moral value and the core of morality relative to created persons is their *being made in the image of God* and their achieving their positive potential by *imitation of God*. A highly plausible view of morality takes moral principles[1] to be, if true, then necessarily true. Monotheists who suppose *God exists* to be a logically necessary truth can take the necessary truth of true moral principles to be grounded in divine cognitive states; monotheists who view *God exists* as contingently true can ground necessarily true moral principles in abstract objects that possess logically necessary existence.[2] On both views, if a moral principle is true, it is true whether God creates or not. A moral principle, being conditional – of the form possessed by *If X is a person then X ought to be respected*, for example – will be true under all possible conditions, including those in which God does not create. On both views, there will be persons[3] to whom moral principles apply only if God creates them.

It is sometimes argued that God cannot be said to be morally good in the same sense in which human beings – say, St Paul – are said to be good. Two arguments often given for this view are:

Argument 1

1 *God is good* is a necessary truth.
2 *St Paul is good,* even if true, is a contingent truth.
3 If "X" in "Y is X" is used in a sentence expressing a necessary truth, and "X" in "Z is X" is used in a sentence expressing a contingent truth, then "X" as used in the one sentence bears a different meaning than does "X" as used in the other sentence. Hence:
4 "Good" as used in "God is good" has a different meaning than does "good" in "St Paul is good."

The problem with this argument is that the principle expressed in premise 3 is false. Consider the sentences "Three is odd" and "The number of coins on the table is odd." The proposition expressed by the first of these sentences is a necessary truth, and the proposition expressed by the second of these sentences is, if true at all, a contingent truth. But "odd" means the same in both cases. Hence premise 3 is false.

The other line of reasoning is that if God is good, still God can do things, and allow things, without ceasing to be good, that no human being could do, or allow,[4] without ceasing to be good. Jill, if she allows a person to suffer terribly when she could easily stop it, or causes someone to die even though her family needs her desperately, is not a good person. God, if God exists, at least allows such things all the time without ceasing to be called good. So "good" must mean something else in heaven than on earth.

This argument ignores the fact that ascriptions of goodness ultimately rest on motives, intentions, ends, and – in the end – character. Two persons, of equally good character, can act differently if their knowledge and powers differ, and greatly differently if their knowledge and powers differ greatly. A man on a train who is in sudden need of a delicate operation will rightly react differently to the idea of a skilled surgeon performing the operation immediately and a sincere lawyer with a knife and good intentions attempting to perform the same operation. Presumably the surgeon may, and perhaps ought, to operate; the lawyer ought to go get help. The claim that God is good is the claim that God's motives, ends, intentions, and character resemble those of a good human person, allowing for difference in knowledge and power. The range of things that God can allow and bring good out of thus vastly exceeds those available to any human being. Especially relevant in this regard is the monotheistic view that while a person's death ends our ability to affect them, it makes no difference to God's power to affect them. So this argument too fails.

Deterministic views

Fatalism: determinism based on logical necessity

Fatalism is the view that these two things are true:

1 Every truth is a necessary truth.
2 Every falsehood is a necessary falsehood.

If one holds that God exists, and is a fatalist, one will think that *God exists* is a necessary truth and also that it, plus various necessary truths about God's nature, will explain other necessary truths about the existence and history of the world.

There can be no such thing as explaining why a particular necessary truth N is *true rather than false* – its having been false is logically impossible and there is no need to eliminate a non-possibility. There is no *possibly being false* to rule out. One can put the point here by contrasting a necessary truth like *Even an omnipotent being cannot fiat the actions of a libertarianly free person* and a contingent truth like *Boston's National Basketball franchise is named the Celtics*. The necessary truth concerning omnipotence and freedom can be explained by making its meaning clear; a detailed explanation of libertarian freedom is offered later in this chapter. But explaining the truth of a necessary truth amounts either to giving an account of its sense or offering an account of necessary truth generally – a theory of necessity such as *Necessary truths are grounded in abstract objects*. Neither of these is a matter of describing some conditions that might have obtained and the obtaining of which would make the necessary truth in question false. There are no such conditions. The contingent truth about the Celtics can be explained in terms of the history of the franchise; what makes it true is a series of events that might never have occurred, so this explanation is a matter of accounting for the fact that it is true rather than false. Even, then, if one is a fatalist – in which case one will deny that there are any logically contingent truths or falsehoods – it is baffling how the truth of one necessary truth could explain the truth of another.

Nonetheless, setting this problem aside, consider a monotheistic version of fatalism. On this view, *Necessarily, God exists* is true, as are each of the following: *Necessarily, God has all and only those properties definitive of God's nature; Necessarily, God's choices are entirely determined by God's nature; Necessarily, whatever is true is true because God chose that it be true*.[5] Then consider the consequences.

One consequence is that God's existence and nature entirely determine

God's choices, which in turn determine everything else. But it is, by hypothesis, logically impossible that God not exist or that God not have the nature that God has. So it is logically impossible that any true proposition is not true or that any proposition that is not true was true. The right way to think of the sort of scenario described is in terms of an axiomatic system in which all the theorems follow by rules of inference from the axioms; the axioms are necessary truths, the rules of inference truth preserving, and so the theorems are also necessary truths. The first consequence, then, would be this: if a theologically based *logical fatalism* were true: every truth a necessary truth, every falsehood a contradiction, then the actual world also the only world possible.

Another consequence is that there would be at most one agent. Suppose that Tess and Tricia are related as follows. Tess has her own thought life, but Tricia thinks only when and what Tess deliberately, specifically causes her to think. Tess can act without Tricia, but Tricia acts only if Tess causes her to act. In fact, every feeling, mental image, dream, movement, attitude, pain, or pleasure Tricia experiences, Tess deliberately, specifically causes her to experience. Tess knows her power over Tricia, but Tricia is ignorant of it. Finally, this relationship between Tess and Tricia is one neither can break; its roots lie deep in the laws of nature. It is logically possible that Tess and Tricia not be so related, but only logically possible. Under these circumstances, however things seem to Tricia, she is not an agent; she does not act on her own, think on her own, feel on her own. But on the scenario with which we began, God is, so to speak, related to whatever persons there are (or appear to be), as Tess is related to Tricia, only more so; here the roots of the relationship lie deep in the nature of a necessarily existing God and in the laws of logic. It is not even logically possible that God not be so related to any persons there may be, or appear to be. Indeed, on the scenario being considered, there is at most one person. On it, God is related to Tess in such a manner that her existence as well as her thoughts, feelings, and actions are entirely determined by God's existence and nature. It is no more logically possible that God exist and Tess not than it is logically possible that Tess exist and God not; *God exists*, on the scenario in question, entails *Tess exists*, and since the former is, by hypothesis, a necessary truth, so is the latter.[6] Thus *Tess exists* also entails *God exists*. Tess is not a person distinct from God; she is at most, as Spinoza would put it, a *mode* – a state – of God's.[7] It is not logically possible that "her" existence and "her" properties, thoughts, and actions exist without God's existing and having the nature that God possesses; the divine existence and nature determine "her" existence and properties in such a way that it is logically impossible that they be otherwise than as they are. In such a world, morality would be impossible. Even if we suppose that Tess is a person, it would be logically impossible that she or anyone act other than as they did, think other than as they did, feel other than as they did. Any suggestion to the effect that anyone might have acted, thought, or felt at some time other than as they did think, act, or feel at that time would be self-contradictory. If all truths were necessary truths, there would be no way things could be other than the way things were. The notions of responsibility and obligation, guilt and innocence, freedom and agency, all presuppose at least the logical possibility of alternatives. *Logical fatalism is true* and *There are moral agents* are logically incompatible propositions; while there is not much controversy concerning this point, there is considerable controversy regarding what sort of world it is within which agents can exist who are free in the sense required if they are to be morally responsible for their choices and actions.

This discussion of monotheistic fatalism raises some interesting questions regarding what is to come. If it is clear that the absence of logically possible alternatives entails the absence of freedom, is there any good reason to think the absence of all but counterfactual alternatives – alternatives available in other possible worlds but not in the real world, alternatives "available" only in a sense compatible with the actions actually performed being in fact inevitable – does not also entail the absence of freedom? If it is true that there is but one agent in a fatalistic monotheistic world, is there any good reason to think that there is more than one agent in a deterministic world?

Determinism not based on logical necessity

Let a tensed universal description (TUD) be an accurate statement of everything that is true in the world at a given time. Each such description should be viewed as tensed to some specific time that is specified in the description. Let LN be a correct account of all of the laws of nature, and LL a correct account of all of the laws of logic. Then *determinism* holds: *For any TUD tensed earlier than time t, that TUD plus LN plus LL, entails any TUD tensed to time t or later*. Thus, if determinism is true, the past determines a unique future. There are logical possibilities alternative to what happens at any given time; it is simply not compatible with the laws of logic, the laws of nature, and what has happened in the past that they be realized. So they will not happen, and there is no more that we can do about that than there is we can do about the truth of the laws of logic, the laws of nature, or what happened in the past.

Compatibilism and incompatibilism

Compatibilism holds that it is logically possible that determinism be true and that persons have the sort of freedom that is required for them to be morally responsible for their choices and actions. The opposite position to compatibilism is *incompatibilism*, which holds that it is not logically possible (non-contradictory) that determinism be true and that persons have the sort of freedom that is required for them to be morally responsible for their choices and actions.

Libertarianism[8]

Libertarianism holds that incompatibilism is true and determinism is false; in order for persons to have the sort of freedom that is required for them to be morally responsible for their choices and actions they must have genuine freedom, not compatibilist so-called freedom, regarding those choices and actions. Libertarians hold that persons do have this sort of freedom. Compatibilists are dubious that there is even possibly any sort of freedom beyond that which they affirm. The notion of libertarian freedom, often called categorical freedom, runs as follows.

(CF) *Jane is categorically (or libertarianly) free with respect to lying at T* entails *Jane's lying is within her power at T and Jane's refraining from lying is within her power at T.*

In turn:

(CFa) *Jane's lying is within her power at T* entails *Jane's lying at T does not require that Jane falsify some total universal description (TUD) tensed to a time earlier than T, make some law of nature false, or make some law of logic false;*

and

(CFb) *Jane's refraining from lying is within her power at T* entails *Jane's refraining from lying at T does not require that Jane falsify some TUD tensed to a time earlier than T, make some law of nature false, or make some law of logic false.*

(CF) is to be understood as containing the definitions provided by (CFa) and (CFb).

Relations between the positions

It may be helpful in understanding these alternatives to see some of their relationship laid out.

1 One can consistently be a determinist and an incompatibilist.
2 One can consistently be a determinist and a compatibilist.
3 One cannot consistently be a determinist and a libertarian.
4 One cannot consistently be an incompatibilist and a compatibilist.
5 *Being a libertarian* entails *being an incompatibilist.*
6 *Being an incompatibilist* does not entail *being a libertarian.*
7 *Being a compatibilist* does not entail *being a determinist.*

Monotheistic determinism and monotheistic libertarianism

A fundamental dispute within monotheism concerns whether possession of compatibilist freedom yields a world sufficiently different from (monotheistic?) logical fatalism to allow for there to be human agents who are morally responsible for their thoughts and actions. Libertarian monotheists think that if the only sort of freedom human persons have is so-called compatibilist freedom then God is cause of whatever evils our thoughts and actions involve. Or they think that God is the only agent, and that human personhood is mere appearance. Compatibilist monotheists disagree. If compatibilism is false, then of course monotheists ought to reject it. There is an interesting and powerful argument against compatibilism.

An argument against compatibilism

Consider the TUD that is tensed to the time just before the last dinosaur died; let that be *TUDdino*. Then suppose that you will decide to have a cup of coffee at 3:00 this afternoon; let the TUD tensed to that time be *TUDcup*; *TUDcup*, of course, includes a statement to the effect that you decide to have a cup of coffee at 3:00. If determinism is true, then:

1 *TUDdino and LL and LN* entails *TUDcup*.
2 One is not responsible for anything that one has no control over.
3 One has no control over anything that is entailed by what one has no control over.

4 One is not responsible for anything that is entailed by what one has no control over (from 2, 3).
5 You have no control over what is true in *TUDdino*.
6 You have no control over what the laws of logic are.
7 You have no control over what the laws of nature are.
8 You have no control over *TUDdino and LL and LN* (from 5–7).
9 You have no control over what *TUDdino and LL and LN* entails (from 4, 8).
10 You have no control over *TUDcup* (from 1, 9).
11 *TUDcup* entails *You decide to have coffee at 3:00*.
12 You have no control over whether you decide to have coffee at 3:00 (from 10, 11).

Note that you and your decision/action "stand in" here for everyone and every one of everyone's decisions/actions. So what follows is that *if determinism is true* then no one is ever responsible for any decision/action. Hence compatibilism, which claims otherwise, is false.[9] Central to controversy over the success of this argument is whether premise 3 – *One has no control over anything that is entailed by what one has no control over* – is true. This claim is sometimes called the *Control Principle*.

Explanation and determinism

If determinism is true, then for any TUD true at time T1 it is not merely the case that *The TUD true at T1 plus the laws of logic plus the laws of nature entail the TUD true at any later time* but that the TUD true at time T1 plus the laws of logic and the laws of nature also *explain* the truth of the TUD true at time T2, and so on. Even if it is a necessary element in explanation, entailment is not sufficient for explanation. The proposition *Either 1 and 3 are 7 or Oklahoma is a state, and 1 and 3 are not 7* entails the proposition *Oklahoma is a state*, but Oklahoma's statehood has not been explained.

The notion of an explanation is notoriously difficult, but this much can be said about it. Let us say that *If X obtains then Y obtains* is true and expresses a law, then there is an *X/Y lawlike connection*; let us also say that if there is a true non-lawlike proposition of the form *If X obtains then an agent with the power to bring about Y will do A* then there is an *X/Y teleological connection*. In order that *X obtains* explain *Y obtains* it must be the case that X does indeed obtain, and the case that there is a true proposition that expresses a lawlike or a teleological X/Y connection. Determinism assumes that for every state *B* that obtains, there is another state *A* such that *A* obtains and such that there is a lawlike *A/B* connection.

In order for determinism to be true, the past must not only entail, but also explain, the future by virtue of there always being such lawlike connections.[10]

The Control Principle

What is most interestingly controversial about the argument, stated above, against compatibilism concerns the third premise, which states a version of the Control Principle: (CP) One has no control over anything that is entailed by what one has no control over. Is (CP), or some appropriate replacement, true? (CP) tells us this: one may properly infer from *Sam has no control over whether A obtains* and *That A obtains entails that B obtains* to *Sam has no control over whether B obtains*. There are two sorts of objection to (CP).

One is that there are analogous inferences that are not proper. For example, neither of these arguments is valid:

Example 1: Sue is obligated to do A; doing A entails doing B; hence Sue is obligated to do B. (Sue is obligated to wash her dog; washing her dog entails shifting the position of some atoms; hence Sue is obligated to shift the position of some atoms.)[11]

Example 2: Sue believes that P; that P is true entails that Q is true; hence Sue believes that Q. (Sue believes that figure F is a triangle; that F is a triangle entails that F's interior angles sum to 180 degrees; hence Sue believes that F's interior angles sum to 180 degrees. Sue can believe that F is a triangle but has learned no geometry sufficient for believing anything about what F's interior angles sum to.)

On the other hand, there are analogous inferences that are entirely proper:

Example 3: Necessarily, P entails Q; Necessarily P; hence *Necessarily Q*.

Example 4: P entails Q; P is true; hence Q is true

are valid inferences. Is it with these, or with the previous examples, that the Control Principle is properly compared? That is just the question all over again as to whether the Control Principle is true. No real progress is likely along these lines, either in favor or against the Control Principle.

Each party to the dispute will simply put forward examples that exhibit their view of the matter, and claim – neither more nor less cogently than the other – that these are the genuinely parallel cases.

The other and better strategy involves looking very closely at what the Control Principle says and endeavoring to find clear counterexamples to it. Suppose *X obtains at time T* is necessarily true of some fact X – that seventeen is prime, or that necessary truths are necessarily necessary. (Such facts will obtain at any time you please.) In such a case, X's obtaining, let us say, is *logically inevitable*. Note that if the occurrence of some state of affairs A is logically inevitable, then A's non-occurrence is logically impossible. Suppose that *State of affairs Y obtains at time T2* is contingently true, as is *State of affairs X obtains at T1*, where T1 is a time *before* any human being existed and T2 is a time well *after* the first human beings came to exist. Suppose, finally, that the conjunct *(X obtains at T1 and The laws of logic are true and The laws of nature are true and Y does not obtain at T2)* is a contradiction. Then let us say that, *given X, Y is in fact inevitable*. When this is so regarding some state of affairs, let us say that it is *in fact inevitable*. Note that if state of affairs A is in fact inevitable, then A's non-occurrence is in fact impossible – *A does not occur* is logically inconsistent with the very complex conjunct composed of the truth about the past, the laws of nature, and the laws of logic. Even the staunchest compatibilist should grant that whether something obtained or not before any human being existed was not something any human being could do anything whatever about, and the same goes for the laws of logic and the laws of nature. Then given things true in our world that we had nothing to do with making true and could not have altered, what occurs now (if determinism is true) is in fact inevitable. So we could do nothing about whether any thing that obtains now did so or not – not even any of our thoughts or actions. What the Control Principle claims is that, regarding things that are either logically or in fact inevitable, and what these things entail,[12] we do not have any control. If determinism is true, whatever occurs is in fact inevitable. So if determinism is true, and the Control Principle is true, there is nothing whatever that we have control over.

Given this understanding of the Control Principle, consider its application to a simple case. Suppose that there is a golden retriever Fairy who makes sure that (R) is true:

(R) *Every golden retriever in the world is well fed.*

Ruth, who owns a golden retriever, has no control over whether (R) is true or not. Obviously (given that Ruth has a golden retriever) (R) entails:

(GR) *Ruth's golden retriever is well fed.*

If (R) is true, then Ruth's golden retriever will be fed, whether Ruth feeds him or not. What can be up to Ruth is simply whether or not *she* feeds him. She can make (GR) true, even though (GR) will be true whether she makes it true or not. What Ruth can have control over, even if (R) is true, is whether

(RG) *It is Ruth who feeds Ruth's golden retriever*

is true. There is a distinction to be made between *cases in which a proposition will be true whether one so acts as to make it true or not* and *cases in which a proposition will be true only if one so acts as to make it true.* What is in one's control in the former cases is what happens by virtue of which a particular proposition is true – whether it is true by virtue of one's own activities or by virtue of something else; what is in one's control in the latter cases is whether anything at all occurs in virtue of which a particular proposition is true. Let us call instances of the former sort cases of *partial* control and instances of the latter sort cases of *full* control.

Suppose that (R) will be true, whatever Ruth does. Since (R) *Every golden retriever in the world is well fed* entails (GR) *Ruth's golden retriever is well fed,* the Control Principle tells us that whether (GR) is true also does not depend on what Ruth does. (RG) *It is Ruth who feeds Ruth's golden retriever,* however, is not entailed by (R). Given (R) and the Control Principle, the truth of (GR) is not under even Ruth's partial control. Given (R) and (GR), the truth of (RG) can still be under her partial control.

If determinism is true, some truths descriptive of a pre-Ruth past, plus the laws of nature and the laws of logic – what we might call some *pre-Ruth package* of truths – either entails (RG) or entails not-(RG). This fact, plus the Control Principle, entails that whether (RG) is true or not is also not even in Ruth's partial control.

Suppose determinism is true, and Ruth herself feeds her golden retriever at time T. Then her doing so is in fact inevitable, and her not doing so is in fact impossible. Suppose that determinism is true, and Ruth does not herself feed her golden retriever at time T. Then her not doing so is in fact inevitable and her doing so is in fact impossible. What is in fact impossible for Ruth is not under Ruth's control. So the Control Principle seems correct in its implications regarding Ruth and the feeding of her golden retriever.

It is worth noting what, if determinism is true, the distinction between partial control and full control amounts to. Consider what, if determinism is true, having partial control means. We may as well consider this concretely in terms once again of Ruth and her dog. If determinism is true, then to say that Ruth has *partial* control regarding whether her dog is fed is to say that the conditional *If Ruth does not feed her dog, her dog will be fed* is *true* (the golden retriever Fairy will become active) but either *Ruth does feed her dog* is in fact inevitably true or *Ruth does not feed her dog* is in fact inevitably true. If determinism is true, then to say that Ruth has *full* control regarding whether her dog is fed is to say that the conditional *If Ruth does not feed her dog, her dog will be fed* is *false* but either *Ruth does feed her dog* is in fact inevitably true or *Ruth does not feed her dog* is in fact inevitably true. If whether her dog is fed or not is in fact inevitable, and whether she feeds it or not is in fact inevitable, it is hard to see how she is free with respect to her dog being fed. Why think that, if determinism is true, anyone is ever free regarding anything?

Compatibilist replies

The natural compatibilist replies to this question amount to this: they find some feature of Ruth that causes Ruth's behavior, and claim that there being a cause of this sort is what it amounts to for Ruth to be free. Suppose Ruth feeds her dog, and her doing so she wants to do, intends to do, and the like. Her body makes all the appropriate dog-feeding movements because of her wants, desires, intentions, and like, and the dog happily eats his dinner. But then Ruth – the compatibilist claims – feeds her dog, and is responsible for doing so. If the sorts of thing she has done are morally right or wrong, she is morally praiseworthy or blameworthy for having done it. So she is free in whatever sense moral responsibility requires.

The incompatibilist, whether she is a libertarian or not, wonders how this can be so, in the light of the considerations previously noted – given that if determinism is true, whatever is done is in fact inevitably done. To answer, compatibilists have to give some account of freedom.

Possibility

It is helpful, in approaching compatibilist accounts of freedom, to highlight three relevant concepts:

Logical inevitability: State of affairs A is logically inevitable if and only if *A obtains* is a logically necessary truth.

In fact inevitability: State of affairs A is in fact inevitable if and only if *A obtains* is entailed by the truth about the past, the laws of nature, and the laws of logic.

These notions contrast to:

Causal impossibility: State of affairs A is causally impossible if and only if *A obtains only if some law of nature is false.*

Compatibilists take it to be possible that a bit of behavior be in fact inevitable and one that one is morally responsible for performing. Compatibilists and incompatibilists typically agree that human beings never perform actions that are logically inevitable or causally impossible. Libertarians deny that human actions are typically in fact inevitable and add that, were they, no one would ever be responsible for them.[13]

Compatibilism and actions versus nonactions

The compatibilist thinks that whether determinism is true or not, and hence even if it is true, we can have the sort of freedom required for moral responsibility. Hence he holds that this sort of freedom regarding some thought or action is compatible with that thought or action being in fact inevitable.

One may be responsible for what one does, but also for what one does not do. A friend who could easily have stopped your progress and knew what would happen if he did not, but nonetheless allowed you to walk into the path of a moving vehicle, is not innocent merely because she did not push you into its path. For simplicity, however, focus here will be on responsibility for what one does. Regarding such responsibility, *Karen is responsible for action A* entails *Karen performed A.*

Let *Karen's states at time T* refer to all of the physical states Karen's body is in at T and all of the mental states her mind is in at T. If determinism is true, each of those states is in fact inevitable, given the content of the past. Let us say that a causal chain *passes through Karen at T* if and only if at least one of its members is also one of Karen's states at T. If some action by Karen is a member of a causal chain – a chain whose earlier members result in Karen performing that action – let us call it an *action chain relative to Karen*; for short, an *action chain*. Any action chain relative to Karen must pass through Karen.

Consider the various sorts of mental states that one can be in that are relevant to how one acts – intentions, purposes, goals, preferences, likes, dislikes, desires, wants, choices, and so on. Let these be *action-inclining states*. Action-inclining states relative to chewing a stick of gum will include desiring to chew it, intending to chew it, having chewing it as a purpose or a goal, and the like. If a chain passes through Karen but contains no action-inclining state of Karen's, then even if it results in some motions of her body, it is dubious that it is an action chain regarding her. There is a difference between *Karen's teeth gnashing* and *Karen gnashing her teeth*, and if determinism being true is compatible with making that distinction between actual cases, presumably the difference will be one between a causal chain passing through Karen that contains none of Karen's action-inclining states (*Karen's teeth gnashing*) and a causal chain passing through Karen that does contain some action-inclining state of her where the target of that state is her teeth being gnashed together (*Karen gnashing her teeth*). An action chain relative to Karen's performing action A must pass through Karen in such a way that it contains action-inclining states which are at least partial causes of A. This is one way, perhaps the most natural, for a determinist to endeavor to distinguish between what is, and what is not, an action: actions are the products of action chains that pass through the person who acts in such a manner that the person's action-inclining states are at least among the action's causes.

Suppose Sam decides to commit murder. If determinism is true, this decision is in fact inevitable given things that occurred in the distant, pre-Sam past. The compatibilist will note that the causal chain that yields Sam's decision "runs through Sam," so to speak, whereas other causal chains do not do so. The earlier portion of the causal chain that yields the pre-Sam events whose occurrence, if determinism is true, render his choice in fact inevitable has in fact run through Sam. The compatibilist will add that there are logically possible worlds in which Sam's decision does not obtain; the events that render Sam's decision in fact inevitable would not obtain if one of those worlds was the actual world. This is the difference between Sam's decision being logically inevitable and its being in fact inevitable. Presumably, if determinism is true, it is not logically possible that the events that render his decision in fact inevitable occur without his decision also occurring – not unless one could have the same events but different causal laws. The core of the compatibilist's position will lie in the development of a notion of *is under the control of* where something is under one's control provided *one could have done otherwise* or one was *compatibilistically free* relative to whether something occurred. Thus compatibilist freedom invites our attention.

Compatibilist freedom

One suggestion regarding what this sort of freedom amounts to is this: let D be a description of what has occurred up to time T, L a statement of the laws of nature, and L* a statement of the laws of logic. Let their conjunct be *the whole past package*. Jane wonders whether or not to lie to John. It turns out that *Jane lies to John* is compatible with the whole past package, and *Jane does not lie to John* is not compatible with the whole past package.[14] The idea is to leave room for Jane's being free even though what Jane will do must be compatible with the whole past package and only one of the logically possible alternatives is compatible with that package; on this view, whatever sort of freedom responsibility requires is constrained by this condition. Given the conditions described, Jane will lie to John, her lying to John is in fact inevitable, and *Jane is morally responsible for lying to John* is compatible with *Jane's not lying to John is incompatible with the whole past package*. Jane's lying, on this account, follows from what has happened prior to her lying, given the laws of logic and the laws of nature.[15]

The range of what can be said to give this alleged freedom content should be explored. If Jane's lying is an action on Jane's part, it must be related to Jane in certain ways – this, we might say, is the *positive story* regarding Jane's freely lying. The *positive story* is the story of the conditions regarding Jane's actually lying, whether it concerns what she did or what was not done to her. Further, if she is free in performing that action, her *not* performing it must have been available to her in certain ways – this, we might say, is the *negative story* regarding Jane's freely lying. The *negative story* is the story of the conditions regarding the availability to Jane of refraining from lying. The combination of the positive story and negative story, where both are told with compatibilist constraints, will be the whole compatibilist story regarding her freely lying. There is no universal agreement among compatibilists as to how this story goes, and we will give a very full account that captures a good many of the elements that compatibilists include in that story. What we say about the version of the story here can also be said about other compatibilist accounts.

Constraints

For an account of free action to be compatibilist, it must be the case that it can be a true account even if determinism is true. Hence *Jane's action is in fact inevitable* (where *in fact inevitable* is understood as we have defined it) and *Jane's action is free and she is morally responsible for so acting* are logically compatible. Our formulation of the compatibilist account will endeavor to give as broad a definition as this constraint allows – to include as many elements as it allows.[16]

The positive story

Jane's lying to John at time T obviously entails *Jane lied to John at T*. We have already noted that, on a compatibilist account, it entails *An action chain that includes Jane's lying to John at T passes through Jane.*

A classic analysis of this sort of freedom goes like this: Jane is free in lying to John at time T if and only if (i) Jane lies to John at T, (ii) Jane wanted to lie to John at T, and (iii) Jane's lying is caused by her wanting to. Let us say that if Jane and her lying are related as (i) through (iii) indicate, Jane's lying is *congenial*. This serves to emphasize that the relevant action chain contains states of Jane that are at least a partial cause of Jane's lying to John, where those states on the whole incline toward rather than against lying.

Here, then, is part of one compatibilist positive story regarding Jane's freely lying to John at time T:

> *Jane's lying to John at time T is a free action* entails *Jane lied to John at T, An action chain that includes Jane's lying to John at T passes through Jane,* and *Jane's lying to John at T is (in the sense defined) congenial to Jane.*

This is compatible with Jane's not liking to do it, but liking any other alternative still less.

If Jim has hypnotized Jane to lie, puts a gun to her head to make her lie, or the like, John *coerces* Jane to lie. If Jane is related to her lying as a kleptomaniac to stealing, Jane is a *compulsive* liar. Suppose neither of these is the case; then Jane's lying is *neither coerced nor compulsed*. Thus far we have at least a fairly complete positive story – one that includes at least a great deal of what is available to such an account:

> *Jane's lying to John at T is a free action* entails *Jane lied to John at T, an action chain that includes Jane's lying to John at T passes through Jane, Jane's lying to John at T is (in the sense defined) congenial to Jane,* and *At T, Jane is neither coerced nor compulsed to lie to John.*

The negative story

If this is (one compatibilist version of) the positive story, there is also a compatibilist account of the availability to Jane of not lying to John at time T. If her not lying is just plain not available to her, then her lying isn't a free action.

Jane's not lying is not logically impossible; it is, in that sense, *logically available*. It is not against the laws of nature; it is, in that sense, *naturally available*. It is within her capacity in the sense that she knows what a lie is and what she will say to John if she lies and she knows how to say those words, she is not dumb or paralyzed, she has whatever range of cognitive, psychological, and physical capacities is required by not lying; Jane's not lying is, in that sense, *competently available*. Perhaps it is true that if she had chosen not to lie, she could have refrained from lying; then, in that sense, Jane's not lying is *counterfactually available*. Even if all this is so, either her choosing to lie or her not choosing to lie is incompatible with the whole past package.[17] Since she lies, her lying is in fact inevitable – it is in fact inevitable that she does not choose not to lie. So even if it is true that if she had not chosen to lie she would not have lied, it is also true that it was in fact inevitable that she did not choose not to lie.

On one version, then, of the compatibilist account,

> *Jane's lying to John at T is a free action* entails *Jane's not lying to John at T is logically, naturally, competently, and counterfactually available to Jane at T.*

Perhaps there is more.

Perhaps this should be added. Suppose that Jane ordinarily has a set of only true beliefs about what one can expect from ordinary computers, but that one morning her colleagues discover her trying to fry eggs on her keyboard. Jane is, in this respect, irrational in the sense that, given beliefs anyone familiar with computers has, she should know that the result of her keyboard-and-egg behavior will not be breakfast.[18] A compatibilist may wish to add that actions that are irrational on Jane's part are not free actions. If so, we then get:

> *Jane's lying to John at T is a free action* entails *Jane's not lying to John at T is logically, naturally, competently, and counterfactually available to Jane at T, and Jane's not lying to John at T would not be irrational.*

It should be noted that *being irrational* here involves such things as having wildly implausible beliefs or reasoning in a chaotic fashion or the like; it is not a sense of irrational in which, for example, acting wrongly is inherently irrational.

Finally, perhaps lack of irrationality in the rough sense broadly characterized should also be added to Jane's act of lying. If we do this, and put the resultant positive and negative stories together, we get this result:

> *Jane's lying to John at T is a free action* entails *Jane lied to John at T. An action chain that includes Jane's lying to John at T passes through Jane, Jane's lying to John at T is (in the sense defined) congenial to Jane. At T, Jane is neither coerced nor compulsed to lie to John,* and *Jane's lying to John at T is not*

> *irrational in the sense of resulting from her having wildly implausible beliefs or reasoning chaotically,* and *Jane's not lying to John at T is logically, naturally, competently, and counterfactually available to Jane at T, and Jane's not lying to John at T would not be irrational.*

Perhaps there remains something that we must add in order to express fairly this sort of analysis of the freedom responsibility requires. But somewhere not too far along the road we have been traveling, presumably one gets to that point without having gotten to the point where both Jane's not lying and Jane's lying are compatible with the whole past package. We have come close at least to that point. For a compatibilist, to reach that point is to have gone too far.

The sort of freedom, if it is such, that we have been describing is a fairly complete rendering of *compatibilist* freedom. One could contest various elements included and perhaps contend for some additions. But it is a fair account of various elements that compatibilists have included in their accounts of compatibilist freedom, and that is all that we need. Is it true that compatibilist freedom is the sort of freedom a moral agent has if she is responsible for her actions?

The Control Principle says:

(CP) One has no control over anything that is entailed by what one has no control over.

The corresponding compatibilist claim is:

(CC) One has control over what one has compatibilist freedom concerning.

The compatibilist will claim that in (CP) "having control of" is given the sense of "has categorical or libertarian freedom regarding" and is thus a claim the compatibilist will reject in favor of (CC). Further, the compatibilist claims, being categorically or libertarianly free is not a necessary condition of being morally responsible. The libertarian response is that one can be neither free nor morally responsible regarding any action that is in fact inevitable. The compatibilist account of freedom may be fine as far as it goes, but it leaves out a crucial element – genuine alternatives that cannot coexist with in fact inevitable actions. The central principle in dispute here has been called the Principle of Alternative Possibilities.

The Principle of Alternative Possibilities

The libertarian typically embraces the Principle of Alternative Possibilities which says that one is responsible for performing an action A on a given occasion only if on that occasion one has categorical freedom regarding performing A as well as categorical freedom regarding refraining from performing A. This principle has met with great resistance of late on grounds worth investigating.

Alleged counterexamples to the Principle of Alternative Possibilities

Recent philosophy has seen a variety of alleged counterexamples to the claim that anyone lacking categorical freedom cannot properly be held morally responsible for anything. The basic idea of the objector is to present cases in which an agent who lacks categorical freedom is nonetheless morally responsible for what she does. Once one sees the relevant recipe, one can construct one alleged example after another; a couple of simple cases will convey the core idea. Suppose that in each case there is a morally right thing to do, and that "responsible" means "morally responsible."

Case 1: John sits in his room. He has a big chemistry exam tomorrow and can either study for it or go out to the Sherlock Holmes Movie Festival. He loves Holmes films and hates chemistry. Yet he decides to stay at his desk and study. Unknown to him, his parents in any case locked his door from the outside, so he could not have left anyway. Yet John is responsible for his choice to stay at his desk.

Case 2: Mary sits reflecting as to whether to send a bitter letter to her aunt, who has angered her greatly. But she also knows her aunt meant well and that it would be wrong to send the letter. Unknown to Mary, her sister Ann, a doctor, inserted a microchip into Mary's brain that allows Ann to monitor Mary's thoughts and control them if she wishes. Ann loves her aunt deeply and is monitoring Mary's thoughts; if Mary decides not to send the letter Ann will do nothing, but if Mary decides to send the letter Ann will make her reverse her decision. Mary decides on her own not to mail the letter, so Ann does nothing.

The argument then goes as follows: in Case 1, John is responsible for having chosen to stay and study, even though he could not have left had he tried; in Case 2, Mary does not send the letter, even though she could not have sent it had she tried. Neither John nor Mary, in the cases described, possesses categorical freedom, but both are praiseworthy for their actions. If they are praiseworthy, then they are responsible. So possessing categorical freedom is not a logically necessary condition of being responsible for what one does. Hence compatibilism is true.

Here is another way to put the argument. Since to make a choice is to act (an action need not be overt), reference to actions covers choices as well. Consider one version of the Principle of Alternative Possibilities:

(PA) If person S is morally responsible for having performed action A at time T in context C, then S could have refrained from having performed action A at time T in context C.

According to (PA), if John is responsible for having stayed in his room, he could have left it; if Mary is responsible for not having sent the letter, she could have sent it. The point of the cases is that in them (PA) is false and John and Mary are responsible anyway. The alleged truth of (PA) is what justifies the claim that only possessors of categorical freedom are morally responsible for what they do. Since (PA) is discernibly false, making that claim is not justified. But that claim is essential to incompatibilism. So incompatibilism is false. The core idea of this argument is this: if (PA) is false of a case in which an agent acts, it is also false of that agent in that case that he possesses categorical freedom, and there are cases in which an agent acts and is morally responsible for so acting even though (PA) is false of that agent.

Reply to the objections

Regarding Case 1, there are various moves open to an incompatibilist. Here are two:

Move 1: She can say that strictly what John is responsible for is not staying in the room (he could not have done otherwise) but choosing not to try to leave and deciding to study (he could have chosen to try to leave, or not to study). This is what he is responsible for, and (PA) is true of this.

Move 2: While Move 1 is correct so far as it goes, there is an additional consideration. Suppose that a person is

> categorically free regarding whether she does something A at time T and in circumstance C, and she knows that, at T and in C, doing A is sufficient for the occurrence of B. Given this knowledge, she does A in order that B may occur. Then she is responsible for B occurring, even if B would have occurred had she not done A. John's deciding to stay in is sufficient for John's staying, and John has categorical freedom regarding how he decides. He is also properly held responsible for what he knows his deciding to stay in is sufficient for.

Move 2 is neither problematic nor uncommon. Suppose a father knows that if he does not promise to pay for his daughter's tuition, her uncle will, but since she is his daughter and he loves her, he wants the tuition to be his gift to her, not anyone else's. What is in the father's power is whether he pays the tuition, but not whether it is paid. He is responsible for the tuition being paid, and his doing so is rightly taken, unless there is special reason to the contrary, as an action he could either have performed or refrained from performing. This fits the pattern described in Move 2.

Another way of seeing the point of Move 2 is to remember Ruth and her golden retriever. The golden retriever will be fed whether Ruth feeds her or not, just as John will stay in the room whether he tries to leave or not. But Ruth is free to decide to do the feeding herself and John is free not to try to leave and free to keep studying, as he is free to try to leave and not to study.

Move 2 does require a clarification of (PA), which should now read:

(PA*) If person S is morally responsible for having performed action A at time T in context C, then (i) S could have refrained from having performed action A at time T in context C, or (ii) there is some action B that S performed such that S could have refrained from performing B, and S's performing B is, at T and in C, sufficient for S's performing A.

Exactly similar moves are relevant to Case 1. So far at least, the incompatibilist is in no danger.

A compatibilist response

The compatibilist case is easily made subtler by tinkering with Case 2. Consider:

Case 3: Mary sits reflecting as to whether to send a bitter letter to her aunt, who has angered her greatly. But she also knows her aunt meant well and that it would be wrong to send the letter. Unknown to Mary, her sister Ann, a doctor, inserted a microchip into Mary's brain that allows Ann to monitor Mary's thoughts and control them if she wishes. Ann loves her aunt deeply and is monitoring Mary's thoughts; *she is able to anticipate what Mary's decisions will be before Mary makes them*. If Mary, uninterfered with, will decide not to send the letter Ann will do nothing, but if Mary, uninterfered with, will decide to send the letter, then Ann will *prevent her from making that decision and cause her to decide not to send the letter*. Mary, uninterfered with, decides not to mail the letter, so Ann does nothing.

Here, Mary cannot decide to send the letter. The only alternatives are these: (1) Mary, uninterfered with, decides not to send the letter, and (2) Mary, interfered with, decides not to send the letter. Mary's choice is not "up to her." (One could, of course, tinker with Case 1 in analogous ways.) Nonetheless, the compatibilist argues, if (1) holds, then Mary is morally responsible for her decision even though both (PA) and (PA*) are false of that decision.

Cases 2 and 3 smack of science fiction. Whether their science fiction will become science or not does not matter to the argument. For one thing, if one can describe logically possible cases in which moral responsibility is present and categorical freedom is absent, then possessing categorical freedom is not a logically necessary condition of being morally responsible, and hence incompatibilism is false. For another, if determinism is true, there is something or other (we may have no idea what) that plays the causal role that Ann's interference *would* play in Case 3 were Ann to have interfered; there is some state of affairs that does obtain and renders the actual occurrence in fact inevitable. The determinist is likely to suppose that talk about microchips and thought monitoring of Mary's decision simply does duty for the properly scientific account of whatever those states of affairs are until we discover how to describe them, if we ever do, though of course that is no argument for anything.

An incompatibilist response

Again, the incompatibilist is not without resources for a reply. How that reply should be cast is a matter of dispute among incompatibilists. Suppose one thinks of an agent as the cause of her choices. In Case 3, as stated, no matter what, Mary will decide not to send the letter. The question is whether she decides on her own – is herself the cause of her choice – or Ann causes her to decide. Then the incompatibilist will make:

Move 3: What remains open even in Case 3 is whether Mary shall cause her choice. If she does cause it, she is responsible, for she could have refrained from causing it. True, had she refrained from causing it, Ann would have caused it for her; in that case, Mary – not being the cause of her choice – cannot be responsible for it. Since she is the cause of her choice, she is responsible for it; but if she is the cause of her choice, (PA*) is true of her choice – she could have caused it (as she did) or not caused it (in which case Ann would have caused it and Mary would not be responsible for her choice).

For Move 3, Case 3 simply requires another application of (PA*). In spite of appearances, it introduces nothing more than this: it brings us up to the point where one sees the very minimal conditions of responsibility, which turn out to be the minimum conditions of categorical freedom.

There is something deeply suspicious, however, about Move 3 as it stands. It makes essential use of the idea that an agent causes her choices. To choose is an action; presumably so is causing a choice. But if an agent chooses to stand up by causing her choice to stand up, presumably she must also cause her causing herself to choose to stand up, and cause her causing her causing herself to choose to stand up, and so on. To choose will involve doing an endless number of causings, causings that are instantaneous and simultaneous or nearly so. We are plainly not aware of doing anything like that, and doing such a magnitude of things seems beyond our powers. Further, there seems no good theoretical reason to suppose that any such thing occurs. In sum: Move 3 requires that an agent perform an endless series of actions in order to make even the simplest choice, which makes making even the simplest choice impossible. The incompatibilist is in trouble if there is no way to state his viewpoint without the assumption that for a person to choose is for him to cause his choices or, more generally, that for a person to act is for him to cause his action.

Correspondingly, the compatibilist account of actions being the results of action chains that include action-inclining states has this feature: the action-inclining states that (at least partially) cause what the compatibilist thinks of as an action are themselves products of other states that are not action-inclining, and as one traces the chain backwards, so to speak, one comes to states that are not only not action-inclining but are also not states of the actor at all. Whether a person acts, and if so in what matter, is rendered in fact inevitable. The incompatibilist is ill-served by joining the compatibilist in accepting this view of what action is.

Consider, then, a different incompatibilist move:

Move 4: If Ann interferes, it is Ann, not Mary, who is doing the deciding – Ann decides that Mary shall not send the letter, and perhaps also that it shall *seem* to Mary that Mary has decided this. But if Ann interferes then Mary has not decided this. She has made no decision at all if Ann interferes. Nonetheless, even if Ann will interfere if Mary, uninterfered with, does not choose not to send the letter, if Mary does so choose then (i) she could have refrained from so choosing on her own, and so (ii) the principle (PA*) is true of *Mary's choosing* that she will not send the letter.

The ideas behind Move 4 bear examination. Move 4 makes no reference to Mary causing her choices; it speaks only of Mary choosing. This apparently small difference is nonetheless important for reasons worth discussing.

As above, let the *whole past package* be the whole truth about the past, plus correct statements of the laws of logic and the laws of nature. An action, then, regarding which Jane has categorical freedom is an action that it is logically consistent with the whole past package that she perform, and logically consistent with the whole past package that she refrain from performing. Let *the almost whole present story* be the whole truth about the present, plus correct statements of the laws of logic and the laws of nature, except the truth about whether Jane performs or refrains from performing the action in question; this story must, of course, be logically compatible with the whole past package. But it is also the case that if Jane's performing an action is in her power, then Jane's performing, and Jane's refraining from performing, that action is logically compatible with the almost whole story about the present. A definition of *in her power* along these lines, then, can be put as follows:

(IHP*) Jane *has it in her power to perform action A* only if her doing so does not require that she make false some truth about the past or the present, some law of logic, or some law of nature; Jane *has it in her power to refrain from performing action A* only if her doing so does not require that she make some truth about the past or the present, some law of nature, or some law of logic false.[19]

If, regarding performing action A at time T, Jane has categorical freedom of the sort defined by

(CF) *Jane is categorically (or libertarianly) free with respect to lying at T* entails *Jane's lying is within her power at T and Jane's refraining from lying is within her power at T.*

and (IHP*) is true, an interesting consequence follows: *it is logically impossible that Jane be caused to perform A at T.*

Since the incompatibilist claims that *Jane is morally responsible for doing A at T* entails *Jane has categorical freedom regarding A at T,* and *Jane has categorical freedom regarding A at T* entails *It is logically impossible that Jane be caused to do A at T,* the incompatibilist position holds that *Jane is morally responsible for doing A at T* entails *It is logically impossible that Jane be caused to do A at T.* It is, then, logically impossible that anyone or even anything causes Jane to make any choice or, more generally, perform any action that she makes or performs categorically freely. Precisely what is essential to something being an action for the compatibilist – that it be caused in a certain way – is logically incompatible with something being an action for the incompatibilist. If one wants the difference put in terms of free action, what necessarily characterizes a free action on the incompatibilist account is logically incompatible with what characterizes a free action on a compatibilist account.

One thing that follows is that, if incompatibilism is true, Case 3 – the third and more sophisticated of the alleged counterexamples to the Principle of Alternative Possibilities – cannot obtain; its description is logically inconsistent and so its occurrence is logically impossible. Hence it is worthless as a counterexample.

One standard complaint regarding libertarianism, which claims not only that incompatibilism is true, but that we have categorical freedom, is that it does not offer a causal explanation of freely performed actions. But if libertarianism is true, it is logically impossible that there be a causal explanation of freely performed actions. Thus the complaint radically misunderstands its target.

Acting not a matter of causing actions

The idea that for Mary to act is not for Mary to cause her action is important enough to receive some further attention. Suppose that the following is true:

(A) Performing infinite (or an endless) number of instantaneous and simultaneous (or nearly instantaneous and simultaneous) actions is logically, or at least naturally, unavailable to any human person.

(B) Necessarily, if for an agent to act, she must cause herself to act, and if causing oneself to act is itself an action, an agent acts only if she performs an infinite (or an endless) number of instantaneous and simultaneous (or nearly so) actions.

If (A) and (B) are true, it follows that:

(C) Performing an action is logically, or at least naturally, unavailable to human persons.

Since (C) is plainly false, and (A) and (B) entail (C), either (A) or (B) is false. Since (A) seems plainly true, presumably (B) is false. This provides another reason for a libertarian to reject the notion of an action as self-caused: no human person could perform the task of self-causing a freely performed action even if it were not logically impossible that a freely performed action be caused.

The incompatibilist, then, in replying to Case 3 – the microchip case where Ann can anticipate Mary's thoughts – had best avoid the notion that Mary causes her actions. The one offering Case 3 need not deny that if Ann interferes, Mary is not responsible, and Case 3 is more plausible if that is not denied. How then, if at all, do our most recent reflections aid the incompatibilist in dealing with Case 3? Consider a refinement of Move 4:

Move 5: If Ann interferes, it is Ann, not Mary, who is doing the deciding – Ann decides that Mary shall not send the letter, and perhaps also that it shall *seem* to Mary that Mary has decided this. But if Ann interferes then Mary has not decided this. She has made no decision at all if Ann interferes. Ann will interfere if Mary, uninterfered with, does not choose not to send the letter. *There remain these alternatives to Mary: freely to choose not to send the letter; not to choose freely not to send the letter. Mary freely chooses not to send it, and relative to that matter she is free. What she is free regarding, she is responsible for.* The principle (PA*) is true of *Mary's freely choosing* that she will not send the letter. Since (in accord with (PA*)) she is libertarianly free regarding freely choosing to send the letter, she is praiseworthy for having so chosen. Since *freely choosing not to send the*

> *letter* is, under the circumstances, sufficient for *not sending the letter*, Mary is also (in accord with (PA*)) praiseworthy for not sending it.

Here there is no requirement that Mary causes her choice not to send the letter; she simply chooses so. The most recent version of the Principle of Alternative Possibilities read:

(PA*) If person S is morally responsible for having performed action A at time T in context C, then (i) S could have refrained from having performed action A at time T in context C, or (ii) there is some action B that S performed such that S could have refrained from performing B, and S's performing B, at T and in C, is sufficient for S's performing A.

Perhaps in the light of Move 5 we should recast this as follows:

(PA**) If person S is morally responsible for having performed action A at time T in context C, then (i) S could have refrained from having performed action A at time T in context C, or (ii) there is some action B that S performed such that S could have refrained from performing B, and S's performing B, at T and in C, is sufficient for S's performing A; minimally, the alternatives will be *freely performing A or something sufficient for A* and *not freely performing A or something sufficient for A.*[20]

Part of what has unfortunately made some philosophers think more of the alleged counterexamples than they should is their focusing only on the contrast between such things as *freely choosing to send the letter versus freely choosing not to send the letter* while ignoring such things as *freely choosing to send the letter versus not freely choosing to send the letter.*

Since (PA**) is true of Mary even in Case 3, the compatibilist has not presented a case in which the Principle of Alternative Possibilities is false and yet the agent in the case is morally responsible for what the agent does. The incompatibilist can thank the compatibilist for helping to clarify the content of a proper statement of the principle, but has been given no reason to abandon incompatibilism.

The fuller map of counterexamples

The range and subtlety of purported counterexamples to the Principle of Alternative Possibilities are greater than we have yet considered, and the argument is not complete until we have considered them. We can begin this process by asking: if determinism were true, how might things work? For the sake of the argument, suppose that a human person is made up of a mind or soul and a body. Consider some human person Jon. Jon's states at any given time T will be just all the states that Jon's body is in at T plus all the states that Jon's mind is in at T. These states, let us say, are *states internal to Jon at T*. The states that things other than Jon is in at T are *states external to Jon at T*. Again for the sake of the argument,[21] assume that a cause always immediately precedes its effect. Then (say) Jon's smiling at T can be determined by only states internal to Jon at T-1, or only by states external to Jon at T-1, or by a combination of internal and external states at T-1.

Among the external states, some will be states of conscious agents who affect Jon by way of endeavoring to get Jon to behave as those agents want Jon to behave, believe it good that Jon behave, and the like. Among Jon's internal states will be conscious states of Jon himself that constitute Jon's own intentions, motives, purposes, and the like, regarding how he shall behave.[22] If Jon is an agent, then Jon has *conscious internal states* and if other agents want to affect Jon's behavior there will be *external conscious states* regarding Jon's behavior. If determinism is true, then, how things work (using the language just explained) is this. Suppose that at time T Jon smiles at Sue to let her know he is glad to see her. Perhaps he is tired and must make a conscious effort to smile at anyone; perhaps he simply unreflectively smiles. But in any case he smiles and his smiling is an action on his part which he intentionally performs.

Jon's smiling, of course, is but a single, simple example of what, if determinism is true, is true of all thoughts and actions whatever. Hence it is appropriate to infer general conclusions from this single case, since the single case is an arbitrarily selected example. If determinism is true, perhaps *Jon's smiling at Sue at time T* must have a cause of one or another of these sorts. Each scenario is intended to state the entire set of causes – conditions sufficient for the effect to occur.[23]

Scenario 1: A set of non-conscious states internal to Jon at T-1.
Scenario 2: A set of conscious states internal to Jon at T-1.
Scenario 3: A set of states internal to Jon at T-1, some of which are conscious and some of which are not.
Scenario 4: A set of non-conscious states external to Jon at T-1.
Scenario 5: A set of conscious states external to Jon at T-1.
Scenario 6: A set of states external to Jon at T-1, some of which are conscious and some of which are not.[24]

Jon intentionally smiled and his intention to smile is an internal conscious state. Jon's smiling presumably involves various non-conscious physical states that are causally intermediate to Jon's smiling; on a determinist model, they occur in a causal chain at which his intention to smile is at one end and his smiling is at the other end. Hence Scenarios 1 and 2 do not fit. Since a state internal to Jon is involved, we can eliminate Scenarios 4 through 6. Only one scenario remains:

Scenario 3: A set of states internal to Jon at T-1, some of which are conscious and some of which are not.

Suppose Jon made a conscious decision to smile before he smiled and consider, not Jon's smiling, but *Jon's deciding (at T-1) to smile-at-T*; we have again six scenarios exactly analogous to our first six. There may be no conscious state of Jon which, on a determinist model, is the conscious cause of his decision. Then Scenarios 2 and 3, each of which refer to conscious states internal to Jon, are eliminated. Since Sue's presence elicited and, on a determinist view, forms part of a causal chain whose earlier members render Jon's smiling in fact inevitable, it is not only Jon's internal states that cause his decision. So Scenario 1, which refers only to Jon's non-conscious internal states, is eliminated. If no conscious states external to Jon play a causal role in yielding his decision to smile then only Scenario 4 remains.

A libertarian can maintain that, under exactly the conditions in which Jon decides to smile,[25] he also could have refrained from choosing to smile, and either choice would be compatible with the truth about the past, the laws of logic, and the laws of nature. A determinist cannot say this. She must hold that *Jon's deciding (at T-1) to smile-at-T* is related to some state of affairs *A* at T-2 such that *A's obtaining at T-2* is, given the truth about the past, the laws of logic and the laws of nature, not compatible with *Jon's not deciding (at T-1) to smile-at-T*. Since a compatibilist must give an account of action compatible with determinism being true, she must agree with the determinist.

If we assume Jon to have come to exist at some time finitely past, then in tracing the causal chain that has *Jon's smiling at T* and *Jon's deciding (at T-1) to smile (at T)* as later members, we will come to a scenario that refers to no states of Jon whatever, either internal or external, and indeed to no states internal to any non-divine person – states obtaining before any non-divine person graced the world's stage. Since this is so, we may as well simplify things and take *Jon's deciding (at T-1) to smile (at T)* itself to be such a state – a state caused by no state internal to Jon (and none internal to any other non-divine person).

Monotheistic determinism

Suppose that determinism is true and that God exists.[26] If determinism is true of God's creation, then God made it so. God, then, directly or indirectly determines, for each thing, that it shall exist when and where and as long as it does, and for every property of every thing, that it has that property rather than not, and for how long it has that property. Since events are matters of things having properties, God determines all events. Our supposition that determinism is true and God exists is the supposition that God exists and causes everything whatever that occurs. Since God is omnicompetent, God will not be caught causing things that God was not aware of causing. So every conscious state of Jon, and of every non-divine person, is the product of a conscious state internal to God – God's intention that it obtain, or the like.[27]

If every thought Jon has is a thought God knowingly caused Jon to have, every act Jon performs is one that God knowingly caused Jon to perform, and indeed every state of any sort Jon is ever in is a state God knowingly caused Jon to be in, a compatibilist must hold that Jon can nonetheless be free and morally responsible with regard to his actions. Theologians and philosophers are sometimes drawn to this view because otherwise God is the agent of evil actions. Sometimes they think that some version of materialism is true, and that materialism entails determinism.

The libertarian, and the determinist who is also an incompatibilist, of course deny this. They will hold it to be false that Jon acts freely. Jon is perhaps a being through whom God acts, but Jon is not an agent at all. Jon does not act; God acts through Jon.

Consider this scenario regarding Jon's smiling at Susan at time T; suppose its full cause is:

Scenario 7: God's conscious state of deciding that Jon shall smile – a conscious state external to Jon – and whatever non-intentional states external to Jon also occur as parts of the deterministic chain to yield Jon's smiling at Susan.

Consider this plausible contention: if those intentional states are caused by someone who is capable of making Jon do whatever they want, and that someone produces them knowing that Jon will thereby be caused to smile at Susan, then Jon is not morally responsible for smiling at Susan – not even if smiling or not is a matter for moral praise or blame. When Mary was not sending her letter, it was rightly said to matter whether Ann interfered or not – whether Ann activated the microchip and thereby caused Mary to act. If any thought or action of Mary's is brought about by Ann using her microchip then Mary no longer is responsible for what Mary thinks or does as a result of Ann's microchip activity.[28] God needs no microchip. But if every thought or action of Jon's is caused by God then Jon no longer is responsible for what Jon thinks and does.

One might wonder if while Ann could not cause Mary's thoughts and actions and leave Mary an agent, perhaps God could cause Jon's thoughts and actions and yet Jon remain an agent. Isn't God's case different? It is, but not in ways encouraging to the suggestion that a Jon all of whose thoughts and actions God causes remains an agent. If an omnicompetent God exists and is Creator, then Jon's coming to exist, and Jon's continuing to exist, depend on God; the remainder of the world in which Jon exists came to and continues to exist by divine courtesy. Far more so than in the relation between Mary and Ann, the relationship between Jon and God, if God causes all of Jon's thoughts and actions, *precludes* rather than *provides for* Jon being responsible for his thoughts and actions.

Nonmonotheistic determinism will offer a different account:

Scenario 8: Only nonintentional states at T-1 external to Jon are required to yield Jon's smiling at Susan at T.

What entirely baffles the libertarian is how, if this scenario is correct, and if the obtaining of Scenario 7 would preclude Jon being morally responsible, the obtaining of Scenario 8 would leave Jon morally responsible. True, in the case of monotheistic determinism, there is Someone Else (someone with a mind) besides Jon who knowingly causes Jon to think and act as Jon does, whereas if nonmonotheistic determinism is true there is merely something else (some non-person distinct from Jon) that causes Jon to think and act as Jon does. But the libertarian holds that the difference between Someone Else and something else is utterly insufficient to make the difference between Jon not being morally responsible for Jon's thoughts and actions and Jon's being morally responsible for Jon's thoughts and actions.

The point, then, is this. For all of the compatibilist maneuvering, if God exists and determinism is true, God and any alleged human agent are related as Tess and Tricia, at the outset of our discussion, were related, only (as we said there) more so.

A parenthetical cross-cultural suggestion

In this chapter, we have considered a dispute between a monotheistic compatibilist determinism and a monotheistic libertarianism over whether, if monotheistic determinism is true, created persons are free, and indeed whether there can even be created persons. In Chapter 12, we considered a dispute between Jainism and Buddhism concerning the nature of persons. From the monotheistic libertarian perspective, on the monotheistic compatibilist determinist account, persons reduce to states of affairs that lack freedom and genuine personhood. From the Jain perspective, on the Buddhist account, persons reduce to bundles of momentary states of affairs that lack memory, responsibility, and genuine personhood. The monotheistic compatibilist determinist, and the Buddhist, at least initially, claim that they can retain the ordinary or commonsense view of freedom, memory, responsibility, and personhood. The monotheist libertarian, and the Jain, denies this. So, concerning monotheism, does Spinoza, and, concerning Buddhism, so does absolutistic Mahayana Buddhism. A suggestion: reflection on these cases is a philosophically informative enterprise.

Divine foreknowledge and human freedom

Here is a standard argument to the conclusion that divine foreknowledge is incompatible with human freedom; it (and the analogous argument below) are concerned only with logically contingent statements. If successful, this argument would show that (i) libertarian monotheism is logically inconsistent, or (ii) that future tense statements are neither true nor false and so cannot be foreknown, or (iii) that for some other reason God does not know the future. Since (ii), as we will see, seems plainly false, we would be left with (i) and (iii).

1 If God knows today what Sally will do tomorrow, then Sally is not free regarding what Sally does tomorrow.
2 If God is omniscient, then God knows today what Sally will do tomorrow.
3 God is omniscient. So:
4 God knows today what Sally will do tomorrow (from 2, 3). So:
5 Sally is not free regarding what Sally does tomorrow (from 1, 4).

Comments on the argument

First, note that *God knows that P* entails *P is true;* but *God knows that P* does not entail *God makes P true*. An omnipotent God can create a world in which things are true that God did not cause to be true. An omniscient God can know things to be true that God did not cause to be true.

Second, we should distinguish between *direction of entailment* and *direction of truth determination. Entailment* is defined this way: *Proposition P entails Proposition Q if and only if "P is true but Q is false" is a contradiction. Truth determination* is defined in this way: *A's obtaining determines B's truth* if and only if *The explanation that B is true is that A obtains*. (To "obtain" is "to be the case" or "to be a fact.")

Third, suppose that Sally will be tempted to lie tomorrow, but will finally decide to tell the truth. Then it is true that (S) *Sally will tell the truth tomorrow*. Consider that claim, plus (G) *God knows that Sally will tell the truth tomorrow*. Note two things: (i) the direction of *entailment* goes *from (G) to (S)* – to get from (S) to (G) one would have to add *God is omniscient;* (ii) the *direction of truth determination* goes *from (S) to (G)* – what makes (G) true is that (S) is true, not the other way round.

Fourth, given that the directions of truth determination go as noted, it is perfectly compatible with (S) being true, and with (G) being true, that the explanation of Sally's telling the truth tomorrow is that tomorrow she freely chooses to tell the truth. Sally can be a libertarianly free moral agent whose decision to tell the truth explains the truth of (S). The explanation of (G)'s being true is just that God is omniscient and (S) is true. This is perfectly compatible with (S) being true because of a free choice by Sally. If this is so, then divine foreknowledge is compatible with human freedom. Hence divine foreknowledge is compatible with human freedom. The argument, then, fails to establish the intended incompatibility.

How not to understand "God knows today what Sally will do tomorrow"

1 *As inferential knowledge*. If X knows today that Sally will do B tomorrow, and X must infer *Sally will do B tomorrow,* then X must know something like this: X must know that *A obtains now* and that *It is a law that if A obtains now then Sally does B tomorrow*. Then something obtains now the obtaining of which is sufficient for Sally's doing B tomorrow. An omniscient being will have no need to make such inferences in order to know anything.

2 *As a probability grid or its product.* It is possible to think along these lines: if Sally does B *freely* tomorrow then her doing B is unpredictable other than probabilistically; if her doing B tomorrow is unpredictable other than probabilistically, then there is some chance that she *not* do B tomorrow; if X knows now that Sally will do B tomorrow, it follows that Sally will do B tomorrow; so if X knows now that Sally will do B tomorrow, then her doing B tomorrow is not to be understood probabilistically; so if X knows now that Sally will do B tomorrow, her doing B tomorrow is not free. But a monotheist who holds both that God has foreknowledge of human actions and that those actions are free is not thinking along these lines nor would or should she think in terms of a probability grid. *That S does A freely* does not entail *That S does A is in principle unpredictable* or *S's doing A is only very probable* or the like. Nor is an omnipotent being in the position of having to be content with probabilistic knowledge. Perhaps a being who *learned* what would happen in the future would suffer this limitation, but an omniscient being has no learning to do.[29]

Truth and the future

Since it does not appeal to the idea that God causes whatever is true to be true, what force the above argument for the incompatibility of divine foreknowledge and human freedom had is also captured by this argument.

1 Every true future tense statement is now true.
2 If every true future tense statement is now true, then determinism is true. So:
3 Determinism is true.

This argument could in principle be given at any time, regarding all future time. If it was always sound and valid, then determinism would be true.

An argument regarding premise 1

The first premise assumes that (1*) Future tense statements can be true. This claim can be defended as follows:

1a It is now true that (i) either (ii) the next President of the US will be a former Celtic center or (iii) the next President of the US will not be a former Celtic center.

1b (i) is of the form ((ii) or (iii))
1c A proposition of the form ((ii) or (iii)) is true only if its components – i.e., (ii) and (iii) – are either true or false. So (from 1a to 1c):
1d (ii) and (iii) are either true or false.
1e (iii) = not-(ii) (obvious).
1f If (ii) and (iii) are either true or false and (iii) = not-(ii), then either (ii) is true or (iii) is true. So (from 1d to 1f):
1g Either (ii) is true or (iii) is true.
1h If (ii) is true, then some future tense statement is true.
1i If (iii) is true, then some future tense statement is true. So (from 1g to 1i):
1j Some future tense statement is true.
1k If some future tense statement is true, then future tense statements can be true. So (from 1j and 1k):
1* Future tense statements can be true.

Further, if some future tense statements are now true, it seems arbitrary to deny that the true ones are now true. But does this entail determinism?

That depends on what makes future tense statements true. Had Aristotle stopped lecturing one day and laconically commented that in the future a human being would stand on the surface of the moon, what he said would have been true. What would have made it true was some human being standing on the surface of the moon at some time later than that at which Aristotle offered his comment. If instead Aristotle had said that some time in the future someone would freely steal a pear, that would be made true by someone freely stealing a pair at some time later than that at which Aristotle's comment was made. There seems no more problem in this case than in the case of the human being standing on the surface of the moon. Or, if there is any problem, it has to do with the relevant notion of freedom, not with Aristotle getting something right before it happened. That a proposition is true at some time T does not entail that what makes it true obtains at T.[30] So present truth of future tense propositions does not (contrary to 2) entail determinism.

Conclusion

After considerable searching, no genuine counterexample to the Principle of Alternative Possibilities has surfaced. Suppose that Tricia is related to God as considered above. If God creates a world in which the initial conditions come from God's hand and everything that comes afterward is in fact inevitable, it is hard to see why the fact that a causal chain passes through Tricia, or that in a world with different initial conditions different behavior by Tricia would have been causally inevitable, provides any reason to think that Tricia possesses any sort of freedom that makes her responsible for anything. What Tricia's possessing compatibilist freedom comes down to is simply that a causal chain runs through Tricia's cognitive makeup and that in a world with different initial conditions different behavior by Tricia would have been causally inevitable. The libertarian seems right in thinking that this is not enough to make Tricia a free and responsible agent. If determinism and monotheism are both true, it is dubious that there can be more than one agent. If this is correct, consistent monotheists will be libertarians.

Questions for reflection

1 How can one tell whether moral values are fundamental within a particular religious tradition?
2 Does it make any difference to morality whether God exists or not? Why, or why not?
3 Explain determinism, compatibilism, and libertarianism.
4 Suppose that God exists, determinism is true, and compatibilism is *true*. Does anything different follow regarding morality that would not follow if God didn't exist?
5 Suppose that God exists, determinism is true, and compatibilism is *false*. Does anything different follow regarding morality than would follow if compatibilism were true?
6 Sometimes religious believers claim that if there were no God, there would be no morality. Sometimes critics of religion claim that all religion perverts morality. Are either right?

Annotated reading

Frankfurt, H. G. (1988) *The Importance of What We Care About*, Cambridge: Cambridge University Press. A very influential contemporary defense of compatibilism.

Honderich, T. (1993) *How Free Are You?*, Oxford: Oxford University Press. Another defense of compatibilism.

Molina, L. (1988) *On Divine Foreknowledge*, Ithaca, NY: Cornell University Press, trans. Alfred Fredoso. The standard presentation of the view that God knows what free persons, created or not, will or would do.

Rowe, William L. (1991) *Thomas Reid on Freedom and Morality*, Ithaca, NY: Cornell University Press. An excellent discussion of Reid's libertarian views.

Van Inwagen, Peter (1983) *An Essay on Free Will,* Oxford: Clarendon Press. A powerful critique of compatibilism.
Watson, G. (ed.) (1982) *Free Will,* Oxford: Oxford University Press. An excellent collection of essays concerning libertarianism.
Zagzebski, Linda (1991) *The Dilemma of Freedom and Foreknowledge,* New York: Oxford University Press. A detailed discussion of divine foreknowledge.

CHAPTER 15
Faith and reason

Faith

Knowledge

Scientism

Propositions

The epistemic status of religious belief

Robust foundationalism

Confirmationism and falsificationism

Ways of being falsified

Theistic arguments and explanatory power

Questions for reflection

Annotated reading

15
Faith and reason

Faith

Religious faith is at its core an acceptance of the diagnosis and cure proposed by some religious tradition accompanied by an attempt to live in the light of that tradition's teachings. In monotheistic traditions, it includes personal trust – trust in God as loving and faithful. In nonmonotheistic contexts, it includes acceptance of the efficacy of particular esoteric experiences achievable by prescribed efforts. There is thus a close connection between *a faith* – the doctrinal content of a religious tradition as embedded in its rites, institutions, practices, and its oral or written texts – and *faith* or acceptance, and life in accord with acceptance, of that tradition. Having faith involves having some understanding, very limited in some cases and quite rich in others, of the tradition within which the faith is had. Whether having faith involves some sort of conflict with reason – believing against evidence, accepting on authority an alternative no more favored by evidence than many others, or the like – depends on what tradition one accepts, and what the evidence is. Our focus here will be on the completion of the overall argument, which requires facing the general question: how, besides appeal to religious experiences and the sorts of arguments already considered, can one rationally assess religious traditions. In terms of the issue we put off until later in discussing the argument from design, how can competing large-scale explanations be evaluated?

Knowledge

There is, of course, considerable skepticism that, if the explanations are religious, rational assessment is possible. Religious belief is often presented as far removed from "ordinary" and from "scientific" belief. The current fashion is to think and speak of religious belief as a private matter – supposedly religion and morality are deeply individual, subjective affairs ruled by "the heart" (which here means something like "idiosyncratic, arbitrary taste and sentiment").[1] This view is neither justified nor workable. Regarding morality: either murderers, child molesters, slaveholders, and drug dealers act wrongly, or they do not. If they do, then laws against them are justified. If they don't – if all there is to acting "rightly" or "wrongly" is "acting in a way privately but arbitrarily liked by some person or group" or "acting in a way privately but arbitrarily disliked by some person or group" – then laws against murder, etc. are also without any justification. Private sentiments are not rightly publicly enforced. Regarding religion: either God exists or God does not exist; either nirvana can be achieved or not. If God exists, God is either trinitarian or not. These things are so, or not so, independent of what anyone thinks. An omnicompetent deity, no less than the planet Pluto or the Green Bay Packers football team, either exists independent of our thoughts, or not.

Scientism

A standard reply is that while perhaps this is so, no one can tell whether God exists or not, so there are just opinions and feelings about such matters. This reply typically is based on the idea that we can only know what science can tell us. The reply is particularly ill-founded, since *We can only know what science can tell us* is not something science can tell us, so if the reply were sound it would itself be just a matter of the opinion and feelings of those who offered it. It may be worthwhile to put this point fully and formally, if briefly, as follows.

Scientism holds:

1 All explanation is scientific explanation.

Note that 1 is not itself justifiable by appeal to science alone; it is a view in theory of knowledge or epistemology – a piece of philosophy, not a piece of science, which neither presupposes it nor otherwise requires it. At this point it is useful to make a simplifying assumption to the effect that:

2 All scientific explanation is explanation in physics.

Almost certainly false, this is the view of traditional believers in the unity of science; if one wishes, one can replace "physics" in this argument by something like "physics, chemistry, biochemistry, biology, geology, and geography" or even by "natural science."

3 Explanations in physics use no concepts and no laws save those of logic and physics.
4 All explanation is explanation in physics. (from 1 and 2)
5 All explanations use no concepts and no laws save those of logic and physics. (from 3 and 4)

Here, a reminder about explanations is relevant. Explanations have two parts. One part is an *explicandum* or *to-be-explained* – an *explainee,* if you like – that tells you what the explanation is an explanation of. This must be described in terms that are accessible to the other part of the explanation. The other part is an *explicans* or *explainer* that tells you what is the reason for the explainee; this by itself is often called "the explanation." A genuine explainee is one that can be related to a genuine explainer. If, as premise 5 says, all explanations are explanations in physics, then all explainers can be described in all ways relevant to explanation only by the concepts of physics. Then all explainees must be related by the laws of physics to the explainers. Then for all purposes relevant to explanation the explainees must be described only by the concepts of physics.

6 For all purposes relevant to explanation, one needs nothing other than physical concepts and laws to explain or describe anything. (from 5)
7 Any (non-ultimate) property that a thing has is a property for which there is an explanation.

An ultimate property, defined in terms of the present argument, will be any property, defined in purely physical terms, that physical theory takes things to have but cannot explain their having.

8 One needs nothing to describe or explain any (non-ultimate) property that anything has except the laws and concepts of physics. (from 6, 7)
9 If one needs nothing other than physical concepts and laws to explain or describe any (non-ultimate) property, and all explanations are explanations in physics, then all of our knowledge is physical knowledge.
10 All of our knowledge is physical knowledge (knowledge in physics, fully expressible in terms of the concepts of physics). (from 8, 9)

Here, we reach the conclusion scientism requires. The problem is that the argument naturally continues as follows:

11 Reference only to physical descriptions and explanation of things will not justify us in thinking that something is an explanation, or in thinking that all of our knowledge is physical knowledge (knowledge in physics, fully expressible in terms of the concepts of physics).

12 If all of our knowledge is physical knowledge (knowledge in physics, fully expressible in terms of the concepts of physics) then all that we have to justify us in thinking that something is an explanation or that all of our knowledge is physical knowledge (knowledge in physics, fully expressible in terms of the concepts of physics) is reference only to physical descriptions and explanation of things.

13 If all of our knowledge is physical knowledge (knowledge in physics, fully expressible in terms of the concepts of physics) then all of our knowledge will not justify us in thinking that something is an explanation, or in thinking that all of our knowledge is physical knowledge (knowledge in physics, fully expressible in terms of the concepts of physics). (from 11, 12)

So scientism is self-defeating.

Belief and knowledge: religious and otherwise

In fact, religious belief and knowledge is in many ways *not* unlike belief and knowledge of other sorts. Understanding this will prepare the way for pointing out some of the ways in which various sorts of belief and knowledge, religious and non-religious, interact and intermingle.

Propositions

We know many things – that two plus two is four, that there are golden retrievers, that oak trees are not made of gold, that we exist, that broccoli does not taste like chocolate, and so on through an enormously large number of pieces of knowledge. We typically say what we know by asserting something. We say that two plus two is four, that there are golden retrievers, that oak trees are not made of gold, that we exist, that broccoli does not taste like chocolate, and so on. What we thus assert is true. If we are multilingual, we can assert the same truths in more than one language. If we are not multilingual, we can do the same thing by using various sentences in the language we know to say the same thing: 2 and 2 is 4; 2 and 2 sum to 4; adding 2 and 2, we get 4; and so on. It is not the sentences that are true; what is true is what we use the sentences to assert. It will be useful to have a term for *what we use sentences to assert*; the term *proposition* is standard. A proposition is the bearer of truth value – anything that is true, and anything that is false, is a proposition.

Necessity, belief-entailment, and contingency

Some of the things we know are true no matter what. If you add two things and two things, you get four things; if you draw a circle then you draw a figure; if you are six feet tall then you are not also not six feet tall. These are *necessary truths*; they are true under any possible conditions and cannot be false. Some of the things we know are not true, no matter what, though they are true, given the way things are. There might not have been any golden retrievers, and we might not have existed. *There being no golden retrievers* and *our not having existed* are ways the world could have been; there are possible conditions under which the world would have been that way. So that there are golden retrievers and that we exist are *non-necessary truths*; since speaking of *non-necessary truths* is an unlovely way to talk, philosophers have instead spoken of such truths as *contingent*.[2]

Among the contingent truths that we know, some have a particularly secure status. I believe that I exist. This belief has the following feature: *it is logically impossible that I believe it and that it is false*. In that respect, my belief that I exist differs from my belief that there are golden retrievers, that oak trees are not made of gold, that broccoli does not taste like chocolate, and even from my belief that you exist. My beliefs that I am conscious, that I can have conscious states, that I do have conscious states, that I can have beliefs, and that I do have beliefs all have the feature that *it is logically impossible that I believe them and that those beliefs are false*. We will describe such beliefs as *belief-entailed*. For each of us, there is a rather small set of beliefs that have this feature; we can call the contingent truths that we know by virtue of having these beliefs *belief-entailed contingent truths*.[3] Having such beliefs precludes having them if they are false. Our comprehending acceptance of necessary truths and of belief-entailed contingent truths, let us say, constitutes *unbreakable knowledge*, and our comprehending belief that such propositions are true *unbreakable beliefs*. Other contingent truths – the vast majority – are *corrigible* truths; they could be believed true even if they were false. Among the things we know, then, are necessary truths, belief-entailed contingent truths, and contingent truths that are not belief-entailed.

Religious believers would like their religious beliefs to be unbreakable. This is not logically possible. Only logically necessary truths and belief-entailed propositions are candidates for being unbreakably believed. This is why they cannot be self-authenticated. Religious beliefs are part of that large set of beliefs that are not unbreakable because they are not beliefs that something logically necessary or belief-entailed is true. What is neither a necessary truth nor a belief-entailed proposition is *necessarily* neither a necessary truth nor a belief-entailed proposition. So religious beliefs are *necessarily* not unbreakable beliefs. There is not only no point in trying to make them so; the hypothesis that they are is simply self-contradictory. Nor is there anything to lament here; it is not sensible to lament that the logically impossible does not obtain. There is no loss here – nothing that could not possibly be so amounts to a loss of anything. That religious beliefs are not unbreakable beliefs should be kept in mind as we consider faith and reason. It will help us do this realistically.[4]

In order to have a neutral expression, let us say that if Kim believes that her golden retriever wants a treat – remembering that *Kim's golden retriever wants a treat* is neither a necessary truth nor something whose truth follows from Kim's believing it – let us say that her belief is a piece of *delicate knowledge* and the belief that constitutes it a *delicate belief*. A delicate belief can be true, well supported by evidence, and reliable. A delicate belief can be false, against the evidence, and unreliable. Much of what we know is constituted by our true delicate beliefs.[5] Delicate knowledge is not a defective version of unbreakable knowledge; it is not any kind or version thereof.[6]

Probability

Delicate beliefs are typically, though perhaps misleadingly, said to be *only probable*. What is meant by this is sometimes clear and sometimes unclear. The proposition *The odds of getting a six with a fair throw of a fair die in a fair environment is one in six* is a necessary truth. But the beliefs that the die, or the throw, or the environment in question are fair are delicate beliefs, and if they have any probability, the proposition ascribing that probability to them is not a necessary truth.

Suppose that it is a probabilistic law that *Given the occurrence of an event of kind A, the chances of the occurrence of an event of kind B is 99.9*. Assuming we know that this is a law and that an event of type A has occurred, we know that the odds are 999 to 1 that an event of type B will occur. Here, we can quantify our probabilities. We can also quantify our probabilities in the absence of any known laws. Suppose that we have 99 marbles in a bag, 33 each of blue, red, and green. Assume that conditions are such that our odds of drawing a red marble from the bag is one in three (being blindfolded, we cannot look into the bag and pick what color marble we want, etc.). A reliable friend tells us that the marble we take from the bag is not green. So we know it is either red or blue. There are now 98 marbles in the bag, and 33 of them are green. Either there are 33 red and 32 blue, or 32 blue and 33 red; we do not know which. So now we can infer that, relative to our knowledge, the odds of our picking a red marble are either 32 in 98 or 33 in 98, but we don't know which. The same goes, relative to our knowledge, for the odds of our picking a blue marble. We may also infer that either the odds of our picking a red marble or a green one are better than our picking a blue one or a green one or the odds of our picking a blue one or a green one are better than our picking a green one or a red one; we don't know which. In such cases, where natural laws are not directly relevant, we can quantify both the objective odds and what the odds are, relative to our knowledge.

Very often, we can do neither. What the odds are, if any, that my computer is on, my window is closed, or my dog asleep are not quantifiable in any real sense. We can say that, since the computer seems to be on, my window appears to be closed, and my dog looks like he is asleep, the odds are better than 5 that these things are so. But that is either metaphorical or else a matter of forcing the notion of quantifiable probability onto a case where it does not fit.

In cases in which quantitative probability is inapplicable, many philosophers nonetheless use the calculus that would apply were the probabilities in question quantifiable. The assumption is that there are non-quantifiable probabilities and that non-quantifiable probabilities behave as do quantifiable probabilities. We can call this the *assumption of universal probabilism*. The issues that concern us in the pages ahead do not concern quantifiable probabilities. We can remain neutral about whether the assumption of universal probabilism is true. What requires saying can be said using such notions as evidence and entailment.

The epistemic status of religious belief

A religious tradition that involved only unbreakable beliefs would be an odd enterprise. Imagine a tradition that accepted mathematical truths of the sort *1 and 1 are 2, 1 and 2 are 3, 2 and 2 are 4, 2 and 3 are 5* and so on and propositions of the sort *I exist, I am conscious* and the like. Their resources for stating, within their chosen framework, either a universal human problem or a solution thereto would be highly limited. No delicate propositions being permitted to stain the security of their tradition, there could be no descriptions of institutions or practices, and so no way of gathering or behaving included in this austere imaginary religion. No such proposition as *Kim needs salvation* could be formulated, since that proposition is neither a necessary truth nor a belief-entailed truth.[7] The very understandable fact is that no religious tradition has ever limited itself to such a slender doctrinal base. But this fact is no defect in religious traditions. Nor has any political, scientific, or academic tradition ever limited itself in this way. Nor is there any reason why they should, and there is excellent reason why they do not.

Robust foundationalism

Robust foundationalism has a high standard for proper belief. According to it, one properly believes a proposition P only if *it is logically impossible that one believe that P and P is false* – only where co-presence of belief and falsehood cannot arise. This limits objects of proper belief to necessary truths and belief-entailed propositions. Even if those monotheists who joined Anselm in thinking that *God exists* is a logically necessary truth are right, few if any religious beliefs can be properly believed on robust foundationalist standards. All or most religious beliefs, in that respect, join *There are trees, Texas covers more territory than Rhode Island, There are pigeons in New York City,* and *London, England is not located in Delhi, India,* as well as almost everything else anyone believes. This is not a source of proper concern, since *It is proper to believe only what robust foundationalism says it is proper to believe* is itself not something even a robust foundationalist could properly believe.[8]

Religious claims

When we deal with such questions as whether seven is greater than five, what twenty-nine times forty-eight is, whether the argument form *If P then Q, Q or R, not-Q, hence R or not-P* is valid, and whether *Necessarily, P entails Necessarily (Necessarily, P)* we deal with things to be thought through without essential appeal to sensory experience. Reports of sensory experiences will not tell us what the answers to these questions are; only abstract reasoning will do that. When we deal with questions of whether there is a tree in the yard, how apples taste, whether crows will be kept from crops by playing rock music in the fields, and what black bears eat, we deal with things to be answered by reference to reports of sensory experiences; abstract reasoning will not tell us the answers. Sensory evidence and abstract reasoning is each precious relative to their knowledge-potential, though they are different; it is foolish not to value both highly if one values knowledge.

If one looks at the sorts of claim that are central to religious traditions

– the ones presupposed or entailed by the diagnoses and cures that such traditions offer – it is obvious that they are not merely sensory reports and they are not merely reports of the result of abstract reasoning. Like theoretical claims in science, they are something different from either sensory reports or reports of lines of abstract reasoning. How, then, might they be rationally assessed? Taking our cue from the noted similarity to theoretical claims in science, let us briefly consider two perspectives in the philosophy of science.

Confirmationism and falsificationism

A light touch on philosophy of science

Some simple definitions will facilitate stating these two perspectives.

Definition 1: X is a *truth condition* of proposition P = P is true if and only if X obtains.

Thus *Sam is sad now* has as its truth condition *Sam's being sad now*. Proving that a proposition is true is also proving that its truth condition obtains; giving reason for thinking a proposition true is giving reason to think its truth condition obtains.

Definition 2: S is an *observation statement* if and only if S ascribes an observable quality to an observable object.

The car is red, The table is brown, The cat is black, This coffee is bitter are observation statements.

Definition 3: G is a *generalization over observation statements* if and only if G is of the form *All X's are Q* and G is formed by inferring it from observation statements of the form *X1 is Q, X2 is Q, X3 is Q* etc. and G is not simply a conjunct of observation statements.

Definition 4: T is a *theoretical statement* if and only if T is neither an observation statement nor a generalization over observation statements and T's truth would explain the truth of some observation statement or generalization over observation statements.

Definition 5: E is a *relevant explanation* of P if and only if (i) *E is true* entails *P is true*, and (ii) *E is true* is either a *scientific* or a *personal* explanation of *P is true*.

Definition 5a: E is a *scientific* explanation of P only if E's truth condition obtaining is related by law to P's truth condition obtaining.

Definition 5b: E is a *personal* explanation of P only if E has the form *Agent A so acted as to bring about P's truth condition*.

Definition 6: T is an *available theory* if and only if T is a *proffered unfalsified relevant explanation of explication-eligible facts*.

Definition 6a: F is an *explanation-eligible fact* if and only if *Fact F obtains* is logically contingent, known to be true, and is possibly explicable.

Definition 6b. Theory T is *unfalsified* if and only if we have examined explanation-eligible facts F such that T *is true* is a relevant explanation of *F obtains* and we have no reason to think that after rigorous examination T is false.

Definition 6c. T is *proffered* if and only if someone offers T.

Attention is limited here to scientific and personal explanations because they are the sorts of theory relevant here, whether or not there are other sorts of explanation. While sometimes a scientific community keeps a theory it knows or has good reason to think false – continues to teach it to students and construct experiments suggested by the theory – this is like driving an oil-burning, gas-guzzling car because one hasn't access to a better one. Only explanations someone actually thinks of can be assessed, so we are inherently limited to actually proffered theories, though since one can proffer theories by thinking them up this limitation need not be suffocating. Confirmationism and falsificationism are theories about theory assessment. They provide different answers to the question: how can we rationally assess available, relevant, unfalsified theories? Each is a complex theory, but a brief account will be useful here.

A light touch on confirmationism

Confirmationism at its core holds that: *If P entails Q and Q is true, then P is supported by Q*. This apparently simple core doctrine is unfortunately more complex than it seems. First, the argument form (If *P* then *Q*; *Q*; Hence: *P*) is invalid; it commits the fallacy of *affirming the consequent*. If it were proper reasoning, one could prove oneself a billionaire by arguing *If I have a billion pounds, then I have at least a pound; I have at least a pound; hence I have a billion pounds* but would be distressed by the result of *If I weigh a billion pounds then I weigh at least a pound; I weigh at least a pound; so I weigh a billion pounds.* Confirmationism, then, has to be stated carefully enough to make it clear that committing this fallacy is not part of confirmationism; it encourages no such absurdities.

Second, "entails" here must bear a specific meaning; it must mean "non-vacuously entails" where this term is defined as follows:

Definition 7: P non-vacuously entails Q if and only if (i) it is logically impossible that P is true and Q is false, (ii) P is not a necessarily false proposition, and (iii) Q is not a necessarily true proposition.

Otherwise, each logically contingent proposition C will entail all of the necessary truths and so will be confirmed by them – by an infinite number of truths that would be true even were C false. Thus if C is a logically contingent proposition, both C and not-C would be "confirmed" by an infinite number of truths. Reading "entails" as "non-vacuously entails" avoids these absurdities.

Third, consider this unhappy argument: *Either (a) the moon is a prime number or the Packers have a winning record; (b) the moon is not a prime number; so (c) the Packers have a winning record.* Since (a) and (b) entail (c), (c) *confirms* ((a) and (b)). But this is obviously false. Similarly, (c) entails (c); but (c) does not confirm (c). So we need something like this: *P's entailing Q and Q's being true* does not confirm P if either Q is identical to P or Q is a component of P.[9] Then that (a) and (b) entails (c) does not by itself *explain* (c)'s being true. All this is implicit in confirmationism.

Perhaps, then, we can more carefully put confirmationism along these lines: *If P entails Q, and P is a scientific or a personal explanation of Q, then if Q is true, its truth confirms P. Q confirms P* means something like *Q's truth supports P's truth* or *That Q is true is evidence that P is true* or the like; it does *not* mean *Q's truth shows or guarantees that P is true.* Suppose that Q is entailed by all of P1, P2, P3, . . . P100. Then if Q is true, and if confirmationism is true (assuming that P1 . . . P100 satisfy the conditions stated above) Q's truth confirms each of P1 through P100.

Typically, *data underdetermines theory* in the sense that any fact or set of facts can be explained by various theories; nonetheless, it is often not easy to think of explanations that both satisfy the conditions stated above and are not known or reasonably believed to be false. Confirmationism claims that a theory that explains a little is confirmed a little and a theory that explains a lot is confirmed a lot, even if neither "little" nor "lot" can be quantified.

Falsificationism

Falsificationism rejects this notion. Why should the fact that *If there is a leprechaun who has absolute power over the location of computers who wants my computer to be on my desk, that will explain my computer being on my desk* and *There is a leprechaun who has absolute power over the location of computers who wants my computer to be on my desk* would explain *My computer is on my desk* be taken to confirm the conjunction (*If there is a leprechaun who has absolute power over the location of computers who wants my computer to be on my desk, that will explain my computer being on my desk* and *There is a leprechaun who has absolute power over the location of computers who wants my computer to be on my desk*)? The idea that it does so, but by so little that one hardly notices it, is more desperation than defense.[10]

Falsificationism accepts these claims:

1 Theory T is a good theory regarding data F if and only if T has not been falsified and if T has explanatory power regarding F.

1a T has *explanatory power* regarding F if and only if *If T is true then its truth explains that F obtains.*

1b T *has not been falsified* if and only if T has been rigorously tested and we still have no reason to think that T is false.

2 *Being confirmed by F* is nothing more than *not having been falsified and having explanatory power regarding F.*

3 While one might have to continue to work within the framework of a falsified theory (one needs some context for research and a false theory may provide a useful context), other things being equal it is better to work within a non-falsified theory.

4 A non-falsified theory is *uninteresting regarding F* if its truth would not explain F's obtaining; there is no point in pursuing theories that are uninteresting regarding the data that we possess.

5 It is *reasonable to believe* any available relevant theory that is unfalsified, has explanatory power, and has no competitors.

6 In cases of competing available relevant unfalsified theories T1 and T2 with explanatory power, it is reasonable to believe (T1 or T2) and to endeavor to falsify one or the other.

6a Theories T1 and T2 are *competing* if and only if (i) the things that each explains are the same as what the other explains, or (ii) some proposition P1 essential to T1 and some proposition P2 essential to T2 are such that it is logically impossible that both be true.[11]

Ways of being falsified

A standard case of falsification is mistaken prediction; it notes that theory T entails that result R will obtain if a certain experiment is performed, the experiment is run, and R does not occur – so T is falsified. What is crucial here is not that the false proposition that T entails is future tense; what matters is that T entails a proposition and we have discovered that the proposition is false. It is *having discernible entailments whose truth value is discoverable* that matters here, and the idea that this is always or essentially a matter of prediction is mistaken.

The false proposition entailed by a falsified theory need not be a mistaken report of observational consequences. There are various grounds on which a theory may be rationally rejected. For example, there are various types of what we might call intellectual suicide. Here are three. The claim *No one can know anything said in English* is self-defeating in that (i) *no one could know it were it true*. The claim *Nothing said in English can be true* is self-refuting in that (ii) *its being true is incompatible with what it says is true. Nothing can be said in English* is self-destroying, (iii) *being an instance of what it says cannot exist*. A more interesting example of self-destruction is the claim *All language is metaphorical*; as a non-metaphorical use of language, it is itself the very sort of thing it says there cannot be. There are deep problems with such claims but the problems do not arise from their entailing false observation statements. Such claims, and views to which they are essential, commit intellectual suicide; there is no chance that they constitute knowledge. A theory defective in any of these ways is rationally rejected.[12]

A theory that essentially contains a contradiction is false. (Theory T contains proposition P essentially if and only if with P, T explains the data it is intended to explain, and without P, it does not.) Any set of propositions that is essentially incoherent cannot comprise a theory. (Propositions *P* and *Q* are coherent if and only if they are (i) logically consistent and (ii) *mutually relevant* to explaining what the theory in which they both appear is intended to explain.) If it is essential to theory T that propositions of kind K1 *be* translatable without remainder into propositions of kind K2, and they cannot be, then T is false. If it is essential to theory T that propositions of kind K1 *not* be translatable without remainder into propositions of kind K2, and they can be, then T is false. If theory T is such that if its truth conditions obtain, it is false, then T is false whether or not its truth conditions obtain. (A theory's truth conditions are just what must exist for the theory to be true.) If theory T is such that *T is true* entails *T cannot be reasonably believed*, then T cannot be reasonably believed. If theory T entails *P*, and we know that *P* is false, then we know that T is false. (Some theories entail that there is no moral knowledge, or that sensory experience is never reliable; if we know that it is wrong to torture infants for pleasure or know by sensory experience that there is a door to our room, these theories are false.) If T's only rationale is that accepting T solves problem Q, and T does not solve Q, then there is no rationale for accepting T. If T does not explain data within T's reference range, then at best T is incomplete. (A theory's reference range is the set of data that it was created to explain.) So disconfirmation has many varieties.

To summarize, confirmationism tells us that we should accept only theories that have been confirmed; falsificationists tell us that we should accept only theories that have explanatory power and have not been falsified.

Theistic arguments and explanatory power

One way of thinking of the standard arguments for monotheism is this: their premises refer to such things as *there being things that might not have existed and are possibly explicable, the accessibility of the world to human cognitive powers, there being a distinction between right and wrong, there being self-conscious morally responsible agents,* and the like. Such arguments are possible only insofar as theism has explanatory power regarding such facts as these. Theism need not be the *only* explanation of these facts in order to have explanatory power regarding them. The monotheistic arguments have any force only if the facts mentioned are such that, if monotheism is true, then it provides (a personal) explanation of their obtaining. Part of a different style of argument for monotheism has the following first premise:

M1 Monotheism has explanatory power regarding things hard to explain otherwise.

Its second premise is:

M2 Monotheism has not been falsified.

In the light of the argument earlier concerning monotheistic belief and religious experience, and stating the premise neutrally between confirmationism and falsificationism, the third premise is:

M3 There are experiences it is reasonable to think veridical that are veridical only if monotheism is true (there is experiential evidence for monotheism).

A falsificationist can accept the principle of experiential evidence used in an earlier chapter, and the reports of persons to the effect that they have had the experiences they report. She can thus accept M3 without inconsistency. Put otherwise, a falsificationist can accept the argument of Chapter 10 without accepting anything incompatible with her falsificationism. So, of course, can a confirmationist. The argument concludes:

M4 If monotheism has explanatory power regarding things hard to explain otherwise, monotheism has not been falsified, and there are experiences it is reasonable to think veridical that are veridical only if monotheism is true, then there is evidence that monotheism is true.

The conclusion is:

M5 There is evidence that monotheism is true.

If M4 is true, it is a necessary truth, and M1–M4 obviously entail M5.

Weak rationality and strong rationality

How is one to understand M5? Here is one more set of definitions:

Definition 1: Rita is *weakly reasonable* in accepting proposition T if and only if Rita accepts T, Rita is not unreasonable in accepting T, and Rita would not be unreasonable in rejecting T (where T is a theoretical proposition).

Being *weakly reasonable in accepting T* is equivalent to something in the neighborhood of *not believing against evidence and not believing something that has no explanatory power*. That proposition P is believed with weak reasonability is compatible with not-P being believed with weak reasonability, and with rational suspension of belief regarding P.

Definition 2: Rita is *strongly reasonable* in accepting T if and only if Rita accepts T, Rita is not unreasonable in accepting T, and Rita would be unreasonable in rejecting T.

Being strongly reasonable in accepting T is equivalent to something in the neighborhood of one's believing against evidence if one rejects T and if one suspends judgment regarding T. Being strongly reasonable in believing that T is compatible with one's having evidence against T so long as one's evidence for T outweighs any reasons that one might have for rejecting T.

Rationality and explanatory power

Plainly, one is strongly reasonable in accepting a proposition for which one knows one has a knowledge-extending proof. One is strongly reasonable in accepting a proposition P that has explanatory power regarding data that one is aware of, provided one has no reason to think P false, and one knows of no other theory that has explanatory power relative to that data, especially if the data in question is hard to explain.[13]

What is finally of interest regarding rational assessment is how things fall when everything relevant, or everything relevant that we can think of, is taken into account. Anything strongly rationally accepted in that context is rationally impressive. Whether monotheism, or any other religious perspective, is strongly rational depends on how it fares relative to its non-religious competitors as well as its religious contraries. The argument here, if successful, gives reason to think that monotheism is strongly reasonable to believe in comparison with the other religious perspectives considered. Whether it is strongly reasonable to accept when compared, say, to materialism is a matter into which we have not inquired.

Belief and blame

The definitions and comments here are not part of what some philosophers call the *ethics* of belief – the attempt to specify conditions under which one is blameworthy or praiseworthy relative to holding some belief, and when one's having a belief is morally neutral.[14] They are part of an effort to say what goes into rational assessment of religious beliefs, not religious believers.

Our discussion has been concerned with how rational assessment of a faith can be conducted. We have argued that, contrary to a widely held view, rational assessment of various faiths or religious traditions is possible, and we have given suggestions and illustrations as to how it can be done.

Questions for reflection

1 Is the critique of scientism offered here successful?
2 How are the critiques of scientism and robust foundationalism similar? How do they differ?
3 Discuss the idea that there can be evidence *against* religious beliefs.
4 Discuss the idea that there can be evidence *for* religious beliefs.
5 Assess the merits and limits of confirmationism and falsificationism.
6 What relevance, if any, has the notion of *explanatory power* to religious belief?

Annotated reading

Mavrodes, George (ed.) (1970) *The Rationality of Belief in God*, Englewood Cliffs, NJ: Prentice-Hall. A good collection of essays on the reasonableness of monotheistic belief.

Mitchell, Basil (1981) *The Justification of Religious Belief*, Oxford: Oxford University Press. A clear presentation of the cumulative-case argument for monotheism.

Penelhum, Terence (1983) *God and Scepticism*, Dordrecht: D. Reidel. Clear discussion of monotheism and skepticism about monotheism.

Swinburne, Richard (1981) *Faith and Reason*, Oxford: Oxford University Press. A detailed account of faith and reason by a philosopher who thinks that one ought to have reasons for one's religious beliefs.

Yandell, Keith E. (1986) *Christianity and Philosophy*, Grand Rapids, MI: Eerdmans. A systematic exploration of issues relevant to monotheistic belief.

Glossary

This glossary defines philosophical terms used in this book, giving them the sense they bear here. Unfortunately, not all of these terms have the same sense whenever they appear in a philosophy book. Terms marked with an asterisk (*) are also defined in the glossary.

Advaita Vedanta A Hindu religious tradition whose core doctrine says that the only thing that exists is Brahman without qualities; its most famous expositor is Shankara.

argument A set of claims (premises) from which another claim (the conclusion) is supposed to follow in such a way that evidence has been provided for the conclusion's truth.

bundle theory The view of persons on which a person at a time is a collection of momentary states and over time is a series of such collections.

Christianity A monotheistic* religion whose central doctrine is that God* became incarnate in Jesus Christ who died for our sins and whose resurrection from the dead is the basis for our hope of life everlasting.

compatibilism The view that we can be morally responsible for our actions even if determinism* is true.

consistency strategy The strategy of arguing that because three propositions, none of which is a necessary falsehood, are consistent with one another, any two of them are consistent with one another.

cosmological argument An argument* to the effect that there being things that might never have existed and/or depend for existence on something else is best explained by reference to a being that cannot depend on anything else and has the power to create them.

determinism The view that only one future is compatible with the past.

diagnosis An account of someone's illness.

doctrine A claim about God, human persons, the human condition, the cosmos, and the like, made by a religious tradition.

dualism The view that there are minds and bodies, each of which belongs to its own kind, neither of which is reducible to the other.

enlightenment The condition of having achieved release from the cycle of rebirth.

entails A proposition P entails a proposition Q if and only if it is logically impossible that P is true and Q is false; *There are three hens* entails *There are at least two hens.*

essence An essence is a set of properties that makes what has those properties the member of a kind; *Water is H_2o* ascribes an essence to water, and *Persons are self-conscious agents* ascribes an essence to persons.

ethical theory A full-dress ethical theory offers answers to the questions *When is moral reasoning appropriate (what makes an issue moral)?, What makes an action right or wrong?, What makes a person good or evil?, Is act morality basic to the morality of persons or is the morality of persons basic to act morality?, What sort of life is worth living?* in a way that is intended to be consistent, coherent, and true.

ethics That part of philosophy concerned with the construction, assessment, and application of ethical theories*.

evil The knowing destruction or diminishing of natural* or moral value* without sufficient moral justification.

faith The acceptance of religious doctrine and the endeavor to live in accord with it; an essential element in faith is trust if the doctrine claims the existence of a cosmic person.

foreknowledge God's knowledge of truths about the future.

formal logical necessity A proposition is formally logically necessary if and only if it has the form *P and not-P* or entails a proposition that has this form; *Bill Russell is not both six feet nine inches tall, and not six feet nine inches tall* is formally logically necessary.

God An omnipotent and omniscient being, Creator of the world and providential in guiding the course of history, and a morally perfect agent.

idealism The view that everything that exists is a mental thing, a state of a mental thing, a quality of a mental thing, or a relation between mental things.

informal logical necessity A proposition* is informally logically necessary if it is logically necessary* (there are no possible conditions under which it would be false) but not formally logically necessary* (it is not of the form *P and not-P* and it entails no proposition of this form); *If William draws a rectangle then William draws a figure* is informally logically necessary.

interactionism The view that dualism is true, that material states cause mental states, and mental states cause material states.

invalid argument An argument* that is not valid*.

Islam A religious tradition that is monotheistic*, holding that God gave a revelation to Mohammed in Arabic, the Koran, through which it interprets the Christian and Jewish Bibles.

Jainism An Indian religious tradition, one of whose core doctrines is that persons enjoy necessary existence and inherent knowledge.

Judaism A religious tradition that is monotheistic*, holding that God gave the law to Moses, called Abraham and made him the father of a chosen people; its sacred scriptures, the Hebrew Bible, includes the books of the Christian Old Testament.

karma The doctrine of karma claims that one receives good consequences for good actions and bad consequences for bad actions, some of the consequences typically coming in a different lifetime than the deed from which they arise.

libertarianism The view that we have freedom of choice, and compatibilism* and determinism* are false.

logical necessity A property of propositions*; a proposition has this property if and only if there are no possible conditions under which it would be false; it is identical to necessarily true*.

logically contingent A proposition is logically contingent if and only if there are conditions under which it would be true and conditions under which it would be false.

logically impossible A proposition is logically impossible if and only if it is not logically possible*; the denial of a logically impossible proposition is logically necessary*.

logically possible A proposition is logically possible if and only if there are conditions under which it would be true; logically necessary* and logically contingent* propositions* are logically possible.

materialism The view that everything that exists is a material thing, a state of a material thing, a quality of a material thing, or a relation between material things.

metaphysical necessity A proposition is metaphysically necessary if and only if it is logically necessary and it either is an existential statement* or states what the essence* of something is.

modal proposition A proposition* to the effect that another proposition is logically possible*, logically necessary*, or logically contingent*; if such a proposition is true, it is necessarily true* and if false it is necessarily false*.
monotheism The view that there exists one God*, in contrast to atheism which holds that there is no God and polytheism which holds that there are many gods but not one God.
moral value The dignity or worth inherent in being a self-conscious libertarianly free agent capable of making choices that are right or wrong.
morality See ethics*.
natural value The worth inherent in the flourishing of a thing that has an essential nature capable of normal development.
necessarily true A property of propositions*; a proposition has this property if and only if there are no possible conditions under which it would be false; it is identical to logical necessity*.
numerical identity Self-identity; the sort of identity a person or thing at one time has with herself or itself another time and anything has with itself at a time; strictly, all identity is numerical identity.
ontological argument An argument* to the effect that it is logically impossible that God not exist.
ontological independence Something X has ontological independence of Y if and only if X does not depend for its existence on Y; something has full ontological independence if there is nothing distinct from itself on which it depends for its existence.
person A self-conscious agent.
phenomenological description A description of how things appear to a subject of experience, whether or not things are as they appear.
problem of evil The problem that exists provided the occurrence of evil is evidence against the existence of God*.
proposition A proposition is anything that is either true or false; we use declarative sentences to express propositions, but the same proposition can be expressed by using different strings of words in one or more languages, so propositions are not sentences.
qualitative identity Perfect similarity.
reason The capacity to see necessary truths*, make inferences, remember, observe and describe, explain and understand, learn, and so on through a rich variety of capacities.
reincarnation The doctrine of reincarnation claims that persons beginninglessly, and endlessly unless they become enlightened*, are born and die and are born and die and are born and die.
religious experience An experience that a religious tradition takes to be significant for salvation or enlightenment.
religious pluralism The view that no religious tradition is true and that every religious tradition produces morally good people except those that do not.
religious tradition A tradition that offers a diagnosis* of what it alleges is our deep and enduring problem and proposes a cure for that problem.
salvation The condition of being rightly related to God*, with sins forgiven.
self-authentication A proposition is self-authenticated to a person by an experience if and only if it is logically impossible* that the person accept the proposition on the basis of the experience and be mistaken in so doing.
semantic logical necessity = informal logical necessity*.
substance theory The theory of persons on which they are self-conscious beings that endure uninterruptedly over time.
syntactic logical necessity = formal logical necessity*.
teleological argument An argument* to the effect that the intelligible order in nature

that makes everyday action and natural science possible is best explained by reference to a Mind in whose image our minds are made.

Theravada Buddhism An Indian religious tradition, one of whose core doctrines is that a person at a time is simply a bundle of states and over time is simply a series of such bundles.

Upanishad A sacred Hindu text; the exact number is disputed, but there are at least over a hundred.

valid argument An argument* such that if one asserts its premises and denies its conclusion, one accepts a self-contradiction.

Selected great figures in the history of philosophy of religion

Dates in medieval Indian philosophy are often, like those asterisked here, approximate.

St Anselm [1033–1109 CE] One might begin with his *Monologium* and *Proslogium* which center on the notion of God as that being than whom no greater can be conceived and the ontological argument.

St Thomas Aquinas [1225–1274 CE] One might begin with *Of Being and Essence* and then dip into *Summa Theologica* [Part I, Question 2, Articles 2, 3 contain his "Five Ways" or arguments for God's existence] and *Summa Contra Gentiles* (I, 12, 13 contains a fuller discussion of the argument for God's existence).

Aristotle [384–322 BCE] One might begin by considering his discussion of God or the Unmoved Mover in *Metaphysics* 12.

Augustine [354–430 CE] One might begin with his discussion of God and time in *Confessions*, Book 11; *The City of God* is his longest and greatest philosophical–theological work.

Averroes [1126–1198 CE] One might begin with *The Incoherence of the Incoherence* which criticizes both Avicenna and Al Ghazali.

Avicenna [980–1037 CE] One might begin with the discussion of God as a necessary being in *The Metaphysica of Avicenna*.

Samuel Clarke [1675–1729 CE] One might begin with *A Demonstration of the Being and Attributes of God*; Part II contains a version of the cosmological argument.

René Descartes [1596–1650 CE] One might begin with his *Meditations on First Philosophy*.

Al Ghazali [1058–1111 CE] One might begin with *The Incoherence of the Philosophers* which attempts to refute twenty philosophical propositions.

David Hume [1711–1776 CE] One might begin with his *Natural History of Religion* and go on to the *Dialogues Concerning Natural Religion*.

Immanuel Kant [1724–1804] One might begin with his *Prolegomena to Any Future Metaphysic*, and go on to the *Critique of Practical Reason*, and *Religion within the Limits of Reason Alone*; the *Critique of Pure Reason* is his most difficult work and most influential relative to the philosophy of religion.

Gottfried Wilhelm von Leibniz [1646–1716 CE] One might begin with the *Principles of Nature and Grace* and *The Leibniz–Clarke Correspondence*.

Madhva [1238–1317 CE]* One might begin with his *Brahma-Sutra-Bhasya*.

Moses Maimonides [1135/8–1204 CE] One might begin with his *Guide for the Perplexed*, I, 71–II, 31, where he considers arguments for the existence of God, and the topic of creation; in the Introduction, he lists twenty-five propositions derived from and summarizing Aristotle's philosophy.

Philo [approximately 20 BCE–50 CE] One might begin with *On the Creation* and *On the Unchangeableness of God*.

Plato [429–347 BCE] One might begin by reading his discussion of the immortality of the soul in the *Phaedo* [esp. 78B–80C] and his discussion of an early version of the argument from design for God's existence in the *Timaeus*.

Plotinus [204–270 CE] One might begin with *The Enneads*, III, 7 on eternity and time, and IV, 7 on the immortality of the soul; VI deals with the kinds of being.

Ramanuja [1017–1137 CE]* One might begin with his *Brahma-Sutra-Bhasya*.

Shankara [700–800 CE]* One might begin with his *Brahma-Sutra-Bhasya*; a *sutra* is a principle (literally, a thread) and the principles of Vedanta are believed to have been collected by Badarayana into a work on which later followers of Vedanta comment.

Baruch Spinoza [1633–1677 CE] One might begin with his *Ethics*, Book I.

Notes

Preface

1 The nonsense line was most famously defended by A. J. Ayer, *Language, Truth, and Logic* (New York: Dover, 1952). Cf. the critique in Alvin Plantinga, "Verificationism and Other Theologia," in *God and Other Minds* (Ithaca: Cornell University Press, 1967). The famous or infamous "University Discussion" between Antony Flew, R. M. Hare, and Basil Mitchell ("Theology and Falsification," in Antony Flew and Alistair McIntyre (eds), *New Essays in Philosophical Theology* (New York: Macmillan, 1957)) and "An Empiricist's View of the Nature of Religious Belief") in John Hick (ed.), *The Existence of God* (New York: Macmillan, 1964) express positions near to Ayer's account. Frederick Ferré responded to this sort of perspective in *Language, Logic, and God* (New York: Harper Torchbooks, 1967), as did the present author in *Basic Issues in the Philosophy of Religion* (Boston: Allyn and Bacon, 1971). A wider range of issues is dealt with very nicely in William Alston, *Divine Nature and Human Language: Essays in Philosophical Theology* (Ithaca: Cornell University Press, 1989).

2 Sometimes this line rests on appeal to some version of relativism; at other times, it rests on the alleged impossibility of cogent argumentation across religious traditions. Cf. the present author's "Some Varieties of Relativism," *International Journal for Philosophy of Religion*, Vol. 19, pp. 61–85, 1986, and Paul J. Griffiths, *An Apology for Apologetics* (Maryknoll, New York: Orbis Books, 1991).

1 Introduction

1 Philosophy of religion is metaphysics, epistemology, and ethics applied to religion. Philosophy, of course also includes logic, history of philosophy (which includes history of philosophy of religion), aesthetics, political philosophy, and so on. My concern here is with philosophy as it relates most closely to philosophy of religion.

2 As well as what there isn't, what isn't known, and what is not good.

3 Nirvana aside.

4 What appears to be an enduring thing is a series of momentary things.

5 This claim, of course, is controversial. So are the varieties of claims that evil is evidence against the existence of God.

6 Advaita Vedanta also appeals to Hindu Scripture.

2 What is philosophy? What is religion? What is philosophy of religion?

1 Everett Hall, *Philosophical Systems* (Chicago: University of Chicago Press, 1958) offers what I take to be the best book ever written on the nature of philosophy, though the final chapter disappoints.

2 Alvin Plantinga's (Professor of Philosophy at the University of Notre Dame) remark to the effect that good philosophizing is just thinking really hard and well is right so far as it goes, and it is what one thinks about that makes one's thought philosophical.
3 Cf. the comments by Everett Hall, *Philosophical Systems: A Categorial Analysis* (Chicago: University of Chicago Press, 1960), 3–6, on what medieval philosophers said regarding *being, truth, and goodness*. Thoughts that something is so are either true or false, and *being true or false* is essential to their nature. So *thing, thought, value,* like *being, truth, and goodness,* come under theory of reality, theory of knowledge, and ethics, which are the core disciplines for the philosophy of religion.
4 In terms of specifics, our focus will be on Judaism, Christianity, Islam, Hinduism, Buddhism, and Jainism – on Semitic and (South Asian) Indian religion.
5 By gods and goddesses as well, if there are any; by every person other than God.
6 Need it be said that these characterizations, accurate so far as they go, do not begin to plumb the complexities of these disciplines?
7 The view that all language, or all religious language, is non-literal is unfortunately widespread. It will be discussed below. As my comments here reveal, I take the view to be false.
8 The degree to which this is, or is not, peculiar to philosophical claims does not matter for our purposes; it is enough that it is true of philosophical claims.

3 What sorts of religion are there?

1 *Proposition Q assumes proposition P* amounts to *If P is false then Q is false* which in turn amounts to *If Q is true then P is true* which amounts to *Q entails P*.
2 I am assuming that an accurate account of a religious tradition, whose accuracy is measured by reference to that religion's authoritative texts, is one that an informed adherent would accept. The sheer fact that some adherent did not accept the account offered here would, by itself and without reference to those texts, be without force.
3 It seems fairest to describe religious traditions in terms that most faithfully reflect their traditional doctrinal formulations. This procedure is followed here. Thus, from the standpoint of orthodox Christianity in any of its forms, so-called "Atheistic Christianity" is exactly the contradiction-in-terms that it seems to be, and someone who offers as a full explanation of the resurrection of Christ that the spirit of Jesus survived death does not believe that the resurrection of Christ occurred. From the standpoint of almost any Buddhist tradition, the Buddhist monks who held that one can give a coherent account of reincarnation and karma only if there is a mental substance that endures through lifetimes are highly nonrepresentative Buddhists. Nonetheless, the *sorts* of considerations applied to religious traditions here apply to non-standard versions as well.
4 Judaism's sacred text, the Hebrew Bible, is largely the Old Testament which, with the New Testament, comprises the Christian Bible (what Protestants call the Apocrypha, Roman Catholics view as part of the Old Testament). Islam accepts both Testaments, interpreting them in the light of its distinctive sacred text, the Koran.
5 Perhaps with the exception of abstract objects.
6 Strictly, what a so-called "cyclical view of time" seems to involve is the idea that a sequence of events occurs that fits a very complex description D, only to be followed by another sequence of events that also fits D, and so on for ever, with no sequence of events occurring that does not fall into this pattern. The book that told the universe's story would be a sequence of identical chapters. This is a view, not about time, but about the

repetition of one pattern of events. A "one-directional" view of time, in the sense intended here, entails that the same story, told over and over, would not match up with what occurs.

7 I Corinthians 15: 3, 4.

8 For Vedanta, the *Vedas* and *Upanishads* with the authoritative commentaries on these texts by Badarayana and others; for Jainism, the *Jaina Sutras*; for Theravada Buddhism, the *Pali Canon*.

9 I must have found this version in A. L. Basham, *The Wonder That Was India* (New York: The Macmillan Company, 1954) but I cannot relocate it.

10 *Maitri Upanishad* I, 3–4.

11 H. C. Warren, *Buddhist Scriptures* (Baltimore: Penguin Books, 1959), p. 186.

12 This is not true for the other varieties of Vedanta, or for all versions of Mahayana Buddhism.

13 Sarvapalli Radhakrishnan and C. A. Moore (eds), *A Sourcebook in Indian Philosophy* (Princeton, NJ: Princeton University Press, 1957), p. 513. Hereafter cited as "RM."

14 RM, p. 269.

15 Herman Jacobi, trans., *Jaina Sutras* (New York: Dover Publications, 1962; originally published in 1896); I, p. 264.

16 *Jaina Sutras*, II, p. 64.

17 RM, p. 260.

18 RM, p. 284.

19 H. C. Warren, *Buddhism in Translations* (New York: Atheneum Press, 1969), p. 146.

20 RM, op. cit., p. 125.

21 Also, of course, nirvana – whose nature will be discussed in a later chapter.

22 This will be clearer after we have discussed the conceptual contexts within which the diagnoses and cures are held.

4 What sorts of religious experience are there?

1 Exactly how many sensory modalities there are seems to be a matter of dispute. Wondering how many current theory offered us, I went to our local bookstore to check out the introductory textbooks in use in psychology, which in the local context seemed at the time not to differ greatly from introductory physiology. Three texts were in use, and while each ridiculed traditional philosophers like Aristotle and Locke for thinking that there were five sensory modalities, they themselves differed as to how many there are; eleven, thirteen, and seventeen were proposed. Nothing argued here requires that there be five, eleven, thirteen, or seventeen sensory modalities. There are at least the five noted.

2 The relevant account here is of course enormously complex; by the time beliefs based on commonsense perceptual experience are purified by filtering them through contemporary theory, it is plausible that (say) experience of God, if it is reliable at all, is the basis for beliefs that need *less* filtering than their perceptual cousins.

3 Or perhaps sub-kind, since all are *sensory* experiences.

4 Anything having this property, or the next, has it essentially.

5 There are two ways of having the property *not being alive* – having been alive and now being dead, and not being capable of life. Corpses have the former, rocks the latter. I do not intend that this way of putting things entails the existence of negative properties – it is fine with me if *not being alive* just amounts to lacking *being alive*.

6 There are complications here that we need not get into in detail. Suppose that

something like traditional monotheism is true, a monotheism that includes (a) *If anything exists that might not have existed, then God exists.* Any actual experience of sort B is something that might not have existed. So if (a) is true, God exists. But *God exists* entails (something along the lines of) *There is a self-conscious being of impressive holiness whose presence elicits worship.* Happily, this sort of complexity can be avoided by using the notion of relevance conditions that relate experiences and claims, as we will do before we consider the question of the evidential force of religious experience. So it is not cheating to ignore it here.

7 Note that the criterion as stated is stronger than it would be were it only required that B differed from A in that it would not follow from B's veridicality that A was not veridical.

5 The importance of doctrine and the distinctions of religious traditions

1 John 14:6.
2 John 3:36.
3 Acts 4:12.
4 George Thibaut, trans., *The Vedanta Sutras of Badarayanna with the Commentary of Sankara* (New York: Dover Publications, 1962; originally published 1896), Vol. II, p. 399.
5 Geshe Sopa and Elving Jones, *A Light to the Svatantrika-Madhyanika*, p. 62; privately circulated.
6 The knowledge in question is not construed as merely knowledge by description, but there is no pretense of a knowledge by acquaintance that does not include some knowledge by description.
7 *Munkara Upanishad* III, i, 3.
8 I, 271.
9 *Digha Nikaya* II, 251.
10 I John 5:20.
11 B'hai and Advaita Vedanta both hold this view; so do various secularized versions of Protestantism and Catholicism.
12 Another factor promoting the same "all religions are the same" line is a popular sort of mind-set that has persuaded itself that religions make no claims at all. Sometimes this rests on some principle of meaning (that is likely not to meet its own standard). Sometimes it is based on a view of what it is to know that something is true (that is likely not to be knowable on its own standards). Sometimes it rests on some sort of relativism (that is likely in turn to make relativistic the view that no religion makes truth-claims). Sometimes it rests on a new account of truth (that will serve its intended purpose only if it is true in a sense of truth of which it provides no account). Each of these perspectives has its own varieties, and it would take some space to describe, and more space to discuss, these views. The present author has argued against such views in *Christianity and Philosophy* (Grand Rapids: Eerdmans, 1984) and *Hume's "Inexplicable Mystery": His Views on Religion* (Philadelphia: Temple University Press, 1990), as well as in "Empiricism and Theism," *Sophia*, Vol. 7, No. 3, October 1968, pp. 3–11; "A Reply to Nielsen," *Sophia*, Vol. 7, No. 3, October 1968, pp. 18, 19; "Some Varieties of Relativism," *International Journal for Philosophy of Religion*, Vol. 19, pp. 61–85, 1986.
13 I have written about these views elsewhere. See "On the Alleged Unity of all Religions," *Christian Scholars'* Review, Vol. VI, Nos 2 and 3, 1976, pp. 140–55, and "Some Varieties

of Religious Pluralism," in James Kellenberger (ed.), *Inter-religious Models and Criteria* (New York: St Martin's Press, 1993), pp. 187–211.

14 Cf. the present author's *Basic Issues in the Philosophy of Religion* (Boston: Allyn and Bacon, 1970), chapter 1.

6 Religious pluralism

1 (London: Macmillan, and New Haven: Yale University Press).
2 (Louisville: Westminster/John Knox Press, 1995).
3 Much of the rest of it will come up during our critique.
4 Professor Hick in *A Christian Theology of Religions*, op. cit. claims

> the religions ask different questions. I want to suggest that these questions, whilst specifically different, are generically the same. They all presuppose a profound present lack, and the possibility of a radically better future; and they are all answers to the question, how to get from one to the other. In traditional Christian language they are all ways of asking, What must I do to be saved?
> (p. 41)

5 Ibid. Professor Hick says, "each of the great world religions is a response to the ultimately real, and that each is a context of human salvation," and "On the one hand religious pluralism leaves the different doctrinal systems intact within their own religious traditions, but on the other hand it proposes the meta-theory that these traditions, as complex totalities, are different human responses to the Real."

6 Ibid.

> Not more than one of these rival belief-systems could be finally and universally true, and yet the traditions within which they function seem, when judged by their fruits, to be more or less equally valid responses to the Real. Now the distinction between the Real in itself and the Real as variously humanly thought and experienced enables us to understand how this can be: namely, the differing belief-systems are beliefs about different manifestations of the Real. They're not mutually conflicting beliefs, because they're beliefs about different phenomenal realities. It's in this sense that they are reduced or "downgraded" in their scope.

7 Ibid. To the question "that's a pretty radical reinterpretation, isn't it?" Professor Hick replies, "Yes; but we really do have to make a choice between a traditional absolutism and a genuinely pluralistic interpretation of the global religious situation."

8 Ibid. As a basis for these claims, Professor Hick asserts that:

> I want to say that what is literally or analogically true of, say, the heavenly Parent of Christian belief – for example, that God is loving, like an ideal parent – is mythologically true of the Real in itself . . . I mean by a myth a story that is not literally true but that has the power to evoke in its hearers a practical response to the myth's referent – a true myth being of course one that evokes an appropriate response. The truthfulness of a myth is thus a practical truthfulness, consisting in its capacity to orient us rightly in our lives. In so far as the heavenly Parent is an authentic manifestation of the Real, to think of the

Real as an ideal parent is to think in a way that can orient us rightly to the Real, evoking in us a trust which can pervade our lives and free us to love our neighbour. And of course I want to give a parallel account of the language about the Ultimate used by each of the other world religions.

9 If one asks what reason there is for thinking religious pluralism to be true, Professor Hick's answer is: "the hypothesis is offered as the best explanation', i.e. the most comprehensive and economical explanation, from a religious point of view, of the facts of the history of religions. A proffered 'best explanation' is not a proof, because it is always open to someone else to come forward and offer what they believe is a better explanation. And so the right response of someone who does not like my proposed explanation is not to complain that it is not proved but to work out a viable alternative." I reject this notion of what "the right" response is. If I propose that the reason why our friend is putting cherry pies into the dishwasher is that she thinks the pies are prime numbers, you do not have to offer another hypothesis in order to show that my explanation would not work. Prime numbers aren't things you can move around.

10 The terms "nice" and "morally nice" serve merely as place-holders for substantive accounts of moral virtue. RP thinks there is deep moral agreement between religious traditions. If one looks at more than overt behavior, this is dubious. It also apparently thinks that morality does not significantly change with changes in metaphysics; this too is highly dubious.

11 Hick, *A Christian Theology of Religions*, op. cit., p.118.

12 This is argued in some detail in the present author's *The Epistemology of Religious Experience* (Cambridge: Cambridge University Press, 1995).

13 Hick, *A Christian Theology of Religions*, op. cit., p. 62.

14 Ibid., p. 71.

15 Ibid., p. 69.

16 Ibid., pp. 62, 63.

17 Ibid., p. 67.

18 A monotheistic doctrine on which human persons are created in God's image can allow that a concept can be human and reliable. So can a view in which the idea of revelation is taken seriously. But RP filters these out.

19 One could simply say that logic generates terms – say, predicates – not properties. Then the predicates are such that a predicate F corresponds to a property if a sentence of the form "X is F" is true. On a widely accepted account, terms replacing "X" in "There is an X" and "For all X" refer to things and terms replacing "F" in "There is an x such that Fx" and "For all x, Fx" are true or false of things. It does not matter to my argument whether or not we speak of terms or properties; it can be cast in either manner.

20 Professor Hick's way of speaking, and mine here as well, is in various ways shorthand for a more careful account. For example: (i) a formal system of logic is not a system of propositions, but of propositional functions – "There is an x such that Fx" and "For all x, Fx" are neither true nor false; they are but logical skeletons of existential and universal propositions, respectively; (ii) hence such things as "For all X, X = X" and "For all x, Fx or not-Fx" are neither true nor false; (iii) the interpretation of a formal system applies it to propositions, and logic applies to things via applying to propositions true or false of those things.

21 Hick, *A Christian Theology of Religions*, op. cit., p. 60.

22 Ibid., p. 63.

23 Ibid.

24 Ibid., p. 67.

25 I've made the point in print twice without its importance being noted. The admission it refers to is itself enough to refute RP.

26 Strictly, I suppose, we'd have one genus – happy properties – with two species: happy properties that are generable from logic, and happy properties that are not. I leave it to the reader to work out the rephrasing of my argument that this point would require.

27 Hick, *A Christian Theology of Religions*, op. cit., p. 62.

28 When Professor Hick says that religious experience is a response to the transcendent Real, he means it is not merely a projection by us. The Real contributes something and we contribute something.

7 Monotheistic conceptions of ultimate reality

1 It is logically consistent with monotheism that there exist abstract objects that possess logically necessary existence. Abstract objects have no causal powers, are not self-conscious or even conscious, and exercise no creation or providence. They are of little if any *religious* interest. It is a necessary truth that *If X has logically necessary existence then there is nothing Y such that Y is distinct from X and X depends on Y for X's existence*. So if *There are abstract objects that have logically necessary existence* is true, it is also true that *There exists something whose existence does not depend on God*. God's status as Creator, and any coherent notion of divine sovereignty, does not require that something that cannot depend for its existence on anything else depend for its existence on God or deny that the existence of such things is logically possible. But the only candidates for being something of this sort would seem to be things that exist with logical necessity.

2 Trinitarian monotheists speak in this fashion, though typically holding God to be three persons in one substance; other monotheists speak of God as personal while adding that it is proper to speak in this way because God is more like a person than God is like anything else. The latter claim rests in part on views concerning the alleged limits of descriptions of God. For a monotheistic tradition to make even the comparatively weak religious claims central to Greek monotheism, God must be self-conscious. For a monotheistic tradition to make the more robust religious claims characteristic of Judaism, Christianity, Islam, or Hindu monotheism, God must be a self-conscious agent – one who knowingly and purposively acts. A self-conscious agent is a person.

3 Roughly Aristotelian in content.

4 If the point isn't clear, consider a parallel case. If I ask for the accurate explanation of the existence of this very duck that walks the shore in front of me, the answer is that it had parents. But if I want to know the explanation of there being any ducks at all, I cannot properly be told about there being duck parents; there being duck parents is (part of) what I want explained.

5 Arguably, this claim is *typical of but not essential to* Semitic monotheism.

6 Exodus, chapter 2 passage in which God, in standard translations, makes self-reference by using the terms "I am" seems not to require a stronger philosophical reading than that expressed by something like *God exists, and it is logically impossible that God depend on anything else for existence*.

7 Of course N(Np) – Necessarily, Necessarily, p – is a second-order modal proposition, and one can go on up the ladder. We will go to third-order in a moment.

8 Here is a little more: 1 P *entails* proposition Q if and only if it is logically impossible that P be true and Q be false (i.e., if *P, but not Q* is a contradiction); 2 No necessary truth entails a necessary falsehood; 3 No logically contingent proposition entails a

necessary falsehood; 4 No necessary truth entails any logically contingent proposition; 5 Every necessary falsehood entails any proposition whatever (this assumes the rules *If P then (P or Q)* and *If (P or Q) and not-P, then Q* or their equivalent); 6 Every logically contingent proposition entails every necessary truth; 7 Every logically contingent proposition entails some, but not all, other logically contingent propositions.

9 The logical relations between these views go as follows. Where NT = necessarily true; NF = necessarily false; CT = contingently true; CF = contingently false, the relationships are:
1 If *NG* is the case, then *CG*, *N(NOT-G)*, and *C(NOT-G)* are NF.
2 If *N(NOT-G)* is the case, then *NG*, *CG*, and *C(NOT-G)* are NF.
3 If *CG* is the case, then *NG* and *N(NOT-G)* are NF and *C(NOT-G)* is CF.
4 If *C(NOT-G)* is the case, then *NG* and *N(NOT-G)* are NF and *CG* is CF.

10 These matters are relevant to arguments to be considered later. It is the case that: (A) A proof of a necessary truth can contain only necessary truths as premises, and (B) A proof of a logically contingent proposition must contain at least one logically contingent proposition among its premises. It is also, of course, true that: (C) No false proposition can be proved, and (D) No argument that contains a false premise is a proof, even if its conclusion is true.

11 "Behave" here is an anthropomorphism which unfortunately is seldom recognized as such.

12 That this is approximate, and not a basic law, does not matter. Anyone who wants more sophisticated examples is free to supply them.

13 Or a feature that follows from its essential features.

14 Strictly, essences typically are thought of as defining *kinds* of things; the view that there are, in addition to essences or kinds of things, also essences of individuals is much more controversial.

8 Nonmonotheistic conceptions of ultimate reality

1 Subject to a philosophical qualification noted in a later chapter.

2 Technically, impermanence and co-dependent arising.

3 *Commentary on the Brahma-Sutra*, II, 3,7.

4 *Pancandasi*, III, 23–4.

5 Further, Shankara's writings contain a sophisticated version of the view that there are experience-independent physical objects.

6 *Chandogya Upanishad* 3.14.1.

7 The passage is from S. Subba Rao, *Vedanta Sutras* (Madras, 1904; 3.3.29, p. 141); cited in J. Estlin Carpenter, *Theism in Medieval India* (New Delhi: Oriental Books Reprint Corporation, 1977); first published by Williams and Norgate, London, 1921, with quotations embedded in the text as indicated.

8 K. Satchidananda Murty, *Reason and Revelation in Advaita Vedanta* (Delhi: Motilal Barnasidass, 1974), pp. 3–4. First published by Ahndra University Press and Columbia University Press, 1959.

9 Strictly, no term more determinate than, say, *substance*.

10 Strictly, it is the *Essay Concerning Human Understanding*, Book II (not the later Book IV) account.

11 Allowing for a particular historical context.

12 Where "the Atman" refers to each "individual person" – the view, of course, entails the remarkable consequence that there is at most only one individual person.

13 We can ignore here whether idealistic Oscar is one collection of present images or a temporally sequenced series of collections.
14 At least for serious purposes in science and metaphysics.
15 I leave "collections of catty images" vague; in fact, there is no replacement for this phrase that satisfies the idealist desiderata of (i) being phenomenologically adequate to our sensory experience and (ii) not referring to what, if it exists, is a physical object.
16 Again, for purposes of metaphysics and high religion.
17 The question remains, of course, as to what can properly replace such sentences as *I am tired*, a topic to which we will return when we come to assess Advaita Vedanta's claims.
18 Jain doctrine is classically expressed in the *Jaina Sutras*. Jain tradition is doctrinally far more homogeneous than Buddhist tradition.
19 *Tattvarthadhigama Sutra*, chapter V, sections 29, 30, 31, 38, 41, 42; Sarvepalli Radhakrishnan and Charles A. Moore (eds), *A Sourcebook in Indian Philosophy* (Princeton, NJ: Princeton University Press, 1957), p. 256. The *Sourcebook* is probably still the most accessible source for the passages that it contains.
20 Ibid., chapter II, sections 7, 8, 29; *Sourcebook*, p. 254.
21 This is a Jain analogue of the doctrine of double predestination (some to salvation, some to damnation), albeit without a predestinator.
22 *Samayasdra*, 325.
23 *Atmanusasna*, 174.
24 Ibid., chapter X, section 4; *Sourcebook*, p. 260.
25 Herman Jacobi, trans., *Jaina Sutras* (New York: Dover Publications, 1962; originally published, 1896) I, 264.
26 Buddhist tradition is far less homogeneous than Jain tradition. While the doctrines that, nirvana aside, nothing is permanent, everything is momentary, and the related thesis that no momentary thing exists independently, come near to being Buddhist orthodoxy, even within Indian Buddhism there is significant doctrinal variety. My focus here is on Theravada Buddhism. The same issues arise for non-Absolutist Mahayana traditions. Absolutist Mahayana tradition is a philosophical sibling, if not twin, to Advaita Vedanta and lies outside the present discussion.
27 *Anguttara-nikaya*, iii, 134; *Sourcebook*, pp. 273, 274; the text is Theravadin.
28 *Visuddhi-magga*, xviii; *Sourcebook*, pp. 284–5; the text is Theravadin.
29 Or, for Buddhist idealism, sensory contents of elements of simultaneous bundles.
30 *Sanmati Tarka*, 1.12; *Sourcebook*, p. 269.
31 Strictly, change requires *that the item that changes retain numerical identity over time*. Whether this is a matter of *permanence*, in the sense of the inherent indestructibility that Jainism ascribes to persons, or a beginningless but nonetheless dependent numerical identity over time that persons enjoy according to Vsistaadvaita and Dvaita, or a non-beginningless dependent numerical identity over time that persons enjoy according to the Semitic monotheisms, is irrelevant here. I use the quoted term "permanence" for convenience; let it stand in for something like "numerical identity over time" of any of the sorts just mentioned.
32 For non-idealist Buddhism, there are bundles that contain no states of consciousness (these being the referents of typical physical object terms) and bundles that contain states of consciousness (these being the referents of typical person terms). For the idealist Buddhist, there are only the latter, and typical physical object terms refer to subsets of bundles of states of consciousness (those containing sensory content).
33 If metaphysical identity is necessary, a Buddhist person could not have lived lives other than the one she did live. This raises questions about any alleged freedom such a person could possess.

34 "Getting them right" of course involves more than being able to pass a true–false exam in metaphysics. It involves deep convictions, basic and firmly held beliefs, associated feelings and practices, and the like – "heart knowledge as well as head knowledge" as some would say. But "getting them right" does include getting them right – believing what is true.
35 I use "memory" here as a "success term" without denying that one can think one remembers when one does not (a view quite open to Jainism). If one prefers, let him for "memory" substitute "reliable memory."
36 If you want to think of various reincarnation "visits" as all comprising a single lifetime, think of the actions as having been done on earlier "visits" than those in which the recompense comes.
37 The role alleged ineffability plays in this notion will be discussed in a later chapter.

9 Arguments against monotheism

1 There may be times in between embodiments, for a given person or for all persons in a condition, in which the physical world spends some time at rest.
2 See Bruce Reichenbach's discussion in *Reincarnation and Karma* and the article by Paul Griffiths, referred to in the Annotated reading at the end of the chapter.
3 For a possible problem regarding the use of the doctrines of reincarnation and karma as a reply to the problem of evil, see Roy Perrett (ed.), *Indian Philosophy of Religion* (Dordrecht: Kluwer Academic Publishers), chapters 1 (section starting on p. 13) and 3.
4 Other sorts of considerations are considered elsewhere – e.g., in our consideration of the concept of God, and the properties of *being omnipotent, being omniscient,* and *being morally perfect.*
5 Or *Probably, God does not exist* or *There is evidence against the existence of God* or the like. It is not a logically necessary truth that *If there is evil then there is evidence against the existence of God.*
6 Perhaps the assumptions are rendered easier to make if one mistakenly takes there to be such a thing as *knowing everything but one thing (being one proposition short of omniscience)* and *being able to do everything except one thing (being one power short of omnipotence).* These assumptions take propositions and powers to be related to one another as are pieces of straw in a haystack (each separable from the others), and this is a dubious view about both propositions and powers. This is so, even if holism (the view that the content of every proposition and power is intrinsically dependent on the content of every other) is also a dubious view about propositions and powers.
7 Perhaps a best possible world should be conceived as also "maximizing" other values besides moral worth. My point here is that, since it is moral evil that is relevant to the objection being considered, the idea of a best possible world is at least the idea of a world with "maximal" moral worth, and that such a world will contain no evil.
8 Philosophers differ over whether such virtues as fortitude, bravery, courage, and compassion have intrinsic worth – possessing them is a logically necessary condition of being a maturely good moral agent, or merely intrinsic worth, so that fortitude, bravery, courage, and compassion are valuable in the way that taking bitter medicine may be valuable – as a remedy for something unpleasant but not as something that is good for its own sake. If *any* evil-requiring virtue has intrinsic worth as an essential element in a fully mature good character, then (N1)'s denial that a best possible world – if that notion makes sense – could contain no evil is mistaken.

9 One can put this premise instead as 2*. If there are apparently pointless evils, then *probably* there is no God, with the conclusion stated as 3*. *Probably* God does not exist. Similar alterations could be made in arguments to come. For simplicity these variations will not be explicitly dealt with, but the discussion applies equally to them.

10 For some relevant considerations concerning actually pointless or gratuitous evil, see the current author's "Divine Existence and Gratuitous Evil," *Religious Studies*, Vol. 25, pp. 15–30.

11 It is one thing to appeal to mystery and another to possess the minimal modesty involved in recognizing that the range of knowledge of an omnicompetent being might include things that exceed our comprehension.

12 Since it is on behalf of an argument we will reject that we make this assumption, its relative unclarity will not be a problem for anything we want to argue for.

13 The definitions of *pointless evil* that follow all refer to our knowledge and our conceptual efforts – to what we can think up. An importantlly different sort of definition would eliminate all such reference. Roughly, on such a definition, a pointless evil would be one that served no point, whatever we thought about the matter.

14 Or, minimally, did not act wrongly.

15 It is controversial whether there are any strictly unimaginably pointless evils. For any evil you like, one could claim that it is a necessary condition of some specific great good – say, the salvation of ten thousand persons – though one admitted that one did not know *in what manner* it served as such a condition. Even if there was no reason to think this was true of that evil, it does not follow that (a) it is not imaginable that it be true, and hence (b) that there may be some great good such that, had we more information, we could see it was necessary to that good, or (c) that even if we are not bright enough to see the connection between a great good and a particular evil even were the connection explained to us, there might nonetheless be one. The point is that strictly *being an unimaginably pointless evil* is tantamount to *being an evil that necessarily has no point* or *being an evil that would be pointless in any possible world in which it occurred*. In order not to make things more complex, I will not directly enter into these matters here. I take it that, to the degree that we understand the notion of *being an unimaginably pointless evil*, there is no good reason to think that it fits any actual evil.

16 One could add *or S's being given the chance to come to have Q, provided she acts rightly* to the definition.

17 Again, one could say *there probably are actually pointless evils* or *it is reasonable to think that there are actually pointless evils* or *it is reasonable to think, and unreasonable not to think, that there are actually pointless evils* in stating this premise. The discussion should make clear what might properly be said about these variations.

18 See previous note.

19 Some have argued that if there are evils that are *either* apparently pointless or neither apparently pointful nor apparently pointless, the existence of those evils, or of our evidential situation regarding them, is evidence against God's existence. One way of putting their point is this: the existence of some evil E which is, relative to our knowledge, either apparently pointless or neither apparently pointful nor apparently pointless constitutes an evil E* distinct from E, and the existence of such evils as E* is evidence against the existence of God. Call an evil that is either apparently pointless or else neither apparently pointful nor apparently pointless a *murky* evil. The same issues arise about murky evils as arise about non-murky evils in a way that seems not to bring about any distinctively new considerations.

20 Should suspend judgment, at any rate, if our total evidence is that the evils in question are of the sort indicated. The same consideration applies regarding 2a** below.

21 See Annotated reading at end of chapter.
22 Or embodied ones of whom we have no trace; the possible scenario sketched here speaks of unembodied agents simply to link up with accounts of angels and demons.
23 One could go on for some time considering possible points and then eliminating any plausible candidates by some further complication of the example. I shall simply assume that any plausible points such evils might serve can be dealt with by suitable qualifications. If this is false, there is *less* to the critic's claim than if it is true.
24 A Rowean will grant that if we have reason to think that God exists, this claim is false. She also is likely to deny that there is any such reason.
25 Or something much like it; nothing hangs here on its being exactly 1–3 and 4–6 that capture a Rowean's position, so long as something similar does so.
26 A Rowean will grant that if we have reason to think that God exists, this claim is false. She also is likely to deny that there is any such reason.
27 See previous note.
28 Unless, of course, its having a point, or not, is itself a matter of how it relates to our cognitive states.
29 Strictly, this is not accurate. Suppose that *having fortitude* is a good, that one can have this virtue only if one has borne pain well, and hence that it is logically impossible that one have the virtue without there having been pains, and that pains are evils. Still, it is not necessary that there have been the particular pains that there were; other pains presumably would have done as well. So the obtaining of the actually endured pains was not, strictly speaking, logically necessary for fortitude to obtain. They were merely some among various possible pains that would so serve; in such circumstances we might say that the actual pains were *disjunctively necessary* for fortitude – it was necessary that they, *or something similar* (i.e., other pains) obtain. Similar considerations apply generally to cases of evils being necessary for goods. It does matter here whether the existence of fortitude in John does provide sufficient point for there being pains which John bears; the point here is simply to be clear about the sense in which it can be true that *Evil E's obtaining is a logically necessary condition of good G obtaining*. A relevant complication is this: might John's bearing pains have a point if they *provide the opportunity* for John to develop fortitude, even if he does not do so? Might a relevant point-giving good be simply *John's having the opportunity to develop fortitude*, whether he does so or not? Obviously, a similar question will arise in the case of other evils and goods.
30 One might propose here something like *(P*) If there is an omnicompetent God then it is immensely probable – or at least more probable than .5 – that there will be no pointless evils*. But why anyone should think (P*) true without thinking (P) true is unclear, and in any case if (P*) is true, it is necessarily true, and if (P) is not a necessary truth the prospects for (P*) being a necessary truth look bleak.
31 Due to Peter Van Inwagen, *An Essay on Free Will* (Oxford: Clarendon Press, 1983).
32 The suggestion here follows an interesting discussion by Peter Van Inwagen.
33 Surviving no doubt would require restrictions on randomness in the sense that there would need to be events that were not *randomness cases*; one could also stipulate that in a chancey world it was random which events were random – i.e., second-order randomness was present as well as first-order.
34 See note 29.
35 If one insists that anything having to do with personal maturity – flourishing as a person – is part of morality, I have no objections; I will then make my point using some such terminology as *morality of common grace* and *morality of special grace*.
36 Or have good reason to believe, or the like.

37 Or, again, we have good reason to believe that there are, or it is likely that there are, or it is unreasonable not to grant that there are, or the like.
38 Or have good reason to believe, or the like.
39 See previous note.
40 For example, I take the following to be a necessary truth: *For any ennumerative class K of things, if K has any purely intrinsic worth, its members distributively have intrinsic worth* (I mean by an ennumerative class one that is defined by its extension). Further, I take natural species to be ennurmerative classes.
41 It is hard to see why the *amount* of animal suffering makes any *evidential* difference. Psychologically, perhaps, some might find it easier to believe that God has a good reason for allowing (say) one-hundredth of the animal suffering God has allowed, but not for allowing the actual amount. But that is *purely* psychological; a sentiment, perhaps, but not a reason. The same holds concerning the number of disappearing species. Presumably if it is wrong of God to allow species to disappear, then it is worse of God to allow many to disappear than to allow a few to disappear. The basic questions remain *whether* the disappearance of a species is an inherently bad thing, and if so whether God could have a morally sufficient reason for allowing this sort of inherently bad thing.
42 Simplicity here can be a matter of kinds of things, number of things, kinds of laws, number of laws, combinations of the above, etc.; none of these ways of understanding *simplicity* will make (N) true.
43 God of course, on this account, loses *purely* intrinsic value if God creates – but this is no real loss – God has just as much intrinsic value as before, and in addition comes to have extrinsic value.
44 *Moral* value is another matter.
45 Much of it, of course, occurred prior to there being any human beings. The view that we should exercise considerably more ecological caution in the future than we have in the past does not presuppose or entail that the disappearance of a great many species provides evidence against the existence of God.
46 The (presumably uncontroversial) assumption being that an omnicompetent God could have prevented the relevant species from becoming extinct.
47 Again allowing for such replacements for "There is no" as "We can think of no" or "To the best of our knowledge, and after careful reflection, we can discern no," and the like.
48 At this point, the question again arises as to whether the notion of *as much natural value as it is possible that there be* is not like *the highest possible integer*, so that any objection based on appeal to it is self-refuting.
49 In the sense intended, *having natural worth* entails *having intrinsic worth*.
50 There will, of course, come a point where someone claims that there is intrinsic unexchangeable irreplaceable worth to there being spotted owls or snail darters and that any God who lets it be true that there no longer are any such things deserves to live in Sing Sing Prison for ever. It is possible to postpone that point for some time, do a lot of interesting philosophical (and presumably theological) work before one gets there. Further, it will be extremely hard if not impossible to show that, say, spotted owls have *unexchangeable* natural worth.
51 Earlier Judaism was in fact highly reserved regarding any notion of afterlife for human persons. Allowing a human person to cease to exist did not seem to them to be something God could not quite properly do. This, of course, does not entail that they thought that God could properly, say, obliterate Abraham when he reached the age of forty and "replace" him with a biologically-forty-year-old Abraham*.
52 Critics tend here to leap to "the hard cases" – to, say, a human whose intellectual

capacities are profoundly limited, less than those typically ascribed to a mature chimpanzee. But the hard cases are emotionally hard (it is psychologically very difficult to think of, let alone experience, biologically human creatures with such limitations) and morally hard (what do we owe such humans, besides not causing them suffering) and intellectually hard (because it is both difficult to think clearly about such matters and controversial about what we actually know regarding such cases – how accurate are our judgments regarding their capacities – and about what future medicine may enable us to do for them). But the critic presumably, in the sort of push-come-to-shove scenarios that are of some help in clarifying thought about such matters, will agree that there is an important difference between the case in which (i) one can save the life of only one of two biological humans – one "normal" child and one of capacities of the sort described earlier, and (ii) one can save the life of only one of two "normal" children. The question as to what to do is much harder in (ii) than in (i). It is hard to explain that fact anything like adequately without accepting something very like the view that persons (defined in terms of their intellectual, moral, and religious capacities) have baseline intrinsic worth. "Person" is not a biologically definable term. It is not at all clear to me that anything short of a person has BIW, or that the critic can both deny this and adequately justify the claim that things that are not persons possess intrinsic natural worth. But going into all of this would require a book on moral philosophy.

53 Claims about BIW starting at the level of persons (and stopping there as well since there can be non-human as well as human persons) will be called "speciesist" and get one booed in various contemporary circles. Nonetheless, name-calling aside, the perspective that so limits BIW seems eminently defensible.

54 Alan Donagan's *The Theory of Morality* (Chicago: University of Chicago Press, 1977) and his *Choice: The Essential Element in Action* (London: Routledge and Kegan Paul, 1987) are very good here.

55 Obviously there are other versions of (b)-strategies, each requiring attention on its own. Even a book-length treatment of some of them would leave out others.

56 Reasonable, of course, in this sense: if it is reasonable to accept P, then it is not also reasonable to accept not-P or to suspend judgment regarding P.

57 With the usual allowance for variant versions concerning probability, reasonability of concluding that, and so on.

10 Arguments for monotheism

1 Proposition P *entails* proposition Q if and only if *P, but not Q* is a contradiction. (e.g., *There are two whales in the bay* entails *There is at least one whale in the bay*, since to assert the former and deny the latter is to contradict yourself). Another way of putting this is: P *entails* Q if and only if *P, therefore Q* is a necessary truth.

2 George Mavrodes, *Belief in God: A Study in the Epistemology of Religion* (New York: Random House, 1970), chapter 2.

3 These examples are due to ibid.

4 For those not aware of the history of the basketball franchise the Boston Celtics, Bill Russell was the center for the Celtics teams that won eleven of thirteen championships, and the greatest defensive center (arguably, the greatest player) ever to play the game.

5 Defending this understanding goes beyond the scope of this book. For a beginning, see Arthur Pap, *Semantics and Necessary Truth* (New Haven: Yale University Press, 1959),

chapter 7, "The linguistic theory of the apriori," and Alvin Plantinga, *The Nature of Necessity* (Oxford: Clarendon Press, 1974).

6 For an accessible review of different relevant views, see Michael Loux, *Metaphysics* (London: Routledge, 1998).

7 If you want another counterexample and are willing to have it more complicated than our other examples, here are two: *For any formal system S, if S is adequate for number theory (e.g., if its axioms are strong enough to entail Peano's postulates) there will be some formula F that is both expressible in S and undecidable in S* and its corollary *For any formal system S, if S is adequate for number theory, there can be no proof within S of the claim S is consistent*. These are hardly uninformative or mathematically trivial.

8 Due to Alvin Plantinga; see *The Nature of Necessity*, op. cit., and *God, Freedom, and Evil* (New York: Random House, 1974). The former contains the full-dress, and the latter a streamlined, version of the argument.

9 Note that, on the principle *For all x, if x is actual then x is possible* that the actual world is (also) a possible world.

10 Note that to be *true in all possible worlds* and to be *included in every maximal proposition* are the same.

11 In am using "empirical" here very broadly.

12 This strategy may also seem attractive if one wishes to hedge one's bet regarding the interpretation of Scripture on how God and the universe are related.

13 Medieval theories of relations is an interesting topic all by itself – one that would take us far afield from our current concerns. Mark Henninger, *Relations: Medieval Theories, 1250–1325* (Oxford: Clarendon Press, 1989) provides an excellent introduction.

14 Some member of the domain must also stand in this relationship only backwardly – must depend on something else but nothing else depends on it.

15 At *De Caelo XII 258* Aquinas offers a series of claims relevant to his Five Ways. It seems worth including them here. Again, we begin with definitions:

Definition A: X has *non-derivative necessary existence* if and only if *X does not exist* is self-contradictory.

Definition B: X has *derivative necessary existence* if and only if *X cannot naturally (without the action of an omnipotent being) cease to exist.*

Definition C: *X cannot naturally cease to exist* if and only if *X contains no matter or the matter that X contains cannot have any essence other than the one that it has.*

Definition D: *X has the power of not existing* if and only if *X is such that X exists only if X has the essence it has but it is possible that the stuff that X is made of come to have some other essence.*

Definition E: *X generates from Y at T* if and only if *There is a Y that exists at T-1 and X at T contains the matter that was in Y at T.*

Definition F: *X corrupts at T* if and only if *There is a Y such that Y exists at T + 1* and the matter that was in X at T is in Y at T + 1.

Definition G: *X is a natural body* only if *X is capable of generation and corruption.*

Aquinas tells us:

1 If X always exists, then X has the power always to exist.
2 If X has the power always to exist, then X lacks the power not to always exist.
3 If X always exists then X lacks the power not to always exist. (from 1 and 2)

4 If X lacks the power not to always exist then X does not generate or corrupt.
5 If X generates or corrupts then X does not lack the power not always to exist.
6 If X has the power not always to exist then X does not always exist.
7 If X generates or corrupts then X does not always exist.

Also involved seems the idea that, in some sense, *Necessarily, in any infinite time all possibilities are realized*, though it is difficult to think of any reading of this claim on which it is true.

16 More fully: for X to change or move is for X to go from potentiality to actuality or from actuality to potentiality regarding quantity, quality, or place.

17 The existence of something with causal powers – the actual capacity to bring about changes in other things – that was not itself changed in so doing – might, by itself, have slight religious relevance, but of course Aquinas has no intention of limiting himself to this one conclusion.

18 And animal mind, if such there be – we need not enter into that matter here.

19 The notion of infinity is of course complex. A nice introduction to various relevant notions is A. W. Moore, *The Infinite* (London: Routledge, 1991).

20 At *Summa* Ia 46 2–7.

21 The strategy here is called Conditional Proof. You assume that P, show that P plus a set of truths entails Q, and conclude *If P then Q*.

22 Let *P = possibly,P; Cx = x corrupts. Then another way of stating the criticism is this: Aquinas shifts quantifiers illegitimately, going from: *A* = (x)*Cx to *B* = *(x)Cx.

23 Let Ex/t = x exists at t; (Et) = there is a t. Then the criticism is that Aquinas illegitimately goes from: *D* = (x)(Et) not-Ex/t to *E* = (Et)(x) not-Ex/t.

24 The Fourth Way is a variety of the moral argument for God's existence, and we will look at it briefly when we consider religion and morality.

25 It does not follow that *being morally perfect* is, like *being omnipotent and omniscient*, an essential property of God. One might (Noel Hendrickson did) suggest that only *always wanting very badly to exist* would be just as good for these purposes as *being morally perfect*. This is a property a morally imperfect being might well have. I leave working out the answer to this objection as an exercise for the reader.

26 Here, "God" is being used as a name, not a definite description.

27 *ST* Ia 15 2 suggests the possibility of the reading that we do not give here.

28 Aquinas is criticized for making an inference from *A* to *B* below:

A. Every generable thing is such that an intelligent agent directs it to seek its own flourishing.
B. There is an end that all generable beings together are directed to seek.

On the present reading, no such inference is required.

29 *Sacred Books*, Vol. 48, pp. 170–1.

30 Ibid., 165 – cf. p. 171 that notes that intelligent agents whom we observe to cause things also have emotions – "are connected with pleasure and the like."

31 Ramanuja thinks of the world as God's body, but a body that depends on God for its existence, in contrast to human bodies in relation to human minds.

32 Ibid., p. 173.

33 Ibid.

34 After an introductory first section, sections 2 through 8 of the *Dialogues* deal with a dialogue concerning the argument from design. Section 9 deals with an argument that is a mix of the ontological and cosmological arguments, sections 10 and 11 with the

problem of evil, and section 12 with natural religion. The present author has discussed all of these issues in Hume's philosophy in *Hume's "Inexplicable Mystery": His Views on Religion* (Philadelphia: Temple University Press, 1988).

35 Two points: there is also a version of the argument that has as a premise the orderliness of the physical world as a whole, rather than the orderliness of particular sorts of natural objects; the fact that we can change the sort of order we find in nature by selective breeding in no way discounts the fact that we did not bring about the order that makes such breeding possible. Both varieties of the argument are discussed further in *Hume's "Inexplicable Mystery."*

11 Monotheism and religious experience

1 Using "a holy, powerful being" as a brief description of the content of monotheistic religious experiences.

2 For other examples, see Sir Alister Hardy, *The Spiritual Nature of Man* (Oxford: Clarendon Press, 1979).

3 And, of course, claims logically entailed by those claims.

4 A fact that is curiously ignored by those who have discussed the similar principle.

5 To describe something completely is to state every truth about that thing. There is nothing whatever such that any human person can completely describe it. Other than the unsurprising fact that we are not omniscient, it is hard to see that anything of particular philosophical interest follows from this.

6 See Caroline Franks Davis, *The Evidential Force of Religious Experience* (Oxford: Clarendon Press, 1989). A strength of this book is its excellent discussion of social science explanations of religious belief. An unnecessary weakness is its assumption that all religious experiences are the same, or of the same sort.

7 For what it is worth, conceptual, moral, and aesthetic experiences are more like religious experiences in these respects than like sensory experiences.

8 Here is one version of an evidential argument from religious experience:

1 Experiences occur which are a matter of their subjects at least seeming to experience God.
2 If experiences of this sort are not canceled or counterbalanced or compromised or contradicted or confuted or logically consumed or empirically consumed, then their occurrence is evidence that God exists.
3 Experiences of this sort are not canceled or counterbalanced or compromised or contradicted or confuted or logically consumed or empirically consumed.

Hence:

4 These experiences are evidence that God exists. (from 1–3)

It continues:

5 If these experiences occur in various cultures, and at various times, to people of various backgrounds and socio-economic status, their evidential force is increased.
6 These experiences occur in various cultures, and at various times, to people of various backgrounds and socio-economic status.

Hence:

7 Their evidential force is increased.

While the claims that appear in the premises of this argument are interesting, controversial, and – in the present author's view – entirely defensible, discussing them in detail would take us far afield – into discussions, for example, of the similarity or otherwise of at least apparent experiences of God as these occur in different times and places and religious traditions.

9 A final issue should be mentioned. If one sees a cup on the table and not unreasonably comes to believe that *There is a cup on the table*, in all strictness one believes more than one's current experience tells. The cup one believes is on the table, if it exists at all, is an enduring thing; one's current experience is momentary. It is not a matter of pure report of sensory experiences if one looks again and has an experience with the same sensory phenomenology that one says that the same cup is still there; it is logically possible that the old cup has passed away and been replaced by a new one. Cups have other sides, and one sees only this side; perhaps one sees only a cup façade. The point is not to provide a basis for skepticism about cups, but simply to note that even a very modest claim about an ordinary object strictly goes beyond the experiential information one currently possesses.

Underdetermination looms larger in scientific theory where there will always be more than one possible way of explaining what is observed, so that claims that various sorts of theoretical entities exist are underdetermined by the data on the basis of which such claims are made. Even religious experiences of a phenomenologically thick sort – Isaiah in the temple in the presence of an awesome holy being in whose presence he senses his own sinfulness and need for forgiveness, for example – underdetermine the claims, for example, that God is omnipotent and omniscient. In religion and theology, as in everyday sensory experience and scientific theory, conceptual experiences join with sensory or religious experiences in more fully determining the concepts used to describe the objects of experience. How this goes in any given case is likely to be complex and fascinating. The next step would be to ask what reasons monotheism can supply for claiming that God is omnipotent and omniscient. But that is another story.

12 Arguments concerning nonmonotheistic conceptions (1)

1 See, for example, the selections from Ramanuja in Sarvapalli Radhakrishnan and Charles Moore (eds), *A Sourcebook in Indian Philosophy* (Princeton, NJ: Princeton University Press, 1957) or George Thibaut, *The Vedanta Sutras* (Oxford: Clarendon Press, 1890–1904), vols 34, 38, 48 of the *Sacred Books of the East*. These volumes contain the aphorisms of Badarayana with the commentaries.

2 That is, no more than one of the alternatives can be true, and (as we shall see) there are other relevant views besides these three.

3 A bit more fully: I take dualism to hold that X is a person if and only if X is a self-conscious being, where X is a self-conscious being if and only if X is sometimes self-conscious and X when not self-conscious nonetheless has the capacity to become so. Further, X continues to be a person only if X is a person and X shall be self-conscious in the future. Dualism, then, holds that *being self-conscious* is not a physical property, that persons are self-conscious mental substances whose essence is (or includes) *having self-consciousness*, and that no mental substance is a physical substance or an abstract object.

4 Philosophers often talk as if the notion of a mental property is obscure and the notion of a physical property is lucid. But when one comes to actual definitions of "physical property" the supposed clarity of the idea becomes shy and hides. Some philosophers talk as if the notion of being self-conscious were itself somehow deeply obscure. There are views (and so much the worse for them) on which it is hard to see how anything could be or become self-conscious, but *being self-conscious* is a clearer notion than is *being physical*.

5 For example, C. J. Du Casse, Alan Donagan, Alvin Plantinga, Howard Robinson, John Foster, Frank Jackson, etc.

6 Whether *X and Y are fully qualitatively identical* entails *X and Y are numerically identical* is a matter of controversy that we need not enter.

7 If the relationship between qualitative so-called identity and numerical identity are not clear, one might consider some relevant necessary truths.

It is helpful, in understanding qualitative "identity" and numerical identity to see how these concepts are related; a bit of reflection should be sufficient to see that each of the following claims is true (indeed, not possibly false, and so necessarily true).

N1 *X is nearly fully identical to Y* does not entail *X is numerically identical to Y*. (Identical twins are possible.)

N2 *X at t is numerically identical to Y at t1* does not entail *X at t is fully qualitatively identical to Y at T1*. (It is logically impossible that anything at one time can be fully qualitatively identical to anything at another time; the definition of full qualitative identity, including as it does spatial and temporal properties, rules that out.)

N3 *X at t is numerically identical to Y at t1* does not entail *X at t is nearly fully qualitatively identical to Y at T1*. (A thing can remain the same thing and yet undergo non-essential change.)

N4 *X at t is fully qualitatively identical to Y at T1* entails *X at t is numerically identical to Y at t1* and entails *X at t is not numerically identical to Y at t1*. (The claim that things that exist at different times are fully qualitatively identical is self-contradictory; see comment after N2.)

N5 *X at t is nearly fully qualitatively identical to Y at T1* does not entail *X at t is numerically identical to Y at t1*. (Something at one time can be very, very similar to something at another time without being identical to it.)

N6 *For all X, X at T is fully qualitatively identical (and hence nearly fully qualitatively identical) to X at T*. (Anything at a time T is qualitatively identical to itself at T.)

N7 *For all X, if X at T is numerically identical to Y at T then X at T is fully qualitatively identical to (and hence nearly fully qualitatively identical to Y at T)*. (See comment after N6.)

8 Where *X is the closest thing to Y* does not entail *X is Y*.

9 That is, each substance in the series exists for two moments, etc.

10 Other possibilities are sometimes proposed – e.g., Bertrand Russell's neutral monism on which mental and physical properties are somehow reducible to other properties that are neither mental nor physical. I doubt that this particular view is defensible. Nonetheless, the discussion deals with the views most relevant to Jainism and Theravada Buddhism, and does not pretend to be a comprehensive discussion of all logically possible accounts of minds and bodies.

11 Indeed, one can intelligently argue about which of these alternatives *is* the Theravada view. Our arguments will be concerned with the *structure* of the view, and not depend on which of these alternative accounts of what makes up that structure is the right reading of the Theravada account.

12 That is, a person(1) can be composed of a set A of states and a set B of states such that were A to exist without B, A would be a person, and were B to exist without A, B would be a person.

13 "Critique," of course, need not mean "refutation, or attempt to refute;" it does mean that here.

14 Whatever relation R allegedly must hold between composite nonendurers in order for them to belong to a single succession such that their being so related gives rise to commonsense descriptions such as "stages of the life of a single person" – resemblance, causality, resemblance-and-causality, or whatever – is such that for any composite nonendurer C at T, both composite nonendurer C* at time T1 and composite nonendurer C** at T1 may bear R to C. Hence both are identical to C if either is. Being distinct themselves, C* and C** cannot both be identical to C. But then neither is identical to C. Thus there being C* and C** at T1 prevents the succession of bundles to which C belongs from continuing, whereas (on a Buddhist-type account) that succession would have continued had only C*, or only C**, borne R to C.

15 Read it as saying that *Whether persons are substances or collections, the substance or collection that is identical to me exists now*; neither a Jain-type nor a Buddhist-type account of persons is built into the first premise.

16 Cloning a person does not destroy her; it simply gives her a twin. *I have a clone at T* does not entail *I do not exist at T*; hence premise 6 is true. This remains the case even if we replace the notion of a clone by the notion of a *clone** so that a clone* is either another person cloned from me or something created *ex nihilo* that is an exact copy of what a clone of me would be (and also bears R to me).

17 Justice, if you prefer.

18 Save, perhaps, for the unorthodox, extremely minority-status Buddhist Personalists.

19 I assume for convenience that the act was itself momentary; otherwise there will also be a problem about the identity of the original agent of the action.

20 See previous note.

21 I take it to be evident that logically necessary truths are internal to all positions, including those that deny them. What is true in all possible worlds is also true in all possible positions; some positions deny this, and in so doing deny what renders them possibly true positions; so they are necessarily false positions.

22 For example, is there within Buddhist metaphysical resources any relation R such that one person(1) bearing R to another person(1) will tie them together into a person(2) in any sense in which a person(2) actually would be a person? Memory relations obviously won't do – *Person(1)X did A and person(1)Y remembers having done A assumes Person(1)X and person(1)Y belong to a single person(2)* and so cannot be used to explain what being a single person(2) amounts to. Resemblance seems irrelevant. Causality is a common candidate, but of exactly what sort (lots of causal relations won't do)? I doubt that any such analysis is even plausible, but that is another matter.

23 It may be helpful here to notice a possible difference between composite nonendurers and composite endurers. All of the elements of a composite nonendurer exist simultaneously. Thus it may be possible for them to be so related that while singly none of them is an organism, together they comprise an organism, albeit a very brief one. The elements of a composite endurer do not exist simultaneously. By the time one element arrives, its preceding elements are all gone. So the elements of a composite endurer

cannot be so related as to comprise an organism. A composite endurer is simply and only a succession of composite nonendurers. If each such nonendurer in a succession is an organism, then it is a succession of organisms.

24 Remember that *E1* and *E2* are composite nonendurers that exist at different times.

25 The temptation is to think that because the elements of a composite nonendurer can be an organism (something somehow more than just its parts), so can composite endurers be organisms. But even if the former is true, the latter is not; a succession of organisms is a succession of organisms, and is not itself an organism. To think otherwise is to embrace confusion.

26 Strictly, of course, if *P* entails *Q* and *Q* is logically inconsistent or self-contradictory, then *P* is also logically inconsistent or self-contradictory – i.e., necessarily false. Hence not only is the complexity view not true; it is not even logically possible that it be true.

27 I think that there are only two logically possible accounts of the metaphysical structure (so to say) of persons. This is argued briefly in "A Defense of Dualism," *Faith and Philosophy*, Vol. 12, No. 4, October 1995, pp. 548–66, in an issue that includes all of the main papers read at the 1994 Notre Dame Conference on the Philosophy of Mind.

28 For example, the Jain view, fleshed out, includes the implausible claims that *Every person is inherently omniscient, though exercise of this capacity is frustrated by our being embodied* and *It is impossible that anything cause a person to cease to exist, though a person can be caused not to be embodied in the body she presently occupies (or in any body at all)*. That our existence involves latent omniscience and necessary ontological independence are claims quite independent of anything discussed here, and I should not like to have to defend them.

29 That is, if Sam at T is identical to Sam at T1, then necessarily, Sam at T is identical to Sam at T1 – which is to be distinguished from *Sam at T enjoys logically necessary existence, as does Sam at T1*.

30 James W. Cornman and Keith Lehrer, *Philosophical Problems and Arguments: An Introduction* (New York: Macmillan, 1974), pp. 238–9.

31 Materialists who are property dualists are often willing to grant that physical things come in at least two kinds – those capable of self-consciousness and those not (or at least those capable of consciousness and those not – though if the *not capable of consciousness/capable of consciousness* distinction is kind-defining or essential, it is hard to see why the same should not be said regarding the *not capable of self-consciousness/capable of self-consciousness* distinction).

32 Some philosophers have embraced the view that there are abstract objects (immaterial substances not capable of consciousness) as well as material substances. But they have continued to reject the idea that there are any mental substances.

33 This is, of course, perfectly compatible with determinism being false.

13 Arguments concerning nonmonotheistic conceptions (2)

1 In fact, the terminology used to refer to the relevant experiences is not as neat as these characterizations suggest. For example, Jainism not infrequently used "nirvana" to refer to *kevala* experiences.

2 One might add something along the lines of *S has seen both that he had E and that it is logically impossible that he have E and P be false*. Nothing argued here will depend on whether we add this last consideration or not, so long as it is not the case that Chandra has E but believes P, not on the basis of his having had E, but on some other basis. Even if E is self-authenticating regarding a proposition P, and person S has E, E does not

self-authenticate P to S if the only reason that S accepts P is not that S had E and E fits a description such that if E occurs then this is (conclusive) evidence for P. For example, if S would otherwise not accept P unless his great-grandfather had asserted P, and would have accepted P on that basis even without having had E, then even if E is conclusive evidence for P, S does not accept P on that basis and so E is not for S self-authenticating regarding P.

3 One might put self-authentication along these lines: E is self-authenticating to Chandra regarding P if and only if (i) Chandra cannot be mistaken about a belief B that Chandra evidentially rests on his experience E, (ii) B cannot be false if Chandra has E, (iii) it is logically impossible that Chandra be wrong about whether Chandra has E, and (iv) Chandra believes that he had E. Again, nothing we say here would be changed if we characterized self-authentication along these lines.

4 These are only one way of putting these views, and do not exhaust the views central to these traditions. But they are accurate and representative, fully fair for illustrative purposes here.

5 Even if some claim is knowable only by someone who has an enlightenment experience it does not follow that it is true only if someone has an enlightenment experience. In fact, the relevant notion of enlightenment experience requires that such experiences essentially involve discovering what has been true all along.

6 Not at any rate so long as they think the doctrines they favor to be logically contingent truths.

7 I assume that we both have sufficient evidence that we are seeing a coin of some sort.

8 With the addition, of course, of claims about consciousness and memory.

9 I think that they are also *reasonably* accepted, save by Advaita Vedantins who claim that all of what could be said on their behalf is "sublated" and so trumped by enlightenment experience.

10 We will not worry here about second-order conscious states – e.g., one's being aware that one at least seems to perceive a tree or is having a headache similar to the one she had yesterday.

11 If there are genuine moral experiences – awarenesses of obligations, for example – they are recognitions of the truth about what one ought to do, whether one is so inclined or not. If there are genuine aesthetic experiences – awareness of beauty, for example – they are recognitions of what is beautiful, whether one thought so or not. They are neither introspective nor sensory. Nor are they relevant to our concerns here.

12 One cannot show that some list of principles of experiential evidence is a complete list, so even showing that, say, forty-seven principles are such that, if any one of them is the right one, enlightenment experience is not evidence for religious belief, would leave open the worry that there was one more principle which was the right one and on it enlightenment experience was evidence. Of course the worry might be small.

13 Philosophers who agree with the rest of what is said here may think that putting the matter in terms of evidence is not quite correct; it won't matter for our purposes whether speaking of evidence is exactly right here. For example, those who think we cannot be wrong about such states will want to talk about something stronger than evidence, which will not affect our basic point.

14 Another answer is that claims that a multiplicity of persons and physical objects exist are somehow self-contradictory, all relational claims are self-contradictory, the notion of a substance (physical or mental) is self-contradictory, or the like. But there seem to be no very good arguments for such accusations.

15 The question arises as to whether *states* is the right word – don't states have to be *states of something*? But similar questions arise about such terms as *qualities (of*

what?), events (aren't events matters of substances coming to gain and/or lose qualities?), processes (don't these occur to something?), and so on.

16 René Descartes, "Meditations on First Philosophy," Meditation II, in E.S.H. Haldane and G.R.T. Ross (eds), *The Philosophical Works of Descartes*, Vol. I (London: Dover Publications, 1931), p. 150. The original edition of Haldane and Ross appeared in 1911 and the first edition of the *Meditations* appeared in 1641.

17 *The Philosophical Works of Descartes*, Vol. II, p. 30. The passage comes at the beginning of the "Reply to the Second Objection."

18 Ibid., Vol. I, p. 150. The passage comes from a section entitled "Argument Demonstrating the Existence of God and the Distinction Between Soul and Body, Drawn Up in Geometrical Fashion," Definition V, at the end of the "Reply to the Second Objection."

19 One sort of dualism will take *being self-conscious* to be the nature of a person; others opt for *being capable of self-consciousness, and sometimes being so.*

20 *Tattvarthadhigama Sutra*, chapter V, sections 29, 30, 31, 38, 41, 42; *Sourcebook*, p. 256.

21 Ibid., chapter II, sections 7, 8, 29; *Sourcebook*, p. 254.

22 Chapter II, section 10.

23 *Samayasdra*, 325.

24 *Atmanusasna*, 174.

25 *Sourcebook*, p. 547.

26 G. Thibaut, trans., *The Vedanta Sutras with the Commentary by Ramanuja* (Delhi: Motilal Barnasidass Reprint, 1962; originally published by Oxford University Press, 1904), pp. 48, 55, 56.

27 Ibid., p. 56.

28 Ramanuja also takes self-awareness to occur in sensory experience – a view that Jainism and (with qualifications) Descartes share.

29 Thibaut, I, i, 1; *Sourcebook*, p. 547.

30 Ibid., p. 58.

31 Ibid., p. 43.

32 David Hume, *A Treatise of Human Nature*, Book One, Part IV, Section VI, "Of Personal Identity," p. 252.

33 *Anguttara-nikaya*, iii, 134; *Sourcebook*, pp. 273, 274; the text is Theravadin.

34 *Visuddhi-magga* xviii; *Sourcebook*, pp. 284–5; the text is Theravadin.

35 *Sangutta-nikaya* iii, 66; *Sourcebook*, p. 280.

36 Substantivalists nonetheless have two advantages in the dispute. Hume admits that we believe that there are enduring substances and has to offer a painfully distended account of our having that belief. There is reason to take the substantivalist report form as the natural one – the one we in fact use in describing such experience. Further, even if it were to be proved that the non-substantivalist report form should be used, this – because of Locke's point – would not establish, or even provide any evidence for, the non-substantivalist point. So if there is a way around the objections offered here to appeals to introspective (etc.) experience, the advantage lies with the substantivalists. Still, the weight falls on the results of asking which view can explain memory, responsibility, self-consciousness, and the like. Appeal to enlightenment and meditative experience is made by both sides, as we have noted.

14 Religion and morality

1 Or *the* moral principle if there is but one.

2 An Anselmian theist could do this too, but it is hard to see what the motivation would be.
3 Other than God.
4 Strictly, one needs to add here "without morally sufficient reason." It is left to the reader to consider the relevance to the argument of adding this needed qualification.
5 Except, if you like, that God exists and has the nature that God has.
6 Indeed, any two necessary truths mutually entail one another. Further, since each truth about Tess's thoughts, by hypothesis, follows from a necessary truth, it is necessarily true, and so entails every truth about every thought that God has. So construed, God's existence, nature, and thought seem as much determined by Tess's as the reverse.
7 One need not put logical fatalism in somewhat monotheistic dress; it is the doctrine that all truths are necessary and all falsehoods contradictions, and *God exists*, for all logical fatalism cares, can be among the latter.
8 This is *metaphysical* libertarianism, to be distinguished from political views that use the same term.
9 For the argument's origin, see Peter Van Inwagen, *An Essay on Free Will* (Oxford: Clarendon Press, 1983).
10 Strictly, of course, sentences like "The past entails the future" are shorthand for sentences like "True propositions about the past entail the true propositions about the future."
11 That Sue is obligated to do A and *Sue does A* entails *Sue causes B* do not entail *Sue is obligated to cause B*. Like everything in philosophy, this example – and any other – will be challenged by someone. If one accepts at least some versions of so-called deontic logic, the entailments will hold. If they did hold, then this wouldn't be what the critic of the Control Principle says it is – an incorrect principle that is analogous to the Control Principle.
12 That state of affairs A obtains entails that state of affairs B obtains if and only if the proposition *A obtains* entails the proposition *B obtains*.
13 In fact, incompatibilists often hold that were determinism true, no one would, strictly speaking, *act* at all, since *Necessarily, if A is an action by Karen, then Karen is free relative to performing A*.
14 There are problems with this sort of claim, to be noted later.
15 Strictly, given a set of propositions for which the laws are truth conditions.
16 Or at least to approximate this goal – sufficient ingenuity can fit a lot into this scope, and we may have left something interesting out. Fortunately, if the account is not quite as inclusive as it might be, it remains true that the account includes many important elements, and the inclusion of some other element of the same sort will not make any difference to our conclusion.
17 For convenience, let "choosing to do A" be a success term – that Jane can choose to lie only if, given that she so chooses, she lies.
18 Compatibilists sometimes suggest that actions out of character are unfree, though this would make most heroic action unfree. There are other possible fine-tunings, but by now the general compatibilist strategy should be clear.
19 Strictly, (HP*) reiterates what (CFa) and (CFb) stated earlier, putting the point in another way.
20 Of course further refinements are possible; for example, perhaps in the last sentence one should thing of "A" as replaceable only by terms describing *basic* actions (roughly, actions performable without performing other actions in order to perform them). But this formulation seems sufficient for present purposes.

21 Assumptions made "for the sake of the argument" can be replaced by other assumptions (e.g., that persons are fully immaterial, or fully material; that causes are simultaneous with, or are both precedent to and simultaneous with, their effects) without affecting the force of the argument; the argument's success as a proof does not require their being true as opposed to some alternative. Thus the premises so assumed could be avoided by using complex disjunctive premises; the cumbersomeness of that procedure motivates the use of "for the sake of the argument" assumptions.

22 Again, there are behavior-relevant states besides intentions, but here let "intentions" represent the entire range of states that are behavior-representing and behavior-relevant. I will not worry here about sorting out "intention-as-representational" and "intentional-as-end-seeking" as this is not crucial to the argument.

23 By "entire set of causes" is meant "the set of phenomena that, given background condition, is sufficient to yield the effect in question," leaving aside the difficult question as to how to mark off background conditions from causes. The argument is compatible with a wide variety of ways of making this distinction.

24 Obviously, there are other scenarios that involve mixed internal-and-external causes; some of these will come up for consideration shortly.

25 A Libertarian can hold the same thing regarding Jon's simply smiling – that this is a basic action that Jon can be categorically free in performing. The slightly more complicated case (decision to smile, then smiling) is helpful in bringing out the details of a deterministic perspective.

26 By determinism's being true, I mean that for any time T at which there is a created universe, determinism is true regarding the universe at that time.

27 Strictly, perhaps God can cause things that God did not intend to cause (for their own sake) but which simply follow from what God does intend to cause for its own sake; God might intentionally cause a yellow cab to exist and thereby cause there to exist tires with a certain size even though God did not care that the cab's tires were that particular size as opposed to various other sizes they might have been. God might decide to produce the tires by some random process that might equally well produce tires of any of hundreds of slightly different sizes. Still, God will not have caused something to exist without knowing it.

28 Arguably, Mary no longer thinks or acts; Ann thinks or acts "in Mary" as well as "in Ann." But we need not get into that here.

29 The temptation to think so arises from noting that if *S* lives in a deterministic world, then what *S* does is both non-probabilistically predictable and unfree, so if what *S* does is free then it is probabilistically predictable. But the reasoning is fallacious. It is exactly parallel to this. Consider a world in which this is a law: *S eats chocolate at time T if and only if S eats peanut butter at time T*. Let this be a *Reese's World (RW)*. If *S* lives in a Reese's World, and *S* eats peanut butter at *T* then *S* eats chocolate at *T*. Suppose that *S* moves from a Reese's World to a non-Reese's World (one where it is not a law that one eats peanut butter at a time if and only if one also eats chocolate at that time). Then *S* can eat chocolate without also eating peanut butter (and conversely). What temptation there was to deny this would go as follows. Let the law whose presence makes a world be a Reese's World be *LCPB*. Let *eating chocolate at T* be *CT* and *eating peanut butter at T* be *PBT*. Then the reasoning would be: since when *LCPB* holds, every *CT* is also a *PBT*, every *CT* is a *PBT* whether *LCPB* holds or not. But of course this is fallacious. Having moved, *S* can now eat her chocolate by itself.

30 This claim should be distinguished from the false claim that *A proposition that says that X will obtain at T can be true even if A does not obtain at T*.

15 Faith and reason

1 Curiously, officially taking this stance regarding religion and morality does not prevent those who do so from treating at least certain of their own moral concerns as proper bases for law or from being sure that, if there is a God, then God will either approve of their lifestyle or at least be decent enough to suspend judgment.

2 "Contingent" here just means "non-necessary." It does not have the meaning of "dependent for existence on," which is another meaning of the word.

3 Philosophers often call such beliefs *incorrigible*; one cannot go wrong in having them.

4 If the ontological argument has a true conclusion, then *God exists* is a necessary truth. So Anselmians will disagree with the claim that no religious beliefs are unbreakable. This will be something to worry about if and when we have a sound and valid ontological argument that extends our knowledge.

5 Exactly what else besides true belief is required for knowledge is highly controversial. Roughly, one party to the contemporary disputes requires only that the beliefs have been formed in the right way (with different accounts of what that is). Their opponents require that the believer be in possession of the right sort of recognized evidence (with different accounts of what that is). It will not be necessary for us to decide that matter here.

6 Indeed, it is logically impossible that delicate knowledge be a variety of unbreakable knowledge. For any person S and proposition P, if P is a necessary truth or it is true that *S believes that P* entails *P is true*, then it is *necessarily* true that P is a necessary truth or that *S believes that P* entails *P is true*. Unbreakable knowledge consists in comprehending belief that necessarily true or belief-entailed truths are true. Kim's holding a delicate belief is a matter of Kim's accepting a proposition that is not a necessary truth and is not such that her accepting it entails its being true. Kim's having delicate knowledge is a matter of her accepting a *true* proposition of the indicated sort. So for any person S and proposition P, it is logically impossible that P be the object of both S's unbreakable and S's delicate belief or knowledge.

7 One reason for this is that *Kim needs salvation* entails *Kim exists* and that proposition is not a necessary truth. That Kim exists is a belief-entailed proposition relative to Kim if Kim believes it, but its truth does not entail that Kim needs salvation.

8 This idea is often thought of as part of Reformed Epistemology. It is an essential plank in that program, but it is also a perfectly detachable plank that was known long before, and independent of, any commitment to Reformed Epistemology.

9 Truth-functional.

10 Consider two scenarios. *One*: a universe U1 exists in which there are a trillion distinct numbered places, one item X that fills exactly one place, and it is not in place 407; if Rita believes that X is in place 500, the fact that X is not in place 407 increases the odds in favor of one's belief – the chances of Rita's belief being true is, not one in a trillion, but one is a trillion-minus-one. *Two*: a universe U2 exists in which there are three places, one item Y that fills exactly one place, and it is not in place 3; if Rita believes that Y is in place 1, the fact that Y is not in place 3 increases the odds that Rita's belief is true – rather than the chances of her belief being true being 1 in 3, it is now 1 in 2. This much is common ground between our disputants. The confirmationist, who likely will begin with *Two*, claims that Y not being in place 3 is *evidence* that Y is in place 1 – and equally evidence that Y is in place 2. The falsificationist denies this. The confirmationist, of course, is also in all consistency committed to holding that X's not being in place 407 is evidence that it is in place 500, although it is also equally evidence that it is in place 1, place 2, and so on for a trillion places minus two (since 407 and 500 are already

mentioned). The falsificationist, who likely will begin with *One*, denies that X's not being in 500 is any evidence whatever for X's being in place 407; she also denies that it is evidence that X is in any of the other places in U1. (Strictly, it is not *X's not being in place 407* or *Y's not being in place 3* that is evidence, but knowledge that these things obtain.) The confirmationist assumes, and the falsificationist denies, that *A increases the probability of P's truth* entails *A is evidence for P's truth*. This is a nice example of what Everett Hall, in his genuinely brilliant but neglected *Philosophical Systems* (Chicago: University of Chicago Press, 1960) calls a *categorial* dispute.

11 One could make the notion of competing theories less restrictive, allowing competition to include cases of only partially overlapping data explained, and in other ways. But doing so is not necessary to the argument here.

12 Reflect on *All our beliefs are culturally determined (and so not valid beyond our culture)* which, if true, is true of all beliefs in all cultures but held in his, and so false. Many seem to believe that *One ought to believe nothing but what science teaches*, but that claim is not something that science teaches, so they are inconsistent in believing it. *Only what passes the Verification Principle of the Logical Positivists is meaningful* did not pass the test of the Verification Principle. It is true that *No view that commits intellectual suicide can be known to be true.*

13 Some would add here that these beliefs regarding the data and the theory and potential theories not involve culpable ignorance; this seems correct.

14 It may be that even if one's evidence is that torture for pleasure is now obligatory, perhaps it would be morally wrong to accept that belief. It may be that one's beliefs are typically not under one's control and that one can bring them under such control only by a rational examination of their grounds. It may be that some beliefs, even when one tends to believe them false, can only be eradicated by engaging in certain practices. An ethic of belief would have to weave these considerations, along with many others, into an overall coherent theory offered with reasons for thinking the theory true. I offer no such thing here.

Bibliography

Alston, William (1967) "Problems of philosophy of religion," *Encyclopedia of Philosophy*, New York: Macmillan, vol. 6.

Alston, William (1991) *Perceiving God*, Ithaca, NY: Cornell University Press.

Bascom, John (1880) *Natural Theology*, New York: G. Putnam's Sons.

Basham, A.L. (1951) *History and Doctrine of the Ajivikas*, London: Luzac Press.

Basham, A.L. (1954) *The Wonder That Was India*, New York: The Macmillan Company.

Bertocci, Peter (1951) *An Introduction to the Philosophy of Religion*, Englewood Cliffs, NJ: Prentice-Hall.

Bowker, John (1973) *The Sense Of God*, Oxford: Oxford University Press.

Bowker, John (1978) *The Religious Imagination and the Sense of God*, Oxford: Clarendon Press.

Braddon-Mitchell, David and Jackson, Frank (eds) (1996) *Philosophy of Mind and Cognition*, Oxford: Blackwell.

Brightman, E.S. (1940) *A Philosophy of Religion*, New York: Prentice-Hall.

Broad, C.D (1953) *Religion, Philosophy, and Psychical Research*, London: Routledge and Kegan Paul .

Burrell, Donald (ed.) (1967) *Cosmological Arguments*, Garden City, NY: Anchor Books.

Burtt, E.A. (1951) *Types of Religious Philosophy*, New York: Harper and Brothers.

Carpenter, Estlin J. (1977) *Theism in Medieval India*, New Delhi: Oriental Books Reprint Corporation.

Carr, Brian and Mahalingham, Indira (1996) *Companion Encyclopedia of Asian Philosophy*, London: Routledge.

Chatterjee, Satischandra and Datta, Dhirendramohan (1950) *An Introduction to Indian Philosophy*, Calcutta: University of Calcutta Press.

Chisholm, Roderick (1976) *Person and Object*, La Salle, IL: Open Court.

Christian, William (1972) *Opposition of Religious Doctrines*, New York: Herder and Herder.

Cohn-Sherbok, Daniel (1996) *Medieval Jewish Philosophy*, Surrey: Curzon.

Collins, James (1967) *The Emergence of the Philosophy of Religion*, New Haven: Yale University Press.

Cornman, James W. and Lehrer, Keith (1974) *Philosophical Problems and Arguments: An Introduction*, New York: Macmillan.

Davidson, Herbert (1987) *Proofs for Eternity, Creation, and the Existence of God in Medieval Islamic and Jewish Philosophy*, Oxford: Oxford University Press.

Davidson, Herbert (1992) *Alfarabi Avicenna and Averroes on Intellect*, Oxford: Oxford University Press.

D'Costa, Gavin (1980) *Theology and Religious Pluralism*, Oxford: Basil Blackwell.

Donagan, Alan (1977) *Theory of Morality*, Chicago: University of Chicago Press.

Donagan, Alan (1987) *Choice: The Essential Element in Human Action*, London: Routledge and Kegan Paul.

Flew, Anthony (1966) *God and Philosophy*, London: Hutchinson.

Frank, Daniel H. and Leaman, Oliver (1997) *History of Jewish Philosophy*, London: Routledge.

Franks Davis, Caroline (1989) *The Evidential Force of Religious Experience*, Oxford: Clarendon Press.

Frankfurt, H.G (1988) *The Importance of What We Care About*, Cambridge: Cambridge University Press.

Griffiths, Paul (1983) "Notes toward a critique of Buddhist Karmic theory," *Religious Studies*, Vol. 18, No. 3, pp. 277–91.

Grittiths, Paul J. (1991) *An Apology for Apologetics*, Maryknoll, NY: Orbis Books.

Haldane, E.S.H. and Ross, G.R.T. (eds) *The Philosophical Works of Descartes*, London: Dover Publications.

Haldane, J.J. and Smart, J.J.C. (1996) *Theism and Atheism*, Oxford: Blackwell.

Hall, Everett (1958) *Philosophical Systems*, Chicago: University of Chicago Press.

Hall, Everett (1960) *Philosophical Systems: A Categorial Analysis*, Chicago: University of Chicago Press.

Hardy, Alister (1979) *The Spiritual Nature of Man: A Study of Contemporary Religious Experience*, Oxford: Clarendon Press.

Henninger, Mark (1989) *Relations: Medieval Theories, 1250–1325*, Oxford: Clarendon Press.

Herman, Arthur (1976) *The Problem of Evil in Indian Thought*, Delhi: Motilal Barnasidass.

Hewitt, Harold (1991) *Problems in the Philosophy of Religion*, New York: St Martin's Press.

Hick, John (1980) *God Has Many Names*, London: Macmillan.

Hick, John (1989) *An Interpretation of Religion*, London: Macmillan and New Haven: Yale University Press.

Hick, John (1995) *A Christian Theology of Religions*, Louisville, PA: Westminster/John Knox Press.

Hick, John and McGill, Arthur (eds) *The Many-faced Argument*, New York: Macmillan.

Hoffman, Joshua and Rosenkrantz, Gary S. (1994) *Substance Among Other Categories*, Cambridge: Cambridge University Press.

Hoffman, Joshua and Rosenkrantz, Gary S. (1997) *Substance: Its Nature and Existence*, London: Routledge.

Honderich, T. (1993) *How Free Are You?*, Oxford: Oxford University Press.

Hume, David (1737) *A Treatise Of Human Nature*, Oxford: Clarendon Press, 1978.

Jacobi, Herman (trans.) (1962) *Jaina Sutras*, New York: Dover Publications, originally published in 1896.

Jaini, P. (1979) *The Jaina Path of Perfection*, Berkeley, CA: University of California Press.

Kellner, Menachem (1986) *Dogma in Medieval Jewish Thought*, Oxford: Oxford University Press.

Kroner, Richard (1956) *Speculation in Pre-Christian Philosophy*, Philadelphia: Westminster Press.

Kroner, Richard (1959) *Speculation and Revelation in the Age of Christian Philosophy*, Philadelphia: Westminster Press.

Kroner, Richard (1961) *Speculation and Revelation in Modern Philosophy*, Philadelphia: Westminster Press.

Larsen, Gerald James and Deutsch, Elliot (eds) (1988) *Interpreting Across Boundaries*, Princeton, NJ: Princeton University Press.

Leaman, Oliver (1985) *An Introduction to Medieval Islamic Philosophy*, Cambridge: Cambridge University Press.

Leaman, Oliver (1995) *Evil and Suffering in Jewish Philosophy*, Cambridge: Cambridge University Press.

Lewis, H.D. (1967) "History of the philosophy of religion," *Encyclopedia of Philosophy*, New York: Macmillan, vol. 6.

Lipner, Julius (1986) *The Face of Truth*, Albany, NY: SUNY Press.

Locke, John (1990) *An Essay Concerning Human Understanding*, ed. Peter H. Nidditch and G.A.J. Rogers, Oxford: Clarendon Press.

Lott, Eric (1976) *God and the Universe in the Vedantic Theology of Ramanuja*, Madras: Ramanuja Research Society.

Lott, Eric (1980) *Vedantic Approaches to God*, London: Macmillan.

Loux, Michael (1997) *Metaphysics*, London: Routledge.

Lowe, E.J. (1989) *Other Kinds of Being*, Oxford: Basil Blackwell.

Lowe, E.J. (1996) *Subjects of Experience*, Cambridge: Cambridge University Press.

McGrath, Alister (1994) *Christian Theology*, Oxford: Blackwell.

McGrath, Alister E. (1998) *Historical Theology*, Oxford: Blackwell.

Macintosh, H.R. (1940) *The Problem of Religious Knowledge*, New York: Harper and Brothers.

Mackie, J.L. (1982) *The Miracle of Theism*, Oxford: Clarendon Press.

Matin, C.B. (1989) *Religious Experience*, Ithaca, NY: Cornell University Press.

Mavrodes, George (1970a) *Belief in God: A Study in the Epistemology of Religion*, New York: Random House.

Mavrodes, George (ed.) (1970b) *The Rationality of Belief in God*, Englewood Cliffs, NJ: Prentice-Hall.

Mitchell, Basil (1981) *The Justification of Religious Belief*, Oxford: Oxford University Press.

Molina, L. (1988) *On Divine Foreknowledge*, Ithaca, NY: Cornell University Press.

Mookerji, Satkari (1944) *The Jaina Philosophy of Non-Absolutism*, Calcutta: Bharati Mahavidyalaya.

Moore, A.W. (1991) *The Infinite*, London: Routledge.

Murty, Satchidananda K. (1974) *Reason and Revelation in Advaita Vedanta*, Delhi: Motilal Barnasidass.

Nasr, S.H. and Leaman, Oliver (1996) *History of Islamic Philosophy*, London: Routledge.

Ormsby, Eric (1984) *Theodicy in Islamic Thought*, Princeton, NJ: Princeton University Press.

Pap, Arthur (1959) *Semantics and Necessary Truth*, New Haven: Yale University Press.

Parfit, Derek (1984) *Reasons and Persons*, Oxford: Oxford University Press.

Patterson, Robert Leet (1970) *The Philosophy of Religion*, Durham, NC: Duke University Press.

Penelhum, Terence (1983) *God and Scepticism*, Dordrecht: D. Reidel.

Perrett, Roy (ed.) (1989) *Indian Philosophy of Religion*, Dordrecht: Kluwer Academic Publishers.

Phillips, Steven, (1995) *Classical Indian Metaphysics*, La Sall, IL: Open Court.

Pike, Nelson (ed.) (1992) *Mystic Union: An Essay on the Phenomenology of Mysticism*, Ithaca, NY: Cornell University Press.

Plantinga, Alvin (1974a) *The Nature of Necessity*, Oxford: Clarendon Press.

Plantinga, Alvin (1974b) *God, Freedom and Evil*, New York: Random House.

Plantinga, Alvin (ed.) (1974c) *The Ontological Argument*, New York: Harper and Row.

Quasten, Johannes (1996) *Patrology*, four volumes, Allen, TX: Christian Classics Reprint.

Radhakrishnan, Sarvapalli and Moore, C.A. (eds) (1957) *A Sourcebook in Indian Philosophy*, Princeton, NJ: Princeton University Press.

Ramanuja (1980) *Sacred Books of the East*, ed. Max Mueller, Delhi: Motilal Barnadisass.
Rambachan, Anantanand (1991) *Accomplishing the Accomplished: The Vedas as a Source of Valid Knowledge in Sankara*, Honolulu: University of Hawaii Press.
Reichenback, Bruce (1990) *The Law of Karma*, Honolulu: University of Hawaii Press.
Rowe, William (1975) *The Cosmological Argument*, Princeton, NJ: Princeton University Press.
Rowe, William (1982) "Religious experience and the principle of credulity," *International Journal for the Philosophy of Religion*, Vol. 13, pp. 85–92.
Rowe, William L. (1991) *Thomas Reid on Freedom and Morality*, Ithaca, NY: Cornell University Press.
Schmidt, William (1931) *The Origin and Growth Of Religion*, London: Methuen and Company.
Sharma, Arvind (1993) *God, Truth and Reality*, New York: St Martin's Press.
Smart, Ninian (1960) *A Dialogue of Religions*, London: SCM Press.
Smart, Ninian (1964a) *Doctrine and Argument in Indian Philosophy*, London: Allen and Unwin.
Smart, Ninian (1964b) *Philosophers and Religious Truth*, London: SCM Press.
Smart, Ninian (1973) *The Science of Religion and the Sociology of Knowledge*, Princeton, NJ: Princeton University Press.
Smith, Wilfred Cantwell (1979) *Faith and Belief*, Princeton, NJ: Princeton University Press.
Smith, Wilfred Cantwell (1981) *Towards a World Theology*, Philadelphia: Westminster Press.
Sopa, Geshe and Jones, Elving *A Light to the Svatantrika-Madhyanika*, privately circulated.
Subba Rao, S. (1904) *Vedanta Sutras*, Madras, first published by Williams and Norgate, London (1921).
Swinburne, Richard (1979) *The Existence of God*, Oxford: Clarendon Press.
Swinburne, Richard (1981) *Faith and Reason*, Oxford: Oxford University Press.
Thibaut George (trans.) (1962a) *The Vedanta Sutras of Badarayana with the Commentary of Sankara*, New York: Dover Publications, originally published in 1896.
Thibaut, George (trans.) (1962b) *The Vedanta Sutras with the Commentary by Ramanuja*, Delhi: Motilal Barnasidass reprint, originally published by Oxford University Press (1904).
Thomas, George F. (1970) *Philosophy and Religions Belief*, New York: Charles Scribner's Sons.
Thomas, George F. (1973) *Religious Philosophies of the West*, New York: Charles Scribner's Sons.
Thompson, Samuel (1955) *A Modern Philosophy of Religion*, Chicago: Henry Regnery.
Van Inwagen, Peter (1983) *An Essay on Free Will*, Oxford: Clarendon Press.
Wainwright, William J. (1984) "Wilfred Cantwell Smith on faith and belief," *Religious Studies*, Vol. 20, pp. 353–66.
Warder, A.K. (1990) *A History of Indian Buddhism*, Honolulu: University of Hawaii Press.
Warren, H.C. (1959) *Buddhist Scriptures*, Baltimore: Penguin Books.
Warren, H.C. (1969) *Buddhism in Translations*, New York: Atheneum Press.
Watson, G. (ed.) (1982) *Free Will*, Oxford: Oxford University Press.
Watt, W. Montgomery (1973) *The Formative Period of Islamic Thought*, Edinburgh: Edinburgh University Press.
Wieman, H.N. and Meland, Bernand Eugene (eds) (1936) *American Philosophies of Religion*, Chicago, IL: Willett, Clark, and Co.

Wood, Thomas (1990) *The Mandukya Upanishad and the Agama Sastra: An Investigation into the Meaning of the Vedanta,* Honolulu: University of Hawaii Press.

Wood, Thomas (1991) *Mind-Only,* Honolulu: University of Hawaii Press.

Yandell, Keith E. (1968a) "Empiricism and theism," *Sophia,* Vol. 7, No. 3, October, pp. 3–11.

Yandell, Keith E. (1968b) "A reply to Nielsen," *Sophia,* Vol. 7, No. 3, October, pp. 18, 19.

Yandell, Keith E. (1971) *Basic Issues in the Philosophy of Religion,* Boston: Allyn and Bacon.

Yandell, Keith E. (1986a) "Some varieties of relativism,' *International Journal for Philosophy of Religion,* Vol. 19, pp. 61–85.

Yandell, Keith E. (1986b) *Christianity and Philosophy,* Grand Rapids, MI: Eerdmans.

Yandell, Keith E. (1990) *Hume's "Inexplicable Mystery,"* Philadelphia: Temple University Press.

Yandell, Keith E. (1993) "Some varieties of religious pluralism," in James Kellenberger (ed.), *Inter-religious Models and Criteria,* New York: St Martin's Press.

Yandell, Keith E. (1995a) *The Epistemology of Religious Experience,* Cambridge: Cambridge University Press.

Yandell, Keith E. (1995b) "A defense of dualism," *Faith and Philosophy,* Vol. 12, No. 4, October, pp. 548–66.

Yandell, Keith E. (1989) "Divine existence and gratuitous evil," *Religious Studies,* Vol. 25, pp. 15–30.

Zagzebski, Linda (1991) *The Dilemma of Freedom and Foreknowledge,* New York: Oxford University Press.

Index